The DECLINE and FALL of the LOVE GODDESSES

Patrick Agan

The DECLINE and FALL of the LOVE GODDESSES

Patrick Agan

Pinnacle Books   Los Angeles

Designed by Jerry Tillett

Published by
Pinnacle Books, Inc.
2029 Century Park East
Los Angeles, California 90067

This book is dedicated to my parents, Marjorie and Eugene Agan, without whose help and support it would not have been possible.

CONTENTS

ACKNOWLEDGMENTS

To my patient and persuasive editor, Evelyn
Grippo, and to the Doug McClelland Collection,
Stephen Lewis, Emily Barney, Lois Kibbee,
Christopher Young, Jack Kuster, Tony
DeMartino, John Clerc-Scott, Larry Baldwin,
Baer Frimer and my friends at Pictorial Parade,
U.P.I., John Canemaker, Joyce Jameson, and a
lovely friend who helped me understand it all—
Hedy Lamarr. With very special thanks to
Beverly Linet.

The DECLINE and FALL of the LOVE GODDESSES

Patrick Agan

Introduction

THEY called them "Pinup Girls" and
"Sweater Queens," thought up adjectives like "It" and "Ooomph" and "Ping"
to describe their teasing charms, and the minions of the movie magazines breathlessly photographed and minutely detailed each new film, each new house, and
each new husband.

They were creations whose natural beauty was enhanced by studio makeup
wizards and whose lives were often rewritten to match the new image. They were
the Love Goddesses, and magazine cover shots were the ultimate testimonials to
their ability to draw people away from real life into the make-believe world of
darkened movie theaters, where, amidst popcorn, Milky Ways, and the *News of the
World,* they proceeded to act out the fantasies of millions.

During Hollywood's Golden Era, the Love Goddesses were a breed apart
from mere mortals; light years away from the everyday worries and cares of the
public. Their carefully constructed appeal was imitated by scores of high-school-
fresh young girls, the Homecoming Queens of every town in America, secretaries,
and salesgirls, who saved their quarters and bussed to Hollywood in hopes of
supplanting them, waiting in the commissary wings or at the extras' makeup table
for the stars to stumble and tumble from their celluloid heaven. And fall they
eventually did; some slowly, some quickly, some happily walking away, some
desperately trying to hang on. The end result was the same, for their legends are
all now just strips of film in silver cans. But for a time they ruled the screen.

Almost without exception, the Love Goddess exuded not only sex appeal but
an elusive sense of humor as well. If one did have a little acting talent, so much
the better. More important, though, was the way she looked through the probing
eye of the camera, and the way the lens caught and held her determined her movie
lifespan.

Offscreen, scores of publicists rewrote biographies, translated high school
diplomas into Ph.D.s, and changed pedigrees at will, further building the salable
image. Over the years, there have been countless girls made famous by the
machinations of studio publicity departments, but making them famous and
making the public accept their creations were two different things. From comets

1

like Veronica Lake and Jayne Mansfield to legends like Garbo, Dietrich, Lamarr, and Rita Hayworth, there had to be the acceptance by the public—through hit pictures and stinkers alike—to keep a career going. When that asset, that interest, was lost, so, usually, was the career. Being boring is the ultimate sin for a Love Goddess. Just ask Elizabeth Taylor.

To millions, the Love Goddesses were surrogate mistresses, ladies of incredible beauty who afforded at least a visual satisfaction that men were able to indulge in even in the company of their wives. The smarter stars never alienated their women fans either, but strove to give them a sexual goal. As a New York movie critic put it about Rita Hayworth, ''Make no mistake about this *Cover Girl.* It's one of those things that men from miles and miles around are going to line up to see. And by an odd chance, there will also be women lining up for miles and miles around, probably each with the thought, 'What has she got that I ain't got—and how do I get it?' ''

The Love Goddesses were an inspiration, Everests of glamour for both men and women, both of whom, in their own way, wanted to scale the heights.

The streets where these dreams were made are gone: once-vast backlots of the major motion picture studios have been sold off for their real estate value. Office buildings tower where, in that long heyday that was Hollywood, imitation villas and villages once housed Lana Turner and Linda Darnell, Ann Sheridan and Susan Hayward. The administration buildings, those that are left, are strangely silent, and the publicity departments that once generated the oil that kept the Dream Machine operating have all but ground to a halt. *TV Guide* has conquered *Movie World.*

Its staunchest supporters insist that the New Hollywood is as vital as the old and offer accounting books and movie grosses to support their statements. But even they must admit the simple truth that things have changed. The days when darkened theaters offered an inexpensive escape from reality are gone. Today, somehow, dreams are more expensive—and they don't last quite as long.

Fortunately, the movie itself—that meticulously mounted and manicured product—remains to remind us of what has gone. The great stars, the great stories, the fabulous faces, those unforgettable closeups still work their magic.

And magic it was—illusion, trick photography, and process shots that created a celluloid kingdom out of a papier-mâché backdrop—and magic it will remain, a Hollywood Olympus where screen gods and goddesses were our stand-ins. They represented our ideals—not only the best we wanted for ourselves, but the best *of* ourselves as well. All of us, to some extent, were touched by them, and more than some of us were named for them.

The men survived better than the ladies, somehow able to adapt more to changing times and styles. But what about the women behind the label of Love Goddess? The often lonely ladies who hung their mansions with mirrors so that at every turn they could see the Image and make sure it was still there. For many, the burden of maintaining it offscreen became more difficult than maintaining it on. The pressures of stardom, the lack of public privacy, the ever present fear that it could all be whisked away tomorrow after a flop picture, and, conversely, the resentment at being merchandised in the first place—all these things combined to bring many of these ladies down. This book is about some of them: the survivors as well as the victims. Yet each in her own way was a victim of the success she struggled so hard to achieve and maintain. In one way or another, they all found the dark side of the American Dream.

You, the reader, may not agree with all the choices or enjoy all the endings; nevertheless, this is the way I have seen them or known them in their prime on *The Late Show,* in their personal late-at-night telephone calls, and in the *National Enquirer/Star* headlines that seem to be their ultimate benedictions. Whatever their stories and whatever their ends, it's to their credit that, however briefly, they earned—and deserved—the cinematic appellation of Love Goddess. They were larger than life, and they made the fans forgo the popcorn so that they would not miss even a moment of those Fabulous Faces.

Frances Farmer*

Listen, I put liquor in my milk. I put liquor in my coffee and in my orange juice. What do you want me to do, starve to death?

Frances Farmer speaking to Judge Marshall Hickson after her January 14, 1943, arrest for breaking parole.

East
Now richly droops wisterias bloom,
While elegant bugs, on separate flourishing leaf,
Luxuriously maneuver.
If we are silent while we feel
How quiet is the night with jasmine,
How sweet the scent of rain upon the pepper tree,
If we but hold our breaths,
One second, while the wind is busy out at sea,
How sharp will seem the sting
Of slug and ant and snail attacking blossoms.

A poem written by Frances Farmer shortly before her death.

AFTER her spectacular performance in *Come and Get It,* Frances Farmer was called the most important movie find since Garbo, the most delicious discovery of 1936. Playing the difficult dual role of a saloon-singing mother and her proper daughter, both loved by timber king Edward Arnold, her fragile blonde beauty and stainless steel acting quality burst over Hollywood like a comet, and, like that high-flying, fast-diving sphere, she rose quickly, only to falter in midflight and fall into a darker night than anyone could have imagined—the darkness of alcoholism, arrests, and mental institutions.

Her main difficulty was that, while Hollywood called her the hottest thing since the Super Swede, *she* never believed them because she didn't want to. A

*Editor's note: The quotations contained in this segment, unless otherwise indicated, are from previously unpublished manuscript notes and correspondence between Frances Farmer and Lois Kibbee, written the year before Miss Farmer's death and given to the author by Miss Kibbee.

rebellious girl from her early teenage years on, Frances proved even more so when the movie industry tried to tuck her neatly into its version of what she should be. She fought that categorization every step of the way and, in doing so, not only complicated what could have been a golden career of many years but strangled her private life as well in a web of degradation and horror that took her the rest of her life to overcome.

As is often the case, Paramount Pictures, to whom she was contracted, was not where she got her big break. Rather, Sam Goldwyn gave it to her when he picked her for *Come and Get It,* a sprawling filmization of Edna Ferber's novel of the north woods. Once it hit, she was compared not just to Garbo, but also to Hepburn, Margaret Sullivan, and Marlene Dietrich. Ironically, her beauty was both the key to her career and the lock against its expansion, for when she returned to Paramount as a full-fledged star, they spotlit that beauty instead of

Frances Farmer in the film that made her a star, Come and Get It *(1936), with Edward Arnold.*
AUTHOR'S COLLECTION

letting loose the considerable acting ability within her. The iron-handed studio heads eventually pounded her into what they wanted, but, at the first chance, she bolted for her first love, the stage, where she starred in the original Broadway production of *Golden Boy* in 1937 and embarked on a disastrous affair with playwright Clifford Odets.

Frances Farmer first won Hollywood's attention after winning a newspaper subscription contest. In later years she was often to wonder whether, if she had it to do again, she would, even in her darkest moments of youthful frustration, have mailed that entry letter? The closing of that mailbox lid was the opening of a life destined from then on to shuttle between Hollywood's heaven and a public hell.

MOST of the difficulties of Frances Farmer's life, she freely admitted, were engendered by her own willfulness and perfectionist sense of never settling for less than *exactly* what she wanted out of life. She came by this streak self-defensively, born as she was a late child to her parents, Lillian and Ernest Farmer, in Seattle, Washington, on September 19, 1913. As she said in her touching, posthumously published autobiography, *Will There Really Be a Morning?* (Putnam), she felt destined always to be "the last of a long and bitter series of encounters between them."

Young Frances Elena Farmer was taught early just what kind of pioneer stock she was descended from—on her mother's side, anyway. The brother and sister-in-law of her maternal grandfather, Zaccheus Van Ornum, were killed in the Snake River Indian Massacre of 1860. Grandfather Van Ornum was one of the Free-Thinkers who disputed the literal interpretations of the Bible and upheld the Darwinian theories of evolution. He passed on this zest for opposing tradition to his thirteen children, finding a particularly ripe pupil in daughter Lillian, Frances's mother.

The three Farmer children, Frances, Wesley, five years Frances's senior, and Edith, older by sixteen months, were exposed to Lillian's thinking from birth, her favorite slogan being, "Make up your own minds. Don't follow the bellwether to the slaughterhouse." She'd proven that herself in her own life when she divorced her first husband, a wild-drinking Irishman, and moved with her daughter by that marriage, Rita, from San Francisco to the Yukon to Seattle, where she opened a rooming house for bachelors. One of them was a young lawyer named Ernest Melven Farmer from Spring Valley, Minnesota, where his father had been a state Supreme Court judge. One of the things that helped bring the couple together was his affection for little Rita—one of the few bonds in a long and stormy married life that began in 1905.

Their first child, a daughter, died of pneumonia after being shunted to a colder room in their modest house when his mother came to visit early in their marriage. Lillian always held this against Ernest (and his mother) and that was the first seed of discontent between them, which would ultimately yield a bumper crop.

The family lived in a middle-class house at 312 Harvard Avenue in Seattle, but even though Ernest was considered a bright young attorney there never seemed to be enough money, with four growing children. Mrs. Farmer became a self-taught dietitian, and her concern for "natural goodness in foods" caused her to launch a campaign against the quality of food being served in Seattle's schools. As Frances would later say, "She became Carrie Nation with a pot holder," and shortly emerged as somewhat of an embarrassment to her husband when she started attacking local bakeries through "The Mothers Want To Know Club," claiming membership of "a million strong and growing every day," and establishing herself as president. While making a noisy name in the process, she did know her subject and became widely respected for her views.

Lillian also had a great regard for the English language and recited works of Whittier, Longfellow, and William Cullen Bryant to her brood, complete with gestures, while Frances "toddled behind her, absorbing by osmosis all the recited eloquence, as well as the impromptu lessons in barnyard biology, garden botany, and everything else in Nature that could be dealt with scientifically without compromising her Puritan restrictions of what the young should know about what went on underneath the female corset." Beyond these subjects, Lillian was also staunchly in favor of the suffragette movement and frequently bared her general opinions about the perfidy of the human male, proclaiming that they were responsible for the woes of the world.

By contrast, Frances's father was a much more passive individual, using a lawyer's logic in place of a loud voice. A man with few social graces, on occasion he'd intentionally annoy his hypertense wife, calling her "Lil," a nickname she hated, and adding, "Trying to make a marriage work with you is like hitching up a good steady mule in the same harness with a high-strung, crazy nag."

Sentimentality and open demonstrations of affection were rarely forthcoming from Lillian Farmer to any of her children, but to Frances the lack of them hurt deeply. "I can still remember the early feelings of loneliness and puzzlement that it induced. I loved my mother with all my heart, but I seldom felt a demonstrative return."

The Farmer marriage seemed a normal one on the surface, but underneath boiled discontent and growing alienation. When Mrs. Farmer was working night and day running her house and writing her treatises on nutrition, things were especially volatile. Her patience worn thin at times like these, she was given to loud emotional outbursts that would send her husband scurrying back to his law books and the children out of sight. Once Farmer thought his wife was close to a nervous breakdown and so wrote her sister, Zella, in Los Angeles. When Zella wrote Lillian about his suspicions, it only intensified the growing rift between them. In Lillian's staunch pioneering and puritanical background, there was no room for the stigma of emotional ill health, and she viewed his letter as a conspiracy against her—a conspiracy she would never forgive him for.

When Frances was four, her mother packed up the children and left Ernest for her sister's home in Southern California. Eventually they moved into a small house of their own directly across from the original MGM studio, where ''once the gatekeeper assured Edith and me that he'd get us into pictures 'any day now,' but the only time he might have made good his promise we were off on yet another nature hike with Mom.''

Money was always a problem, since Farmer was often late with his monthly support payments and therefore a constant irritant to his estranged wife. World War I was in full swing, and looking for a project she threw herself into the war effort. One erratic result was a red, white and blue chicken which she got by crossing a Rhode Island Red, a White Leghorn and a Blue Andalusian. After producing this mutation, she promptly donned an Uncle Sam suit and called a press conference to show off her patriotic results, a somewhat bewildered bird who was quickly made famous by the Los Angeles press.

After five years Lillian moved her children to Chico, California, where at first they lived in a rustic one-room cabin built on the foundations of the original Van Ornum homestead. They acquired an old Star automobile, and, in general, it was an untroubled time, although money remained tight. Lillian made ends meet by various means, including making food displays for the County Farm Bureau and the State Agricultural Department. The one sad spot, ''the saddest day of my nine-year-old life occurred when someone poisoned our two pet dogs. Mom bought us steak that night, a rare treat in those days, but for once none of us could get it past the lump in his throat.''

Early in 1925 when Frances was eleven, Lillian decided to devote herself completely to her nutrition research and sent her children back to Seattle to live with their father, by then ''an interesting stranger who was known to us only by hearsay as a 'big lawyer in a big town.' '' Unfortunately Ernest Farmer had not prospered over those years, and they returned to a beaten man whose practice was composed primarily of impoverished laborers and small tradesmen. ''For Wesley, Edith, and me the move back to Seattle was both an exciting adventure and a distressing one. I remember the feeling of loneliness and confusion when we said goodbye to Mom. . . . I think I was a little wary, too, of meeting the stranger who was our father.''

While their mother stayed behind, Aunt Zella drove the children to Albany, Oregon, the halfway point where their father picked them up and herded them onto a train for home. ''In certain ways, that train trip represented the end of my dependent childhood. I began to understand that there were certain things one could expect from adults, and others that one could not expect . . . being shunted from one household to another was a new adjustment, a fresh confusion, and I groped for ways to compensate for the disorder. Whatever the developments in my nature, I think that from that point on I was no longer a child.''

Within days of their arrival, the three children came down with the chicken pox, and shortly thereafter Lillian's house in Chico burned to the ground, destroying much of her nutrition research material, which desolated her. Until then she had been resisting Ernest's pleas to reunite the family. "For God's sake, Lil, come up here and take care of these kids," he would say. She decided, finally, to accede, but only on the condition that he move out of the house. "From then on we had a 'weekend' father. He would come and see us every week and putter in the garden or fix whatever needed repair in the house. About ten o'clock on Sunday evening, he would put on his hat and take the trolley back to his hotel room on the other side of town. It was a custom to prevail for many years to come."

In such a divided house, Frances had no reliable parent to go to for advice and began falling back on her mother's dictum to "decide for yourself," establishing this individualistic streak at an early age. It was a lonely, confusing time for the young girl, soon complicated by her growing awareness of her sexuality. An autographed picture of Douglas Fairbanks, Sr., her idol, became the source of a family joke to which Frances retorted, "Someday I'll be a movie star, too." "Oh Sister," her mother would say, "where do you get such ideas? Now eat your lunch." For Lillian Farmer there was no problem that couldn't be solved by a nutritious meal.

By the time Frances entered West Seattle High School at age fifteen, she had "already begun to show signs of an acutely intense nature." She liked studying, learning—"except chemistry"—and became a fixture in extracurricular activities like the school newspaper and the debating society, "possibly because controversy was a natural climate at home."

Frances became a controversial figure when she entered a national essay contest and won first prize for her entry entitled "God Dies," paralleling her disappointment at losing a prized possession as evidence of the obvious absence of a God who would let such a thing happen. Frances did believe God had died—"It wasn't murder. He just died of old age"—but her views soon stirred up a storm of controversy that began with headlines such as SEATTLE GIRL DENIES GOD, WINS PRIZE.

The pulpits of Seattle and elsewhere shook with sermons denouncing her, although, in fairness, some saw it as simply an adolescent search for answers and took no offense. They were in the minority however, and the hysteria over it all had her soon wondering "what sort of monster I'd unleashed. I had merely tried to put down my own thoughts and ideas about God, and, to me, it seemed an honest enough attempt." Mother Farmer, on hearing that one particularly virulent minister was planning his entire next sermon about Frances and the threat of atheism in general in public schools, rose from her pew during his oratory and leveled a ringing denunciation that brought more newspaper attention to the essay, "while I nearly expired from embarrassment."

At home things were equally stormy. Mrs. Farmer was desperately trying to divorce her husband, even threatening suicide by throwing herself into Puget

Sound when particularly vexed. The divorce was finally granted in 1931, but Farmer was often late with his alimony payments of $100 a month. This upset his ex-wife to the point that one day she went to a hardware store, bought a revolver and six blanks, and proceeded to his law office where she stormed in and emptied the gun at her husband, who had quickly dived under his desk. Wesley bailed her out and Ernest didn't press charges, but it brought home to Frances once again that her mother was a far from stable woman, especially in a time of crisis. This realization would ultimately be renewed countless times.

In the fall of 1931, Frances entered the University of Washington intent on becoming a writer. She raised her own tuition through a variety of odd jobs, including those of camp counselor, singing waitress, and worker in a soap factory. Before long, though, she became attracted to the glamour and intellectual excitement of the drama department, especially as personified by Sophie Rosenstein, a young university instructor. "She was a witty and stimulating person and talked at length and with enormous enthusiasm about the art of the theater, and the importance of raising it above the commercial levels of Hollywood and Broadway. She had an almost religious fervor for the theater and it was infectious. What first had begun as a provocative notion became a driving ambition." Frances soon changed her major from journalism to drama and began immersing herself in the study of the theater, "the interest becoming all-consuming as I realized I had entered a new creative world with complete confidence and none of the frustrations I had experienced in my writing courses."

By now a striking beauty with deep-set eyes and elegant cheekbones, she was a natural choice to play the lead role in *Helen of Troy* in her sophomore year. In her classes, an unforced natural talent began to blossom, and the following year she starred again in a campus production of *Alien Corn* in the role originated by Katherine Cornell. It was a great success, running for fourteen consecutive weekends at the Studio Theater (in the round, an experimental technique in those days), and garnered Frances her first set of glowing reviews. A local critic declared, "The name of Frances Farmer, who has a divine, intangible maturity to her acting, is destined for electric lights on Broadway." It was then that the dream began to take firm shape as she rose to the heights of the university theater department. Surpassing even her own strict expectations, she delved deeper and deeper into her studies of the then-budding Stanislavski method school of acting, the cornerstone of which was "the idea that art needed leisure to achieve the depth and intensity of fulfillment."

By the time she was a senior, Frances had decided that she wanted to be a professional actress and try Broadway, but getting there was the problem—one that would soon be solved in a bizarre series of occurrences.

In the spring of 1935, a radical Seattle newspaper, *The Voice of Action,* announced a contest. The seller of the most new subscriptions to the working-men's newspaper would win an all-expense-paid round trip to Moscow, via New York, plus $100, all timed to coincide with Russia's May Day celebration. At first Frances was too busy in her off hours as an usher in a local movie house to think much of it, but her friends, spearheaded by Sophie Rosenstein, decided that since she was the best actress in the school she should win the contest. They began assembling subscriptions among themselves, entering them all under Frances's name. "Within a month I received incredible news—I had won the trip to Russia by the small margin of two dollars and fifty cents." She was wild with excitement. "The trip, I reasoned, would have a double significance to me. First of all, there was the opportunity to visit the famed Moscow Art Theater, the shrine of Stanislavski. But above and beyond that, it meant I would end up in New York—an unbelievable opportunity for my theatrical ambitions."

Unfortunately, before Frances could impart this enthusiasm to her mother, the newspapers called Lillian and announced her daughter's feat, touching off a storm of argument by quoting Lillian as saying, "No daughter of mine is going to Russia." "Her wrath was positively Olympian, if, I thought, a trifle over-extended," but try as Frances might to explain that she wasn't out to overthrow the U.S. government, her mother chose not to listen or understand. Turning to her father, she explained that the trip would give her the chance she so desperately wanted to try New York and that the Moscow trip was only a means to that end. He advised her, "Then go you must, Frances," and she felt, "I knew he was right; I must."

Seattle's Hearst-owned *Post Intelligencer* made such a fuss over the award that shortly it was picked up by the wire services "and I became a national celebrity overnight," albeit via headlines such as:

MOTHER TRIES TO STOP COED'S TRIP TO RUSSIA

and

PARENT UNABLE TO HALT GIRL'S TRIP TO SEE REDS

Lillian even appealed to the public prosecutor's office at one point to stop the trip, "but since I had reached the age of twenty-one the previous September, she found no aid there. What was termed in the press as my 'pilgrimage' to Russia became a *cause célèbre*. I suppose every child suffers embarrassment by a parent at one time or another. I know I suffered acutely from Mom's public outbursts, and fervently wished the whole thing would just disappear.

"In the sum of things, of course, I did what I had to do. It was Mom's own edict that she had drummed into me since childhood, 'Make up your own mind!' I wanted mother's love, I needed her approval, and I suffered painfully under her deep anger at my anarchy."

Frances didn't think of herself as unfeeling or defiant. She always maintained that "the most dominant thing in my nature is that I must be who I am, regardless of the circumstances, the penalties or the people involved. I was taught early that I had the right, even the obligation, to decide for myself what I must be and what I must do. Perhaps that intense awareness of a preoccupation with self was the thing that opened some long, dark and seemingly endless corridors in my life, but I have an idea that it was also responsible for my emergence as an actress."

On April 10, 1935, Frances left Seattle by bus for New York with $100 and a third-class steamer ticket in her pocket and a new hat from her friend, Sophie, on her head. The heaviest burden she carried was her mother's disapproval, and "even though I would return to Seattle many times in the future, I knew I could never really go home again."

While waiting to sail, Frances made her first contact with the Group Theater in New York, and "I was fascinated and immensely impressed by the experience, for it was the Group that had spearheaded the Stanislavski method of acting in the U.S. in 1931 and by '35 had already left a decisive impression on the American theater." At a party she met playwright Clifford Odets and was "speechless" at being near the embodiment of the Group's daringly experimental theater.

Frances sailed for Russia on the *Washington* and promptly found herself romantically involved with an Englishman, John McKenzie, a first-class passenger who quickly whisked her from near-steerage onto the upper decks and into his arms. When they parted, she agreed to meet him in Paris. She then proceeded to Russia by train, joining a group of students from other countries, "and except for the planned events and views of Moscow's sights I was left very much alone and had no feeling of being under 'surveillance' at any time" for the week she spent there. "To the Russians I was just another student tourist and certainly no 'tool' for them to manipulate."

As agreed, Frances stopped over in Paris for a romantic interlude with McKenzie. From there they went to London, continuing their affair. "By then I was ready to accept him on any basis, permanent or not. He made several business trips a year to the States, and when we said goodbye at the dock, we made arrangements to meet again in New York." Sailing on the *President Harding,* Frances had her first chance in weeks to fully assess herself and her future, now spiced by the romance of her recent affair. For most of the trip she thumbed through McKenzie's parting gift, a copy of *The Spirit of Man,* inscribed "To Frances—As it was in the beginning."

Having landed in New York, she looked up an old friend from college, Jane Rose [later a veteran character actress seen on TV's "Phyllis" series], and promptly moved in with her in Jane's tiny westside apartment. Some jobs modelling hats brought a little money into the household, but it was a tough time for them both. Frances cashed in her return ticket to Seattle, netting twenty-five dollars, and wrote several articles on her trip for *The Voice of Action* as well as a long letter of apology to her parents, who were still being hounded by the press. She explained that she wanted to try New York for a career and expressed her deep concern over having caused them so much trouble. "One doesn't deliberately create situations like this, they creep up on you and smack you in the rear before you know it. . . . It's my ambition that someday I shall make you inordinately proud of me."

Through a shipboard acquaintance, Frances was introduced to Shepard Traube, a young Broadway producer who immediately signed her to a personal contract. But with the theater in the summer doldrums, he didn't have anything for her to do. Instead of a role on stage, he decided to create one off, capitalizing on her recent publicity. He presented her at a press conference as being able to give "important statements" on the status of commercial American sports as opposed to those she'd seen in the Soviet Union. "What I knew about the sports world I could have put in his eye, but the newspapers picked up the story," and she soon came to the attention of Oscar Serlin, the New York talent chief for Paramount Pictures.

Though her deepest feelings were with the legitimate theater, she went along with Serlin's suggestion of a screen test because she couldn't afford to reject it, and "in those days film companies tested just about every female in sight as long as she was still warm and breathing and had the required number of features." Assigned a scene from *The Lake*, in a role originated by Katharine Hepburn, she was to test opposite another youngster, Allyn Joslyn.

So much had happened to her in just three short months that Frances began feeling slightly overwhelmed by it all. Writing to her sister Edith, she said of her leaving Seattle, visiting Russia, and living in New York, "It's something you look forward to in a haze and look back on in a mist. You never have it alive and kicking in your grasp."

Before making the test there were weeks of laborious rehearsal, which she loved, and dieting, which she didn't, but Paramount had decreed that she lose weight. She was alone but not really lonely, for she realized that solitude was a very important part of acting. "For the first time I have been able to work on my acting with complete concentration and I glimpse progress for the first time, and I like the feeling of everything being done in its natural time, without fear of being interrupted. . . . I feel I'm putting my best foot forward in this test and if it fails, I'll blame it on fate."

For Frances as for thousands of young girls before and since, the glamour of New York quickly faded. She felt that "right now [it's] a hot, dirty and uninteresting place—filled mostly with objectionable people shouting on the streets, and last spring it was the mecca of my all!"

Then, as if out of nowhere, came a call from a man who identified himself as a friend of John McKenzie, who asked her out to dinner. He was, like McKenzie, a gallant and handsome charmer, and Frances let herself be swept up in the evening of posh restaurants and bars and, ultimately, into the friend's bed. Next morning "I was horrified at myself and terribly ashamed," for how could she care so deeply for McKenzie and allow herself to sleep with his friend?

Shortly afterwards she heard from McKenzie himself. He was on his way to New York and wanted to see her. "I met him at the ship's landing and we went immediately to the luxurious apartment he kept as a permanent residence on Park Avenue." Instead of sweeping her into his arms, however, he acted cool and aloof, and she was stunned when he told her their affair was over and that he was returning home never to see her again. "I was devastated, feeling that I had failed him in some way and that it was my own inadequacies that had forced his decision. I didn't realize until later that he had sent his friend as a kind of ambassador to find out what kind of girl I was and if I were worth the trouble of a divorce. It had been a simple case of comparing notes, as even sometimes gentlemen do. In any event the rejection was a crushing emotional blow. I was heartbroken.

"In retrospect, John McKenzie was the most significant love relationship of my life . . . but I found out that even if he desires it, nobody dies of a broken heart—except in opera."

Before she had time to brood, though, it was time for the screen test and Frances' first brush with the illogic of Hollywood that would ultimately be her undoing. A makeup artist was dispatched to do her over, and do her over he did, shaving her eyebrows almost completely off, lightening her already blonde hair a shade, and reshaping her face entirely. As she eyed the results in the mirror she thought, "It certainly isn't *you,* Miss Farmer!"

The test was duly shot and the performers dispatched with the routine "we'll call you," but as August came and went Frances began to think they never would. Almost broke by now, she struggled by with a few more modelling jobs, eating many twenty-five-cent lunches.

In early September Oscar Serlin called Shepard Traube to offer Frances a seven-year contract with Paramount, starting at $100 a week with six-month options. "I felt like an heiress and wrote my mother about my incredible fortunes." Telling her how she remembered what lack of money "has done to your life," she declared she'd dedicate herself to getting her family out of the state of quasi poverty that had always stalked them. "So hold on, Mom, and, God willing, things will be different some day."

Frances's success erased her mother's displeasure over the Russian trip, and for one rare moment the Farmers were all united in their approval of Frances and each other. To Frances, Hollywood was a golden trinket "dangling in front of me. I wanted to reach out and take it, yet I wanted something else; to be a serious actress in the legitimate theater. On the other hand the movie contract would save me from the jaws of poverty. All right, I thought, if I don't make a success in Hollywood, I can always come back to New York and try again."

On September 19, 1935, her twenty-second birthday, Frances signed the Paramount contract and boarded the Chief for Los Angeles. Traube and makeup man Eddie Senz, the same man who'd remade her face just weeks before, saw her off, with Eddie handing her a toy bulldog puppy as a going-away gift. Five months before, she'd left Seattle, a young university student bound for Russia, and now, "fifteen thousand miles later, I arrived in Hollywood as a screen starlet."

Unlike the other novices in Paramount's starlet stable, Frances was ready to work, and within a short time she had a reputation in the drama department as a "creature of intensity." She threw herself wholeheartedly into the acting classes, rehearsing scenes and working on interpretation techniques and speech. The only facet of studio life that she instantly hated was the glamour angle. At first studio heads tried to change her name, saying that she sounded like a cookbook, but she adamantly refused to consider that, just as she refused to cooperate in what she thought would be a loss of identity by giving in to their demands that she spend more money on her appearance, as did so many of the talent department's beauty-contest winners and handsome, muscle-flexing beachboys. There was a competitive intensity among this assortment of young people, all anxious to become "stars," and as the ranks thinned out, it became only more so.

Ironically Frances gradually broke through the personal coat of ice that she'd assumed to avoid personal complications. She became friendly with a young actor, "a handsome blond god who called himself Leif Erickson." His real name was Wyecliffe Anderson. Nicknamed Bill, he had been a vocalist with a band before striking studio contract gold. His two most attractive qualities, to her, were his dogged determination to act and his unsophisticated enthusiasm about it all. To Frances those qualities seemed to denote a stronger character than that of other classmates, who were more interested in Ciro's than cinema technique. Though she thought his choice of a screen name frankly absurd, their friendship slowly grew with their spending many evenings together going over scenes "sprawled on the floor in uninhibited analyses of scripts and characters. We had fun together." Besides, the studio heads thought they looked good together and began publicizing them as a pair, as well as assigning them scenes to do together in class.

After a bit part in a Community Chest trailer, Frances got the word that she was to be "groomed for stardom," and she was amazed and angry that the thin studio walls rebounded with the news practically as soon as she herself heard it. It was then that she made up a personal list of Hollywood hates that included gossip, the lack of sensitivity and individuality, the crude language, and the intrigue, which she thought worthy of a Middle Eastern court.

During filming of her first movie, a "B" picture called *Too Many Parents*, Leif showed up at her apartment one night and proposed marriage, saying, "My mother says I ought to marry you." By this time they had become lovers, but marriage was far from Frances's mind as she was still trying to cope with the immense changes in her life. However, since the studio had already been pushing their fan-magazine friendship, and since Frances did have a deep feeling for Leif, if somewhat less than love, she agreed, and they eloped to Yuma, Arizona. Leif had been, and remained, the only friend she'd made since landing in Hollywood. Conversely she also hoped that he would afford a buffer between herself and the studio's growing publicity demands, demands that made her short of temper and increasingly uncooperative both on the set and off. She neither loved him nor was in love with him, yet on a Sunday morning in early February of 1936, she woke up in a desert town as Mrs. Leif Erickson.

Within the week Frances learned that she was to make her first "A" production, starring opposite Bing Crosby in *Rhythm on the Range* (1936). Although she thought the screen coupling of the crooner and the method actress ludicrous, she later recalled it as one of the happiest times she had spent before a movie camera. Crosby's style of "tell me where to stand and what to say" eased her newcomer nerves. Also, "I had had a crush on him since my high-school days, and stood in awe of the fact that in my first important film I was actually working as his leading lady." Also in the picture was raucous Martha Raye, but Bing's easy-going manner helped immensely to keep the set calm. At the time one of Paramount's biggest stars, he enjoyed nothing more than a relaxed set but, in a pinch, was not above using his box-office weight to make a point.

It was a big break for Frances because co-starring in a Crosby picture automatically brought her to the attention of the studio heads—not to mention the prestige she gained in her mother's eyes, doubly delighted at having a daughter "with her feet on the ground now that she was married, and a movie star to boot." All the past recriminations were shunted aside with Lillian's new enthusiasm for her daughter, the first she'd ever really shown for her offspring's activities.

The good reviews for *Rhythm* heartened Frances, but instead of a juicy role, she got a call from studio chief Adolph Zukor instead, who told her frankly that now that she was a rising star she'd have to start acting like one. It was the old story of looking good at all times and especially "getting rid of that disgraceful old car." It was image-making time, he said, and she must conform. He berated the young girl at length over the responsibilities that movie stardom demanded and screamed for more glamour. Frances let him scream and went on wearing the comfortable slacks and sweaters she preferred. She did, however, get a new car—but only because it was offered her by an agency in return for some publicity work. Her lack of attention to the rest of Zukor's edict, however, was her first step towards making an enemy of the mogul. In true Hollywood fashion, Paramount's publicity department started playing up her "eccentric" way of dressing and labeled her "the star who would not go Hollywood." Frances thought it all silly and, anyway, what did all those trimmings have to do with acting—"A Dusenberg wouldn't transform me into a Duse."

She and Erickson lived in a simple Laurel Canyon house, and columnists were increasingly critical of the fact that they seldom showed up at the mandatory Hollywood parties and openings, preferring instead to stay home and work or absent themselves totally on weekends on camping trips. On the rare occasion when she did speak to the press, it was usually a putdown of the movie industry, which further alienated her from the studio heads. She was a growing property, though, and was shortly destined to become even bigger when Sam Goldwyn asked to borrow her for the dual lead in *Come and Get It*. Zukor rented her for top dollar, but Frances got only her hundred-dollar-per-week contract fee, which was standard Hollywood procedure but which she felt was unfair; another chalkmark against the industry in which she was becoming more important.

She later said that she'd never worked harder on a picture than she did in *Come and Get It,* even to the point of donning a black wig and haunting the red-light district of Los Angeles to see firsthand the ways of the girls of the street and how they picked up men. She mimicked their dangling cigarettes and mannerisms

17

for the part of the saloon-singing mother who falls in love with Edward Arnold. So immersed did Frances become in the part that she often took home the wasp-waisted corsets and costumes to wear around the house in order to fully relax in them. Under Howard Hawks's direction, the part became a challenge she willingly accepted.

Midway through production, however, the director and Goldwyn had an argument over the story line and Hawks was replaced by William Wyler, a man Frances didn't even pretend to get along with. From then on the set was tense, and despite the support of other cast members like Joel McCrea and Walter Brennan, Frances was only mildly pleased with her performance in the second half of the picture as the innocent daughter who falls in love with her mother's former lover. As for Wyler, he was quoted as saying that the best thing he could say about Frances was that she was "unbearable."

Since the picture was set in the Northwest, the studio decided to premiere it in Seattle, Frances's hometown—in fact, at the very theater at which she'd once worked as an usher. Once she got there all was forgiven. The press and the populace seemed to have totally forgotten the cloud under which she'd left town a scant year before, but while her mother insisted on not "dredging up the past," Frances felt that even despite the Local-Girl-Makes-Good headlines, there were still unsolved tensions between them. As with other avenues of publicity, Frances thought the whole project worthless and time-wasting but consented, this once, to please her family. Also, it let her have her personal last laugh at the citizens who'd so violently berated her.

Come and Get It was a smash hit and reviewers were ecstatic in their praise of Frances, with "one overwrought writer proclaiming me 'Another Garbo'!" Delighted that she had succeeded as an actress, Frances was not happy when that success turned the floodlights of publicity on her, with her phone constantly ringing with some new cheesecake gimmick and other "contrived bits of fiction that staggered the imagination. 'She starts each day standing on her head, yoga-fashion, munching carrots in order to retain her figure.' I seriously considered painting myself blue to give them something authentic to print."

Communicating with the press as little as possible, she was labeled aloof and a snob who disdained the town that had brought her fame and fortune, thereby planting the seeds of ambivalence toward her that would one day leave her stranded and alone when she could have dearly used a friend or some sympathetic publicity. Actually Frances was only trying to be herself and adjust in her own manner to the new role of movie star. Instead she was branded from the first as a troublemaker and a rebel.

After the success of *Come and Get It,* she was rented out again, this time to RKO, to play opposite Cary Grant in *The Toast of New York.* The story of wall street tycoon Jim Fiske and his mistress Josie Mansfield, it had potential for honesty, but Frances's hopes for such a script evaporated as the censorship of the time laundered Josie from an unscrupulous vixen to "an ingenue fresh from Sunnybrook."

Rebelling, she shocked studio heads by giving out belittling interviews, fought with the director, Rowland V. Lee, and implored the scriptwriters to put more meat into her role—all to no avail. The picture, when released, was a success—but not for Frances. She hated it, and herself for making it, feeling that she had sold out her talent and had let her will be ground down by movie bureaucracy. She held it against the industry just as they held her attitudes against her. As for working with the screen's number one glamour boy, she later recalled him as aloof and remote, solely intent on remaining Cary Grant the personality which in Frances's eyes had nothing whatever to do with acting. People said she was letting success go to her head "but a more just appraisal would have been that I found in Hollywood success none of the satisfaction I'd imagined would be there."

Frances's political activism didn't help her position with the moguls either. She worked hard to make money for the Loyalist cause in the Spanish Civil War and other causes that were unfashionable among the decision makers of the studios.

In 1937, Paramount put Frances opposite Fred MacMurray in a newspaper yarn called *Exclusive,* and that same year she made a Technicolor adventure called *Ebb Tide* with Ray Milland, both, to her, commercialism at its crassest. The shooting schedules overlapped, and she often worked sixteen hours a day. Twice within six months she was hospitalized because of overwork. By now the glamour had worn very thin, and the surface underneath seemed riddled with tensions, discontent, and the beginning of a strong desire to escape, not only from Hollywood but from her failing marriage to Erickson as well.

That escape happened when Frances accepted a stage offer in the East where she was seen by Clifford Odets and Howard Clurman, then preparing Odets's new play, *Golden Boy,* for the prestigious and controversial Group Theater. They offered Frances the female lead. She was so flattered by the offer and the chance of working with the Group that she didn't take into consideration that one of her primary assets was her movie name, which would help get the project going. She loved the part, though, and was determined to do it. Paramount wanted her to come back home for *Beau Geste* but she pleaded to do the play and they acquiesced, although they made two stipulations. She could do only the New York run, and while doing it she was to be suspended from salary. Even that didn't matter, though, for being back onstage made her feel revived, reassured about her talent, and happier than she'd felt in a long time. At the time the Group was struggling financially even though it had had several successful productions and was backed up by talents like Jules (later John) Garfield, Lee J. Cobb, Franchot Tone, Stella and Luther Adler, and Karl Malden.

Golden Boy cost only $19,000 to produce, yet ten days before opening night, the money still had not been raised. Finally Clifford Odets and his wife, Luise Rainer, along with several others, were able to get it together, and the curtain rose on an unqualified success both for Frances and co-star Luther Adler. The play proceeded to guide the Group Theater into its first period of prosperity. Shortly after the play's opening, in November of 1937, Frances was joined in New York by her husband. One of the reasons he came east was to quelch the rumors that Frances and Odets had embarked on a stormy affair, as, in fact, they had.

To Frances, Odets had always been a romantic figure. When Luise Rainer left for Europe and he made the initial overtures, she leapt into the relationship with a savage conviction that it would work. Erickson stayed in New York to do a stage play but by then the marriage was all but over. The gossips had been right, the goodnatured fellow Frances had married now frankly bored her, and she realized she'd made a serious mistake by trying to use him to mask her own insecurities about Hollywood and its effect on her. With Odets and the success of *Golden Boy,* she realized she no longer needed Erickson, and while she didn't want to hurt him—in fact, she still felt affection for him—she no longer wanted to be his wife.

Golden Boy ran for 248 performances, and Frances was elated when she heard of a planned London production, determined to star in it, Paramount or not. She was heartbroken, though, when another actress got her part after offering to help finance the production. She felt betrayed. When the chips were down, it seemed, the Group was all too capable of selling its artistic integrity for cold, hard cash. Losing the role was an enormous blow to her ego and undermined all the new-found strength she'd gained with Odets and his play. It was during their affair that Frances became dependent on liquor to salve her often bruised ego, as Odets manipulated her back and forth across an emotional grenade-studded battleground of lovemaking and recrimination.

Retreating temporarily, she returned to Hollywood. Paramount teamed her with Erickson, of all their actors, for *Escape From Yesterday,* and she surprised everyone on the set by her docility. No one guessed that her change of attitude was because she had been so dangerously shaken. After *Escape* she managed to tour with *Golden Boy* in the United States and went back to Broadway for *Thunder Rock,* directed by Elia Kazan. It was a resounding flop for both Frances and the Group Theater, which left her feeling even more bereft and shaken.

An even more crushing blow was swift to follow, however, when Odets jilted her. After promising marriage and continued Broadway stardom, he dropped her cold with a note saying, "My wife returns from Europe today and I feel it best for us never to see each other again." And that was the last she ever heard from him. (Luise Rainer must have heard plenty about her, though, for the Odetses divorced shortly after her return.)

Odets made his escape from their affair just a week before Frances was to start rehearsals for another Broadway play, *The Fifth Column,* but as 1940 dawned the commitment seemed overwhelming. The prospect of doing the Hemingway play seemed more a penance than a joy, assuming ominous complexity. "For days I went around in a state of shock . . . liquor seemed to dull every instinct and I indulged with great frequency until I received a call for the first rehearsals. In the days that followed I lived in a state of suspended animation and functioned in a kind of blind, desolate haze. I attended rehearsals but couldn't work without collapsing in a flood of tears." In her misery at losing Odets and trying to cope with the new play, she turned to Howard Clurman "in a kind of straw-clutching panic." It was the first of a series of brief affairs that added the burden of guilt to the already heavy load of personal traumas she was juggling. She felt she couldn't continue and handed in her notice to the Theater Guild, producers of *The Fifth Column,* who promptly brought her up on charges of unprofessionalism before the Actor's Equity Union. She was fined $1,500, which nearly cleaned out her bank account, but at least she was released from one difficult obligation.

Barricading herself in her New York apartment, Frances began delving into philosophy in hopes of finding an answer for herself, a key to understanding, but the locks of her troubled mind remained tightly sealed. The only place she could think of to go was back home, but after two disastrous weeks in Seattle she returned to Hollywood.

The press greeted her with a barrage of snide tales fed by her failed marriage, the flop of *Thunder Rock,* and the debacle of *The Fifth Column.* The Golden Girl who was going to show Hollywood had returned tarnished and ill.

By now Paramount felt that the public's interest in Frances had crested, and they quickly forgot their promises of saving her for important roles. Almost as if to punish her, they began loaning her out to other studios for Technicolor trash such as *South of Pago Pago* in 1940, in which she played a goodtime girl traveling with Victor McLaglen and other assorted heavies who find an island cove loaded with pearls. Swaggering around as Ruby, she managed to give the part some spunk despite the ridiculous script, luring native Jon Hall away from the island so McLaglen and crew could entice the other natives into raiding the oyster beds. From that exotic outpost she went to Warner Brothers to star with ex-Group-member John Garfield in *Flowing Gold.*

Having finished that, she went back east for more summer stock, almost as if this hectic activity would in itself keep her growing demons at bay. During off hours she barricaded herself with a bottle, growing more debilitated and more confused. After spending a lonely winter in New York, she drove alone all the way back to Hollywood, stopping at out-of-the-way places and disguised in a black wig. Once there, Frances made an erratic decision that since she was a movie star, she'd live like one and, throwing caution aside, she rented a lavish Santa Monica mansion that had once belonged to Dolores Del Rio and installed a staff. Still alone, she rattled around the place for several weeks, brooding and more unhappy than ever. Her mother visited and for a brief moment they came together, Mrs. Farmer relishing her role as movie star mom. For once Frances had won her mother's approval—but not for long.

In April of 1941, Frances started *World Premiere* with a tragically dissipated John Barrymore, and, while the film was a poor one, she relished the chance to work with him even though, by then, the electricity of his acting was almost totally gone. After that came *Among the Living,* starring the young Susan Hayward, a "B" picture mildly received at the time, but which has acquired a late-show following over the years. Frances couldn't have cared less, though, as she was still seeking in work a respite from her personal struggles. Harold Clurman showed up in

Hollywood and set up residence with her in Santa Monica for a time while she starred as Calamity Jane in Universal's *Badlands of Dakota* opposite Robert Stack. Again she incurred studio wrath by demanding they rewrite the glamour out of the character and give her back her original grittiness. Again she lost the battle and another mark was chalked up against her name on Hollywood's list of troublemakers. At home, ironically, her mother seemed to have no reservations about Clurman setting up house with Frances, and Lillian returned home to Seattle satisfied, never grasping the tenuous emotional state her daughter was in. Mrs. Farmer saw only the externals, and for once she was pleased.

Clurman left suddenly when he patched up his marriage to Stella Adler, leaving Frances more alone than ever. Now the rumors were building of her decreasing mental stability. She managed to finish *Son of Fury* with Tyrone Power late in 1941, playing an unscrupulous beauty in league against him with George Sanders, but after that there were no more offers. Almost a year dragged by before Paramount came up with a part for her with Rosalind Russell in *Take a Letter, Darling*. Frances agreed, but by then she was hardly able to make decisions and stick to them, as evidenced by her immediately starting to skip costume and makeup tests, offering neither explanations nor apologies.

What few friends Frances had made were alienated by this time and she was alone, at a crisis point, with no one there to help or listen. Her willfulness had driven away her few supporters, and on the night of October 19, 1942, she found out just how alone she really was.

After a rare appearance at the studio, Frances stopped off for a couple of drinks before heading out to Santa Monica. On the way home she was overwhelmed with a hopeless wave of emotion, and she pulled the car over to the side of the road, bursting into tears. She neglected to shut off her headlights, though, which were on high beam, and was soon jerked out of her anguish by an irate policeman, who informed her she was in a dim-out zone, a World War II blackout restriction enforced in all coastal areas of the country, which required the driver to use only his low beams. By now Frances had been trying to solidify the demons that were chasing her, and in the policeman she saw the embodiment of them.

She screamed at him, yelling, "You bore me," and shot off in her car. He pursued and stopped her, smelled her breath, and accused her of being drunk. Frances yelled again, and since she'd forgotten her driver's license, she couldn't even prove her identity. The policeman took her into custody to the Santa Monica jail, where she was booked on a misdemeanor for violating dim-out restrictions and drunk driving. In the melee that erupted in the courtroom, the night-court judge forgot this was her first offense and sentenced her to 180 days and put her on probation. She was put into a cell, and, by the time her agent arrived eight hours later to bail her out, she was in a frenzied state. When reporters asked her to comb her hair, she told them to go to hell and take their pictures. They did, and the pictures splashed across front pages showing her disheveled appearance and the undeniably growing strain in her eyes.

Frances Farmer makes a phone call from L.A. jail prior to removal to County Hospital for observation (1943). UNITED PRESS INTERNATIONAL PHOTO.

Two days later the head of Paramount, Buddy Da Sylva, called and asked why she'd been missing appointments. Her agent, visiting her at the time, took the phone and said she'd be there promptly the next morning. She wasn't, and Paramount simply cancelled her contract.

With her driver's license suspended and her car impounded, Frances holed up in her Santa Monica mansion, barricading herself against the press and everyone else, including her mother. In the middle of November 1942, her agent got a call from an independent movie producer who wanted her for the lead in a film adaptation of John Steinbeck's *Murder at Ludice*. Thinking it would be a good time for her to get out of town and let the publicity cool down, he advised her to take it, and she was soon flown by chartered plane to Mexico City. When she got there, Frances found that there wasn't a completed shooting script. Just before she left she also got the news that she was a free woman, since Erickson had picked up a Nevada divorce decree in Reno. This new-found freedom was meaningless, however, for she had been totally on her own for some time and was growing more unstable by the day.

The film never did get off the ground, but Frances found plenty of drinking buddies among the footloose cast to keep her company—and strangers, too. So many in fact that after one alleged all-night rumpus at the hotel, which included breaking furniture and Frances's throwing a punch or two, she was asked to leave the country and was escorted by Mexican police all the way to El Paso, where she was unceremoniously dumped at a hotel. The incident is "alleged" because Frances herself didn't remember anything about it when Mexican police told her that she was being shipped out on charges of disturbing the peace and being drunk and disorderly. She only knew that she was stranded and broke in a remote Texas city. Cabling her brother, Wesley, she got the money for train fare back to California and entered a period of almost surrealistic personal horror.

When she went home she found her Santa Monica house inhabited by a strange family and all her possessions gone from it. It seems, and Frances always contended, that her sister-in-law and her mother had taken it upon themselves to strip the house and "store" Frances's possessions. Gone were her clothes, automobile, books, records, files, and, most important, the autobiographical manuscript she had been working on as a means of therapy in solving the increasing puzzle her life was becoming. Everything was gone except for a few clothes, which she was advised were waiting for her at the Knickerbocker Hotel in downtown Los Angeles where a room had been rented in her name. "I suppose it seems peculiar that I never asked questions, or received an accounting, but I didn't give a damn. At the time I neither knew nor cared." She never saw any of her things until a few years before her death when a cut-glass decanter was sent her. At the time it was a mystery she couldn't be bothered trying to fathom, and the near future would make it unimportant.

Almost broke as 1943 rushed at her, Frances was lucid enough to realize that she needed to make some money, so she took the lead in a low-budget film called *There's No Escape* at Monogram Studios, the poverty row of Hollywood, haven of used-up starlets and washed-up stars. The title of the picture was more prophetic than she realized, and her behavior became increasingly erratic, alternating between fits of laughter and ear-shattering tantrums. The first day of shooting arrived with Frances, acting wild, demanding a total script rewrite, and flying into another tantrum when the producers tried to talk her into doing a scene that required she be bound and gagged.

A week into shooting, the fragile bubble of Frances's sanity burst. In her dressing room, when her hairdresser started combing her hair, Frances exploded into anger, struck out at the woman, ripped off her wig, and dislocated her jaw. That was the last straw for the producers, and she was replaced by Mary Brian. Licking her wounds, Frances retreated to her hotel, where trouble erupted again when she became drunk in the bar, slid out of her sweater, and threw a glass at a mirror behind the bar, smashing it. Later she took a sleeping pill and went to bed. Several hours later she was awakened by a pounding at her door. Nude, she refused to open it, whereupon it was broken through, and a naked Frances was confronted by a police matron and two policemen. In her deteriorating mental condition, Frances had given no thought to her probation and had never reported to a parole officer. The police had a bench warrant for her arrest because of this oversight and took her into custody, with Frances struggling all the while. She ran into the bathroom, but they knocked that door down, too, and they finally got her dressed and under control. They dragged her kicking and screaming through the hotel lobby and took her to the police station. There the officers, who had been searching for her for two weeks, got a new jolt when she listed her occupation as "cocksucker" (as reported in Kenneth Anger's *Hollywood Babylon*).

At the court hearing she created more disturbance when she saw the large group of reporters and photographers present. "Rats!" she called them as they shot her disheveled appearance. When Judge Marshall Hickson asked her about the hotel bar brawl, she denied taking part in it, in fact, didn't remember it at all. When he asked her about her drinking, though, she came through loud and clear with an answer. "Listen, I put liquor in my milk. I put liquor in my coffee and in my orange juice. What do you want me to do, starve to death? I drink everything, including benzedrine." At that, the red-faced judge rose from his chair and re-activated the suspended 180-day sentence to be served in the Los Angeles City Jail. Frances yelled "Fine," adding, "Have you ever had a broken heart?"—an obvious reference to her failed marriage and her disastrous affair with Odets. Then she picked up an inkpot and threw it at the judge, hitting him with stunning accuracy. As she was being led away the reality of her situation began to seep through. They were going to lock her up. She whispered, "We must find the men who gave me this part. Only they can release me." Then she turned violent again after being denied a phone call. She floored one policeman and hit a matron, finally being subdued with a straightjacket and put in a cell, all of which was photographed by newsmen.

Frances's parents had appeared by this time, and Mrs. Farmer spoke to the press with her usual zeal, saying, "They might be planning a picture for her with jail scenes in it and want her to be able to give a performance based on actual experience.'' She seemed not to realize the seriousness of her daughter's condition, and when told of her daughter's admission of heavy drinking, readily agreed, saying ''Of course that's Frances's trouble. She does it as an escape from herself and her frustrations. She has had bad advice in her professional life from people more interested in her money-making abilities than in her personal welfare.'' Mrs. Farmer also darkly hinted that her daughter's penchant for supporting left-wing causes was also partially to blame for her condition.

The newspapers had a field day far in excess of the relative news value of the incident; it was a Hollywood scandal, and they relished it. At a sanity hearing two days later, Frances sat quietly as the chief county psychiatrist testified, ''I have examined Miss Farmer on successive days during her stay here, and I have found her to be mentally ill. She is in need of care and treatment and I would recommend that she be placed in a sanitarium.'' The Screen Actor's Guild came to her aid and placed her in the Kimbel Sanitarium in the San Fernando Valley.

At first Frances responded well to the peaceful place and the first rest she'd had in years. But after several weeks there, her doctors began treating her with insulin shock treatments, which she later said were at least partially to blame for her many memory lapses. Over the eight months she was there, she was subjected to ninety of the shots—''ninety sweating comas''—a brutal and inhumane treatment, which has subsequently been deemed ineffective in the treatment of mental illness. They did make her more docile, though, which was probably the original intention.

After her release from the sanitarium, Frances went home to Seattle, and the publicity subsided to occasional snippets in the columns, capped by Louella Parsons's pronouncement that the ''Hollywood Cinderella Girl has gone back to the ashes on a liquor-slicked highway.'' Her mother was appointed her legal guardian, but the uneasy truce between them deteriorated; shortly after Frances's return to Seattle, her mother had her committed to the state asylum. After three months Frances was released as being totally cured but had to return to the family home. There was nowhere else to go. Mrs. Farmer now assumed the position that Frances had disgraced her, and she took her daughter's troubles as a personal affront. She wanted Frances to resume her movie career, saying that during her hospitalization there had been several tentative inquiries as to whether she'd be able to work again. But Frances rebelled against the very idea of going back to Hollywood.

That stalemate lasted almost a year until a huge fight erupted when Mrs. Farmer grandly summoned a visiting Zasu Pitts to the house, supposedly to cheer Frances up. Frances didn't even know the actress, and, what's more, didn't want to, but Zasu was a favorite of her mother, who was mortified and furious when Frances refused to even see her. Mrs. Farmer continued with her grandiose plans for Frances's Hollywood return, undeterred by her daughter's negativism, until finally they came to blows. Frances threatened her mother's life if she continued badgering her, and she slugged her father when he tried to intervene—ineffectually, as usual. For Mother Farmer that was the last straw, and on May 22, 1945, she had Frances recommitted to the state hospital. Frances was thirty years old.

For the next five years the privileges of a Love Goddess were incinerated in the fire of her incarceration, and all the glowing reviews that had heralded her career at its beginning couldn't save her from the hell of each day.

Since Frances was a readmission case, she was treated as incurably insane and was subjected to outrageous treatment by staff and inmates alike. For an independent woman, being trapped inside this snake pit was a monumental punishment for wrongs, many of which she was not even capable of remembering. As she described in her autobiography, *Will There Really Be a Morning?* she was assigned to the violent ward, where she was forced to work long, inhumane hours in the clothing dispensary, watched over every moment of the day by sadistic matrons who tormented her with verbal and physical abuse. At first, she said, she struggled against her fate, screaming nights away until they put her into solitary confinement, a mean cell which didn't even contain a toilet. It was there, early on in her confinement, that Frances's strong will asserted itself and she made a personal vow to survive, somehow to come out of it all intact, although, for her, there was no end in sight. There were no seasons, no holidays, no release from the ever present anxiety of knowing she was a social outcast, forgotten by the world and unloved even by those few people she should have been able to expect it from. She had been confined to a mental death sentence, and it was only her almost perverse streak of determined pride that gradually helped her cope with it all until she could come up for review by the board of directors.

Surrounded by the hopelessly insane, women who had torn themselves apart emotionally and were now doing it physically, fighting at the fence at the end of the ward for the few scraps of almost inedible food, Frances fought, too, for the food and against the injustice. When her mother had petitioned for her readmittance, she asserted, among other things, that Frances had tortured her pet dog. This fact was later held against her when a cat somehow managed to crawl into the ward only to be ripped apart at the hands of the savage women. According to Frances, she tried to save the cat and, found holding its bloody remains in her hands, was accused of killing it. The reward for her attempted kindness was to be thrown into one of the silent, filthy black rooms where the time of day or night was ascertained only by the slit of light or darkness underneath the door. This incident, too, is described in her autobiography.

While she watched other women sink deeper and deeper into black abysses of madness, the desire to survive, to be well, grew slowly but strongly in her. She played by the rules, keeping quiet when her nerves were ready to burst into screams at the horrors of her surroundings. Women cried for God, but help never came, and she was reminded of her long-ago thesis that God was dead. Now she had visible proof that her adolescent idea was true in the meanest terms imaginable.

Finally, on the morning of March 22, 1950, a glimmer of hope appeared. At first, Frances suspected it was just a ruse, another cruel trick. She was told to appear for a parole hearing. By then she had all but resigned herself to spending the rest of her life in this living purgatory, and the summons took her totally by surprise. She was allowed to bathe and wash her close-cropped hair, but she was not allowed to shave the five-year growth of hair under her arms and on her legs. The staff asked her a few cursory questions about the weather and had her count to fifty and back, and that was it. On their records, which she herself didn't see until years later, were notations that she had become more docile and had been helpful to less fortunate patients. These notations, her interview, and a simple letter from her father unlocked the doors that had held her captive so long. (The letter requested her release, since she was needed at home to help care for her mother, who had suffered a slight stroke.) Three days later her father came to pick her up.

In later years Frances admitted that she was obviously out of her mind for some time but recognized that it was her own strength of will that ultimately pulled her out of it, certainly not any help that she got at the institution. She pulled, clawed, and worked her own way out of the maze of madness that had entrapped her, surviving as she had vowed she would—but not without terrible scars that never really healed.

Her reception at home was a frantic one, with her mother still the domineering woman she'd always been, only more so now that her mobility was hampered by ill health. Frances's ineffectual father was more a nuisance than a parent, yet Frances followed every command, laundered all the soiled bed linen and washed every dish without complaint. The reason? She thought that at a moment's notice her parents could have her recommitted. Frances never knew until several years later that, one year after her release, as of March 25, 1951, she had been discharged from the jurisdiction of the Western State Hospital as fully recovered by order of the Superior Court. Her parents never told her she was free, however, and they tormented her with threats of "sending you back" long after the year was up. It was a cruel trick to ensure her presence, to keep the much-needed "slavey" at home.

When her father became seriously ill and was put in a nursing home, the friction between Frances and her mother intensified. In June of 1953, with her father gone, Frances took a cautious step and wrote to the superintendent of the mental institution asking to appear before the staff to petition for a final discharge. He replied that her father had already requested and accomplished that, and that her civil rights, denied all adjudged mentally ill, had long since been restored to her.

Still disbelieving, she insisted on returning and making the appearance, and on July 1 she willingly but with great trepidation approached the institution that had been her personal hell for so long. She told them she had been unaware of the change of status and wanted proof. They gave her the necessary proof and she left, returning a few days later for a formal Superior Court discharge in "The Matter of the Insanity of Mrs. Frances Anderson." (Anderson was Leif Erickson's real name and the one she used.) That resolved, she petitioned to have her mother removed as her legal guardian. That too was granted, and Frances was finally free after nearly nine years.

The first thing she did was to find a job, as a valet at Seattle's Olympic Hotel. The one-time Golden Girl of Hollywood subsisted on an income of seventy-five cents per hour, earned by taking and delivering hotel guests' laundry.

Her mother was growing increasingly senile, but in the back of Frances's mind lurked the idea that if Lillian could have had her put away once, she might, somehow, be able to do it again. With cold calm she decided to take a further step toward independence and safety: she decided to get married. The man she chose was an employee of the city engineering department named Alfred H. Lobley, Jr. whom she met on a blind date set up by a co-worker. He was a calculated choice. He provided stability and security for her, in return for which she provided the dubious glamour of marriage to Frances Farmer the actress. She never professed to love him, but she did her best to make the marriage run smoothly. One hindrance was that they moved in with her mother, who was becoming increasingly incompetent, so much so that within a month of the marriage Frances had to leave her job to stay home and care for her.

The end of the mutually tormenting mother-daughter relationship finally came. Frances called her half-sister, Rita, who agreed to have her mother come and stay with her for a while. En route to the airport, Frances, Alfred, and her mother picked up her father at the nursing home. The quartet then went to the airport, where Mr. Farmer clung emotionally to his wife. They said goodbye to Lillian, and Frances returned her father to the home. That was the last time she was ever to see either one again.

Something about her emotionless attitude toward her parents obviously upset her husband, and that night drank himself into a fury. By the weekend he had destroyed much of the new livingroom suite he had purchased in an attempt to perk up the old house. Frances sat on the side porch while he rampaged inside, and after he had passed out on the floor, calmly took sixty dollars from his wallet and walked out. Feeling neither elation nor regret, she went to the bus station and bought a ticket for as far as the money could take her. That destination turned out to be Eureka, California, a geographic compromise costing forty-two dollars in the 1954 economy.

For the next three and a half years Frances submerged herself in the small town, taking a job as a typist/secretary for a commercial photographer, trying to forget the Frances Farmer that was and get a hold on the reality that faced her every morning in the bathroom mirror of her small rooming house. She made no friends and never told anyone who she was, and no one asked. Having been out of the public eye for a decade, she wasn't surprised at this, only grateful. Living and working under the name Frances Anderson, she made no contact whatsoever with her husband or her family until she was finally tracked down through the local social security office. She was then informed that both her parents were dead and the estate was being settled.

Her days were spent in the tedium of organizing graduation and wedding portraits, and her nights were spent in trying to exorcise the demons of the past that came back to haunt her. Gradually she began drinking again as a way to help calm these mental foes. Knowing she was playing with fire, she regulated her drinking so it wouldn't interfere with her work, stealthily hiding her lunchtime drinking with chewing gum and working steadily, surviving. She bought her wine at different stores, knowing that Eureka was a small town and gossip-prone, like any other. Old fears sprang up and she took to locking her liquor in a suitcase chained to her bedstead.

She had no social life whatsoever outside her work until one night when, on a booze-buying spree, Frances stopped at a waterfront bar. With her two shopping bags of liquor at her feet, she only wanted to buy a pint of vodka and be on her way when a man came up behind her and said, "You're Frances Farmer, aren't you?" Caught off guard, she told him yes, and asked how he knew. The stocky, middle-aged man looked at her and said simply, "I remember you."

His name was Leland Mikesell, a salesman of radio advertising spots, and he immediately became overwhelmed with plans for a Frances Farmer comeback. A fast talker, he convinced her to withdraw her savings of $400 and come with him to San Francisco, where he would personally re-launch her. Until then she had never thought of trying to revive her career, dead as it was, buried under an avalanche of personal tragedies and public ostracism. Her isolation in Eureka had gotten her nowhere, and she found herself open to his platitudes and promises.

He wanted to marry her, but first he wanted to revive her career. He laid out a ground plan: she would begin working as a reservations clerk at San Francisco's Park Sheraton Hotel, and after a short time there they would tell the hotel people who she was and call a press conference. It worked, and in mid-June of 1957 her name appeared in the headlines: FRANCES FARMER FOUND AS HOTEL CLERK. Hollywood's hard-luck, headstrong girl was back in the news and, shortly, in show business, although she faced that prospect with concern over whether the public still wanted her and, for that matter, whether she truly wanted them. The fire of fame had once almost consumed her, and, without Mikesell, she might never have been tempted near it again.

Considering all she'd been through she looked remarkably well, the blonde beauty somewhat diminished by her ordeals but still there nonetheless. Ed Sullivan contacted her to appear on his television show and she consented. It was the first time the public had seen her in over fifteen years and, ironically, they heard her sing "Aura Lee," her famous song from *Come and Get It,* recently revived by Elvis Presley as *"Love Me Tender."* Clad in a striped *crepe de chine* skirt and simple black sweater, she perched nervously on a rustic chair, strumming the simple melody on a guitar. The reaction to her appearance was personally rewarding to her, and Sullivan asked her back for another appearance. She was then signed by the Bucks County Playhouse to appear in *The Chalk Garden,* which earned good reviews even though all were prefaced by a capsulized history of her downfall. She learned to sidestep impertinent interviewers, though, granting them time only when it was important to the production. In July of 1957 she sued to have her marriage from Lobley dissolved, and when the divorce went through almost a year later she married Mikesell.

Like any small-time opportunist who latches onto a famous name, Mikesell took over her career possessively and did accomplish a lot, considering their stormy offstage relationship. She returned to Hollywood for a "Playhouse 90" and then, in a show of poor judgment, accepted a bid to appear on "This Is Your Life." It was one of the few times that the program's producers approached a star ahead of time, wanting to take no chances with the famous Farmer temper. The program turned out to be one of the most personally insulting shows, as again her past was dredged up and, in front of television cameras, she was asked to recount

Frances Farmer sings on "The Ed Sullivan Show" in 1957. It was the first time the public had seen her in fifteen years. PICTORIAL PARADE

31

her past: the drugs, the alcohol, the mental institutions. It was torture, compounded by the fact that none of her old friends or co-workers would consent to appear with her. In Hollywood, feuds and ill will last long, and all she got out of it was the type of publicity she didn't need, and an Edsel.

In 1958 she returned to her old home studio, Paramount, for what would be her last film, a teenage quickie called *The Party Crashers,* in which she played the mother of another Hollywood tragedy, Bobby Driscoll (who would die, alone, ten years later of a drug overdose in an abandoned New York City tenement).

Mikesell arranged another summer stock tour, which ended in his hometown of Indianapolis, but their marriage, highlighted by her still-frequent drinking bouts, was disintegrating quickly. After the run of the play she was approached by the local NBC affiliate TV station to host a daytime movie show to be called "Frances Farmer Presents." She grabbed the offer.

By now the Mikesells' private difficulties had extended to public displays on his part, something now abhorrent to her in light of her past. They divorced in 1963. Like the other men in her life, husbands and lovers, he was a mistake, another in the string of men she self-destructively attracted and was attracted to, but he, at least, was the last mistake of this type that she would make.

Meanwhile the television show went remarkably well, and she had visiting celebrities such as Ginger Rogers, Helen Hayes, and Vivian Vance on it, and one poignant interview with Leif Erickson, their first meeting since their divorce. In 1964 she was named Indiana's Businesswoman of the Year and went to New York for a "Today Show" appearance. But her personal life was still basically one of loneliness, drinking, and frustration. The day that Clifford Odets died she appeared on camera in such condition that they had to stop the show and send her home. Shortly after that, in March of 1964, suffering from low blood pressure aggravated by her continued drinking, she appeared on camera again slurring her words, incoherently announcing "Frances Farmer Prevents," and that was the end. Her show was cancelled.

A few years later, in 1968, she decided to try to set her story down on paper. She began negotiations to collaborate with Lois Kibbee on the work. It was a soul-searing experience for her, one that would often have to be eased by liquor. By now, though, she had finally found something she had never really had before, a friend. Her name was Jean Ratcliffe, and they lived together simply in a large old farmhouse just outside Indianapolis on Mollner Road. There Frances was able to enjoy an ever-growing brood of cats, and she felt a greater sense of personal peace than she'd ever known before. She and Jean formed a corporation to market a line of cosmetics, but that ultimately broke down. Frances wrote poetry, performed as artist-in-residence at Purdue University, and, in general, tried to juggle the pieces of her life into a satisfactory whole.

Her correspondence with Miss Kibbee reflects that attitude along with an occasionally insightful sense of humor. One morning in June, for example, when she awoke to find the book material spread across the family room floor, courtesy of her cats, she wrote, "Must I explain they had a ball, literally, not with yarn this time but with editorial material. Oh well, no harm done . . . nothing eaten or digested . . . everything just exuberantly rearranged. Shades of Hedda Gabler! And I've always had a hankering to play the part of that bored woman! We're trying to get the garden wrung out and the stone work decorative, for when you come back in August you must see that we are good housekeepers out-of-doors as well as in. Sport, my dog, will want to look his best for you, too.''

Jean Ratcliffe kept asking Miss Kibbee to encourage Frances to tape-record her life story for the book, an experience that would often leave Frances rattled and furious as she looked back over the tattered landscape of her life. ''Just make her work,'' Jean wrote once, ''or I'll lose my mind . . . and if I do that, who'll mix the drinks?''

After a brief illness Frances wrote, ''There's a beastly hopelessness in sitting out the aches and pains of mortal flesh. You live, you survive, wondering what for. Recovery brings back the spirit and the answer.''

When her oldest cat was killed, Frances was philosophical. ''We lost Lennie, struck down and mangled by a car on the street out front. I can't say what a shock it was to us to have to admit . . . he's dead. A gentle, deaf, loving creature, he seemed so much more involved in the world of human beings than the other critters who make their home with us here. 'Well, in the midst of life we are in . . . ,' I heard myself blankly uttering to the vet when he announced the verdict. Why is it that truly deep feelings evoke nothing but the most blatantly trite quotes at first? I wasn't about to forgive God for this. Then I wept. So Lennie won't be here anymore.''

A particularly difficult job for Frances was reading the finally assembled medical reports of her years in the institution, but she read with interest how she was eventually ''cured,'' knowing full well that she'd done most of the job herself by sheer force of will. But happily there were other things to help, like her home. ''Summer definitely seems to be on the wane tho the sun is still hot and the Kentucky Wonder beans have grown way beyond the reach of human touch or step ladder,'' she wrote in August of 1969. ''The tornados are striking and the crickets are bellowing in the bushes. Spiders are madly weaving veils over everything inside and out, sure signs according to the Hoosier almanac that there's going to be a winter. Sure signs that I ought to get out broom and dust cloth for autumn cleaning, but I ignore them. My mother used to say she never saw a cobweb in the house until her best friend and most meticulous housekeeper came up the front path. *I*, no doubt, will be running for the vacuum sweeper when Gabriel comes to call.''

Assembling various material brought to light things she'd never known and gave her a perspective by which to reassess old relationships. ''I've been thinking about that letter my sister, Edith, wrote to Louella Parsons re: libel, threats of suit, etc. Extraordinary! Naturally she never mentioned it to me then or ever. I gathered it up among the other things stashed away with what purpose in mind God knows. Among my protectors she stands out as embarrassingly naive. I find that people *will* interpret you behind your back as well as to your face in spite of the fact that you too speak English and have a voice of your own. Silence has been my defence, not always a successful one. But then I grew tired of fighting a long time ago. There have been times when I've been compelled, under the impetus of too much wine and anguish, to cry out, like Miss Madrigal in *The Chalk Garden,* 'Quoted, yes! But *if* quoted, quoted *rightly!*' One gets fired for that sort of thing and the misquotes go on in the end. So you learn to become the judge as well as the judged. . . . [Edith] will spring up to defend herself as well as me. She will diagnose, accuse, protest, and rationalize all of her animadversions and ideas-fixe concerning the Hollywood actress who went wrong. The human being, her sister, she *will* not know.''

The humor kept surfacing, though, to support her, as it did in March of 1970 when she noted, ''This is one of those days. . . . At the crack of dawn they hauled the motor out of the well pump and took it away with vague promises of return. I grow more bath-and-humor less as the day wears on. . . . The will to persevere grows fainter and if it weren't for Lent I'd relent and get swacked . . . to hell with it.''

Though she didn't know it for a while yet, these were the last months of Frances Farmer's life. The book she was working on with Lois Kibbee was never completed, but another did appear after her death entitled *Will There Really Be a Morning?,* assembled by Jean Ratcliffe. Frances contracted cancer of the esophagus in the spring of 1970 and was hospitalized for three weeks. After that she was able to go home to her beloved cats, cornfields, and friends—but only for a while.

She died on August 1, 1970, at age fifty-six. In death she received her final notices, and they were kind ones. The torments of sexual insecurity and professional conflicts ended quietly in the Indianapolis Community Hospital on a summer afternoon. Happily for her, when death finally did come it came quickly, unlike the larger portions of her life in which she lived in slow agony and threatening shadow.

FILMOGRAPHY

Frances Farmer

TITLE	YEAR	DIRECTOR	LEADING PLAYERS
Too Many Parents	1936	Robert McGowan	Lester Matthews, Porter Hall, Henry Travers, Billy Lee
Border Flight	1936	Otho Lovering	John Howard, Roscoe Karns, Robert Cummings, Grant Withers
Rhythm on the Range	1936	Norman Taurog	Bing Crosby, Bob Burns, Martha Raye, Lucile Gleason
Come and Get It	1936	Howard Hawks William Wyler	Edward Arnold, Joel McCrea, Walter Brennan, Andrea Leeds

TITLE	YEAR	DIRECTOR	LEADING PLAYERS
The Toast of New York	1937	Rowland V. Lee	Edward Arnold, Cary Grant, Jack Oakie, Donald Meek
Exclusive	1937	Alexander Hall	Fred MacMurray, Charlie Ruggles, Lloyd Nolan, Fay Holden
Ebb Tide	1937	James Hogan	Ray Milland, Oscar Homolka, Lloyd Nolan, Barry Fitzgerald
Ride a Crooked Mile	1938	Alfred E. Green	Akim Tamiroff, Leif Erickson, Lynne Overman, John Miljan
South of Pago Pago	1940	Alfred E. Green	Jon Hall, Victor McLaglen, Olympe Bradna, Gene Lockhart
Flowing Gold	1940	Alfred E. Green	John Garfield, Pat O'Brien, Raymond Walburn, Cliff Edwards
World Premiere	1941	Ted Tetzlaff	John Barrymore, Eugene Pallette, Virginia Dale, Ricardo Cortez
Badlands of Dakota	1941	Alfred E. Green	Robert Stack, Ann Rutherford, Richard Dix, Broderick Crawford
Among the Living	1941	Stuart Heisler	Albert Dekker, Susan Hayward, Harry Carey, Maude Eburne
Son of Fury	1942	John Cromwell	Tyrone Power, Gene Tierney, George Sanders, Roddy MacDowell, John Carradine, Elsa Lanchester
The Party Crashers	1958	Bernard Girard	Mark Damon, Bobby Driscoll, Connie Stevens

Betty Grable

I am what I want to be. Just give me the lines that lead into a song-and-dance routine. I'm the kind of girl that truck drivers love.

Betty Grable talking in 1942
about her screen image.

Everyone has to have a gimmick and I've been standing on mine for years.

Betty Grable talking in 1968
about her screen image.

Iᶠ ever a star had a trademark, or in Betty's case, two, it was those gorgeous Grable gams. In the dark days of World War II, they became a symbol of everything the boys abroad were fighting for. And unlike other Love Goddesses, Grable was always down to earth enough to be grateful for the fame her legs, and her undeniable talent, brought her, and she never tried to embroider on it. If the public wanted her in tights—and they assuredly did considering she grossed an incredible $100 million at the box office during her peak years of stardom—that's just what she gave them. For the year 1946–47, the Treasury Department listed her as the highest salaried woman in America, at $300,000, and her home studio, Twentieth Century Fox, insured those famous legs for $1 million, making them more valuable than Fred Astaire's or Marlene Dietrich's.

Her specialty was the naive girl on the make, who was usually trying to make it in show business. And in countless films she played just that—backstage, front-stage, and, especially, onstage, showcasing her legs, the bright, happy smile, and the resilient heart-of-gold personality that made her the most popular pinup girl of the war. In fact, she virtually originated the term "pinup."

From Germany to Japan her pictures accompanied our servicemen, who hastily tacked them up over a million barracks beds in a thousand quonset huts.

Betty Grable in a typical starlet pose—in a typical starlet hat (circa 1938).
THE DOUG MCCLELLAND COLLECTION.

Clad in a white bathing suit topped by a hurricane of blonde curls, she looked over her right shoulder with a come-hither glance that made every G. I. want to get the fighting over with and get home. On many a faraway atoll, those famous legs tapped their way into G. I. dreams, and when in 1941 she sang "You Started Something" in *Moon over Miami,* each one took it personally.

There was nothing exotic or aloof about Betty Grable. She epitomized the kind of girl that any guy, with a little luck, might meet. She was an All American Love Goddess, projecting a straightforward, sweater-filled allure; the dream girl of Everyman and one of the most popular movie stars of all time. Betty was witty and wisecracking, warm and quite wonderful, stretching what she herself always thought was a minor talent into a bouncy legend.

When she hit the box office Top Ten for the first time in 1942, a grateful studio promised her Technicolor for the rest of her career. And a colorful one it was, too, until the early fifties when she was unseated in the affections of the public by another blonde bombshell—Marilyn Monroe.

For a while Betty tried to compete with Monroe. In fact, she co-starred with Monroe in the classic *How To Marry a Millionaire* in 1953. However, she could read the handwriting on the wall through her slipping box office receipts, and, though it saddened her greatly, she walked away from her movie career in 1955 after *Three for the Show.*

She worked through the thirties to become a star, topped the heap during the forties, and dropped it all halfway through the next decade—still a star, still a name that conjured up happy memories for millions all over the world. Her prime films had been as welcome as an extra gas ration ticket or a letter from home. At her funeral in 1973, her Las Vegas pastor said simply, "She kept up our spirits and made us proud to be Americans." After mom and apple pie, the hottest contender for third place in America's affections was Betty Grable.

BETTY's life began in much the same way as many other screen stars' did. In fact, maybe a little better. There were no slums to crawl out of as with Betty Hutton and Susan Hayward; no ghetto prejudice as with Dorothy Dandridge. Neither was she born into a family of troupers and thus committed to a career from childhood on, as was Rita Hayworth. The only thing she had in common with most was a determined stage mother whose own lack of career proved the impetus for Betty's.

Ruth Elizabeth Grable was born December 18, 1916, in St. Louis, Missouri, the daughter of Conn and Lillian Grable. He was a bookkeeper who later achieved success as an investment counselor, while Lillian was a frustrated actress. The mother of two daughters, she channeled her efforts into making something of Betty, when Betty's older sister quietly but firmly rebelled.

It's unlikely that Betty would ever have gravitated to the performing life without her mother's influence, but gravitate she did, from the first dance lesson her mother arranged. That lesson was the start of a regimen which covered the ground from tap to ballet to acrobatic. "I don't think I missed a thing except eccentric dancing. I dreaded every lesson, and I especially hated acrobatic dancing." For good measure, Lillian also gladly dipped into the family coffers for money to pay for the study of the saxophone, the ukelele, and the trap drums. "Mother was determined not to miss a trick. I got my start in a children's show playing the saxophone. I was dressed as if I were a piece of coral. Later I did a bit where I played and tapped at the same time. We cut that short but quick; it almost loosened my teeth."

Betty's formal schooling was at the exclusive Mary's Institute, but she was constantly jerked away from that staid atmosphere when her mother entered her in kiddie shows at the St. Louis Odean on amateur nights, which were emceed by visiting celebrities such as Jack Haley and Frank Fay at the Missouri Theater.

Some Grable family friends and family members objected to Lillian's attempts to steer her youngest daughter into a theatrical career, something still considered a bit low class at the time. So Mama Lil plotted out another avenue for her daughter to display her budding talents. Whenever the family went on a vacation, Lillian had Betty virtually sing for her supper at various hotels along the way, figuring that Betty needed the exposure. Meanwhile, Betty recalled, "I died inside at the thought of it."

Lillian shortly came to the conclusion that the best place for her, *and* her daughter, to vacation was Hollywood. The family first went west in 1928. While the others saw the sights, Lillian saw casting directors, scouted out the studios, and set up auditions for her very young daughter. Nothing happened. They returned the following year, and Betty resumed auditioning, until one day she came home smiling.

"Mother," she said, "I had to lie and pretend I was 15, but I got a chance to dance in the chorus of *Let's Go Places.*" She was actually thirteen at the time.

Mrs. Grable convinced her husband to return home to St. Louis, while she and the girls stayed West, and, like the father of Linda Darnell nine years later (Chapt. IV), he listened. In the annals of Hollywood, a mother with a starlet-to-be daughter always proved to be ultimately persuasive.

Unlike Linda, though, Betty's career didn't take off into immediate starring roles. For her the thirties were to prove a hectic, painful time, with mostly chorus-girl campus-cutie bits and a brief career as a Goldwyn Girl. Sam Goldwyn liked what he saw of her in his 1930 Eddie Cantor starrer, *Whoopee,* changed her name to Frances Dean, and, the following year, used her in *Kiki, Palmy Days,* and *The Greeks Had a Word for Them.* After *The Kid from Spain,* he dropped the youngster because he didn't think she was star material. But how could he really tell? His makeup department had made over the teenager in a ridiculous attempt to Garbo-ize her, a tactic that totally obliterated her natural sparkle.

For a while she sang with Ted Fio Rita's orchestra and, after a few more small parts in movies, got a good break in 1934 in the Astaire-Rogers classic *The Gay Divorcee.* Another star of that film, Erik Rhodes, recalls that "She was full of pep, Betty was. When she did her big number with Edward Everett Horton, *Let's Knock Knees,* we all knew there was something special about her, something appealing that made you feel good inside."

George Raft obviously felt the same way when he met the young dancer and asked her to accompany him to the six-day bicycle races. Betty might not have known a line when she heard one, but mother Lillian did. She said Betty could go but had to be home by 11:30 P.M.—an early hour for a six-day race—and had to take her sister with her. At the time, Raft was one of Hollywood's reigning Lotharios, as famous for his performances offscreen as he was on. But even for him a teenager was stretching the point, and his friends joshed him about being a cradle robber.

He fell genuinely in love with Betty, though, but realized the facts of life, Hollywood-style, and told a friend, who promptly told Betty, "I'm giving her back till she grows up." That's exactly what he did, too, according to *George Raft* by Lewis Yablonsky (McGraw Hill). But throughout the thirties, he watched her blossom from overripe child into fully ripe woman. Later they were to resume their romance replete with headlines.

In the meantime, Betty kept chipping away at a career. She later said that she couldn't act any better, sing any better, or dance any better "than a dozen people I can name." Yet, while others quickly flashed and fell by the wayside of Hollywood and Vine, Betty continued moving upward—although she was the first to admit it was a long, hard, and slow climb.

During the Depression year of the Thirties, Hollywood was a mecca for every pretty girl from every no-name town in the country. Gleaming on the West Coast like the Emerald City of Oz, Hollywood was a place where dreams could be made to come true. For years, Betty was just another of the many talented and ambitious youngsters who peopled its bungalow courts and cottages and puttered up and down its newly laid-out streets in roadsters and Model-T Fords. Said Betty later, "I was lucky, that's all; just lucky." Also, she had the constant encouragement of her mother.

Thanks to Lillian's diligence, Betty was always trying new avenues to success. She performed song and dance stints with Jay Whidden's orchestra at the Mark Hopkins Hotel in San Francisco and headed down the coast for similar appearances at Santa Monica's Miramar. RKO used her in *The Nitwits* in 1935, and *Old Man Rhythm* and *Collegiate* the following year, the latter starring Joe Penner and his duck.

After that she was in another Rogers-Astaire movie, *The Fleet's In,* and began a romance with former child star Jackie Coogan. At first, Betty's mother was against the affair which smoldered in the gossip columns for months. As always, Betty listened to her mother and promised that no matter how serious things got, she wouldn't marry anyone until she was twenty-one. She was desperately in love with Jackie though, and four weeks before her twenty-first birthday her mother relented. They were married on December 20, 1937.

At the time, the actor who had starred in classics like *The Kid* (1921) with Charlie Chaplin was twenty-three years old and out of work, but Jackie was confident their marriage would get off to a great start because "I'm soon going to receive a million dollars. I made it when I was a kid." Betty couldn't have cared less about the money at the time, but later, when it became evident that he wasn't going to get it, her feelings about the money changed drastically.

He was to have gotten the money (estimated as high as $4 million) when he was twenty-one, but it wasn't until he became serious about Betty that he decided to fight for it, taking his mother to court over the savings. Jackie's father had died in 1935, and his mother had then wed the family's financial manager, Arthur Bernstein. While Jackie's movie career slipped away as he grew up and out of stardom, the Bernsteins were living a life of extreme luxury on his money. The court fight that ensued was a bitter one, with charges and counter-charges flying back and forth—and all over the headlines—between mother and son. Said Mrs. Bernstein at one point, "I'm not really bitter at Jackie. I'm just filled with regret that I should have put so much time and spent so much money trying to make the right sort of man out of him only to discover that he is really very stupid." Coogan said his mother had been influenced by Bernstein and that if his father had lived, "this suit would not have been necessary."

At the time there were no laws regulating the earnings of child stars, but the tragedy of Jackie Coogan brought one about. After the Bernsteins were forced to pay him the miniscule (considering) sum of $126,307.50 in settlement, the California courts enacted the Child Actor's Bill, shortly dubbed the Coogan Act, to protect future cinema moppets from overspending parents and guardians.

The settlement money went quickly to pay off Jackie's debts, and the marriage was off to a rocky start. Betty kept working (*Pigskin Parade* at Twentieth with a young Judy Garland), and together, riding the crest of publicity engendered by the trial, the Coogans toured in a vaudeville act that was well received. Everyone was anxious to see the former star and his gorgeous young wife.

Jackie had apparently inherited a talent for spending money as fast, if not faster, than he earned it, and he was singularly immature about handling it. Betty gave him support in his legal battles and career, but it quickly became evident to Hollywood at large that she was growing up a lot faster than he was.

Career-wise she also seemed to be doing better than he when in 1937 Paramount asked her to step into Shirley Ross's part in *This Way Please,* starring Jack Benny and his wife Mary Livingston. Ross had left the production because Benny kept building up his wife's part.

The studio was so pleased with Betty's replacement duty they put her right into *Thrill of a Lifetime* and signed her to a contract. She supported Martha Raye in a couple of 1938 Raye vehicles (*College Swing* and *Give Me a Sailor*) and was eventually starred with husband Jackie in *Million Dollar Legs*—a prophetic title even if the legs, in this picture at least, belonged to a football team.

Betty listened to the studio's plans for launching a massive publicity campaign to build her into stardom. But she had the rug pulled out from under her when they suddenly scratched their plans. Like Goldwyn several years before, they gave the reason that she wasn't yet ready for the big time.

She and Jackie tried vaudeville again, and she made *The Day the Bookies Wept* at RKO, but by now the marriage was foundering. Her husband's spending habits and her career frustrations combined to bring the marriage down. They separated in 1939, and, the following year, when the divorce became final, Betty found that after all her years of hard work, her biggest claim to fame was as "Coogan's ex."

With nothing happening in Hollywood, Betty accepted an offer of the second female lead in Broadway's *DuBarry Was a Lady,* starring the formidable Ethel Merman. Since Betty had no illusions about her singing voice, Merman didn't see her as a threat as she had with other newcomers (like Betty Hutton), so both of them were surprised when Betty quickly became as big a hit as the show itself.

After the Broadway run, there was a lengthy road tour which ended abruptly when Darryl F. Zanuck, the head of Twentieth Century Fox, called Betty back to Hollywood under circumstances right out of a Busby Berkeley musical.

At the time, the reigning musical queen of the Fox lot was another blonde, Alice Faye, then scheduled to start production on a major movie, *Down Argentine Way,* with Don Ameche. Just as filming was about to begin, she came down with appendicitis, and a desperate Zanuck offered the part to Betty after seeing her photo in a newspaper and remembering her. The picture was in Technicolor and had Betty lavishly done up as a wealthy American in Argentina looking for race horses. It boasted a cast of the studio's prime character actors, including lanky Charlotte Greenwood, zany Carmen Miranda, and J. Carroll Naish. After a decade of hard work, Betty Grable had hit her stride. The sweat and tears of buildup and rejection had finally paid off—and the best was yet to come.

Off camera, Betty had been dating bandleader Artie Shaw, and many onlookers thought they'd marry. He and Betty were all over the gossip columns, but Shaw had another blonde on his mind, too, and, on February 9, 1940, Betty's romance came to a screeching halt when she opened the morning papers to see headlines screaming of Shaw's elopement to Las Vegas with Lana Turner: Reports had her grieving furiously over the union, but, when asked about it, blithe Betty replied she wasn't all *that* distraught, but she did allow that "It must have come on him very sudden." The Shaw-Turner marriage ended as suddenly as it had begun—within the year—but by then Betty was back with George Raft.

Before that happened, though, an ebullient Fox decided that if one blonde was great box-office, two of them would be a bonanza, and they teamed Betty and a recovered Alice Faye in *Tin Pan Alley,* another rousing musical. The film contained an elaborate, and for its time quite risqué, harem number, with the stars floating through it in sequined halters, diaphanous veils, and see-through harem pants to the unabashed delight of "sheik" Billy Gilbert.

Predictably, columnists (not without the help of Fox's publicity department) promptly invented a feud between the blondes, but that was not the case. Alice gave Betty a portable radio during the filming, and they attended each other's parties. (Ironically, they would both marry orchestra leaders, eschew Hollywood life for seclusion, and have two daughters.) Betty's open-faced charm and down-to-earth manner precluded any such foolishness as jealous rivalry, but it was good publicity for the film, a smash hit.

Faye was entering a complacent stage of her career, secure in her position as Fox's top star, yet seemingly more interested in her homelife with new husband Phil Harris. Alice was more mature looking than Betty in the picture, and her waistline was thick in comparison to that of the only four-years-younger Betty. It's interesting to note that despite the women's friendship and the studio's later pleas, they never worked together again.

Perhaps the essence of Betty Grable's screen charm surfaced in her next film, *Moon over Miami,* in which she portrayed a carhop who came into a small inheritance. She then coerced "aunt" Charlotte Greenwood and "sister" Carole Landis into helping her invest the money in trapping a millionaire. The trio sets off for the millionaire's playground of Miami Beach, with Betty posing as an heiress, while Landis took over secretarial duty and auntie played the ladies' maid. The comic complications of the basically good-natured ruse started immediately upon their arrival, when, in short order, Betty met two millionaires: Don Ameche and Robert Cummings.

As they both view for her attentions, Betty changed from one gorgeous outfit to another, singing one of her signature tunes along the way, "You Started Something." She was obviously the girl on the make, but she did it with such a refreshing charm that no one seemed to mind; she was simply the kind of girl who recognized her assets and wanted to make the most of them, a girl very much like Betty herself. After all, a girl only has so many chances. . . . She might cheat occasionally on the truth, but those white lies were invariably forgiven when the pink and white blonde fell into the right man's arms at fadeout.

Betty's arms, at the time, were being filled by George Raft, recently resurfaced in her life, thanks to Betty's old friend Mary Livingston. Raft had watched Betty's rise to stardom and her unhappy marriage with increasing interest, but had been reticent to approach her again for fear of being rejected. After all, he was movies past, while she was obviously movies not only present, but future as well. Enlisting the aid of Jack Benny's wife, though, he found out that Betty had never quite forgotten him, and would like to see him again. Betty took sick on the night of their first date and had to cancel. She was sure he'd never call her again. But he did.

They went dancing at the Mogambo on Sunset Boulevard, and Betty, in pale satin, a white gardenia clasped in her golden hair, and her pink complexion alight with a combination of interest and promise, swirled around the dance floor in the arms of the virile man she had never forgotten. They floated by Ty Power and Annabella, Lana Turner and Greg Bautzer, Linda Darnell and Pev Marley, two stars in a tiny galaxy all their own. Raft took her to her door on that sweet-smelling California night and asked to see her again.

She replied, ''When?''

''Tomorrow night?''

She merely smiled, her eyes full of agreement.

''That's a date then,'' the tough guy of a hundred movies said. ''And don't you get sick.''

Betty didn't. The Grable-Raft romance was one of the hottest of the times, equaling in press coverage the romantic exploits of Lana, Hedy, Rita, and other Goddesses. George and Betty night-clubbed their way from Sunset Boulevard to Santa Monica, from LaRue's to the Trocadero. They drank ice-cream sodas and went to baseball games, the horse races at Santa Anita, and, on Tuesday and Friday nights, the fights.

Everything was romantically perfect until the reality of the situation began to seep into Betty's soul: George was married, and his wife wasn't about to give him a divorce.

Betty tried to forget it all during the shooting hours of *A Yank in the RAF* with Ty Power, Fox's hottest male sex symbol. It was a flag-waving comedy-drama about an American showgirl doing her bit for the war effort in London. For the film, she traded in her low-cut gowns for tailored uniforms, complete with shirt and tie, and a fatigue cap that covered most of her golden hair, which looked darker than usual in this black and white production. The love theme was ''These Foolish Things Remind Me Of You, and her slightly pug-nosed, corn-fed, apple-cheeked face reflected a prototype of wistful beauty that was particularly American.

Betty projected an obvious sexuality, rare at the time, and, when she stared up into Power's face, saying about that evening's date, ''I can't wait,'' her eyes flashed with an open sensuality, healthy in its honesty. Fox was careful to include two dance numbers between the buzz bombs, ''Hiya Love'' and ''Another Little Dream Can't Do Us Any Harm,'' which showcased her nicely.

Fox had already found the Betty Grable formula with *Down Argentine Way,* but with Alice Faye up for most of those roles, they experimented a little with Grable. *Yank* was a hit, and her fan mail was steadily rising, so they decided to try her acting talents in something different, a thriller called *I Wake Up Screaming.* It was the first of several teamings with Victor Mature; in this one, the plot had them working to uncover the murderer of Betty's movie sister, Carole Landis. Fox's resident heavy, Laird Cregar, was on the right side of the law for a change as the detective who initially thought Betty was the one who had done her sister in. Grable accepted the role and did well with it, although it was obvious that her true talents were not being best exploited in black and white mysteries.

She didn't complain about it, though; in fact, Betty didn't complain at all during her initial years of stardom. Coming as it did after so many years of hard work, she realized that the studio knew what was best for her, and she never stormed the front office demanding better scripts or a specific leading man. She was that rarest kind of movie star—she listened.

Betty's romance with Raft continued. It was one of the most publicized of the time, with every new fur coat or piece of jewelry getting extensive fan magazine coverage. Those were the Golden Days of not only the movies, but of the fan magazines as well, and hundreds of thousands of copies of such publications as *Photoplay* and *Screen Stars* were sold every month to eager, war-deprived moviegoers who slavishly read of the life and romances of their favorites. You may not have been able to get butter for *your* kitchen, but you could peek into Lana Turner's and see how she was coping with the problem! The studios fed the magazines pictures and stories, happily setting up interviews for their stars with the leading reporters.

The fact that Raft was married was not overlooked by the press, and, as the months wore on, it became increasingly apparent to the press and to Betty herself that Raft would *stay* married. His wife Grayce Mulrooney whom he'd married in 1923 was a staunch Catholic and had no intention of granting him a civil divorce. Grayce obviously enjoyed her status as Mrs. Raft, as neglected a position as it was, because technically she could have gotten a divorce. As a Catholic, though, she would never have been able to remarry as long as George lived. Since she would remain stuck with the marriage in any case, she quietly determined to keep it legal, to George's increasing dismay.

Footlight Serenade put Betty back on screen with Victor Mature, and the standard Broadway-background musical was another rousing hit. Fox wisely realized that Betty was best in color and quickly followed *Serenade* with the lush *Song of the Islands,* again with Mature.

The fan letters were reaching the thousand-a-week level, and Betty made the box office Top Ten in 1942. Photographer Frank Powolny's white bathing suit pinup was being sent out by the mail bag full (ultimately some three million copies would be distributed), and the songs "Sing Me a Song of the Island" and "O'Brien Has Gone Hawaiian," from her latest film, were hits in sheet music sales. Fox rewarded Betty by promising her nothing but Technicolor and big-budgets from then on, a shrewd move on their part.

As Betty was attaining full-scale stardom with magazine covers and endorsements all over the place, her romance with Raft was gradually fizzling out. The furs and diamonds he lavished on her were not enough; Betty wanted a homelife that consisted of more than just nights on the town and a visit home to her mother, but she knew the dream wasn't about to be realized with him. Sadly they separated. Raft would never get over her, and Betty told Louella Parsons, Hollywood's unofficial den mother, "I would have married George Raft a week after I met him, I was so desperately, so deeply in love with him. But, when you

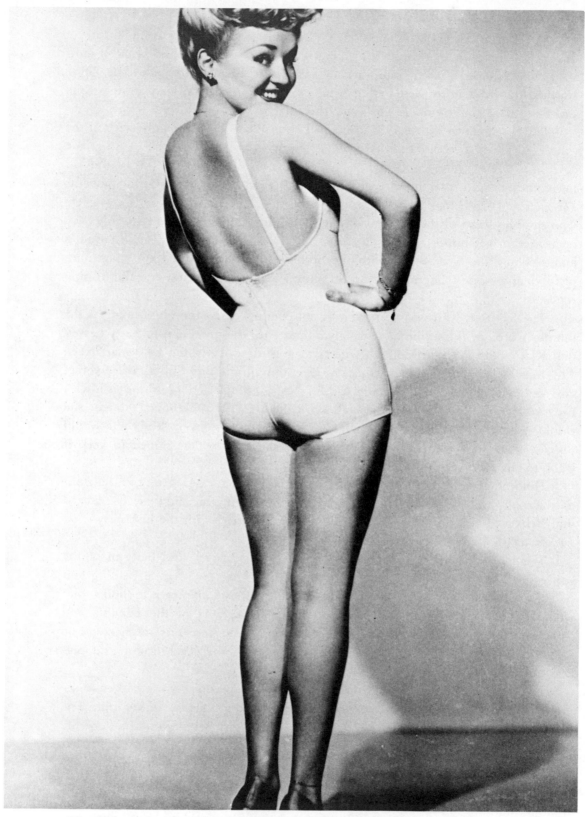

The picture that launched a million dreams. Betty as the pinup girl (1942).
THE DOUG MCCLELLAND COLLECTION.

wait two and a half years, there doesn't seem to be any future in a romance with a married man. . . . I don't expect to get over George today, tomorrow, or next week. But I do know there's no turning back.''

During a personal appearance tour in Chicago in 1940, Betty had met bandleader Harry James, and they renewed their acquaintance when James and his orchestra were hired to back up Betty in her next film, *Springtime in the Rockies.* James was married to singer Mary Louise Tobin but was in the process of getting a divorce. Besides meeting on the set, Betty and James kept bumping into each other at the Hollywood Canteen where, like many other stars, their romance was born. One night James asked to take her home, and she agreed. She told her mother, ''He's easy to be with. It's relaxing to be with him.'' That relaxation shortly turned into something more high powered when they started dating in earnest. It was the launching of one of the longest and happiest relationships in Hollywood, but, as with most launchings, there were a few rough seas to be crossed, one in particular named George Raft.

One night Betty showed up at a Hollywood nightclub where Harry and his band were playing, and Raft came in. He approached her table, but she told him to leave her alone, not unkindly, but firmly. Raft, in short order, got into a fistfight with James over her; Harry came out the winner. The resultant headlines convinced Betty of one thing—at long last she'd found her champion. The hit song from *Springtime in the Rockies,* ''I Had the Craziest Dream,'' proved prophetic. Betty's personal dreams of happines were soon to come true.

Sleekly handsome and one of the greatest trumpet players of that or any other time, James had a charisma and an easygoing life-style that complemented Betty's own. They both loved horse racing and spent many an afternoon mingling with other film stars at Santa Anita. James was making movies at the time, albeit relatively minor ones, and was building up a bobby sox following that was quite impressive. The main problem was that he was constantly on the road, but Betty soon determined that she'd make changes in her own life so that his career wouldn't disrupt their affair. When he went to New York in the spring of 1943 for an engagement at the Astor Roof, Betty went too, and was a constant ringsider. Everything was going well for her at that time. One of her most popular films, *Coney Island,* had just been released. The press received it with the same kind of joyous notices that were becoming routine, and the box office was golden.

Harry's divorce became final on July 5 of that year, and, six days later, Betty and Harry eloped to Las Vegas where, at 4:15 on the morning of July 11, they were married by a Baptist minister in the Little Church of the West. The honeymoon had to wait, since the following day Betty was due to report for the starting of *Sweet Rosie O'Grady,* while Harry was scheduled for a guest shot in MGM's *Swing Fever.* Betty didn't care, though, since she'd finally found the man in her life, and they'd work it out.

Since the war years were a time of upheaval and quick emotional decisions, Betty didn't lose a fan by her marriage. Men and women understood how love worked in the atmosphere of war and separation, and nobody wondered a bit when eight months later, on March 4, 1944, the world's favorite pinup girl gave birth to her first daughter, Victoria Elizabeth, delivered by Caesarean section. The new mother remained the darling of the boys overseas. The famous Eighth Air Force named a B-17 bomber the ''Betty Grable,'' and she was into her third year as one of the ten top stars according to the Money Making Picture Herald-Fame Poll. (She would stay a fixture there until 1951.)

In *Sweet Rosie O'Grady,* Betty stepped into a bathtub to sing ''My Heart Tells Me'' which helped that picture to be another huge hit.

It seemed as if Grable could do no wrong. She appeared as herself along with Alice Faye and Carmen Miranda, in *Four Jills in a Jeep,* a film about a group of actresses entertaining the boys abroad. Later in 1944, she starred in what amounted to almost a biography of her life, *Pinup Girl.* It was one of her weaker vehicles, despite the presence of Martha Raye and Joe E. Brown, but was popular anyway. An outfit in the South Pacific, after viewing a print of the film one sultry night, promptly dubbed one of their fighter planes ''The Pinup Girl'' and plastered a huge picture of Betty over the fuselage.

Betty's films were grossing so well they gave Fox profits enough to experiment with ''classier'' products such as the biography of President Wilson. At the time, Zanuck jokingly said, ''If *Wilson* doesn't do well, I'll never make another movie without Betty Grable.'' It didn't, and he almost didn't!

Harry and Betty appeared together in 1945 in *All Star Bond Rally* along with Bing Crosby, Frank Sinatra, Harpo Marx, and Carmen Miranda, among other patriotic stars.

She was then set off like a twenty-carat, blue-white gem in *Diamond Horseshoe,* a spectacular musical based around Billy Rose's famous nightspot, in which she introduced another hit, ''The More I See You.'' Fox knew that any leading man would pale next to their Golden Girl, so they used newcomers occasionally in order to test their wings—in this case the rather flimsy ones of crooner Dick Haymes, then trying to make the grade as a picture personality.

Away from the screen, the Jameses lived a free-flowing outdoor life centered around their 103-acre ranch, managed by Betty's father Conn Grable. Betty's mother was also on the family payroll as Betty's secretary, while James himself shortly made a stab at becoming a movie star, thanks to Zanuck.

James's good looks and bobby sox appeal made Zanuck think he just might have the stuff of which movie stars are made and fashioned *Kitten on the Keys* for him in 1945. Zanuck was unhappy with the results and virtually reshot the entire film, releasing it as *Do You Love Me?* the following year. In it James played a trumpeter—type casting?—who romanced a college dean, played by Maureen O'Hara, only to lose her—to Dick Haymes! Betty was reportedly so incensed over the ending that she demanded it be rewritten so that when the rejected James came out of O'Hara's apartment to his car he would find—you guessed it—Betty Grable waiting for him for the fadeout. Surprise ending or not, it didn't do much to help either the picture or James's budding movie career.

About this time, Alice Faye decided to retire. Zanuck virtually begged her to come back to Fox for *The Dolly Sisters* with Betty, but when she left the studio, it was for keeps. After she'd finished *Fallen Angel* (1945) with Dana Andrews and Linda Darnell, "I drove right through the gate and left the key to my dressing room with the guard, along with a note for Mr. Zanuck. I never went back. Zanuck pleaded with me to do *The Dolly Sisters* with Betty Grable, but I never answered his calls. I didn't want any part of that place again. . . . Never even cleaned out my dressing room. I just left everything hanging where it was." Alice had had it and wanted nothing more than to stay home with husband Phil Harris and quietly raise their two daughters.

Ironically the lady who inherited the part, June Haver, had made her screen debut in Alice's *The Gang's All Here* in 1943 and had subsequently attained stardom the following year in *Home in Indiana*. Blonde, talented, and freshfaced, she virtually got the same kind of break that Betty herself had gotten in *Tin Pan Alley*—a chance to share equal billing with the studio's hottest property. Betty welcomed the relative newcomer in her typically unselfish way, and the two of them brought off the Technicolor production with consummate ease and enormous charm. Fox's flagship theater, New York City's rococo *Roxy,* reported record-breaking business when the film opened.

Zanuck was putting together another "prestige" picture to welcome back Tyrone Power from the war—Somerset Maugham's *The Razor's Edge*—and approached Betty about playing the lead in the heavy drama. She laughed in his face at the idea—"People would have expected me to come on like a chorus," she later said, emphasizing the fact that by now she knew exactly what the public expected of her. Unlike her successor, Marilyn Monroe, Betty Grable had a no-nonsense approach to her talent and appeal, one that saved her enormous heartbreak in the end. While Monroe would later cripple the same studio with her demands to be presented as an "actress," Grable knew her value—and image—was as a sex symbol, and she didn't fight it. The last thing the public wanted from Betty was black-and-white bitchery, and *Razor's Edge* went to Gene Tierney.

Around this time, like Faye before her, Betty was thinking more about her family than she was about her career, especially when she was called upon to play a "typewriter" (read secretary) in a period musical called *The Shocking Miss Pilgrim,* again with Dick Haymes. The film was an early (very) attempt to show the independence of women who were then truly being recognized for their own worth, thanks to their numerous contributions to the recent war effort. It was a very mild entertainment.

The Jameses had added a sixty-nine acre horse-breeding ranch to their holdings because of their mutual interest in the ponies, and they wanted to spend as much time there as possible. Harry's popularity as a bandleader faded, as the Big Band Era itself did, and he was just as happy at home, especially when Betty was with him. After finishing *Miss Pilgrim,* Betty found herself pregnant again, and their second daughter, Jessica, was born on May 20, 1947.

Later that year, a man whose wholesome good looks and talent ideally complemented her own entered Betty's life and together they became one of the most popular screen teams of the decade. He was Dan Dailey, an ex-Broadway hoofer, and their first film together, *Mother Wore Tights,* was an out-and-out delight. Directed by Walter Lang, it was one of her most popular films and brought full-fledged stardom to Dailey after years of so-so work in Hollywood.

By now motherhood had slightly matured Betty's charms, but that was gorgeously disguised in her next picture, a wonderfully old-fashioned piece of costume tomfoolery entitled *That Lady in Ermine.* Costarred with the scion of movie masculinity, Douglas Fairbanks, Jr., it was co-directed by Ernst Lubitsch and Otto Preminger. In it, Betty stepped out of a portrait and proceeded to tantalize all concerned, including two of the screen's suavest charmers, Reggie Gardiner and Cesar Romero. Lubitsch's fading light touch wasn't helped by Preminger's omnipresent heavyhandedness, and it wasn't one of Betty's best received films.

Fox cleverly pulled her right back to what her public appreciated most and reteamed her with Dailey in 1948 in *When My Baby Smiles at Me.* The film was full of songs and poignancy, and featured them as a vaudeville team once again, this time updated to the thirties. And instead of recalcitrant children (as in *Mother Wore Tights),* this time they were plagued by stardom when Betty got a Broadway call and left Dailey behind. It was one of the best critically received of Betty's films and was auspicious for Dan, too, who received a Best Actor Oscar nomination for his role as the half of the act who gets left in the sticks.

At the end of the forties, director Preston Sturges was approaching the end of the decade of intuitive humor and incisive filmmaking. In the past, he'd made such classics as *Sullivan's Travels,* with Veronica Lake and Joel McCrea, and *The Miracle of Morgan's Creek,* with Betty Hutton. Sturges's gifts were waning with the period, though, as evidenced by Grable's next film, *The Beautiful Blonde from Bashful Bend.*

It showed a darker side of Betty Grable that the public had never seen before. Sturges cast her as a gun-toting dancehall girl who's mistaken for the arriving schoolmarm by some small-town citizenry. In the film, Betty uses her six-guns to bring some of the local youngsters into line in a frightening scene where she shot inkwells off their heads. Cesar Romero and Rudy Vallee supported her, but even those two, as well as Olga San Juan and Hugh Herbert, couldn't keep the film from being one of the major disappointments of 1949.

Fox began to think that Betty alone was no longer good box office, especially in anything that varied from the "Grable formula" (although exhibitors still listed her on their Top Ten lists). They tried to turn back the clock by teaming her with former co-star Victor Mature in a remake of one of her most successful films, *Coney Island*—this go-round called *Wabash Avenue.* The neighborhood changed, but the story remained the same; revealing Gay Nineties costumes, with Betty as a saloon star showing lots of leg and involved in the standard backstage love triangle. It's one of the few times that a major star has remade one of her own pictures, but was done with such verve and enthusiasm that it proved to be a smash hit, proving the "formula" still worked when packaged properly.

By now Betty's happy homelife had her down to one picture a year. Late in

1950 she was back with Dan Dailey in the charming *My Blue Heaven,* about two radio stars out to adopt a child. It was a contemporary story without a bustle or a chorus line in sight, but Betty was totally believable, supported by Jane Wyatt, David Wayne, and a studio newcomer, Mitzi Gaynor. Gaynor got most of the publicity from the picture in her debut role as a showgirl, but Betty watched the competition with a surprising amount of good cheer. As would later happen with Marilyn Monroe, she welcomed Mitzi onto the lot, and they became close friends.

It was a bona fide hit, and Fox immediately reteamed Betty with Dailey in *Call Me Mister,* the story of a soldier who goes AWOL to patch up his marriage. Betty played a showgirl traveling in Japan with a USO troop, with husband Dailey in hot pursuit, and the resultant fun and box office made Fox realize that Betty was indeed worth the $300,000 a year they were paying her.

They were confident enough to let her go it alone again in *Meet Me After the Show* with an up-and-coming leading man, Rory Calhoun. It was a return to the Grable show-biz storyline formula, albeit modernized, and showcased her beautifully.

As soon as it was finished, Fox wanted her to start *The Girl Next Door,* but Betty balked. She'd just finished one film with the dance routines all scheduled for the end of production, and now they wanted her to start another with the musical numbers at the start of the shooting schedule. She gave them a flat no, saying she was tired and needed a rest and some time with her family. The studio bosses answered her by putting her on a contract suspension—with no salary—that lasted some ten months. It was the first of several suspensions that Betty would shortly be chalking up as the studio began to place more and more emphasis on Marilyn Monroe, especially in light of the lean box office of *Meet Me After the Show.*

Betty rode out her suspension with Harry, spending a lot of time at their horse ranch at Calabasas. Money wasn't a problem at the time for Betty had carefully invested most of her earnings, and the Jameses' horse, Big Noise, raked in $100,000 worth of purses in 1951 alone.

When a studio is out to undermine the ego of a recalcitrant star, their methods would do justice to a Borgia court, with intrigues and strategies hatched in air-conditioned conference rooms rather than Italian throne rooms. The studio heads knew that Betty was only interested in doing musicals; that she knew not only what she did best, but also what the public wanted her to do. Nonetheless, they decided in September of 1952 to throw her a ringer—a script entitled *Blaze of Glory* which would star Richard Widmark. Betty took one look at the storyline about secret agents and Communists and the floozie who's the go-between and threw it right back at them, saying, "I wouldn't work in a picture like that. I want to work in movies I can take my daughters to." The film was made as *Pickup on South Street* with Jean Peters, but Betty's refusal to do the part landed her on suspension again for eight months more.

And pivotal months they were, too, with Monroe's *Niagara* released to spectacular notices and an avalance of publicity. Suddenly Fox had a new Golden Girl.

But they also still had Betty Grable with a large enough contract to make them bring her back in a major picture, a remake of an old Janet Gaynor film, *The Farmer Takes a Wife.* The days of the movie musical that made Betty Grable famous were waning, but Fox went all out on this one to see if the genre could still bring in the people. There was a charming score by Harold Arlen and some lovely location shots of Lake Erie. There was no backstage plot in this story of an 1800s couple trying to make a go of marriage and farming along the Erie Canal. Unfortunately, the magic and/or appeal was missing, and, despite Betty's good performance and Dale Robertson's burgeoning sex appeal, the film was poorly showcased and not a hit. It marked the end of Betty's personal reign as the musical queen of the Fox lot.

Fox tried to loan her to Columbia for something called *The Pleasure Is All Mine,* but Betty decided against it and took another suspension.

That ended shortly when the studio put together one of the all-time comedy classics about girls on the make—*How To Marry a Millionaire.* Marilyn got top billing over Grable in the latter's fortieth film, but, surprisingly, Betty didn't seem to mind all that much. Her role as a dizzy, slightly over-age showgirl looking for that last big break was one of the choicest of her career, affording her a final chance to prove she was more than just a pair of legs. As if in answer to all those films she made in which she was indeed looking for a millionaire, in this one Betty opted for love with honest forest ranger Rory Calhoun.

Always an open and friendly woman, Betty, when Monroe came to her for advice, was happy to give it, although deep inside there must have been the saddening knowledge that her heyday was over and that her days of top stardom were running out. The intriguing thing is that Grable didn't fight it as others had. Instead she accepted it as a fact of Hollywood life, for after over two decades there, Betty had few illusions left. She'd known rejection, replacement, the joy of winning top billing, and, now, at last, the inner agony of losing her position. But she also knew there were other things to life, and, when Marilyn asked for help, Betty gave it.

One day Monroe showed up in Betty's dressing room distraught. She didn't know how to walk in one scene; could Betty help her? "Sure honey," said the blonde of 10 million daydreams, "just do the same thing I've been doing, only enlarge on it about a hundred times." Betty and Marilyn often had dinner together, with Grable cooking up a steak and some french fries. The famous story goes that on the set of *Millionaire,* when she saw, finally, who was coming out on top, Betty told Monroe, "Honey, I've had mine. Go get yours."

For three years, from 1946 to 1948, Betty had been the highest salaried woman in America. The memories were beautiful ones, and she had a career to be proud of, with very few compromises. And she had Harry James.

She once said that when she married him she expected their home would turn into a combination music hall and dance academy, but it hadn't worked out that way. Whenever he was on the road, he'd call her nightly to speak to her, and their private life, although movie-star lavish, also had a definite down-to-earth feeling about it. The Jameses' racing stables' colors were red and white, and Betty often wore outfits of those colors to the races and decorated her studio dressing room in those tones. She loved her private life and admitted, "We aren't very social. Harry's work keeps him out late, and we're too tired by the weekend to entertain."

Betty was no one's fool though, as far as her tenure at Fox was concerned. They'd made $100 million off her and now kept her waiting on the sidelines all day after calling her for a shot in the morning that they *knew* they wouldn't get to until late afternoon. The coddling went to Monroe, with Betty playing a far-second fiddle.

After finishing the picture, Betty left the Fox lot, but unlike Alice Faye, she did "shed a little tear." Marilyn Monroe took over her dressing room, but there's little reason to believe she ever enjoyed it as much as her predecessor.

When asked what she'd do next, the pragmatic star told reporters, "If Harry wants me, I'll join his band. But he's the boss. We've been so happy for ten years, he might think it wouldn't be good for us to work together. Whatever he says goes. I got a kick out of playing a straight comedienne role in *Millionaire* with no singing or dancing. But at heart I'm a musical comedy hoofer—and everybody should stick to his own line. I'm no great shakes as an actress—I've never been within gunshot of an Oscar, but I think I've entertained people."

The year 1954 started out badly for Betty. In January her father died. Though he and her mother, Lillian, had been divorced since 1939, Betty had kept the family together, if at separate addresses. Conn had managed the James' second ranch, "The Baby J" in Woodland Hills, while Lillian managed her daughter's secretarial work.

One month after losing her father, Betty's self-doubts were stubbed out when Columbia offered her a glamourous musical return in *Three for the Show,* an offer she promptly accepted. On the first day of shooting, as had been his custom on every new film since their marriage, Harry James showed up on the set to wish his wife well.

The plot was familiar, perhaps too familiar, to Grable fans: a Broadway star torn between two men—only this time the star was married to both of them. Jack Lemmon played her presumed-dead spouse who returned home to find her in the confident arms of Gower Champion. The 5'4" blonde weighed in at 114 lbs. and was photographed to emphasize the fact that she still had a remarkable figure, measuring at the time 36-24-35. The musical was a remake of Jean Arthur's *Too Many Husbands.* It contained one lavish number in which Betty got in her last licks as a Love Goddess. It was an almost direct ripoff of Monroe's "We're Havin' a Heat Wave" from *There's No Business Like Show Business.* In fact, for a minute, it looked like Betty had sneaked back to Fox just long enough to purloin MM's old costume, a semi-midriffed, sequin-flounced affair with the mandatory half wrap-around skirt designed for showcasing the still legendary legs. The number was complete with native bearers, tropical setting, and a dazzling blonde centerpiece.

When the film was finished, Sam Goldwyn called Betty to talk about her playing the forever-congested Adelaide in his upcoming *Guys and Dolls*. But, "It happened that on the same day my dog, who was fourteen years old and like one of the family, hurt his paw, and I had to rush him to the hospital. So I sent word to Mr. Goldwyn I could not keep the date. When Mr. Goldwyn heard I broke a date with him because of a sick dog, he sent word that he never wanted to see me again." In such ways are movie moguls mollified by their sense of power and actors denied roles that could give their careers an entire new aspect. Broadway's original Adelaide, Vivian Blaine, a former Fox Golden Girl herself, got the part.

Three for the Show wasn't the hit Columbia had been hoping for, but Fox executives took notice, especially when Monroe refused to report for her next film, *How To Be Very Very Popular*, and took off for New York instead to form Marilyn Monroe Productions. They suddenly wanted Betty back, and she came. The Jameses had recently run into some minor money troubles which, for a time, had the Calabasas horse ranch attached by a law firm over the payment of some legal fees.

If Betty thought she was coming back in triumph, though, she was quickly disenchanted when the studio publicity guns started aiming their major barrels at Sheree North, a "new Marilyn Monroe" they'd manufactured in hopes of keeping the original in line. It didn't work—not for Sheree, Betty, or the film, which turned out to be a widescreen dud. The big number, "Shake, Rattle and Roll" went to North, while Betty held up the sidelines. The end result was limpid and very very unpopular with critics and the public at large.

Afterwards, Betty issued a statement that she'd do no more movies unless the "right" property came along.

She made her television debut in a comedy called *Cleopatra Collins*, opposite Max Showalter, the following year. She had gained a little weight by then, and, in a dream sequence where she was the real Cleo to his Marc Antony, she told him to cover her bulging belly with his armor. "But it'll crush you," he exclaimed. "It can only help," she replied, laughing.

Betty and Harry worked together at the El Rancho in Las Vegas for $12,750 a week, with a twenty-week contract spread over two years. She was happy there, and the audiences were delighted to see the former pinup queen in the flesh. The Jameses worked their schedule around the annual winter meet at Santa Anita race track, and they and their daughters spent several weeks at the Westerner Hotel. It was a quiet life in comparison to the one Betty had left behind, but it suited her. She played golf, had her horses, and thought less and less about the fact that no movie offers were coming in.

She put together a pastiche of all her old movie numbers and, in early 1958, played at Hollywood's Moulin Rouge. The show was appropriately called *Memories*, complete with a rousing finale of "Katie Went to Haiti." She took the show to New York the following year for a successful run at the Latin Quarter and again gave her fans her best. "I don't have a secretary (her mother had retired from that position in 1955) or personal maid; no entourage. I do my own nails, hair, and makeup." She went on to add that she was a "frustrated perfectionist" who always worked to give her fans the glamour they expected of her—"I worry about everything"—when it came to a public image.

In 1959 the James family decided to get out of Hollywood altogether and sold their house on North Beverly Drive in Beverly Hills to make Las Vegas their home base. They moved into a $100,000 house behind the Desert Inn, right on the golf course "where we can play all year round."

She and Harry played the El Rancho, but that was the last the public was to see of her for a while. Daughters Vickie and Jessica were now teenagers, and Betty seemed happy to spend the years as a family unit quietly watching the girls grow up and, of course, making good use of the nearby golf course.

It was a time for reflection, and she told old friends she didn't miss Holly-wood at all. "I've made more friends here than I ever did in California, and, besides, Harry and I get to spend more time together." To another friend she said, "It really is the best place in the world as far as I'm concerned. When I came here, many of my L.A. friends asked me how I could live right smack in the middle of the desert where temperatures are high for six months of the year. They must have been kidding! Don't they realize that heat isn't bad as long as the air is clean?" Like her one-time movie rival and still friend Alice Faye, Betty opted for isolation rather than stay in a town that no longer appreciated her. (Faye still lives in Palm Springs.)

After three years of sun and golf, though, Betty began to chafe at the lack of activity in her life. (The only news she made was in March of 1961 when the IRS filed a $46,654 tax lien against her and James for the 1959 earnings.) As her daughters grew more independent, she thought she'd like to work again. One night she and former co-star Dan Dailey sat down together and laughingly talked about the good old days. They shortly hatched the idea of working together again and decided the perfect vehicle would be *Guys and Dolls*—with Betty as Adelaide at long last.

Unlike Rita Hayworth, Betty wasn't a captive of her screen image or its limiting expression of her talent. When she decided to try a legitimate stage career, she endeared herself quickly to directors by saying, "You know, in the movies all I ever had to say was 'Hello Harry' or 'Goodbye Harry,' so everything else you'll have to teach me—word by word."

They opened just before Christmas of 1962 at the Dunes Hotel in Vegas in a truncated version of the Broadway hit, shortened to accommodate two shows a night. The reviews were solid gold; the Grable-Dailey punch was as powerful as it had been a decade before on the screen. It played for eighteen SRO weeks, with such good box office that they were teamed again the following year in another musical revival, *High Button Shoes*.

On August 18, 1964, Harry gave his oldest daughter, Victoria, in marriage to William Bivens, a student, while a radiant Betty looked on. It was virtually the last public appearance they would make as Mr. and Mrs. Harry James.

The following year was to be one of Betty's most traumatic. Just after New Year's, the woman who had steered her into her career and then managed much of it, mother Lillian, died at seventy-five following a heart attack. Since she'd stopped working as Betty's secretary ten years before, she'd been living in Hollywood near her older daughter, Mrs. David T. Arnold of Beverly Hills. Ironically, she died in Santa Monica's St. John's Hospital, the same one Betty would later be in.

On the surface, the James household still seemed a happy one. Harry was touring a lot again with his re-formed band, finding success on the wave of nostalgia that was just beginning to sweep the country. They necessarily began spending long stretches of time apart. With his revived popularity with the public, Harry also found a revived popularity with the ladies, and it was soon no secret that he was dating other women not only on the road, but even closer to home. Betty was heartbroken. He was the enduring love of her life, and during her movie heyday she had come close on several occasions to compromising her career to be with him and their children. All that loyalty and devotion went quickly down the drain, though, and the public was enormously shocked when she filed for divorce. Betty and Harry James? Divorced after twenty-three years? As impossible as that seemed, it was sadly true.

Forty-eight-year-old Betty looked decidedly matronly—and downcast—on October 8, 1965, when she went to court for a private divorce hearing. Wearing a white hat pulled down over her golden hair, she appeared there alone. Harry didn't show up. Betty divorced him on the grounds of "extreme cruelty" and "mental cruelty." However, the decree was handed her in a sealed judgment, and the true details of their divorce have never been revealed. Betty did not ask for alimony, and her attorney said there would be no statements from either, that it had been an amicable split, and "both parties remained friends." But long after the divorce, it was said that Betty still carried a torch for James.

The year 1965 was the year of the "Dollies," and, when Betty was offered the lead in a Vegas version of *Hello Dolly,* she threw herself into rehearsals with a vengeance in an effort to exorcise the jolt of the divorce. Her old friend Max Showalter played Horace Vandergelder to her Dolly Levi, and it was one of the most memorable experiences of his career. He calls her "one of the most wonderful gals I ever knew."

Dolly was a godsend for Betty. She worked feverishly to prove to herself and the public that Betty Grable still had what it took, and when the show opened just before New Year's of 1966, reviewers were quick to note that she did indeed still have it.

Her work schedule was heavy—two shows a night, seven nights a week—and after each night's show she usually threw parties for the cast and stayed up late having fun with the gypsies. Showalter had regular checkups and vitamin shots to keep in shape for the demanding run which went on for months, but when he suggested Betty do the same, she just pooh-poohed the idea saying, "I haven't been to a doctor in twenty years."

When Mary Martin came back from Vietnam with her *Hello Dolly* troup, Betty was offered the lead for the national tour, and she grabbed it. She,

Showalter, and the other principals went from Vegas to Chattanooga to join the company and start the extended run.

In the troupe was a young dancer named Bob Remick, some twenty-one years Betty's junior, and the two quickly hit it off, developing an immediate rapport. As the tour progressed, their affair deepened, although any time they were in or near a town where Harry James was playing, Betty always gathered together some of the cast and off she'd go to see him. Their paths crisscrossed around the country, and it was at times like those that it became apparent no one could ever really replace Harry in her affections.

She and Remick decided to keep their romance a secret, as Betty felt people might misunderstand or ridicule her affection for a younger man. Bob agreed, and the affair was kept under wraps for the next seven years.

At the end of the national tour, Betty inherited the Broadway *Dolly* spot from her old friend and co-star Martha Raye, and New York welcomed her in the spring of 1967 with open arms. By that time Dolly had been played by many veteran stars, including Ginger Rogers. When Rogers ascended to the part, producer David Merrick introduced her with "Cast, meet your star," to which La Rogers graciously bowed. When he did the same thing for Betty, she just looked around her and yelled "Help!" That endeared her to the company, and she became one of the most loved Dollies backstage as well as onstage.

They played for weeks to full houses, with Betty showing those glamourous gams only once during the finale when she sang, "Look at the old girl now, fellas," and every time she did it it brought the house down. Betty loved the part and the company, and, on her last night in the role, she was so choked up, she could hardly finish. At the very end when she and Showalter sang their final number, she broke down, and whispered to him, "Hold me, just hold me," and as the spotlight narrowed, they turned, his arm around her, and walked offstage.

During the run there had been a constant string of autograph seekers lined up at the stage door, positive proof that the All American Love Goddess hadn't been forgotten. Sometimes a middle-aged man would pull out a tattered snapshot and say, "Remember me? We danced one night at the Hollywood Canteen." The press had been equally kind, and when they asked her if she minded being "The Girl with the Million Dollar Legs," she quipped, "Not at all. Everyone has to have a gimmick, and I've been standing on mine for years." She left New York tired, but absolutely delighted about the enormous success she'd had.

Back home in Las Vegas, she and Remick lived together in her luxurious home, but shortly the sunshine and golf again began to pale. "I just can't sit still for long."

No one was surprised, then, when in early 1969 she announced she was going abroad for the first time in her life—to London, where she'd star as a saloon owner in the Old West in a musical called *Pieceful Palace*. It evolved into *Belle Starr*, which opened in the West End the following May.

The opening night audience loved her, yelling out, "You're wonderful," during her six curtain calls, but the show was a badly done hodgepodge, and the

Betty in the ill-fated London production of Belle Starr *(1969).*   PICTORIAL PARADE.

58

critics ripped into it like a wolf pack after a wounded deer. *The Daily Mail* called it "excruciating rubbish, wonderfully bad" and described her famous legs as "well-matched, pretty, and able to dance effortlessly for several seconds at a time." *The Daily Telegraph* allowed that her voice was "huskily pleasant," but that in her role as the madam of a western saloon, "She is just left standing there while the company rampages around her."

Said Betty, "I gave up reading reviews years ago, and I'm not going to start reading them now. The British audiences are wonderful, and that's more important." Even Grable's legs couldn't hold up *Belle Starr* for long, though, and it folded after twenty-one performances.

When she left her London hotel for the last time, there were fans with placards saying, "We Love You" and "Hurry Back in Something Good." She was deeply touched "to see that I wasn't forgotten," but returned home quickly.

Happily, American summer stock producers were eager to have her, and she toured, sometimes with Remick as a member of the cast, in things like *Plaza Suite*. In 1971 she checked into the famous Bevery Hills Hotel to shoot a television ad for Geritol. The All American Love Goddess endorsed the All American tonic, complete with both her married daughters and their four children. It might have made millions of people feel a little older, but it did prove that Betty was the country's most glamorous grandma.

Shortly after that, Betty received an offer to travel to Australia to star in *No, No, Nannette* and agreed to make the trip. She enthused to a friend, "Maybe after my six months there I'll take a round-the-world trip. I'm becoming very excited about traveling. There are so many things I haven't done in life that I suddenly realize I'd like to do."

That unbounded optimism was to be tragically stymied when Betty was told to report for a complete physical for insurance purposes. She never was to make it to Australia. Instead, she entered St. John's Hospital in Santa Monica for the treatment of lung cancer. Remick was by her side, and it was at this point that their relationship became public knowledge, thanks in part to an exposé in the *National Tattler*.

Once it was out in the open, Betty spoke candidly about it to her friend writer Bridget Walsh, almost as if to take her mind off her awesome problem. "Yes, he's younger . . . a *lot* younger. But he's so much more mature than some forty-five-year-old men I've known. Age is all relative. He's very good for me. He's a Libra and doesn't have a nerve in his body. I've never heard him lose his temper. Sure it's very flattering to have a younger man interested in you. But though Bob says he absolutely idolizes me, he's not stupid about it. No, there's no marriage planned. My God, I'm a two-time loser. First Jackie Coogan, then Harry. And why should Bob and I want to marry? Our relationship is great the way it is. It's great to have a man to lean on." And she shortly needed him more than ever.

Doctors operated on her for six hours, and she came out of it with their assurance that she'd recover. She believed it herself—until she read in a gossip column that she was dying! "I don't know what I would have done without Bob," she later said, "Here I thought I was getting better; then I read that column, and it frightened the hell out of me."

By the end of July, reports came out stating that she *did* seem to be recovering. Her response to the cobalt treatments she'd been taking was deemed "phenomenal," and she went back to Vegas in a jubilant mood. To celebrate she tossed a big party for pal Debbie Reynolds and the cast of Debbie's show and sparkled that evening, on Remick's arm, with all her old radiance.

The treatments and a great deal of rest continued for the next few months, until Betty felt well enough to work again. She kicked off 1973 by happily accepting an offer to tour in *Born Yesterday*. She played the zany role that had won Judy Holliday a Best Actress Oscar with enthusiasm and charm—so successfully in Jacksonville, Florida, that she ran for eight weeks. The producers asked her back for another engagement in Tampa the coming summer, and Betty, optimistic as always, said yes.

She told friends, "I'm feeling okay, holding my own. It looks like everything is under control. Of course I'm seeing the doctor often now. I'll never be so foolish again. From now on I'm urging all my friends to have physical checkups at least once a year. Vickie and Jessica both promised me they would. And I'd like to do an ad or testimonial for the Cancer Crusade. I'm grateful for this second chance."

That was the public Betty; the private Betty was struggling hard to hold on. The Florida tour had been exhausting and painful, she'd collapsed during one performance. Her second chance was slipping away at a rapid pace, and, as the certainty of it crystallized, it became harder and harder to keep up a smiling front. Remick was the only one who was allowed to see the gradual chipping away of her health as she slipped into her final illness. Betty's daughters didn't approve of him, but that didn't deter him from taking care of the woman he loved.

Unselfish in the extreme, Bob tried to make life as easy for her as possible. When she was too weak to come to the dinner table, they ate together in her bedroom, sharing what they now undeniably knew would be their last hours of any kind of freedom.

As she weakened, her doctors advised that she return to St. John's in Santa Monica and she realized they were right. Stoically she set about finding someone to care for her dogs and put her business affairs in order. She did it quietly and just as quietly left the city that had been her home for almost fifteen years.

Remick, sensing the discomfort of a plane flight full of curious onlookers, contacted a close friend, and together they rented and set up a luxuriously appointed camper to drive Betty to Los Angeles. They took turns driving through the cool Nevada night so that one of them would always be beside Betty if she awakened and needed help or just wanted some conversation.

Betty insisted that all this be done quietly, and it was several weeks before the news leaked out that she was again hospitalized. She had told a close friend, "Why worry a lot of people needlessly? After all, what can anyone do, except perhaps pray.'' When the news did come out, she was again deluged with cards and flowers from Hollywood and all over the world, just as had happened the year before. She tried to answer as much of her mail as possible and remained as gallantly optimistic as always. In fact, one wonders if she really accepted the fact that her illness was terminal? On June 21 she wrote columnist Jim Bacon a note saying, ''I am feeling quite well now. I am resting a little and contemplating a return to work later in the season.'' Hardly the words of a dying woman—yet she wouldn't let her friends come to visit her in the hospital, preferring to talk to them on the phone, always cheerful, trying to allay their fears and her own. Betty may not have realized the extent of her illness, but others did, and there was a morbid interest in not only how she was handling it but what toll it had taken of her fabulous face. One Hollywood photographer was offered $5,000 by a scandal sheet to sneak in and take a picture of her in her hospital bed, ''But I turned them down flat. Betty had given me and millions of other people such happiness that I couldn't possibly betray her when she was at her lowest point. That's the business, though. They like to see you up there, but they like to see you down too. They (the paper) never did get the picture, and I think that's saying something in favor of Hollywood loyalty. Betty was a good and generous friend to many people, and, in the end, that loyalty at least afforded her some privacy when she needed it most.''

Remick kept vigil with her almost constantly, and, on the rare times he wasn't there, Betty sang snatches of her old movie numbers to cheer herself up. The last few days of her life she spent slipping in and out of a coma, Remick always there to hold her hand when she awakened. He was there on July 2 when Betty rallied for the last time. She died that day, her hand in his.

The real tragedy was that had Betty had a physical checkup sooner, the cancer might have been arrested. She'd admitted to her friend Bridget Walsh the year before she became ill that her voice was becoming progressively hoarser and that ''I'm not feeling well in general.'' She went on to say she'd always had an unreasonable fear of doctors—''No particular reason for it, that's just the way I am. Did you see *The Hospital* with George C. Scott? Since that movie, I can't even go to a hospital to visit a friend. Oh, I've been meaning to make an appointment for some time now, but my life has evolved into such a lethargic pace here in Vegas that I somehow just don't get around to doing a lot of things. I'm basically lazy. Always have been.

''And in the past I always relied on others to make appointments and decisions for me. First it was my mother. Then it was the studio. . . . Then, after I married Harry and had two daughters, I somehow went in for checkups because they did.''

By the time she was finally forced to see a doctor, the disease was too extensive to be arrested, and Betty Grable, the dream girl of World War II, died at fifty-six.

Some 600 people gathered two days later for her funeral at All Saint's Episcopal Church in Beverly Hills, including both ex-husbands, Coogan and

James, the man that got away, George Raft, and the one who stuck by her, Bob Remick. Other good friends like Alice Faye, Dorothy Lamour, Mitzi Gaynor, June Haver, and Dan Dailey were there as well, and, as the organ played her signature tune, "I Had the Craziest Dream" from *Springtime in the Rockies,* all eyes filled with tears.

When the service ended, Harry James got up from his seat beside his two daughters and left by a side door, speeding away in a waiting car. Of all there, he had the most dreams to remember.

FILMOGRAPHY

TITLE	YEAR	DIRECTOR	LEADING PLAYERS
Let's Go Places	1930	Frank Strayer	Joseph Wagstaff, Lola Lane, Walter Catlett, Dixie Lee
Whoopee	1930	Thornton Freeland	Eddie Cantor, Eleanor Hunt, Paul Gregory
Kiki	1931	Sam Taylor	Mary Pickford, Reginald Denny
Palmy Days	1931	A. Edward Sutherland	Eddie Cantor, Charlotte Greenwood, Charles Middleton, George Raft
The Greeks Had a Word for Them	1932	Lowell Sherman	Madge Evans, Joan Blondell, Ina Claire
The Kid from Spain	1932	Leo McCarey	Eddie Cantor, Lyda Roberti, Robert Young
Probation	1932	Richard Thorpe	John Darrow, Sally Blane, Clara Kimball Young
Hold 'Em Jail	1932	Norman Taurog	Wheeler and Woolsey, Edna Mae Oliver, Edgar Kennedy
Child of Manhattan	1933	Eddie Buzzell	Nancy Carroll, John Boles, Jane Darwell
Cavalcade	1933	Frank Lloyd	Diana Wynyard, Herbert Mundin, Ursula Jeans, Margaret Lindsay, Clive Brook
What Price Innocence?	1933	Willard Mack	Jean Parker, Minna Gombel, Willard Mack
Student Tour	1934	Charles Reisner	Jimmy Durante, Charles Butterworth, Maxine Doyle
The Gay Divorcée	1934	Mark Sandrich	Fred Astaire, Ginger Rogers, Alice Brady, Erik Rhodes, Edward Everett Horton
The Nitwits	1935	George Stevens	Wheeler and Woolsey, Evelyn Brent, Hale Hamilton
Old Man Rhythm	1935	Edward Ludwig	Charles (Buddy) Rogers, Barbara Kent

TITLE	YEAR	DIRECTOR	LEADING PLAYERS
Collegiate	1935	Ralph Murphy	Jack Oakie, Joe Penner, Frances Langford
Follow the Fleet	1936	Mark Sandrich	Fred Astaire, Ginger Rogers, Randolph Scott, Harriet Hilliard
Pigskin Parade	1936	David Butler	Stuart Erwin, Judy Garland, Patsy Kelly, Jack Haley, Johnny Downs
Don't Turn 'Em Loose	1936	Ben Stoloff	Lewis Stone, James Gleason, Bruce Cabot
This Way Please	1937	Robert Florey	Charles (Buddy) Rogers, Ned Sparks, Jim and Marian Jordan
Thrill of a Lifetime	1937	George Archainbaud	Yacht Club Boys, Judy Canova, Ben Blue
College Swing	1938	Raoul Walsh	George Burns, Gracie Allen, Martha Raye, Bob Hope, Edward Everett Horton
Give Me a Sailor	1938	Elliot Nugent	Martha Raye, Bob Hope, Jack Whiting
Campus Confessions	1938	George Archainbaud	Eleanore Whitney, William Henry, Fritz Feld
Man About Town	1939	Mark Sandrich	Jack Benny, Dorothy Lamour, Edward Arnold, Binnie Barnes
Million Dollar Legs	1939	Edward Cline	W. C. Fields, Jack Oakie, Andy Clyde, Ben Turpin, Dicky Moore, Billy Gilbert
The Day the Bookies Wept	1939	Leslie Godwins	Joe Penner, Richard Lane
Down Argentine Way	1940	Irving Cummings	Don Ameche, Carmen Miranda, Charlotte Greenwood, J. Carrol Naish
Tin Pan Alley	1940	Walter Lang	Alice Faye, Jack Oakie, John Payne, Esther Ralston
Moon over Miami	1941	Walter Lang	Don Ameche, Robert Cummings, Carole Landis, Charlotte Greenwood, Jack Haley
A Yank in the R.A.F.	1941	Henry King	Tyrone Power, John Sutton, Reginald Gardiner
I Wake Up Screaming	1941	H. Bruce Humberstone	Victor Mature, Carole Landis, Laird Cregar, Alan Mowbray
Footlight Serenade	1942	Gregory Ratoff	Victor Mature, John Payne, Jane Wyman, Phil Silvers
Song of the Islands	1942	Walter Lang	Victor Mature, Jack Oakie, Thomas Mitchell, Billy Gilbert
Springtime in the Rockies	1942	Irving Cummings	Carmen Miranda, Cesar Romero, Charlotte Greenwood, Edward Everett Horton
Coney Island	1943	Walter Lang	George Montgomery, Cesar Romero, Charles Winninger, Phil Silvers
Sweet Rosie O'Grady	1943	Irving Cummings	Robert Young, Adolphe Menjou, Reginald Gardiner, Virginia Grey

TITLE	YEAR	DIRECTOR	LEADING PLAYERS
Four Jills in a Jeep	1944	William Seiter	Kay Francis, Martha Raye, Carole Landis, Mitzi Mayfair, Phil Silvers, Alice Faye
PinUp Girl	1944	H. Bruce Humberstone	Martha Raye, John Harvey, Joe E. Brown, Eugene Pallette
Billy Rose's Diamond Horseshoe	1945	George Seaton	Dick Haymes, Phil Silvers, William Gaxtan
The Dolly Sisters	1945	Irving Cummings	John Payne, June Haver, S. Z. Sakall, Reginald Gardiner
Do You Love Me?	1945	Gregory Ratoff	Maureen O'Hara, Dick Haymes, Harry James, Reginald Gardiner
The Shocking Miss Pilgrim	1947	George Seaton	Dick Haymes, Anne Revere, Gene Lockhart
Mother Wore Tights	1947	Walter Lang	Dan Dailey, Mona Freeman, Connie Marshall, Vanessa Brown
That Lady in Ermine	1948	Ernst Lubitsch Otto Preminger	Douglas Fairbanks, Jr., Cesar Romero, Walter Abel, Harry Davenport
When My Baby Smiles at Me	1948	Walter Lang	Dan Dailey, Jack Oakie, June Havoc, James Gleason
The Beautiful Blonde from Bashful Bend	1949	Preston Sturges	Cesar Romero, Rudy Vallee, Olga San Juan, Porter Hall
Wabash Avenue	1950	Henry Koster	Victor Mature, Phil Harris, Reginald Gardiner, James Barton, Margaret Hamilton
My Blue Heaven	1950	Henry Koster	Dan Dailey, David Wayne, Jane Wyatt, Mitzi Gaynor
Call Me Mister	1951	Lloyd Bacon	Dan Dailey, Danny Thomas, Dale Robertson, Richard Boone, Jeffrey Hunter
Meet Me After the Show	1951	Richard Sale	Macdonald Carey, Rory Calhoun, Eddie Albert, Irene Ryan
The Farmer Takes a Wife	1953	Henry Levin	Dale Robertson, Thelma Ritter, John Carroll
How To Marry a Millionaire	1953	Jean Negulesco	Marilyn Monroe, Lauren Bacall, William Powell, Rory Calhoun, David Wayne
How To Be Very, Very Popular	1955	Nunnally Johnson	Robert Cummings, Charles Coburn, Sheree North, Fred Clark

Rita Hayworth

I like having my picture taken and being a glamorous
person. Sometimes when I find myself getting impatient
I just remember the times I cried my eyes out because
nobody wanted to take my picture at the Trocadero.
All women like being fussed over and I'm no exception.
I think it's damned nice!

Rita Hayworth, quoted in the New
York Times, *1942.*

Men fell in love with Gilda and wakened with me. A lot
of people are unfaithful in marriage. I preferred to
marry five times.

Rita Hayworth, quoted in W
magazine, 1974.

Margarita Carmen Cansino grew up
to become Rita Hayworth, the titian-haired Love Goddess of World War II whose
picture was plastered on the side of the first atomic bomb. As the erotic symbol of
millions of male fantasies, it seemed appropriate that she, of all the great screen
beauties of the time, should be singled out as the most potent and most potentially
destructive of them all. That unasked-for distinction proved prophetic, for destructive she certainly was but, sadly, her most affected victim has always been herself.

During the 1940s she reigned as the gem of Columbia Pictures, showcased by
a canny Harry Cohen in a series of pictures artfully designed to show off her sex
appeal, which was always tempered by the innate innocence of a girl who'd fallen
into unbelievable good luck and was determined to stay there. When cornered she
fought like a tigress, but she always knew just when to give in. Her private life
was one of the most public of the century, thanks in large part to her marriages to
Orson Welles, Prince Aly Khan, and Dick Haymes, but audiences never held it
against her, for they were always able to recognize that she was a woman with a
simple aim in life—calm happiness—an almost impossible goal in light of her

Rita Hayworth evolves into a Love Goddess in Tales of Manhattan *(1942).*
THE DOUG MCCLELLAND COLLECTION.

image and fame, and one that, except for brief moments, she has yet to attain. Time and again she issued ''I'll-never-be-happier'' statements, only to have them shattered in a blaze of usually unsavory headlines. Shy and often self-conscious to the point of embarrassment, Rita Hayworth was taught early on to please the men she let control her life, all of whom used her to fulfill their own egos, leaving hers to starve. Ultimately the teasing temptress of the screen was trapped by her greatest creation. As she has often said one way or another, ''They went to bed with Gilda and woke up with me.''

THE daughter of a well-known Spanish dancer and his Ziegfeld Follies showgirl wife, Margarita Cansino was born in New York City, the Upper West Side to be exact, on October 17, 1918—an inauspicious day as far as her father was concerned. ''When I looked at Margarita a few minutes after she was born I was terribly disappointed. I had wanted a boy. What could I do with a girl?'' Canny Eduardo quickly solved that problem by sticking a pair of castanets in her hands ''instead of a rattle'' and taking the first steps to bring her into the family business, a vaudeville act called The Dancing Cansinos. ''From the time I was three and a half,'' she has said, ''as soon as I could stand on my own feet, I was given dance lessons.''

And dance she did, slowly, painstakingly developing the only true talent she ever had. Much later it was her dancing ability that helped create the facade of the hair-tossing tease who, while she masqueraded under names like Salome and Carmen and Sadie Thompson, was undeniably the Everywoman that every man thought of whether he admitted it or not. Her childhood was a patchwork of rehearsal halls and dressing rooms as she accompanied her family on their dancing tours. There was little time for formal education or making friends, and, although the young girl didn't know a better life, she did realize that she didn't much like the one she had. Her parents' dedication to dancing didn't rub off, ''but I didn't dare tell my father so I took the lessons,'' hoping by doing so to earn, and keep, his approval.

She eventually earned a modicum of that approval, but not because of her dancing. While watching his fourteen-year-old daughter perform a torrid flamenco in the live prologue at the 1932 opening night of the movie *Back Street,* he observed that she had the body of a budding goddess. ''All of a sudden I wake up. Wow! She has a figure! She ain't no baby anymore.'' The body that would attract men like William Randolph Hearst and Howard Hughes ripened early, and it wasn't long before others noticed it as well. During what lengthened into an eighteen-month stay in Tijuana, Mexico, where The Dancing Cansinos were performing at the Foreign Club, Eduardo took careful pains to safeguard his maturing daughter from the advances of the admiring crowds by locking her in her dressing room between shows and sending her back across the border to join other family members at Chula Vista every night.

The next stop for the troupe was at the famous Agua Caliente Hotel two miles south of Tijuana, then just coming into its own as a favorite getaway spot for Hollywood types looking for a playful weekend out of town. By then Rita was partnered with her father, and they were so sensational together that the original four-week engagement stretched into seven months. It was lucky seven for young Margarita, since one particularly warm evening the vice-president and west coast production head of the Fox Film Corporation came in. His name was Winfield Sheehan, and his business was packaging beauty for the movie cameras. In the darkhaired young girl with the flashing legs, he saw the potential of a screen presence, the raw clay he specialized in molding into "personalities." Rita's naiveté and quiet enthusiasm impressed him, and shortly Eduardo and Sheehan were locked in negotiations over the future of the voluptuous teenager. Since her formal education was almost nonexistent (her father had long believed "school for a dancer is nonsense"), she had no way of knowing that Eduardo's contractual approval was the beginning of a new life, one that would make her an international sex symbol thanks to a series of powerful men who would mold and shape her into one of the most titillating personalities the screen has ever seen.

Sheehan arranged her screen debut, as a Spanish dancer, in *Dante's Inferno* (1935) in a routine choreographed by her father. It was impressive enough to bring a $200-per-week studio contract plus an on-the-lot slot for Eduardo as studio dance instructor.

As dark-haired Rita Cansino (she became a red-head later on) she spent the next year decorating several Fox westerns with her sultry Latin looks (which were orientalized in 1935 for *Charlie Chan in Egypt*). Sheehan picked her to star with Gilbert Roland in a remake of *Ramona,* but before that could be finalized Fox Films merged with Twentieth Century Pictures and he was out of a job. So was Rita. Taking advantage of the publicity she'd received, she quickly got acting jobs, freelancing primarily in low-budget westerns at studios like Crescent and Grand National. They weren't much, but by now she was eager to learn and was no longer responsible for half the family's income, now that her father's dance studio at the corner of Hollywood and Vine was a success. For the first time she had a bit of independence, but it wasn't to last long.

By acquiescing to her father's demands over the years and thereby gaining the disciplinarian's approval, Rita had unwittingly set a pattern of behavior that would last her whole life: when a man was in a power position, she obeyed him. She had a knack for attracting predatory men, and soon another one appeared— literally—on her doorstep. He was Edward Charles Judson, a forty-year-old foreign-car salesman and sometime oil-scheme promoter. Judson had seen the Technicolor tests of *Ramona* at Fox before Sheehan was ousted and was so impressed by Rita's beauty that he decided to track her down and meet her. He called her, asked her out, and was quickly turned down. "But my father doesn't know you," Rita said. This problem was quickly solved when Judson soon gained Eduardo's approval to escort his comely daughter. Intrigued by both her beauty and the complacent personality that went with it, Judson decided he'd stumbled on a mother lode just waiting to be properly mined, and he devoted himself to making it pay off. Rita's somewhat overweight figure had been carefully whittled down by constant work at the gymnasium and at the family dance studio. Starting with an even stricter diet than the one she had been on, Judson became almost sculptor-like in his attention to Rita's looks and Svengali-like in his approach to her career. By offering an executive at Republic Pictures a discount on a car, he got her the female lead in *Hit the Saddle* (1937). Shortly after that he proposed marriage and she accepted.

His biggest coup was landing her a contract at Columbia Pictures. A con man of no mean proportions, he took on Harry Cohen, Columbia's peripatetic chieftain, and came up with a seven-year deal. After signing it, Judson remarked to Cohen, "What bride ever received a better wedding gift than a movie contract?" to which Harry replied, "It looks to me as if an old man has just found himself a seven-year meal ticket with free room and broad."

At that time there was no scarcity of Latin types around Hollywood, so Cohen's first decision was to Americanize his new starlet. Taking her mother's maiden name of Haworth, he added a *y,* and shipped her off to studio hairstylist Helen Hunt, who changed her hair color from brunette to a shimmering auburn. Rita accepted all this with patience and shy excitement, even the electrolysis she had to undergo to raise her hairline, particularly unpleasant for a girl with a low pain threshold.

But Judson didn't rest once he'd maneuvered her into Columbia. He knew by instinct that the best way to make somebody want something was to make him think it was hard to get, and he quickly launched his own personal promotion campaign to make Rita Hayworth just such an unattainable commodity. He wangled evening dresses from fashion houses and hired a publicity man to get her name into the gossip columns. After a string of "B" efforts at Columbia, Rita was given a choice role of a mantrap in *Only Angels Have Wings,* with Cary Grant and the publicity-shy Jean Arthur. So good was she in it that Judson was able to sell the studio on the idea of putting the big publicity guns behind her career, a notion the PR department was only too happy to explore, since their efforts with Arthur were constantly stymied by her avid desire for personal privacy.

Meanwhile Cohen decided to let his new actress develop at someone else's expense, and he lent her to Warner Brothers to replace Ann Sheridan, their resident Oomph Girl, in *Strawberry Blonde,* opposite Jimmy Cagney and Olivia DeHavilland. From there she went to Twentieth for the coveted role of Dona Sol, the temptress who leads Tyrone Power very much astray in *Blood and Sand.* She won the part over thirty-seven other actresses and scored her first Technicolor triumph, with the public at last getting a look at the burnished bronze of her hair. When she left Twentieth after finishing the picture, she left as a star, having the last laugh on the studio that had axed her from their contract list six years before. Back home, Cohen rewarded his new star with two classic musicals opposite Fred Astaire, *You'll Never Get Rich* (1941), and *You Were Never Lovelier* a year later.

Ironically, as Judson's faith in his young wife's career paid off in terms of better parts and, more important, a much better contract, the more he wanted to keep her to himself, sequestering her in their Westwood house. The marriage had already begun showing signs of trouble. One of their few outings together was to New York for the opening of *You'll Never Get Rich* at the Radio City Music Hall, and that night she was escorted by four servicemen representing each branch of the Armed Forces, which left Ed very much in the background. Back home their difficulties increased, aided and abetted by Harry Cohen, who figured that the less influence Judson had on Rita, the better things would go for him. At forty-five and with his masterpiece completed, Judson had to face the fact that his days of power were waning, although even he didn't guess how quickly they would be over for good.

The beginning of that end came when Rita went back to Twentieth to replace Alice Faye in the splashy Technicolor musical *My Gal Sal* opposite "that gorgeous hunk of man," Victor Mature. In him she quickly found a playmate who was only too willing to take her to all the public posh spots, and in only a matter of weeks their romance became Hollywood's topic A. It was an imprudent affair at best, and Rita threw herself into it with all the abandon of a high school girl on her first date, a comparison not far from the truth. In September of 1942, she filed for divorce, citing extreme mental cruelty. Judson filed a countersuit and threatened to make public an agreement that Rita had signed during a flush moment of her new romance which specified that she would pay her husband a total of $12,000 if he agreed in writing that he would "not imply, directly or indirectly, that she had committed an offense involving moral turpitude under federal, state or local laws, or that she had conducted herself in any manner which would cause her to be held in scorn, or which would damage her career." His reason for threatening the disclosure? Rita had stopped sending checks after four monthly installments of $500 each.

Smelling big trouble, Cohen stepped in, and again the pair met—the con man and the mogul—and again the topics were Rita and money, only this time only Cohen was concerned about her future. Reportedly it cost Cohen $30,000 to make Judson forget the action and quietly let Rita go. Said Rita, "I married him for love but he married me for an investment. I got a divorce to be myself again. From the first he told me I couldn't do anything for myself. 'You're such a child,' he'd say. I didn't have any fun those five years we were married. I was never permitted to make any decisions. He robbed everything of excitement. He was a husband-nursemaid."

Reputation salvaged—in fact, enhanced by her romantic migrations—Rita was nonetheless on the receiving end of one of Cohen's famous tongue-lashings on the responsibilities that go with being a full-fledged movie star, rather a moot point, since by then Mature had decamped for a tour of duty in the Coast Guard.

But she got over that quickly, too, thanks to good friends like Tony Martin and David Niven, plus all the other things she had going for her. After all, she was a star, she was independent for the first time in her adult life, and she'd just met an intriguing man whom everyone was hailing as the town's newest genius, Orson Welles.

Rita and Welles were quickly dubbed Beauty and the Beast by the Hollywood press, but instead of a beast Welles turned into a Svengali, seeing in Rita the ultimate Trilby, anxious to be stretched and molded into not only the physical but intellectual epitome of sex. In a matter of weeks he swept away the memories not only of Mature and Gilbert Roland but of Howard Hughes, both of whom she had been dating as well. Welles's initial act in the re-education of Rita was to bring her into his magic routine, where every night he sawed her in half and then put her together again. (When Mature heard this, he reportedly commented, ''That's a hell of a way to woo a girl!'')

To Rita, Welles was ''a brilliant man, a stimulating man,'' but, despite the undeniable glow on her face, she had one serious problem to deal with: Louella Parsons. Louella had long championed Rita's rise as a star and was her confidante, so naturally when she saw Welles loom into Rita's future Louella was forced to defend her position as Queen Bee of the Hearst newspaper chain, whose founder, William Randolph Hearst, had been chipped away at so well by Orson in his *Citizen Kane*.

One of the most flattering epithets Miss Parsons used for him was ''awesome Orson—the self-styled genius,'' while on the other hand she was one of the few people to spotlight Rita's efforts on behalf of the British War Relief Association, namely her nightly L.A. stage appearances in *Charlot's Revue,* all proceeds of which went to the relief fund. Parsons found herself in the unenviable position of having to choose between bread and affection, and it was only the sincerity of her friendship with Rita that kept her from aiming her heaviest guns at the blossoming romance. As it was, she did get in a few broadsides, accusing Welles of stealing Rita away from serviceman Mature while avoiding military duty himself. (Welles did try to enlist but·was refused for reasons of health.)

Meanwhile Rita remained overwhelmed by Welles much the way Marilyn Monroe would be a decade later when she married Arthur Miller, and she threw herself enthusiastically into his mini-education program. For the first time in her life she truly wanted a man to make decisions for her. Also, it took only a glance at his recent romantic track record with Dolores Del Rio to make her realize that the quicker she got culture the stronger the bonds between them would be.

Welles's last picture, *Journey into Fear* (starring Del Rio), was released in 1943 to less-than-spectacular box office, and his ''genius'' status in Hollywood was already shaky. One wonders if it hadn't been, would he have been so willing to devote so much time to Rita. But she wasn't thinking of that aspect when they were married in a Santa Monica civil ceremony on September 7, 1943, the day her divorce from Ed Judson became final.

They started building a fantasy house in Carmel, California, while he gently insinuated himself into her career decisions, a fact that Harry Cohen was anticipating but hardly relishing. On Orson's advice, Rita turned down *Once Upon a Time* opposite Cary Grant but did show up for shooting on *Coverl Girl,* a lavish Technicolor musical which teamed her with Gene Kelly and Phil Silvers. On loan from MGM, Kelly found Rita's dancing ability everything perfectionist Fred Astaire had a few years before, and the film was a dazzling success. Their number entitled *Long Ago and Far Away* helped make it a top grosser for Columbia, made Kelly more valuable on his return to MGM, and solidified Rita's image as Betty Grable's movie-musical equal. Meanwhile Welles kept making up reading lists, noting museums to visit, and collecting classical records for Rita to study in their private hours. "He's a genius," she told reporters, "and let's face it, I'm no Einstein—but I'm willing to learn. Orson's the most stimulating man I've ever known, and remember, he *did* ask me out to dinner before he sawed me in half!"

But saw her in half he did, picking her apart and then putting the pieces back together to suit his own demands and desires. Though to millions Rita was already perfection, Orson couldn't resist tampering and tinkering with her, and though Rita trusted him implicitly during this period, she would surely have felt the strain of the pulling and mending going on inside her brain and emotions. Once again a strong man was making her over *his* way, but at least, she consoled herself, this time a *bona fide* genius was doing the reconstruction.

Though Hollywood had decided that Welles was unreliable as a money-making director, in those pre-bulbous days he was desired as a leading man in films like *Jane Eyre* and *The Stranger.* But Rita's career far outshone his own. She started the glorious *Tonight and Every Night* musical about wartime London but shortly into production found out she was pregnant. Their daughter, Rebecca, was born on December 17, 1943, three months after completion of the picture, but the euphoria of motherhood was shortlived when just a month after her daughter's birth, Rita's own mother died. Volga Cansino had been a supportive character in her daughter's hectic life, especially so during the divorce from Ed Judson, when she appeared in court with Rita. A former showgirl, Volga had known in advance some of the pressures her daughter's famous life would give her, and she was always there to comfort her. Her sudden death from peritonitis came as a severe blow to Rita.

For a while, retirement rumors flurried around Hollywood, but Columbia had gained enormous status from the success of Rita Hayworth. "Two months after Becky was born I was back rehearsing production numbers for *Gilda.*" The brainchild of screenwriter and producer Virginia Van Upp, Gilda was a lady who, once in Rita's life, would stay with her forever. It remains her ultimate screen triumph and also has become the mark to which all subsequent performances were compared, especially in light of the frequent contract suspensions and "comebacks" that ultimately cheated her audiences of watching her gradually mature away from that singluar aspect of herself.

Ironically, it was the permanence of Gilda rather than another man that began to chip away at the Welleses' marriage. He wanted to make pictures abroad

As Gilda *(1946), the woman no man in his right mind could resist.*
THE DOUG MCCLELLAND COLLECTION.

where his reputation was still potent, while Rita had to stay behind, studio-bound, and star in *Down to Earth,* this time playing the mythical goddess of dance, Terpsichore. She begged Harry Cohen to let her film abroad, too, but no go. Thanks to Judson's astute contract, she was tied to Columbia for another ten years, and "it was a horror. We [Orson and Rita] were jailed, both of us, by that contract, victims of our own success."

Concurrent with her receiving international publicity by having her photograph pasted on the side of the Bikini Atoll atomic bomb—"It was Harry Cohen's idea to put my picture on that bomb . . . and they threatened to put me on suspension if I put up a fuss. Harry was the beginning of the Gestapo at Columbia."—she learned that Welles seemed more than slightly interested in Italian actress Lea Padovani.

Before Orson departed for Italy, though, he'd received a $50,000 advance against a film for Columbia, and, even though the Welles-Hayworth union was by this time shaking at the foundations, Cohen still wanted the film, and agreed to let Rita star.

Deserted by her Svengali, Rita was once again at the studio's mercies, and the terrific grosses of *Gilda* brought new life to some of her older films including the reissued *My Gal Sal,* which went out with a new, sultry ad campaign complete with the tagline "It takes a girl like Rita to play a Gal Like Sal." Singer Anita Ellis recalls one night at a producer's house when she was asked to sing "Put the Blame on Mame" (which she'd dubbed in *Gilda*) from behind a screen while Rita stood in front and mouthed the words. Both ladies turned the producer down, "but can you imagine him even asking? It was like that scene in *Singin' in the Rain,* for God's sake." The ironic part of it all was that Rita had a good singing voice, but Cohen never felt it matched her onscreen image and always had her voice dubbed by other singers. Rita may have disliked the idea, but, says Ellis, "On the set I never saw any displays of temperament. She was always quiet, always agreeable."

The grosses from *Gilda* and *Down to Earth* (a print of which was encased in a time capsule scheduled for opening in 2047) gave her the leverage to rework her contract and form her own production company, Beckworth, which would guarantee her a 25 percent cut of all her pictures plus almost a quarter of a million dollars per year in salary. To get this deal, she agreed to make two pictures a year for the next seven, excluding the one she would do with Welles, *The Lady from Shanghai.*

By the time Welles wandered back to Hollywood, the couple were formally separated and rumors were flying that the picture would never be made unless the pair reconciled. But Rita scotched the rumors, saying, "Of course not! I made an agreement and I'll stand by it! I owe it to Orson." Sentiment aside, she also believed that their daughter Rebecca would ultimately benefit from the film's profits.

"Orsie," as Rita called him, took the male lead in *Shanghai* and then broke another newsflash to Harry Cohen—he was going to cut off Rita's hair and dye it blonde! "Everybody knows her most beautiful feature is that hair," Cohen fumed, nearly apoplectic at the thought, but Welles went ahead, and studio photographers were there to immortalize the event. Rita was understandably nervous, and a makeup man approached to powder her because she was sweating. Said the gallant Welles, "Miss Hayworth doesn't sweat; she glows." Said the not-so-gallant Cohen, "Oh my God! What has that bastard done?"

Now a closely cropped topaz blonde, Rita left with Welles for Mexico, where most of the picture was to be shot aboard Errol Flynn's yacht, the *Zaca*, in Acapulco harbor. (Flynn was then married to Nora Eddington, who was later to crop up in Rita's life when she met Dick Haymes, at which point Nora was Mrs. Haymes.)

The picture was completed in mid-1947. Cohen looked at *The Lady from Shanghai* and didn't know what to do with it. Taking it away from Welles, the studio editors recut it into a reasonable length and let it out in 1948 to terrible box-office results. As sleekly beautiful and as dangerous-looking as a stainless steel scalpel, Rita's "new look" bombed with her public, but she remained loyal over the years to both the picture and its director. "See, Orson was trying something new with me, but Harry Cohen wanted The Image—The Image he was gonna make me till I was *ninety*!"

On a personal level, however, the film did nothing to reunite Rita and Orson. A goddess left in the lurch doesn't forgive easily, and she filed for a divorce on November 10, 1947. "I couldn't take his genius twenty-four hours a day any longer. I was married, yet I didn't have a husband." Stories broke that Welles had conducted all-night production conferences in their bedroom, and Rita could either leave the room or try to sleep through it all. "He told me he never should have married in the first place, as it interfered with his freedom in his way of life."

Disappointed by the film's lackluster showing with her fans and disillusioned with her failed marriage, Rita was at odds with herself, and when Harry Cohen offered her a "free" vacation to Europe—on the condition she show up at various European premieres of *Tonight and Every Night*—she took him up on it. Cohen's motive was actually threefold, for, besides the extra publicity her appearances would create, she would also have a chance to let her hair grow out and he would be able to take care of preproduction on her next film, *The Loves of Carmen,* a return to the temptress-type role her public so obviously wanted.

Naturally, the Love Goddess at large caused wide speculation, and Rita turned to her old friend David Niven for help in planning her trip. Realizing she'd be catnip for every newsman between Hollywood and Helsinki, Niven mapped out a quiet meandering journey through France once her premiere duties were over. Staying at country inns and small hotels, Rita would end up at the Hotel La Reserve in Beaulieu-sur-Mer, one of the choicest spots on the Riviera.

When she left on the trip she said that all she wanted to do was "just to roam, to live for a year like the natives." If that were truly her wish, she missed it by countless miles, for Rita Hayworth quickly found there was no place of quiet refuge for the fantasy figure of the world's males. After attending various film openings, she arrived in Paris only to be felled by a virus infection that required her to receive several blood transfusions. By the time she did reach the Riviera she was exhausted and looked forward to nothing more strenuous than relaxation and catching up on some local pals such as social lion-hunter Elsa Maxwell, with whom she'd shared the stage in *Charlot's Revue* during the early war years.

In those days, Elsa Maxwell was the queen of café society and gathered around her table everyone from the Duke and Duchess of Windsor to all sizes and shapes of visiting firemen of celebrity status. When she learned that Rita was in town, she decided to pull together a small dinner party of her most interesting friends to cheer her up. That dinner soon became the topic of widespread speculation, because one of the guests was Prince Aly Khan, son of the Aga Khan, the immensely wealthy religious leader of twenty million Ismailian Moslems, and at the time his presumed successor. "I had no idea who he was. He had something to do with a famous family, that's all I knew. I think this rather amused him." Still pale from her recent illness, highlighted by her again red hair, and sheathed in white, Rita was a ravishing picture, irresistible to Aly, then steadily acquiring a reputation as the playboy of both the eastern and western worlds despite his strained marriage to British brewery heiress Joan Yarde-Buller.

The son of an all-powerful father, Aly had two grand passions in his life, women and horses, although no one could ever quite figure out which was of paramount interest. His father sent him at an early age to an Egyptian *hakim*, a doctor versed in the arts of lovemaking, particularly the development of an awesome staying power. In fact, so staying were Aly Khan's powers purported to be that among his friends it was known that he could make love to five women in one day, earning in the process a reputation as a woman-pleaser, since he ejaculated only about once a week. (At the time of his death in an auto crash outside Paris in May of 1960, these lovemaking tricks were beginning to catch up with him in the form of a difficult prostate problem.)

The attraction between the prince and the movie queen was almost instantaneous, and while Maxwell thought that Rita's initial interest in Aly might have been to rekindle the attention of Welles, that was quickly forgotten when in a matter of weeks Rita embarked on one of the most famous romances in contemporary history. For a girl who had been disappointed in love twice and temporarily deserted by her fans (although her European appearances were highly successful), Aly Khan must indeed have appeared as a prince, but instead of a white charger, it was a sports car that carried her with him away from Cannes and into Spain, where at every stop from Toledo to Madrid to Lisbon, hordes of newspaper reporters waited for the latest news flash, which Rita wasn't long in delivering by look if not by public statement. She left little doubt that she was living up to her label of Love Goddess to its fullest.

Knowing by now that when Rita was in love business went out the window, Harry Cohen began cabling her to report back home for *Carmen*. Incensed by her silence, he uncharacteristically flew to Spain for another of his famous heart-to-heart talks, the result of which was her return to Hollywood to shoot the tragic tale of the gypsy girl, "a creature of a thousand moods . . . whose arms were kind . . . whose lips were maddening." Undoubtedly Cohen reminded her that she stood to make a great deal of money through her new company by making *The Loves of Carmen*. Remembering the failure of *The Lady from Shanghai* (and its nonexistent profits for her daughter Rebecca), Rita seemed to sense that this picture might well be her last chance at big time money since, in her heart, she was ready to walk away from it all now that she'd found a man whose sole goal in life was *not* to make Rita Hayworth into an even bigger star. Cohen soon shipped her and co-star Glenn Ford, as a somewhat unlikely Don José, to northern California for location filming of the Technicolor love story, which he hoped would ignite the same kind of box office fires their *Gilda* teaming had done. The press had yet another field day when Aly showed up in Hollywood while she was away, impatiently waiting for her to finish her camera chores. At last she'd found a man who wanted a wife instead of a goddess—or so she thought.

And if Rita thought that *Carmen* would be her last chance at Hollywood money through her production company, Beckworth, there was more than a little reason for her to believe it would be her last crack at showing everyone she was a star. In the lushly colored drama, complete with a wildly sexual flamenco choreographed by her father, Eduardo, there was an earthiness, a crackling sensuality about her, the freshened sexuality of a goddess who'd finally found things offscreen as glamorous as people had always expected they were for her. It was a vibrant Rita cavorting amidst castanets and Spanish corporals, and with the hint of off-screen scandal, it helped her live up more fully than ever before to all the adjectives that had been pinned on her over the years.

Her character in the movie contrasted greatly with the woman she would soon become. As Carmen she fought like a tigress to get the man or the bracelet she wanted, playing off lover-against-husband-against-lover and back again. But offscreen she would shortly find herself swept away in a tidal wave of headlines that outlined a life of truly epic proportions, only to find out, too late, that her role was as consort, almost lady-in-waiting to a man whose rule of life was that everything had its proper place, according to his own priorities.

When *Carmen* was in the can, Rita flew to Cuba with her daughter, Rebecca, where she was soon joined, in a series of highly publicized "coincidences," by Aly. From there they sailed for London aboard the *Britannica*, stopping there long enough to be criticized by the British press, who objected to Rita's dragging her daughter along on such an obviously romantic outing. From there they went to Switzerland, where, "coincidentally," Rita and Aly arrived at the same hotel on the same day. Before leaving Hollywood though, Rita had done two things: she picked up her final divorce papers from Orson Welles, and left Columbia stranded with an expensive western they'd mounted for her, which Harry Cohen would remember for the next several years.

By the beginning of 1949, Rita was the most publicized romantic figure on the face of the globe. Her every movement was duly chronicled, including Aly's proposal, complete with twelve-carat ring, and her formal acceptance by Aly's father, the Aga Khan. (Rather belatedly a group of American women's clubs voted to boycott her films in future, which cued father Eduardo to reply about this anti-Rita publicity, "I told her to go back to Orson . . . it didn't work. Now I keep my advice to myself.") When they announced their wedding date of May 27, 1949, they set off a stampede towards Aly's Château d'Horizon in Cannes where the nuptials were to take place. The only Hollywood correspondent to get a legitimate invitation was Rita's old friend Louella Parsons—much to the chagrin of Hedda Hopper, who had steadfastly stated that the marriage was but a dream in the movie queen's head. Louella looked on while Hedda fumed outside in the hot, crowded street. True, Rita had said, "I am lost in a kind of dream world," but she made the dreams come true. She certainly looked the part, too, standing there in the town hall of the French resort town clad in blue crepe designed by Jaques Fath, repeating the civil vows of marriage later recapped religiously at the chateau. One wonders whether she waved to Hedda as she and her new husband stepped into his cream-colored Cadillac for the ride to the reception? One also wonders whether Hedda knew Louella had commandeered the Communist mayor's telephone to breathlessly relate the events to the world.

One of the few invited guests in the Western Hemisphere not to appear that day was Harry Cohen, who opted for the dictatorial regime of Columbia Pictures rather than play the part of the unwilling father/potentate watching his favorite daughter make a match he could only consider ill-starred due to its obvious effect on the company's stock. Let Hedda hop in Cannes; he was staying home.

The party lasted until dawn, but then it should have, considering each guest at the reception had been alloted fifteen bottles of champagne. After the Moslem ceremony, Rita began to collect gifts fit for a Love Goddess, including an impressive collection of jewels, a sports car, an undisclosed cash dowry and four of Aly's favorite racehorses. She could not know then how much that particular gift would mean in her life. Horses were Aly's main passion, and their first public trip after the wedding was to the races at England's Epsom Downs.

The move from movie star to princess, a fantasy figure's transition to an even more glamorous fantasy, captured the attention of the world—not just the devotees of movie magazines. Where once she'd graced the covers of *Photoplay* and *Movie World* as screen siren, Rita and her new husband were now photographed with equal zeal by society photographers from *Town and Country*.

On the surface, at least, the image was one of contentment. But how Rita felt, in her few private moments, was a matter of speculation. Less than a decade later, Grace Kelly would make the move from the sound stage to the inner sanctum of international society with almost disarming ease, but Grace had a Philadelphia Main-Line background to help pave the way. Despite her new title and her husband's celebrated cronies, Rita was still Margarita Cansino inside, a shy girl often more comfortable with the grips and technicians of her movie sets than with her co-stars.

Like her own father, Ed Judson, Orson Welles, and Harry Cohen, Aly Khan was a dominant man who knew what he wanted and was used to getting it. For all appearances, Rita tried once again to play the dutiful daughter, the ''good little girl'' doing what was expected of her to please a strong father figure. Part of her problem, it may well be, was that she'd been so transformed by the studio from little girl to Love Goddess that her own emotions as a woman hadn't had a chance to evolve at a pace equal to her career.

Rita had always been reticent about her innermost self, wary of betraying real emotions to a public interested in the fantasies she created on—and now off—the screen, and now she had another secret to keep to herself. With it came the pressure of knowing that it would be only a matter of time before her secret was revealed. Seven months to the day after the heralded wedding, Princess Yasmin, Rita and Aly's daughter, was born in a Swiss clinic, and once again the publicity was great, especially among finger-counters. As soon as she'd recovered, the couple took off on a far-flung trip to Aly's various religious domains and tried to forget the hullabaloo. They even took their own cameraman along to film the fun, which, briefly, was to show up on a few film screens under the titles *Champagne Safari* and the prophetic *Safari, So Good.*

At the time there had already been rumors of discord betweeen Aly and Rita, and this second honeymoon was supposed to smooth things over as well as present Rita to her future subjects. Besides the cameraman there was also a truckload of refrigerators stocked with champagne, assorted bridge-playing French socialites, and various secretaries, valets, cooks, and maids. It was quite a honeymoon, and a trip that finally gave Rita true insight into the man she'd married. She wasn't a wife: she was a possession, and the ensuing scenes between them reportedly provided the gist of the film *The Barefoot Contessa*—a role Joe Mankiewicz had the nerve to offer Rita! It was the tragic tale of a gypsy dancer turned star-into-noblewoman with the riches shortly becoming shackles of worn-out honor.

Harry Cohen dangled *Born Yesterday* in front of her, but Rita showed great determination for over two years in staying away from films, despite the growing difficulty of the most challenging role of her career. As a Hollywood-queen-turned-princess, she was inundated with responsibilities far beyond the demands of any movie script, and she became more and more withdrawn, glimpsed at race tracks in chiffon hats and white gloves, looking regally sadder as time wore on. Every expression was still being carefully catalogued for posterity, and as Harry Cohen read the headlines and looked at the money *Carmen* had made—not to mention the $20 million from her three previous pictures, excluding *The Lady from Shanghai*—he must have cried many a stockholder's tear.

As the safari wore on it became more intolerable for Rita. Though she deeply loved Aly, she felt that the burden of royal responsibility was not something she could live with. Instead of the quiet days they'd spent after their marriage at one or the other of his several houses from southern Ireland to the French Riviera, with Rebecca and before the birth of Yasmin, there was now the entourage of a crown prince to contend with, and they rarely had a chance to be alone. Was the Love Goddess lonely on her honeymoon? That was the verdict when she packed up her children, left Africa for Paris, and from there sailed home. Aly eventually followed her to Hollywood, but despite his attempts to play husband and father, the pressures remained and only seemed to loom larger in her life. Amidst another splash of headlines, they separated. All she wanted was a three-million-dollar trust fund set up for their daughter, nothing for herself.

When Rita married Aly there had been much consternation among American church people because of his Moslem religion, but all that was quickly forgotten when she landed back home, where her first comment to panting newsreel cameramen was, "I want a hot dog."

The all-American sex symbol was home after two and a half years of an adventure trumpeted from Toledo to Timbuctoo. She came back a disheartened, financially insecure woman of thirty-two with two children to support and not at all sure her public was still interested in paying to see her. Most important, she came back alone—straight into the hands of a waiting Harry Cohen.

Technically on contractual suspension, and after a period of seclusion, Rita sent out feelers to Cohen, who jumped at the chance and began putting together a comeback film. As usual he opted for something old and something borrowed— Glenn Ford and a Gilda-like lady with a shady past named Chris, in a black and white thriller called *Affair in Trinidad.*

Again a creation of Virginia Van Upp, Rita stormed onscreen doing the famous "Trinidad Lady" number, a torrid song and dance constructed to hit the male heart square in the middle. In her absence newcomers like Elizabeth Taylor and Marilyn Monroe, as well as old friend Ava Gardner, had taken up much of her Love Goddess leg-room. A widow in the film, her character, like the woman herself, was contrite now, and tired. The adventures of her recent past showed onscreen in the demeanor of the lady named Chris Emory. All in all, *Affair in Trinidad* was *Gilda,* a little lower on the ladder on which she'd stood so optimistically high just seven years before. But the ladder was shaky now—so shaky, in fact, that the decline of the Love Goddess had begun.

After a screen absence of almost four years, the Rita the ads trumpeted "is *back*!" was not the same girl the public remembered leaving, and even Harry Cohen and the power of Columbia couldn't heat the picture up to her former white hot boiling point. Expensive to film and delayed by script revisions demanded by its star, *Affair* made money, but it was evident that millions of people who used to flock to see her were now more firmly established in front of ten-inch screens in their living rooms. Chastened, she told Louella, "I feel I have so much to live for in my two little girls. I'm going to keep working hard to take care of them and give them the advantages they should have." The public had a long memory and decided that her days and nights as a princess had robbed her rather than enriched her. Harry Cohen's solution to the dilemma? Make her a princess again, one of the most notorious of all—Salomé.

Much later she would say to interviewer John Hallowell of *The New York Times,* "I can certainly tell you some of my non-favorite [films], honey. Certainly *Salomé* and her stupid seven veils." But at the time, Rita had to make it. The financial settlement between herself and Aly was nil; she wanted nothing for herself but insisted on a trust fund for Yasmin which took several years and many court battles to solidify. Personally, though, she was alone again and still bound to Columbia Pictures. She tried to buy out her contract, but Cohen checked the grosses of *Affair in Trinidad* and put an impossible price on her head. She was her own bounty hunter but couldn't get together the ammunition to extricate herself. (Shortly Cohen would start to build Kim Novak as a replacement for his wayward superstar and asked a publicity man what he thought of her screen tests. Swallowing hard the man replied, "Harry, with proper care you've got the makings of the last great silent movie star," to which Cohen replied through clenched teeth, "Do you think it will take you more than ten minutes to get your desk cleaned out and your ass off the lot?" Upon hearing the story about her new competition, Rita muttered mournfully, "Some people have all the luck.")

Hoping to cash in on the success other studios had had with the Bible (*The Robe, Samson and Delilah*), Harry modestly called *Salomé* "The Screen Achievement of 1953" and spent a fortune producing it in vivid Technicolor, casting pros like Charles Laughton, Judith Anderson, and Stewart Granger. Rewriting history in typical movie fashion, Harry's Salomé danced to *save* the head of John the Baptist, and the Dance of the Seven Veils was indeed the high point of a somewhat soggy epic, helping it ultimately to gross a healthy $4.75 million. With her revised contract Rita could now collect 25 percent of both *Trinidad*'s and *Salomé*'s profits, so the news wasn't all bad, even though writer Gene Ringgold would dub her performance as a sort of "Gilda goes to Galilee."

With two semi-hits, it looked as if Rita might just regain the career momentum she had spurned for Aly Khan, but, for all her statements about her dedication to acting, her love life was always her top priority, as it soon would be again when she met singer Dick Haymes, in a quirk of fate from which she'd professionally never recover.

Haymes was Rita's age and a former all-American boy in films like *State Fair* (1945), and he was once considered a singing threat to Frank Sinatra. When he and Rita met he was in the process of divorcing his third wife, the former Nora Eddington Flynn, Rita's old chum. He was also settling some Internal Revenue problems over back taxes and having trouble keeping up ex-wife Joanne Dru's alimony payments. His varied vulnerabilities were one reason Rita fell for him, and as his problems increased, her loyalty grew. Not the least of his worries was with the U.S. Immigration Office, which had a deportation case against him for avoiding service in World War II by technically remaining an Argentinian citizen even though both parents were U.S. citizens; he'd lived here since his teenage years and made a considerable amount of money, but had never applied for American citizenship.

When Rita, some ten pounds heavier than she was in *Salomé,* showed up in Hawaii for location filming of *Miss Sadie Thompson,* her second release of 1953, Haymes followed shortly, further complicating his immigration case by leaving the territorial United States without informing the department. In short, it was a front-page mess with Rita caught square in the middle, causing her to lose much of the public support she'd gained when Aly Khan, even as he protested that he still loved Rita, took off after Gene Tierney.

Haymes began issuing statements that Rita was "the only woman I have ever loved" and she listened, swept along and obviously believing him, proclaiming, "I'll stand by him even if he is deported." Attesting to her good frame of mind is Ted Hook, who played one of Sadie's love-starved soldiers in the torrid "The Heat Is On" number in *Miss Sadie Thompson* and now the owner of Ted Hook's Backstage Restaurant in New York City. "She was a ball to work with. I remember one day she ordered real beer for us all during a take on that number and eight hours later we were all plastered."

Filming finished, Rita returned home, gathered up her two daughters, and flew directly to the Sands Hotel in Las Vegas where Haymes was appearing. When it became apparent that she and Dick would marry as soon as his divorce was final, Aly's minions went to work, and on September 14, 1953, she received a threat of death if she didn't return to him. Frightened and under tight security, she nonetheless went ahead with her plans and married Haymes on September 24, the day after he picked up his decree from Nora. The ceremony, in the Gold Room of the Sands, was carefully contrasted with her previous diamond-studded nuptials and was described by *Life* as a "skid into the rhinestones."

During all this, *Sadie Thompson,* in 3-D, presented a waiting world with a sweaty Rita in three dimensions. In the lurid Technicolor melodrama co-starring a hammy Jose Ferrer, she was nevertheless shown as an actress of considerable versatility, swaggering through masses of salivating soldiers, swinging the inevitable handbag, and leaving her corset in the closet. But instead of letting the thirty-five-year-old legend reveal the same physical problems of other thirty-five-year-old women, the studio brushout artists came in, scraped away her waistline for the ads, and tried to foist on the public a Rita who no longer existed. If they had presented her honestly, her image, her career, and her private personality might have been allowed to change gracefully from goddess to maturing woman, but the studio wasn't about to let her outgrow the Love Goddess image. She was betrayed by Harry Cohen's art department.

The critics carped loudly over her performance as the tropics' number-one shady lady, but no less an authority on the subject than her creator, W. Somerset Maugham, said glowingly, "Of all the actresses in Hollywood I can think of no better choice than Miss Hayworth. . . . She has everything to disturb a man's senses, and whatever she does to Davidson in the film of my story, she will do to all men in the audience. I couldn't be more delighted that it was in a screen version of one of my stories that she proved just how superb an actress she really is."

Maugham's plaudits were among the few good things happening to Rita, since a month after their marriage Haymes was arrested for defaulting on his alimony payments to Joanne Dru. Freed on bail, he accumulated a few more lawsuits while Rita fretted and followed him to his singing dates, which were ever less frequent. So distracted was she that she turned down the part that Deborah Kerr ultimately played in *From Here to Eternity*. Shortly after that, while the couple

Rita as Miss Sadie Thompson, *the vamp of the South Seas (1953). (Note the carefully retouched waistline.)*   THE DOUG MCCLELLAND COLLECTION.

was in Florida, Rita was accused of child neglect after leaving Yasmin and Rebecca up north in the care of a housekeeper, who panicked when one of the girls caught a slight virus infection and she couldn't immediately locate Rita on the phone. Both Welles and Aly Khan stepped forward in her defense, but it was one of the darkest moments in her life as the latest setback was blared in headlines from coast to coast and around the world.

With $50,000 advanced by Harry Cohen and the modest profits from *Salomé* and *Miss Sadie Thompson,* Rita and Dick were able to struggle by, but when they finally returned to Hollywood it was to a conservative apartment and not a Beverly Hills mansion. Haymes, with time to spare in his own ailing career, decided to take over Rita's and had her dissolve her Beckworth company and set up Crystal Bay Productions with himself as president. In the meantime Harry Cohen had expensively prepared *Joseph and His Brethren* for Rita, in which she would star as the sultry Queen Zuleika. Going over the script for his wife, though, Haymes decided that *he* would be ideal in the title role, and so informed Harry and the film's producer, Louis B. Mayer. Rita's new contract (signed in December of 1954 and reportedly geared to earn her $1 million) had an added clause that Columbia would indeed look for movie roles for her husband but they had nothing in mind as important as the lead in the multi-million-dollar epic, a favorite project of Cohen's. "That crooner told me that either he played Joseph or his wife was out of the cast." Living up to her end of the deal, Rita showed up for work on the unsettled production on March 8, 1955, but nightly thereafter had to cope with the harangues of her increasingly demanding husband. After exhausing days of wardrobe fittings, makeup, and tests, she would come home to face arguments fueled by the fire of his own career impotence. It was enough to test even the most loyal of wives—which Rita had surely proved to be up to that point. Though she never complained publicly, her friends knew that the marriage was dissolving in a sea of alcoholism and abuse leveled at her by her husband. It's also interesting to conjecture whether Hayworth's own drinking problems didn't stem from this period: an uncertain, shaken goddess wary of the public and even warier of her husband.

Though she denied reports of her subsidizing Haymes—"Do I look as if I've reached the point where I have to support a husband?"—it soon became apparent that the Haymes household was far from a domestically settled one. By mid-April the situation reached a boiling point, and Rita walked off *Joseph* after five weeks' work. Cohen, true to fashion, reacted both characteristically and prophetically. He told Rita, "When you came here you were nothing, a nobody. All you had was a beautiful body and Harry Cohen. Now you just have the body." The film was shelved.

Haymes had made two minor musicals for Columbia in 1953, *All Ashore* and *Cruisin' down the River,* but their failure to cause a ripple of interest at the box office, his complicated personal life, squabbles with Joanne Dru over back alimony, and his immigration problems had made him a nervous wreck, and for a time he was hospitalized. He said "I don't know what I'm going to do. I'm going insane. My nerves are shot, I don't know where to turn. I want to work. I'm trying to work, but they won't let me."

Like *Joseph and His Brethren,* the Haymes-Hayworth marriage was also shelved after he allegedly punched her in the face one night at a Hollywood party. When Rita showed up in New York in August of that year, she admitted to friends that it was all over. By the end of August she'd filed separation papers, and a few months later, with Yasmin in tow, she filed for divorce in Paris during a visit with Aly. The divorce was granted five weeks later—in absentia for both parties—in Reno, Nevada. Said a harried Rita, "I stood by him as long as he was in trouble but I can't take it anymore." Haymes finally did win his case to stay in this country, and recently he talked candidly about his drinking problem—but not about Rita, perhaps repaying her now for the loyalty she showed him then.

By now Harry Cohen was leveling his publicity guns at making Kim Novak the sexual centerpiece of Columbia, and he reached a final compromise with Rita: two more pictures for a sum total of $300,000 and she'd be free. Various properties were pitched at her, including *Solomon and Sheba* and another reunion with Glenn Ford, *The Notorious Landlady*—later made starring Novak—but Cohen, almost perversely, decided to shake the Gilda character out one more time in a $2.4-million-budgeted melodrama called *Fire down Below.*

Though Rita spent less than two years as Mrs. Dick Haymes, her absence from the screen extended into almost four, so it was once again to a wary public that she had to present herself. Co-starred with Bob Mitchum and Jack Lemmon, the trio was supposed to cause "spontaneous combustion" at the box office in *Fire down Below*—one ad for which shows the fire to be aimed directly at Rita's crotch, a far cry from the elegant presentations of *Gilda* and *Affair in Trinidad.* The combustion never occurred, though, among these "three of the biggest in one of the best" and for many it marked the final blow to her reign as a Love Goddess.

Floundering in her personal life, she evidenced the same lack of direction in *Fire down Below* as Irena, a sort of Sadie Thompson after the party had finally ended. At age thirty-nine, in a wardrobe designed by Balmain of Paris, Rita looked and acted more like an overworked cocktail waitress looking for a place to sit down than Irena, a European temptress looking for refuge. As one character in the film describes her, "She came from Lithuania . . . or Estonia, or someplace. The story changes."

The one flash of the old Rita came during a frenzied dance number at an island festival that sufficiently heats up Robert Mitchum to make him follow her back to their ship where he corners her in her cabin, grabs her, only to find her cold in his arms. "What are you waiting for?" he mutters as the cameras swing in over his shoulder, hitting her full-face. "I'm waiting for someone to touch me with kindness," she replies.

The sexual attraction between Rita and Mitchum in their roles was the sort engendered by two weary barstool-sitters after several lonely hours in an out-of-the-way watering hole; as screen time passes each looks better to the other. They finally fall into each other's arms more out of desperation than any real affection.

Rita would stick to smalltime smuggler Mitchum after sending curly-haired Lemmon back to middle American hearth and home telling him, "You don't know me. . . . I'm no good. I'm all worn out. I've been passed from hand to hand. . . . I've lived among the ruins. Armies have marched over me."

Playing this lady so shady that she could cast a shadow at high noon, she must have known that her sex-symbol days were ending. When the picture was released her personal reviews were good, although it barely recouped its costs at the box office. She had a good time filming in the tropics, though; so good, in fact, that Dorothy Mitchum had to fly in at one point to calm down her carousing husband, who'd met his match in Rita for having fun.

When the final results were in, she realized that her place in the fantasy pantheon had been usurped—or filled by default—by Ava, Kim, Marilyn, and Liz. Said she, a hint of good humor surfacing, "It's comforting to know it took a quartet of dames to replace me!"

To wind up her contract, Harry Cohen cast Rita in *Pal Joey* as the society matron Vera Simpson opposite then-hot Frank Sinatra. He paid Sinatra a fortune to play the part and also threw in Kim Novak as Sinatra's chorus girl love to give the cast an extra boost, not to mention the satisfaction of seeing Rita being pitted against the younger blonde. There was one dream sequence when both ladies danced with Sinatra, and even at forty Rita showed there was still plenty of spark left when properly handled. In her "Bewitched, Bothered and Bewildered" number, alone in a lavish bedroom, she was a standout, and while gossips had a field day beforehand trying to figure out who'd get top billing between her and Sinatra, he gallantly handed it to her saying, "Who else but Rita should get top billing? After all, in my mind, she always was and always will be Columbia Pictures! The studio may have built her into a star but just remember it was Rita Hayworth who gave Columbia status."

When the day came for Rita finally to leave Columbia—at the same period when Glenn Ford and Bill Holden were also leaving—Harry Cohen found a minute to get sentimental, saying, "There go my three kids. It's the end of an era." Said Rita, a bit less sentimentally, "I don't look back. I did what I had to do. I was the property of Columbia . . . and since I could sing, dance and act I never felt like one of those movie queens they used to manufacture in Hollywood. I had sexy genes, I guess, and that helped." When asked about new celluloid sexpots like Monroe and Mansfield, she added, "Marilyn and Jayne can have the headlines. I've had enough! From now on the only ones I want are for my acting. I'm in a new phase of my career." Stating that she could have stayed at Columbia if she wanted to, she reiterated it was time for a change and that "I looked at all the parts I had done and realized that, no matter how they were sliced, it was still Salomé."

At a party for *Fire down Below,* Rita had met producer Jim Hill, a handsome forty-one-year-old bachelor who was partnered with Burt Lancaster in his Hecht-Hill-Lancaster company. Hill was known as a man about town, and Rita was the first woman he'd ever seemed really interested in. A gentleman, quiet as she was, his interests apart from his work lay in classical music and his art collection. His current project was *Separate Tables,* based on Terrence Rattigan's two one-act plays about the lonely lives of a group of people living in a remote English seaside hotel, which was scheduled to start shortly starring Lancaster, Laurence Olivier, and Vivien Leigh. When the Oliviers dropped out of the production, Hill asked Rita to take over the role of Ann Shankland, an aging beauty out to recapture her estranged husband (Lancaster). Flattered by the offer "of the kind of role I've been waiting all my life to play," Rita's interest in him escalated even though he, at first, expected her to refuse the part. Production started with old friend David Niven in the role vacated by Olivier, which would win him an Academy Award. The producer-star relationship gradually warmed into something stronger. On February 2, 1958, with both daughters in attendance, Rita married Hill in her Beverly Hills home. It was to be a union both placid and unrealistic for Rita, in that it marked a new phase of her career, one far removed from her sex-appeal-only days. Though still front-page news, the wedding itself was almost staid in its simplicity, with both husband and wife returning to work on *Separate Tables* immediately.

Rita's reviews for *Separate Tables* were excellent, but it was quickly apparent that her marriage to Hill marked the end of her sex-symbol image. On his advice she sought roles that would present her—finally—as exactly what she was: a maturing beauty who could also act. She went back to Columbia for *They Came to Cordura* but found the place drastically changed, Cohen having died since her departure. News features on the picture made much of the fact that she had left glamor behind, story after story showing the classic WWII pinup picture side by side with the dirt-strewn face she wore as the abused Adelaide Geary in *Cordura.* Co-starring Gary Cooper as a war-weary Army major shepherding a dubious bunch of heroes across revolution-torn Mexico, with refugee Rita thrown in for good sexual measure, the film was a lavishly mounted, Technicolor, $5-million, box-office dud that added luster to neither Rita, Cooper, nor the rest of the cast, which included Tab Hunter and Richard Conte.

Like Welles before him, Hill tried hard to show more of Rita's talent as an actress and next had her signed to star in *The Story on Page One,* clumsily written and directed by Group Theater founder Clifford Odets. It garnered her a great set of reviews—*Time* magazine said she'd mastered the art of the beat-down broad—but wasn't very popular.

Thinking the solution to her script problems might lie in total control, Hill and Rita shortly formed their own company, Hillworth, and chose a script called *The Happy Thieves,* purportedly a sleek comedy about sophisticated art swindlers headed by Rita and Rex Harrison. It was a critical and financial disaster, and rumors quickly started that the marriage was failing fast.

They announced another film, *I Want My Mother,* but it was unexplainedly dropped twenty-four hours before principal photography was to begin. Its cancellation was a deep disappointment to Rita, who was looking forward to the juicy role as the mother of a psychopathic killer. Its cancellation also seemed the final straw for Rita, and in September of 1961, three years after their marriage, she filed for divorce from Hill, wanting no money and sighing the by-now familiar refrain that she had mistakenly married a man more interested in her career than in herself.

With her fifth marital strike-out, Rita reacted belligerently, announcing that she was heading for Europe, and "I may even decide to live there. That's what Ava [Gardner] has done. But she's smart. She knows the score." Arriving in Madrid with old friend Gary Merrill, former husband of Bette Davis, she spoke vaguely about making a movie but instead began a meandering, hippie-like odyssey through Spain and into Italy, drinking heavily and getting involved along with Merrill in numerous public brawls with photographers, fans, and reporters, all of whom censured the former beauty for her childish behavior and again dredged up the romance and luxury that had surrounded her first trip when she'd met Aly Khan. Aly had recently been killed in an auto crash outside Paris, and speculation was rife that part of Rita's public rebellion was due to the tragedy that struck a man whom many said she'd never stopped loving.

Whatever the reasons, she seemed locked into a black journey of self-destruction that took a terrible toll on both her health and her looks. When she and Merrill eventually returned home, they surfaced in New York, where they began to work on a Broadway play called *Step on a Crack,* but by then Rita was in such poor physical shape, suffering from anemia and extreme fatigue, that she was hospitalized amid rumors of overweight, severe stage fright, and the breakup of her relationship with Merrill.

Once out of the hospital, a disheartened Rita Hayworth returned home to Beverly Hills and went into virtual seclusion. She appeared less and less around town and turned down what few offers came her way, usually bids to head up a television variety hour. At the 1964 Academy Awards she presented the Best Director Award, looking bloated and acting nervous, so much so that she mispronounced the winner's name, Tony Richardson for *Tom Jones,* as "Tony Richards."

A comeback of sorts occurred that year when she traveled to Spain to co-star with John Wayne in Samuel Bronston's *Circus World,* as an aging aerialist, a part she pulled off quite well in the otherwise sodden epic, which one reviewer compared to having an elephant sit on your lap for two hours and fifteen minutes. Later, in a British-published interview, veteran director Henry Hathaway claimed that Rita's heavy drinking held up production of the sawdust saga on many occasions, but the picture triggered interest in her back home where NBC presented "The Odyssey of Rita Hayworth" as a segment of their "Hollywood and the Stars" TV series. The show, a compilation of old film clips including a fascinating sequence of the many times in movies that Rita had slapped Glenn Ford and vice-versa, ended with an in-person interview at her home, picturing her as a lonely woman, living a solitary life save for a housekeeper and several dogs, who, when she was not wandering the perimeter of her small swimming pool, played a lot of golf.

Of all the great screen teams of Hollywood, Rita's with Ford had always been one of the most potent, and when she had a chance to try to rekindle some of the fire she grabbed it in an MGM-produced cop-thriller called *The Money Trap*. While Ford was the male star, Rita was assigned the small part of an ex-flame of his, a washed-out waitress named Rosalie whose end comes when she's thrown off the roof of her sleazy tenement.

At that time one of Rita's closest friends was George Masters, the makeup man and hairstylist to stars like Jennifer Jones and Ann-Margret, who recalled doing Rita for that picture. Since he had no screen guild card as a makeup man, he couldn't work on the studio lot, so Rita set up quarters in a trailer across the street from the studio gates, where one long day they both waited for her call—for a close-up shot of her body after the roof fall . . . the Love Goddess in the mud. The shot was delayed again and again, and with time on their hands, Masters and Rita kept playing with his makeup skill and her champagne, adding more blood and more mud as the afternoon wore on and the wine took its toll. Finally she was called at 7:00 P.M. but was by then unable to make it across the street, looking so muddied and befouled as to be unrecognizable. The shot was rescheduled.

Yasmin visited her on the set of this picture as she had earlier on *Circus World,* and unlike Rebecca, seemed to have a close and warm relationship with her mother. While the film itself turned out to be a muddled and virtually unseen affair, *Time* magazine again pointed out the fact that Hayworth, "at forty-seven has never looked less a beauty, or more an actress." Unfortunately there was little available in the way of parts to capitalize on the fact that Rita had advanced as an actress. It was to become a situation faced by other excellent actresses in the seventies, such as Natalie Wood, Shirley MacLaine, and Anne Bancroft.

The parts that did come along were mostly cheapies such as the lamentable 1966-produced *The Naked Zoo,* in which Rita is again killed off, this time by her young lover who forces a quart of liquor into her, thus instigating a heart attack. The author is one of the few people ever to have seen this wreck, financed and produced by a Florida used-car salesman and yanked out of New York City theaters just days after its "premiere."

Journeying to Italy, Rita took the role of an alcoholic mother in *The Cats* when Joan Crawford turned it down, and she recalls it as one of the meatiest parts of her career. It has never been shown in the United States, although it was sold to television some years back. In 1971 she got a call from *Fire down Below* co-star Bob Mitchum, and she said "yes" before she even read the script for *The Wrath of God,* which garnered her another set of good reviews for a smallish mother role that required five gruelling months of location-shooting in Mexico.

About that time there seemed to be hope for the beginning of a television career when Rita appeared on "Rowan and Martin's Laugh-In," "The Carol Burnett Show" (after personally calling Burnett after the comedian had done a spoof of *Gilda*), and "An Evening with Rita Hayworth" on the "Merv Griffin Show." But the new career stalled on her second Griffin appearance, when it became all too apparent to both Griffin and the studio audience that she was simply too drunk to continue, and was escorted offstage during a station break. Sensitive, shy, and no longer secure in the beauty that had made her a goddess, Rita had tried to compensate for her insecurities by drinking in the dressing room, and it proved her undoing.

Much was made of her taking over the lead in Broadway's *Applause* from Lauren Bacall in 1971, but after weeks of rehearsal she abruptly left New York before appearing in so much as a preview. People close to the production said, sympathetically, that the actress simply couldn't remember her lines in what is a marathon role. Trained for movie scenes, sometimes done over and over, she would get Act One down pat only to forget it by the time she'd learned Act Two. Rita blamed the fiasco on too little rehearsal time.

In 1972 she accepted the lead in a British-produced horror quickie called *Tales That Witness Madness,* playing a talent agent, but by now her strange behavior caused her literally to disappear after four days in front of the cameras. Doctors attested that she had the flu, but when the producers tried contacting her at London's Dorchester Hotel, they found that she'd checked out and was on her way back to the United States. Ironically she was replaced in the part by Kim Novak, the girl Harry Cohen had long ago groomed as a threat to Rita at Columbia.

Just before her London sojourn, Rita had appeared at the San Francisco Film Festival tribute to her with a question and answer period following the showing of old film clips. During it she seemed to have softened in her remembrances of her old boss "who put me on suspension so many times even I can't remember them all!" She added candidly, "I think if he could have ever been in love with anyone, he was secretly in love with me." To a startling question as to how she felt when she looked in the mirror in the morning and no longer saw the Love Goddess looking back, she quipped, "That's one problem I don't have, honey. I never get up until the afternoon." Her reply brought the second standing ovation of the evening, the first happening when she initially came onstage.

Despite the fact that her public appearances evaporated, interest in Rita's personal life continued, almost as if the public couldn't, or wouldn't, give up their love affair with the lady no matter how unseemly the details began to get. The World War II soldiers who fantasized about her from Alaska to Guadalcanal now began to read about the cracks in their wartime idol, as chronicled by people like Rex Reed who reported he'd seen her at one Hollywood party drunk and on the floor.

Her romance with a furniture-salesman-turned-artist, Bill Gilpin, became common knowledge when he did a front page story in *National Enquirer,* recounting how he'd approached her for a date on a golf course and got it. She also made news when she complained bitterly that neighbor and former co-star Glenn Ford's TV antenna was spoiling the view from her house.

For a time she was barred from several chic Hollywood clubs for showing up in jeans and sweatshirts and then proceeding to drink herself under the table. And she made few new friends when she showed up at an industry awards dinner to share the podium with Ford and proceeded to break into a "Put the Blame on Mame" bump-and-grind. Whether it was an attempt at kidding her own image or laughing at the industry that had forgotten her, it didn't work. Ford walked off, leaving her to finish it alone.

The Blackglama mink coat company was more interested in her *Gilda* character, though, and signed her for their "What Becomes a Legend Most" campaign. They whipped up a replica of her famous black satin gown for her to wear, and for her troubles she got a new mink coat, the standard fee. But she was sadly surprised at the later news that, of all the "legends" from Rosalind Russell to Claudette Colbert to Barbara Stanwyck, her ad, with her short-cropped hair, was the least recognized by the public.

In 1974 she gave a rare interview to *W* magazine, a fashion industry tradepaper, appearing ill at ease but anxious to please. "It's lunchtime," she said at one point. "I'd offer you a sandwich, only my refrigerator is empty. I don't keep food in the icebox, because it all just spoils." After backhanding the press—"the minute a star stops going out every night, they say she's 'gone into seclusion.' It's absolutely wicked"—she mentioned the possibility of a film in France and later expressed her personal disappointment that she couldn't commute to see her daughter, Yasmin, living in New York and studying opera, because she frankly couldn't afford it. "Yasmin can, but she only visits once or twice a year. She calls me on the telephone sometimes."

By this time Rebecca Welles was married and living with her sculptor husband, Perry Moede, in the northeast, and, while they were far from rich, Rita was stung by the publicity that had them living in poverty. Adding that she'd provided college educations for both her girls, she concluded that she couldn't live their lives for them. To a specific quote of Becky's that her mother had spoiled her by raising her in luxury and it was so hard now being poor, especially in that area, Rita caustically replied, "Then they should move to another area."

For the next two years there was little heard or seen of Rita except for a brief appearance on a late-night ABC special in which she talked briefly about having had a face-lift. She looked lovely but seemed absentminded, which only added fuel to the fire of gossip that she was becoming more and more reclusive. Her ultimate decline started innocently enough in early January of 1976 when she made a trip to London for a television interview and then arrived there, on January 19, so incoherently drunk she didn't want to get off the plane. Eventually airline personnel assisted her off, struggling, straight into the glare of the ever present photographers. Instead of the Rita Hayworth they were expecting, though, they were shocked by the disheveled state she was in. Obviously the long flight had triggered the old fears of rejection and inevitable competition with a dead image. As those fears surfaced Rita apparently tried to quell them with liquor. The closer the plane came to London's Heathrow Airport, the closer also came the inevitable barrage of news photographers with their layouts already primed with the "before" picture and aching to take the "after." The Rita who arrived gave them a picture even they found hard to believe: that of a sad and lonely lady crying

''No'' to an unanswering and uncaring world as she was helped off the plane by airline personnel. The resultant pictures were on front pages around the world.

The following day she called a press conference on a golf course and said she'd become ill during the flight, and happily posed for photographers. She looked strained but smiling, but unfortunately the damage was done, and she quietly returned home to her unprepossessing house on Hartford Way up behind the Beverly Hills Hotel.

In March of that year trade papers noted that Rita would go to Rome where she'd star as Natasha Rambova opposite Helmut Berger in yet another *Valentino*. The project, like so many others—including a little number called *Horror Hotel* purportedly to star her, Hedy Lamarr, Lana Turner, and June Allyson—never materialized, and for a time it seemed almost a game to use Rita's name to launch a PR item.

Like so many other former sex symbols, Rita found herself more welcome abroad than at home and journeyed to several film festivals for more tributes. In

Rita in London in 1976, the morning after being carried off a transcontinental flight.
LONDON DAILY EXPRESS.

October she was frightened badly in Buenos Aires when she arrived at her hotel to find that only a few minutes before a bomb had been discovered and detonated by the police. There was no indication that it was meant for her, and she was greatly heartened that evening at a screening of her most famous film when crowds chanted "Geelda! Geelda!" outside the auditorium.

The only piece of concrete news came when she sued a former business manager for more than $1 million, charging him with breach of fiduciary duty in guiding her into a series of bad business deals for tax shelter purposes. To guard against bankruptcy proceedings, she then deeded over her house to daughter Yasmin, because she'd fallen behind in the monthly mortgage payments of $386.61—the amount of a dinner tab in her heyday. To all outward appearances, Rita relied on the "users" of the industry and came up empty. Ever since the age of fourteen, or perhaps from that first pair of castanets at age four, her career and life had been guided and directed by men until she reached the age when the interest was over, the white fire of Gilda was finally out.

But that would not happen totally before another set of flame-filled headlines.

It was early in 1977 when she decided to appear at an art gallery opening in Newport Beach for her old boyfriend Bill Gilpin. As the afternoon wore on, it quickly became apparent that she was in a precarious mental state and should not have been out of bed, let alone out of the house, trying to function through the hot crowds of jostling acquaintances and members of the press—all there at Gilpin's invitation. Finally, sensing she was near the breaking point, he took her off to nearby Hoag Memorial Hospital with the reporters in close pursuit, again there to chronicle yet another step down from her pedestal, this the most serious of all.

The attending doctor, James Miner, hospitalized the actress and soon issued a statement saying that she was "gravely disabled as a result of mental disorder or impairment by chronic alcoholism." At his request, a petition was filed a few weeks later, on March 7, to have her estate and affairs taken over by a temporary conservator because, he said, she was unwilling or unable to accept treatment for what was by now a desperate condition.

This action prompted her lawyer, Leonard Monroe, to whisk her out of the hospital and out of the state after a decision on the petition was handed down appointing public guardian James E. Heim as the conservator.

With Rita out of the state's jurisdiction, Monroe then contacted Yasmin, who had been in close touch with him and her mother since Rita's initial admission for alcoholic poisoning, and arranged her appointment as guardian of her mother's affairs. For weeks the public didn't know Rita's whereabouts, until on May 10 syndicated columnist Dorothy Manners broke the news that she was staying at Silver Hill, Connecticut, in the exclusive private hospital that had become a well-known retreat for others in Rita's situation, such as Joan Kennedy. Once there, intensive treatment began and, with Yasmin's support, both financial and moral, Rita began to come around, thanks to a stabilized diet and plenty of golf. Once she began feeling more herself, though, Rita decided she didn't like the place no matter how exclusive or expensive ($2,000 per week) it was, and finally, as she told a reporter, "I just checked myself out. I wanted to come back to Hollywood. There was no special regimen there, but I didn't complete the course. The weekends were dreary . . . too much idleness there, and I was convinced I could recover faster back home."

She surfaced in Palm Springs with quotes of "It's great to be back" making the papers along with pictures of her looking more rested than the public had seen her in some time. She announced that she'd had some picture nibbles but wouldn't elaborate on what they were. Former silent-screen star Billie Dove was one of the people who saw her there and said, "She looks absolutely fantastic—and you can quote me."

Back in Hollywood she got in touch with one of her few stalwart friends, George Masters, who did her hair and face radiantly for her first public appearance since the scandal, a re-premiere in the original 3–D process of *Miss Sadie Thompson* at a small Sunset Boulevard theater called the Tiffany. The event, on July 20, gave her the first taste of American movie-star treatment she'd had in years as she stepped from her limousine into wave after wave of American applause, as Kodaks clicked the moment into memory. During the screening there were several ovations given her performance, in particular after the sensuous "Blue Pacific Blues" number in which she lies on a sweaty cot surrounded by soldiers, swigging off a bottle of beer as the rain beats on her windows.

To questions on her health she replied that she was feeling fit and fine, eating sparingly and playing plenty of golf, adding "I'm taking it easy for the next three months with this schedule, then I'll be completely perfect and ready for work." Lawyer Monroe added obsequious statements about finding "just the right picture" for her, and let Rita have her moment in what looked like a renewed sun. Reporters were also tipped as to how many of Rita's old friends had flocked to her aid, such as Elizabeth Taylor who'd invited her to spend some time at the Warner Farm in Virginia, and Frank Sinatra, who had inundated her with flowers during her hospital stay along with an invitation to visit at his nearby Palm Springs palazzo. For reasons of her own she didn't take him up on it, although they had remained friends since their *Pal Joey* days. Rita also stated that she was looking forward to spending part of the autumn in New York with Yasmin prior to the girl's debut in opera, which she'd been studying since her college days at Bennington.

What wasn't said was that besides the tribute, an undeniable ego balm for the affection-starved actress, another reason she was at the theater was that she'd been promised a new television set, her own being broken and she being unwilling, or unable, to have it fixed. A new portable was delivered the next day.

It soon became obvious that a complete role switch had taken place between Rita and Yasmin in that the daughter was now mother to the woman, supervising her financial affairs, personal activities, and public appearances. The offspring of one of the century's greatest love stories, who had spent her childhood touring movie sets around the world with her famous mother, was now, at twenty-seven, in control of the woman who had borne her, providing the money to run her by-now unpretentious home on the strict condition that Rita complete treatment for the alcoholism that had come so perilously close to incapacitating her. A dark-haired beauty, Yasmin inherited much of her mother's looks. Now she inherited the responsibility as well.

Hollywood is an odd town. When a star hits rock bottom, it perversely brings out the best in the survivors, and, to a degree, that happened for Rita Hayworth on November 19, 1977, when the Thalians, a noted group of actresses and industry wives, put on their annual charity ball for a mental health clinic at Cedars-Sinai Hospital and named it in honor of Rita, "You Were Never Lovelier." Rita showed up with Yasmin and a group of friends, including lawyer Monroe, for an evening highlighted by onstage tributes from many of her old co-stars, from Glenn Ford to Phil Silvers. It was a touching, nostalgic journey of film clips and reminiscences with wave after wave of applause saluting Rita's memorable movie moments, including a re-enactment of her famous *Mame* number by Thalian president, Debbie Reynolds. One poignant tribute was given by Lana Turner, Hayworth's forties co-leader in the glamor brigade, who stalled her own entrance until just before showtime so as not to draw away any of Rita's limelight. Among the guests were June Allyson, Dame Judith Anderson, Janet Blair, Lloyd Nolan, and Barry Sullivan, but the highlight was the lady herself.

At the end of the show the movie screen suddenly filled with the number from *Down to Earth* when Rita runs down a long, windblown rampway as Terpsichore, Goddess of Dance. The film clip started, the Technicolored deity ran and ran until she reached the bottom of the ramp, the lights dimmed, came up again, and there was Rita in person, swathed in an emerald green caftan and obviously overcome by the magic of the evening.

Unabashedly nervous, she perched on a white stool as her former co-stars swarmed over the stage to greet her. Glenn Ford took her face into his hands and planted two deep kisses on her smiling lips. Gene Kelly, her co-star in *Cover Girl,* presented her with the Thalian Award for her contributions to motion pictures. Accepting it, she mumbled something to Ford and then stepped forward. "Glenn told me I should say 'thank you,'" she started as the huge burst of applause died down, "and, well, I guess I've said it." Taking over the microphone, Debbie Reynolds hastened to add that "our Rita's very shy and we promised her she wouldn't have to make a speech," and with that the scarlet folds of the rectangular curtain fell around the stage, shielding the lady from the audience.

Will the curtain rise again for an encore, a movie or a television show? The hundreds gathered in the ballroom of the Century Plaza Hotel certainly hoped so, but only one person knows the answer. And for the time being, at least, Rita Hayworth isn't talking.

FILMOGRAPHY

Rita Hayworth

TITLE	YEAR	DIRECTOR	LEADING PLAYERS
As Rita Cansino			
Under the Pampas Moon	1935	James Tinling	Warner Baxter, Ketti Gallian, J. Carroll Naish
Charlie Chan in Egypt	1935	Louis King	Warner Oland, Pat Paterson, Thomas Beck
Dante's Inferno	1935	Harry Lachman	Spencer Tracy, Claire Trevor, Henry B. Walthall, Scotty Beckett
Paddy O'Day	1935	Lewis Seiler	Jane Withers, Pinky Tomlin, Jane Darwell
Human Cargo	1936	Allan Dwan	Claire Trevor, Brian Donlevy, Alan Dinehart, Ralph Morgan
Meet Nero Wolfe	1936	Herbert Biberman	Edward Arnold, Joan Perry, Lionel Stander, Victor Jory
Rebellion	1936	E. B. Derr	Ton Keene, Duncan Renaldo
Trouble in Texas	1937	Edward F. Finney	Tex Ritter, Horace Murphy, Yakima Canutt
Old Louisiana	1937	E. R. Derr	Tom Keene, Robert Fiske
Hit the Saddle	1937	Sol. C. Siegel	Robert Livingston, Ray Corrigan, Max Terhune, Yakima Canutt
As Rita Hayworth			
Criminals of the Air	1937	Charles C. Coleman, Jr.	Rosalind Keith, Charles Quigley, Marc Lawrence
Girls Can Play	1937	Lambert Hillyer	Jacqueline Welles, Charles Quigley, Guinn "Big Boy" Williams
The Shadow	1937	Charles C. Coleman, Jr.	Charles Quigley, Marc Lawrence, Arthur Loft
The Game That Kills	1937	D. Ross Lederman	Charles Quigley, John Gallaudet, Paul Fix
Paid To Dance	1937	Charles C. Coleman, Jr.	Don Terry, Jacqueline Welles, Charles Kennedy, Bess Flowers, Thurston Hall, Ann Doran
Who Killed Gail Preston?	1938	Leon Barsha	Don Terry, Robert Paige, Wyn Cahoon, Marc Lawrence
There's Always a Woman	1938	Alexander Hall	Joan Blondell, Melvyn Douglas, Mary Astor, Frances Drake, Jerome Cowan
Convicted	1938	Leon Barsha	Charles Quigley, Marc Lawrence, George McKay, Doreen MacGragor
Juvenile Court	1938	D. Ross Lederman	Paul Kelly, Frankie Darro
The Renegade Ranger	1939	David Howard	George O'Brien, Tim Holt, Ray Whitley

TITLE	YEAR	DIRECTOR	LEADING PLAYERS
Homicide Bureau	1939	Charles C. Coleman, Jr.	Bruce Cabot, Robert Paige, Marc Lawrence
The Lone Wolf Spy Hunt	1939	Peter Godfrey	Warren William, Ida Lupino, Virginia Weidler, Ralph Morgan
Special Inspector	1939	Leon Barsha	Charles Quigley, George McKay
Only Angels Have Wings	1939	Howard Hawks	Cary Grant, Jean Arthur, Richard Barthelmess, Thomas Mitchell, Allyn Josslyn
Music in My Heart	1940	Joseph Santley	Tony Martin, Edith Fellows, Alan Mowbray, Eric Blore
Blondie on a Budget	1940	Frank R. Strayer	Penny Singleton, Arthur Lake, Larry Simms
Susan and God	1940	George Cukor	Joan Crawford, Frederic March, Ruth Hussey, John Carroll, Nigel Bruce
The Lady in Question	1940	Charles Vidor	Brian Aherne, Glenn Ford, Irene Rich, Evelyn Keyes
Angels Over Broadway	1940	Ben Hecht and Lee Garmes	Douglas Fairbanks, Jr., Thomas Mitchell, John Qualen
The Strawberry Blonde	1941	Raoul Walsh	James Cagney, Olivia De Havilland, Jack Carson, Alan Hale
Affectionately Yours	1941	Lloyd Bacon	Merle Oberon, Dennis Morgan, Ralph Bellamy, George Tobias
Blood and Sand	1941	Rouben Mamoulian	Tyrone Power, Linda Darnell, John Carradine, Nazimova, Anthony Quinn, Laird Cregar, Lynn Bari
You'll Never Get Rich	1941	Sidney Lanfield	Fred Astaire, John Hubbard, Robert Benchley, Osa Massen
My Gal Sal	1942	Irving Cummings	Victor Mature, John Sutton, Phil Silvers, Carole Landis, James Gleason, Walter Catlett
Tales of Manhattan	1942	Julien Duvivier	Sequence A. Charles Boyer, Thomas Mitchell, Eugene Pallette
You Were Never Lovelier	1942	William A. Seiter	Fred Astaire, Adolphe Menjou, Leslie Brooks, Adele Mara
Show Business at War	1943	Louis de Rochemont	The cast included every major star in Hollywood from Ethel Barrymore to Loretta Young, including Hedy Lamarr, Jack Benny, James Cagney, Bette Davis, Marlene Dietrich, John Garfield, and Clark Gable.
Cover Girl	1944	Charles Vidor	Gene Kelly, Phil Silvers, Jinx Falkenberg, Lee Bowman, Eve Arden, Jess Barker
Tonight and Every Night	1945	Victor Saville	Lee Bowman, Janet Blair, Marc Platt, Leslie Brooks, Florence Bates
Gilda	1946	Charles Vidor	Glenn Ford, George Macready, Joseph

TITLE	YEAR	DIRECTOR	LEADING PLAYERS
			Calleia, Steven Geray, Gerald Mohr, Joseph Sawyer
Down to Earth	1947	Alexander Hall	Larry Parks, Marc Platt, Roland Culver, James Gleason, Edward Everett Horton
The Lady from Shanghai	1948	Orson Welles	Orson Welles, Everett Sloane, Glenn Anders, Ted De Corsia, Erskine Sanford
The Loves of Carmen	1948	Charles Vidor	Glenn Ford, Ron Randell, Victor Jory, Luther Adler, Arnold Moss
Champagne Safari	1952	Jackson Leighter	Aly Khan. A travelogue of Rita and Aly's African honeymoon
Affair in Trinidad	1952	Vincent Sherman	Glenn Ford, Alexander Scourby, Valerie Bettis, Torin Thatcher
Salomé	1953	William Dieterle	Stewart Granger, Charles Laughton, Judith Anderson, Sir Cedric Hardwicke, Alan Badel
Miss Sadie Thompson	1953	Curtis Bernhardt	Jose Ferrer, Aldo Ray, Russell Collins, Peggy Converse, Charles Bronson
Fire down Below	1957	Robert Parish	Robert Mitchum, Jack Lemmon, Herbert Lom, Bernard Lee
Pal Joey	1957	George Sidney	Frank Sinatra, Kim Novak, Bobby Sherwood, Barbara Nichols, Elizabeth Patterson
Separate Tables	1958	Delbert Mann	Deborah Kerr, Burt Lancaster, David Niven, Wendy Hiller, Gladys Cooper, Cathleen Nesbitt
They Came to Cordura	1959	Robert Rossen	Gary Cooper, Tab Hunter, Van Heflin, Richard Conte, Michael Callan, Dick York
The Story on Page One	1960	Clifford Odets	Anthony Franciosa, Gig Young, Mildred Dunnock, Hugh Griffith
The Happy Thieves	1962	George Marshall	Rex Harrison, Joseph Wiseman, Gregoire Aslan
Circus World	1964	Henry Hathaway	John Wayne, Claudia Cardinale, Lloyd Nolan, John Smith, Richard Conte
The Money Trap	1966	Burt Kennedy	Glenn Ford, Elke Sommer, Ricardo Montalban, Joseph Cotten
The Poppy Is Also a Flower	1966	Terence Young	Senta Berger, Stephen Boyd, Yul Brynner, Angie Dickinson, Hugh Griffith, Jack Hawkins, Omar Sharif, Trevor Howard, Gilbert Roland
The Rover (L'Avventuriero)	1967	Terence Young	Anthony Quinn, Rosanna Schiaffino, Richard Johnson
Sons of Satan (I Bastardi)	1969	Duccio Tessari	Giuliano Gemma, Klaus Kinski

TITLE	YEAR	DIRECTOR	LEADING PLAYERS
Road to Salina (Sur la Route de Salina)	1971	Georges Lautner	Mimsy Farmer, Robert Walker, Ed Begley
The Naked Zoo	1971	William Grefe	Fay Spain, Stephen Oliver
The Wrath of God	1972	Ralph Nelson	Robert Mitchum, Frank Langella, Victor Buono, John Colicos

Linda Darnell

Before I came to Hollywood I dreamed that movie people led lives of ease and luxury, that their wants were filled before they could mention them and that life was a smooth succession of pleasure. So what did I find? For one thing I didn't discover the true meaning of work until I got out here. I've never worked so hard or so steadily.

> *Linda Darnell in a 1941 interview.*

Let's have some laughs. Let's all stay up and watch *Star Dust.*

> *Linda to her friend and former secretary, Jeanne Curtis, shortly after midnight on April 9, 1965, just five hours before the fire that killed her.*

IN 1939 Linda Darnell was sixteen. While other girls were studying their high school homework, Linda Darnell was studying the lines for her first starring role opposite Tyrone Power in *Daytime Wife.* In this release she communicated, despite her age, a mature warmth that classified her as one of the screen's great natural beauties.

With her Texas-bred complexion, raven hair, and brown eyes capable of captivating movie men like Power, Henry Fonda, Cornel Wilde, and every other leading man Twentieth Century Fox could muster, she graduated from dewy-eyed innocence to full-blown voluptuousness in what is perhaps her best-known film, the highly touted *Forever Amber,* in 1947.

The search for Amber was equalled only by that for Scarlett O'Hara some nine years earlier, and when Linda Darnell won the part it seemed as though her years of training had finally paid off in superstardom. Linda's full-bodied beauty, cameo-perfect face, and inherent sexiness only served to highlight the stubborn chin that showed she clearly meant business as the English Restoration heroine/

100

vixen of the bestselling book, a woman who battled her way from tavern wench to the royal court—and bed—of Charles II.

Hampered by the censorship of the times and the heavy-handedness of director Otto Preminger, the film itself didn't live up to its publicity, but it did enable Darnell to ensconce herself in the Hollywood hierarchy where she would stay another six years.

Over the fourteen years she was under contract to Twentieth Century Fox, she covered the ground from virginity (*Blood and Sand,* 1941) to venality (*Hangover Square,* 1945) to ultimate and ironic vulnerability when she was burned at the stake in *Anna and the King of Siam* (1946). When Fox gave her the chance, she was excellent, and even when they didn't, she was good, always imparting just the right hint of allure and charm, earthiness and exoticism with period style or forties pizzazz.

At her peak Linda Darnell was the embodiment of historical fantasy, and, while she played those kinds of roles until her death in 1965, she also wove a

Linda Darnell (left) *in the movie she was watching the night she died, 1940's* Star Dust.
THE DOUG McCLELLAND COLLECTION.

unique web of twentieth century womanhood—the woman on the make (*A Letter to Three Wives,* 1948) and the woman on the loose (*Fallen Angel,* 1945). She helped launch careers, as with Tab Hunter in *Island of Desire* (1952) and solidify them, as with Paul Douglas in *Everybody Does It* (1949), but she never promised more than she could deliver.

From an early age she was brought up to think of her career as the most important thing in her life, and that determination sustained her through a career that lasted twice as long as the careers of other girls perhaps equally lovely but without that inner fire of seductive sincerity. As a virgin—in fact *the* virgin in *The Song of Bernadette*—or as a vixen like Amber St. Clair, Linda always gave the public her best shot. When she died in 1965, alcoholic and overweight, the public chose to remember her beauty and the pleasure she'd given them rather than the tragic figure she'd become.

PEARL Darnell always wanted to be a movie star. Instead she ended up as the wife of a Dallas postal clerk and the mother of five children. Of the five, though, there was one outstandingly pretty one, and Pearl determined when her daughter was four years old and taking her first tap dance lessons that, even if she would never realize her dream, little Monetta Eloyse would. To that end she worked tirelessly and vicariously shared the glory when her child, renamed Linda Darnell, became one of the great beauties of the silver screen.

Monetta Eloyse was born on October 16, 1923, although later press releases would backdate this to 1921 to make the teenager appear older. She was an early bloomer, nubile enough that by age eleven she was able, at her mother's instructions, to pass herself off as sixteen in order to get jobs modeling clothes in local department stores and working as a greeter at fairs and expositions.

Her mother wanted her to get acting experience as well, and when she learned that the Dallas Little Theater had the temerity to charge $1,500 a year to take on apprentices, she put her daughter to work with the Catholic Players of St. Matthew's and with Dallas's New Theater group. Linda said later, "She really shoved me along, spotting me in one contest after another. I was going to be a movie star or Mom was going to bust in the attempt."

A small, shrewd lady, Pearl Darnell scanned the papers daily for news of any visiting talent scouts, and when Monetta Eloyse was fourteen, she egged her into an interview with Ivan Kahn, in town for Twentieth Century Fox. After looking at assorted photos of the five-foot, four-inch girl modelling clothes and posing for publicity shots as an official greeter of the city of Dallas, he left saying, "Maybe you'll hear from us later."

That was good enough for Pearl, and she set off with her daughter, hot on Kahn's trail. Impressed by both the mother's determination and the daughter's beauty, Fox tested her but decided she was too young and sent her back home. Though her enthusiasm was dampened, it was far from doused, and it wasn't long before Pearl got her daughter entered in RKO's "Gateway to Hollywood" contest as Dallas's official entry. Back they went to Hollywood, but RKO was as stymied as Fox had been. Still technically a child, Monetta was too well-developed for kid parts and obviously not experienced enough to play women. So they did nothing. When her contract expired mother and daughter went back home again, "and it was hell," Linda said later, "to go home to Dallas and have everybody ask you, how are you making out in Hollywood? I hadn't even a film to point out. I didn't even have an answer. I was just miserable, I guess."

She wasn't miserable for long, though, because people at Fox had been keeping their eyes on her, and when they learned that she was at liberty, they contacted her. She went back to Hollywood again, and had a screen test under the watchful eye of ace cameraman Peverell Marley. Marley helped the nervous young girl to relax, and the test was so successful that the studio signed her to a contract at $750 per week and immediately cast her in *Elsa Maxwell's Hotel for Women,* a showcase production for the studio's unknowns.

The studio publicized her birthdate as 1921 so that the eleventh-grader could believably pull off the roles she seemed a natural for. She was also renamed Linda Darnell, and overnight the little girl from Dallas became a starlet, one that studio chief Darryl F. Zanuck had big plans for.

Along with her mother and a younger brother and sister, Linda moved into a small Hollywood apartment while father Calvin and the rest of the family stayed behind in Dallas. He was a man dedicated to his job, had been at it almost thirty years, and was determined to stay put, his wife's dreams notwithstanding. Even though his daughter was making good money, Calvin insisted on paying the rent for their Hollywood home. Her money, he insisted, should be put away for her. Calvin had no intention of moving further west until he'd picked up his pension, but he still intended to remain the head of the family.

Linda's reviews for *Hotel* were so encouraging that, at great expense, Zanuck yanked her out of a small part she'd already started in *Drums Along the Mohawk* and teamed her with one of their top box-office draws, Tyrone Power, in *Daytime Wife.* This was a gigantic break for the Texas teenager, giving her a first-hand crack at grabbing the attention of audiences all over the world. Power, at the time, was rivaled only by MGM's Robert Taylor for the kind of popularity that Paul Newman and Robert Redford won in the early seventies. To be given the assignment was tantamount to immediate stardom, and overnight Linda became Hollywood's "Cinderella Girl." So pleased were they with the teaming that in 1940, Fox heads cast them together again as young lovers in *Brigham Young,* Henry Hathaway's ode to Mormonism starring Dean Jagger in the title role.

Her third picture, *Star Dust,* was co-written by the man who originally spotted her in Dallas, Ivan Kahn, and its plot was practically the story of Linda's own life—a beautiful young girl brought to stardom through the interventions of a talent scout. (One wonders whether Kahn could in fact have been thinking of Linda when he wrote the script. After all, she'd recently lived it, and drama and melodrama are often scripted on the facts of life, as romantically elusive as those facts might seem to a Kansas City salesgirl.) Her co-star was another youngster, John Payne, who played a football star also brought to Hollywood. It was an entertaining yarn and a popular one. Linda Darnell was definitely on the rise.

The studio publicity mills were churning out story after story about the new beauty, combining a charming sense of her childlike qualities with increasingly lovely stills. They mentioned that her father's nickname for her was "Tweedles" and that she had three dogs, three turtles, and a rooster named "Weedy" which had been an Easter present from Dad. "Weedy" had a special bed and ate at the family dinner table.

The releases also informed the public that for fun she enjoyed horseback riding and sketching, but when she got nervous she bit her nails. The nail biting, they said, required a wardrobe girl to follow her around with a supply of artificial nails—at twelve dollars a set. It was innocent stuff, playing up the naïveté of the young girl who was about to take another giant leap forward in the swashbuckling *The Mark of Zorro,* again opposite Power.

Directed by Rouben Mamoulian, he gave her shrewdly lit close-ups that made her more beautiful than ever. A rousing hit, one of Power's biggest, its impressive cast included gloomy Gale Sondergaard, evil Basil Rathbone, and fusty J. Edward Bromberg as the addlepated governor unseated by Zorro.

The Fox heads were so happy with the results that they teamed the young pair yet again in the lavish Technicolor *Blood and Sand,* which featured the burgeoning screen personality of Rita Hayworth as the temptress who leads bullfighter Power astray and, briefly, away from wife Linda. A remake of Valentino's silent classic, it was the public's first chance to see Linda and Rita in color, and each acquitted herself very well indeed. It was a big break for Hayworth (Hedy Lamarr had turned the part down), and it was a big money-maker. Linda's wide-eyed virginal appearance helped solidify her growing image as the screen's sweetest young thing.

Fox kept her that way opposite Henry Fonda in *Chad Hanna,* a circus story with Dorothy Lamour, and the pleasant *Rise and Shine* with Jack Oakie. By 1941 she was clearly on her way to her mother's goal.

Unfortunately for Linda, though, her mother was more star-struck than she was, and with every step Linda took forward, her mother was right behind acting out her own fantasy. Though she issued statements that the Darnell clan in Hollywood lived just as they did back home, it couldn't be proved by Pearl's actions. She changed her first name to the more glamorous Margaret and took to affecting odd costumes. Once she showed up on the Fox lot with a snake writhing about her shoulders and, in general, made herself a nuisance not only to studio personnel but to Linda as well. Fortunately Linda had a close friend in Peverell Marley, the cameraman, who always stood by her when her mother's antics got out of hand, as they often did. Margaret paraded around with the pet rooster, "Weedy," and when it died she insisted on giving it an elaborate funeral. She also made it clear that she wanted her daughter to consign some $100,000 in future earnings to a Darnell Family Fund and then inveigled Fox into using its influence to get her husband transferred from Dallas to a post office in Beverly Hills.

Calvin resisted his wife's maneuvers only so long before giving in and moving to Hollywood. Once he got there, though, Linda made a decision. She wanted out of the family nest and felt that at eighteen she deserved a little privacy. "I had been thinking of moving away for some time," she told writer Jack Holland. "I hadn't been happy for months." She said there had been so many demands on her time at home that "I felt stifled. I couldn't even paint or read a book without interference. But, above all, I was never actually alone. And I'm a person who has to have solitude most of the time to be really happy. Then, too, Mother had always depended on me, and that put an extra strain on the whole setup. When I told Mother that I was going to get an apartment she hit the ceiling, as I expected. She argued that I wouldn't be able to take care of myself." She moved into a four-room apartment which had its own tiny swimming pool, while she filmed *The Loves of Edgar Allen Poe,* a murky biography of the writer's life. It was a box-office dud. She bragged that she was learning to cook and was proud of the results so far—"I even wash the dishes. Oh, it's wonderful, this life," she said as she settled in. One of the few people whom she invited over was Peverell Marley, as always a staunch friend and profferer of good advice.

Mother Darnell didn't give up easily, though, and called constantly to check up on her independent daughter, giving bits and pieces of advice. Linda listened, but she relished the first freedom she'd ever had in her life too much to give it up. She needed time alone because there were problems cropping up suddenly that needed her full attention.

She had begun to realize she was in a rut, and that the studio realized it, too. Linda wanted badly to expand her image, specifically in the direction of the lead role in *The Song of Bernadette,* but "I found my looks stood in the way of my ambition." Executives told her, "You could never play Bernadette. She just wasn't beautiful. She was just a peasant girl." The part went to Jennifer Jones (who won a Best Actress Oscar) while Linda ended up—unbilled—as the Blessed Virgin Mary in the film's vision scenes.

The public, too, was tiring of her untouchable image, and she later said of this period, "After three years people just got tired of seeing the sweet young things I was playing and wham—one morning I found myself at the bottom of the heap."

Studio head Zanuck liked Linda, though, and that, plus the fact that he'd already invested a great deal of money in her, made him decide that a change of image might pep up her career. While he was planning a massive publicity attack to this end, Linda began relying more and more on Marley, the man who photographed her first screen test and her first three films, and who had remained a close friend throughout. Three times married and three times divorced, Marley tried to maintain a respectable distance, although he later admitted he'd been in love with Linda from the first moment he saw her but thought the situation was hopeless. There was their age difference as well as the fact she was a mother-ridden starlet with a career ahead of her.

Linda had been dating boys her own age, but she made it clear early on that she was "allergic" to actors and would never marry one. In January of 1942 she accompanied press agent Allan Gordon on the turbulent Las Vegas elopement of Lana Turner and Steve Crane, and gossip had it that she and Gordon would marry. Instead, Luscious Linda, as the press called her, began seeing more and more of Marley.

Kind and understanding, he always had Linda's best interests at heart. He was crazy about her and she developed a deep trust and affection for him. When he left for the Army toward the end of 1942, she realized just how much she had depended on him and how much she missed him. When he came back on leave, he proposed marriage and she quickly accepted. They knew there would be opposition to their marriage and decided to keep it under wraps. Remembering the Lana Turner weekend of the previous year, Linda planned one of her own with best friend Ann Miller, and on April 18, with Ann standing up for her, she and Peverell Marley became man and wife in Las Vegas. She was nineteen to his forty-one.

The following day Linda reported back to Fox, where she'd just started work on a musical called *The Girls He Left Behind*. It was a Tuesday morning and she appeared wearing a homemade bandage on her leg saying she'd injured herself doing a dance routine. The Fox executives looked her over and, surprisingly, understood. They took her off the picture and granted her a six-week leave for a honeymoon. Zanuck realized that with the marriage a *fait accompli,* he'd just have to make the most of it. To critics of the marriage Linda said, "He's what I want. I need an older, experienced man to guide me"—which he did, safely away from the overweening attentions of Pearl/Margaret Darnell.

Marley was to have an auspicious effect on the life of his young bride. First of all, it was reported that he was astonished to learn that she had never menstruated. This problem was corrected with hormone injections, but Linda was unable to bear children. Her marital status made her truly a woman in the eyes of her studio, though, and they used the marriage to launch the "New Linda Darnell" in 1944, opposite Joel McCrea in *Buffalo Bill*. Linda was effective as a dusky Indian girl, but it was only a harbinger of things to come.

Fox decided to make a movie based on Chekov's *The Hunting Party* and cast Linda as a sultry mantrap opposite urbane George Sanders, with Edward Everett Horton as the unlikely but effective third party in a fatal (to Linda) love triangle. The studio widely publicized their "new" star with poses very reminiscent of those circulating of Jane Russell in *The Outlaw,* with Linda sprawled decoratively over a pile of hay. She was gorgeous in *The Hunting Party* and garnered the most respectable set of acting reviews that she'd gotten thus far, projecting a sensuality both promising of things to come yet vaguely reminding people of the virginity she'd just recently left behind.

Coupled with a slight but noticeable improvement in her acting ability in Rene Clair's *It Happened Tomorrow* with Dick Powell, the new campaign paid off, and she found herself back on top as Fox's resident brunette sex symbol.

After appearing in Benny Goodman's *Sweet and Lowdown,* Linda was starred in one of the great period thrillers of the forties, *Hangover Square* with Laird Cregar. During his brief career (he died shortly after completing this film at age twenty-eight), Cregar specialized in madmen in films like *The Lodger,* and *Hangover Square* was no exception. As a psychopathic composer he was hopelessly in love with Linda, who brandished a hard-eyed allure as a befeathered temptress in turn-of-the-century London. He also had another problem besides Darnell, his sporadic outbursts of murder. After a chilling scene in which Linda tried to throw him out of her room, he strangled her with his talented hands and left her to burn. It was a

The "New Linda Darnell" launched in 1944.   THE DOUG MCCLELLAND COLLECTION.

spine-tingling climax to a nerve-wracking film that firmly established Linda as a top purveyor of cold-hearted sex.

As an actress she scored again in *The Great John L.*, about the life and loves of John L. Sullivan, the boxer, and she was then cast in *Fallen Angel,* to be directed by Otto Preminger.

Preminger, a tyrant on the set, didn't bother to conceal his discontent over Linda's limited acting ability. Her beauty was undeniable, but Preminger wanted more, and the pair quickly developed an antagonism toward each other. Under contract to Fox at the time, Preminger had to accept Linda and vice-versa. They were stuck with one another.

Fallen Angel was a thriller planned as a change of pace for fading musical star Alice Faye. Faye was hopelessly out of her element as a small town church organist in the black and white drama, but it gave Linda another chance to be cheaply alluring as a waitress—and also another chance to end up dead, this time done in by Dana Andrews.

When the film was finally finished, both Preminger and Linda heaved a mutual sigh of relief, but it was a shortlived breathing spell, for they were soon ordered to work together again. This time it was the lavish *Centennial Summer* with Cornel Wilde and Jeanne Crain, a leisurely, plush musical of the Philadelpha Exposition of 1876, with a pleasant score by Jerome Kern. Luckily Linda didn't have to do much heavy emoting in the bright Technicolor outing, which had both girls chasing after Wilde.

Fox realized, even if Preminger didn't, that Linda's beauty was the key to her screen personality, and played up that simple fact by casting her as Tuptim in *Anna and the King of Siam,* her second film of 1946. As the unlucky concubine who meets her fate at the stake for being unfaithful to the king (Rex Harrison), Linda gave her role unexpected realism when it came time to shoot the execution scene. She had a lifelong fear of fires and being burned that surfaced when she was slightly injured during the filming. She noted to a reporter that in other films she had died horrible deaths—by stabbing, strangulation, and shooting—but that of them all, her current movie fate was the most horrible. "Never again. Next time I prefer being stabbed or shot. At least that kind of dying is painless."

From that she went right into a very good western, *My Darling Clementine,* with Henry Fonda and Victor Mature. It was a retelling of the famous feud between Doc Holliday (Mature) and Wyatt Earp (Fonda), in which she played a saloon singer named Chihuahua, in love with Mature. The pair, both known mainly for their good looks, acquitted themselves admirably as actors this time out, with Linda exuding a somewhat contemporary allure in her part. It was a lean and fast-paced success.

During filming of *Clementine,* Fox was in the planning stage of one of its most ambitious projects of all time, *Forever Amber.* When the studio bought the rights to the torrid bestseller in 1946, it was considered quite a brave step, since the book had been condemned by the Catholic Church and the Hayes Office, Hollywood's own bastion of morality. Despite objections, though, Fox went ahead with its project, with Zanuck personally determined to make it an even bigger hit than *Gone with the Wind.* The journey of the notorious Amber St. Clair from Kathleen Winsor's pages to Zanuck's Technicolor success is a fascinating one.

First the studio launched a search for Amber in much the same way that David O. Selznick had searched for his Scarlett nine years before. It was surefire publicity for the film, and it increased the heartbeat of many an established Hollywood star who yearned for the role, particularly Lana Turner. For months Zanuck ran a guessing game as to who would play the part.

Originally he wanted an English actress for the part and offered it to both Vivien Leigh and Margaret Lockwood, but both ladies turned him down. He tested stars and unknowns alike, some 213 in all, before settling on a young ingenue named Peggy Cummins, whom he whisked off the London stage and imported to Hollywood with appropriate hoopla. The film was started under the direction of John Stahl, but when it was half-finished Zanuck had a terrible decision to make when he realized that Cummins simply wasn't projecting the necessary fire for the part. The film was shelved—after an expenditure of more than $1 million—while Zanuck regrouped his forces.

He soon decided that Preminger should take over the film, and to re-cast Amber. Preminger went to him and declared that he thought the only actress right for it was Lana Turner. But Zanuck wanted someone he had under contract, believing that whoever played it would end up a superstar. Why should he do Louis B. Mayer (MGM and Lana's boss) a favor? He was amply satisfied, after seeing rushes of *Clementine,* that Linda could carry it off and, against Preminger's loud opposition, handed her the part.

Linda's hair was dyed the necessary blonde, and the shooting schedule was revived, with Preminger issuing such statements as "She has the animalistic quality we need," which must have stuck in his throat. Preminger had done his best to get Turner, even masterminding a dinner party at which she flirted shamelessly with Zanuck, to no avail.

The shooting script had honed Amber's lovers down from twelve to four in an effort to placate the censors, but the end result was a compromise that ultimately benefited no one. For a moment, though, Linda basked in the popular acclaim of her role. She was the new Scarlett, the most talked-about star in Hollywood, the town's hottest property. And, sadly, she had to face all that alone.

During all this, her marriage to Peverell Marley hadn't been going well, and for six months of 1946 she and Marley had separated—indeed, so close to a divorce that a property settlement had been arranged. As he got older, Marley began getting more and more distant from his young, still-blossoming wife. He began resenting her career and seemed to blame himself for creating a beautiful Frankenstein's monster and then finding it difficult to live with.

In fact, Amber St. Clair emerged on the screen as a sort of patched together, Frankensteinish version of the lusty original. An overdubbing was added to the opening credits, stating that this was the tragic story of a sinner whose only rewards for her lack of virtue were exile and loneliness. (It didn't, however, obscure the fact that, for the most part, Amber had a very merry time of it en route to these melancholy destinations.) Considering the bastardization of the story, the antagonism between her and Preminger, and the mental upset of a fragile marriage, Linda gave an excellent account of herself, as she stalked her way among screen lovers John Russell, Glenn Langan, Cornel Wilde, and George Sanders, and screen husband Richard Haydn. She established in the part of Amber the same kind of stubborn, petulant sexuality that Scarlett had, even though their backgrounds were very different—Amber the Puritan, Scarlett the surviving aristocrat—both willing to compromise to get what they wanted.

A harrowing moment came during the Great Fire of London scene in which Amber (Linda) is locked in her bedroom as the blaze roared closer and closer around her and husband Haydn. Even though the set was perfectly safe and had been lined with asbestos Linda was too terrified to perform. Preminger literally had to drag her onto the set, her lifelong fear of fire surfacing again.

Fox opened the feature in one of the first mass bookings—900 theaters across the country on the same day. An enormous publicity build-up helped the film quickly to gross some $6 million, according to Otto Preminger, but the critics ripped into it like piranhas on a picnic. There are those who consider it one of Hollywood's biggest flops, but actually it did make money—although nowhere in the neighborhood of what Fox had expected.

The picture's pubicity brought Linda to the attention of Hollywood playboy Howard Hughes, who invited her along on TWA's star-studded coast-to-coast inaugural flight on February 15, 1946. At first, though, Linda didn't want anything to do with him. When he approached her agent, Bill Shriffrin, about setting up a meeting she said, "I know what he wants but I am married. My contract with Twentieth Century Fox has several years to run, so I don't need to know him." Hughes persisted though, and caught her on the golf course one day where he wheedled a luncheon date out of her. She agreed on the condition that her agent come along, too.

Their date was set for the next day at noon, at which time Hughes chugged up in his battered Chevrolet to her Bel-Air door. Linda and Shriffrin were waiting and Hughes drove them to his private airfield and calmly ushered them aboard his Constellation. With Hughes at the controls, the three of them then proceeded to fly to San Francisco, where a car met them, whisking them off to the Fairmont Hotel where Hughes had rented an entire floor. A small orchestra played while a lavish buffet was spread before the startled star, who couldn't help but be impressed by the curious luxury of her eccentric host. They became friends, but she eventually returned to the security of Marley, from whom she was not yet divorced.

Both Zanuck and Linda were stunned by *Forever Amber's* poor reception by the public, and it was months before he decided just what she'd do next to reaffirm her reputation. He settled on teaming her with Cornel Wilde again in *The Walls of*

Jericho, but the story of a smalltown lawyer who lets his marital affairs interfere with his career was a boring and dreary entry.

Linda was in a quandary. At twenty-five she was a top star, world famous, but with a career that was stymied. Turning away from it, she tried to bring her personal life back into order, and in 1948 she and Marley adopted a five-week-old daughter, Charlotte Mildred, whom they promptly nicknamed Lola. For a time it looked as though Linda's career was over, but Fox came to her rescue, in the person of director Preston Sturges, with a stylishly brilliant comedy called *Unfaithfully Yours,* pairing her with Rex Harrison. It was Linda's first contemporary role since *Fallen Angel* four years before, and she played Harrison's wife with a thoroughly modern charm. Harrison played a symphony conductor who suspected his wife of being unfaithful and plotted her demise during a concert. It was a good deal of fun, aided greatly by the support of Edgar Kennedy and Lionel Stander, and gave Linda a resurgence of popularity.

A blonde Linda and a dashing Cornel Wilde in Forever Amber *(1947).*
THE DOUG MCCLELLAND COLLECTION.

Linda lucked out again when Joseph L. Mankiewicz was shaping up his classic *A Letter to Three Wives,* the story of three troubled marriages. In her he saw the perfect actress to play Lora May Hollingsway, a girl from the wrong side of the tracks who set her sights on department-store-owner Paul Douglas in one of the most trenchant dissections of marriage ever filmed. Linda's Lora May was a straightforward creature who recognized what she saw in the wealthy and social Douglas and set out to get it. She also knew what she had to offer as in the scene when she was getting ready for Douglas to pick her up for a date.

Said her mother's best friend, played by Thelma Ritter, "Why dontcha show more of what you got? Wear some beads."

"What I got don't need beads," Linda snapped back, going on to prove just that. Buttressed with a heavyweight cast including Jeanne Crain, Kirk Douglas, Ann Sothern, and Jeffrey Lynn, it was one of the best films of the year.

The success of *Letter* should have finally opened the Fox executives' eyes to Linda's now undeniable acting ability, but if they saw it they chose to ignore it, throwing her into a minor action film with Veronica Lake and Richard Widmark called *Slattery's Hurricane.* Directed by Lake's husband, Andre de Toth, it was a lackluster outing for all concerned.

Management smartened up a bit when they cast her again with Paul Douglas in *Everybody Does It,* a comedy about a businessman who unwittingly starts an opera career. Linda played a diva who gave the fledgling baritone some professional help, a stylish part that showcased not only her beauty but her comedic timing as well.

Mankiewicz came to her aid with a decidedly dramatic part in his rugged story of racial unrest, *No Way Back.* As gangster Richard Widmark's voluptuous girlfriend, she aided him in starting a race war to avenge the death of his brother, Linda's late husband. Ahead of its time, the film was powerful but, alas, not very successful, although all concerned turned in excellent performances, including Sidney Poitier in his screen debut.

Yet Linda was beginning to feel threatened and hemmed in by the slapdash way she was being treated by her home studio, then just beginning to tremble over the rising threat of television. For every good part she got a stinker or two and decided to try to reaffirm her image—in fact, break new ground in her career—by turning to the stage. She left Hollywood for Phoenix, where she appeared in *Roomful of Roses.* She got some respectable notices for her work, but her triumph was shortlived when she returned home to find herself in financial trouble. Her business manager, to whom she'd given power of attorney, embezzled her life savings of $65,000 and left her liable for back taxes, which he said he'd paid but hadn't. This was the beginning of financial troubles that would dog her the rest of her life, often causing her to have to sidestep any hope of career advancement by waiting for the right part. Linda took just about everything that came along in order to keep her career afloat.

During this time Marley's career was also flagging, which created further tensions in an already troubled existence.

In 1950 she made a western with Jeff Chandler, *Two Flags West,* playing the third point in a triangle involving him and Joseph Cotten. Unfortunately, the battle scenes got the best reviews.

Later that year she was ordered to work again with her nemesis Otto Preminger in *The Thirteenth Letter,* the first Hollywood picture shot entirely on location—in this case, Quebec. Top-billed as the sultry Denise, Linda gave a fine performance as a love-starved cripple doing her best to complicate the life of village doctor Michael Rennie, the target of a series of poison-pen letters linking him with the wife of his medical superior, Charles Boyer. The poignant scene where the doctor discovered her shoeless in her bedroom and she had to hobble past him to get her specially built-up shoes was a startling example of just how good an actress she was when given a chance. Filmed in black and white, it was not a major film but a worthwhile payoff for Darnell's fans.

Returning home Linda realized that not only was her career going poorly but her marriage was virtually over. The Marleys' adopted daughter had done little to mend the widening rift between Linda and her fifty-three-year-old husband and on July 19, 1950, he moved out of their Bel-Air home.

Linda went back to work opposite Paul Douglas and Joan Bennett in a football drama called *The Guy Who Came Back,* as a vamp again, but though she didn't know it at the time, it would be the last picture she would make for Fox under her $2,250-per-week contract.

On February 20, a chic-looking Linda showed up in court for her divorce hearing, nervously puffing a cigarette in the witness box before being sworn in. The clerk told her to put it out, which she did before proceeding to tell how her marriage had dissolved. The twenty-seven-year-old star told how she often had to "hold back the tears" over Marley's behavior. "He used to go to bed while guests were still in the house. He refused to attend affairs given by my fellow film workers. He criticized my friends and relatives. I decided I couldn't go any further with our marriage." Her testimony took all of two minutes after which she was awarded custody of their daughter plus seventy-five dollars a month child support, but no alimony. The divorce was granted on the grounds of "mental cruelty."

With nothing on her work schedule Linda went to New York for a while, where she briefly dated Ethel Merman's estranged husband, Robert D. Levitt, and, a few months later, made more news when her Warwick Hotel suite was robbed of $12,500 worth of furs and jewels.

The gossip in Hollywood was that Fox was not going to renew Linda's contract, although they didn't officially announce the parting until October of 1952. Linda had mixed feelings about leaving Fox after thirteen years. Although on the one hand she hoped that she'd be able to use her freedom to find better parts, she wistfully told a friend, "I feel like a girl leaving home."

Those early fifties were the years when most of the big studios were dropping their contract players, and the scrambling for roles became more fierce than ever before. She made a not-so-funny comedy at Universal called *The Lady Pays Off,* but it was strictly double-bill material. In the press, however, she was still hot copy and startled quite a few readers that year when she announced, "I'm bored with not being in love. I'm looking for a steady boyfriend. Being in love is the most wonderful thing that can happen to anyone. I've only had four dates in the past two months, although two were with nice men: Robert Taylor and Vittorio de Sica." She added with a sigh, "My social life isn't just a void—it's a king-sized vacuum." That statement sounded schoolgirlish, but perhaps she had every right to sound that way. She had until then been more or less sheltered by her family, her studio, and a much older husband. It wasn't surprising that Linda now wanted a man her own age, especially since her career appeared to be going nowhere.

Like most big names she was able to work at smaller studios and elicited a burst of sexy publicity quite by fluke when she starred in an otherwise mediocre picture for United Artists called *Island of Desire*. That picture launched the film career of Tab Hunter, who quickly became a teenage idol. The amount of press he got upon *Island*'s 1952 release couldn't help spilling over on Linda. As a World War II nurse stranded on a desolate island with Tab, she was the envy of every teenage bobby-soxer in America, although she displayed a maturity well beyond her twenty-eight years. In the eyes of the public she *was* mature, since she'd been around for some thirteen years and, until *Island*, they seemed to be getting tired of her.

After making *Night Without Sleep* with Gary Merrill, she starred in a familiar lady-in-distress role in *Blackbeard the Pirate*, a rousing sea yarn starring Britain's Robert Newton in the title role. It was big with the Saturday matinee crowd but no great shakes for the adult trade.

Later that year Linda decided to take the path being taken by many other big stars of the forties, like Paulette Goddard and Hedy Lamarr, and journeyed to Europe looking for film work. She wound up in Italy to discuss a project with producer Giusseppe Amato. "The Italians are so natural and free," she enthused. "I want to learn their technique. I travel a lot between pictures anyway. After thirteen years at the same studio—Fox—I'm ready for something completely new. And you can't blame an old crone of twenty-nine for trying."

Within a month reports filtered back that she and Amato were having an affair, but she denied it. She did sign to make a film for him, something called *Angels of Darkness* in which she played a heart-of-gold prostitute along with Valentina Cortese and Giulietta Masina. Anthony Quinn was in it too, but it was a sad waste of all concerned and received few U.S. bookings.

Upon completing it Linda came back to Hollywood, but her dissatisfaction with her career was growing. She made *Second Chance* with Robert Mitchum—in 3-D—but she was type-cast again as a gangster's girl being stalked by killer Jack Palance. In 1953 she bought a ranch in Roswell, New Mexico, and began splitting her time between there and her Bel-Air home on Siena Way. "Ranch life is economical. If I'm going to pick and choose roles for their professional value rather than to bring in money, the long green stuff might come in handy. I'll never have to worry about that as long as I have the ranch.''

She left the sagebrush behind to return to Hollywood for a very good part in *This Is My Love.* Playing the neurotic spinster whose sister (Faith Domergue) is always stealing her boyfriends, Linda said she liked the part better than any she'd ever done. Stripped of glamour, she was convincing in the role and commented, ''No, I don't get the man. But then I almost never do. Even in *Forever Amber* I didn't get the man I wanted.''

Amato called her back to Italy for another movie, and she was only too happy to go. The film was called *The Last Five Minutes* and starred her with Vittorio de Sica and Rossano Brazzi, but it was never released in the United States. ''I love it over here,'' she told reporters when she landed, but she quickly squelched the recurring rumors of romance with Amato by saying in her forthright manner, ''My Italian director friend can't handle me. He goes toddling up the street ahead of me and I say, 'Hey bud, you're with me.' He says, 'You American women aren't women. You're men.' I tell him 'We like it that way.' I don't want to get married to anybody. I'm having too much fun free.''

She was singing quite a different tune within the year, though, after meeting New York beer king Philip Liebman, president of Liebman Breweries and the man who invented Miss Rheingold. She was thirty-two years old then, and he was thirty-nine. For months they kept their romance a secret; in fact, Linda was denying it right up to the day she married him in Mexico on February 25, 1954, and even after. She didn't let the public in on it until the following July at New York's Idlewild Airport when she introduced him to the press as her new husband. She'd been hinting broadly that changes were taking place in her life during that period when she issued statements to the effect that ''Hollywood—I've had it. I'm not interested in living here any longer. I'm sick of Hollywood. I'll be back only long enough to make a good film if I'm offered one. I have low blood pressure and I need the altitude in New Mexico.''

Liebman began planning a film production company and lining up scripts for his wife to star in when they returned from their honeymoon in Venezuela. They left on July 1 but were back home eight days later, reportedly because of his business. They tried to honeymoon again later in the month, heading for Spain and Italy, but were once more stymied when Linda had to fly back to Hollywood from Rome to attend the funeral of her good friend, agent Bill DeHaas. Pictures of her in tears at Rome's airport started rumors that all was far from idyllic in the Liebman household. An aggressive businessman, her husband was quickly discovering the penalties for marrying a public figure.

They tried again for a honeymoon a few months later, this time taking Linda's six-year-old daughter with them, but it quickly became apparent that they were an ill-matched pair. Linda was drinking—not beer—and Liebman's patience was running out. Their previously established lifestyles just didn't mesh as Linda had hoped. Liebman didn't want to submerge his identity as a movie star's husband, and he also decided that he didn't want to get into the movie business. It all happened very quickly, and on December 2, 1955, Linda went in secret to Mexico to obtain a divorce. Arriving there with her attorney, she was spotted by reporters, but she told them she was there for business purposes "which I prefer not to discuss." She sued on the grounds of incompatibility and asked for no alimony. She also said there was "no bitterness" between them, but she must have choked a bit on those words when, five days later, Liebman married a reservations clerk for a Beverly Hills auto leasing company. The entire friendship and marriage had lasted a mere twenty-one months.

Alone again, Linda turned to the only thing she knew, her career, and tried to resuscitate it with a western at Republic called *Dakota Incident.*

Shot in Trucolor, Linda had top-billing as Amy Clark, a hard-bitten, red-satined, saloon-singing beauty. It was a gritty tale of a group of misfits caught in an Indian raid, and Linda approached the predictable script with humorous enthusiasm. "A lot of people are going to be surprised to find some emotional range in this ex-dollface." Linda looked great, but any emotional range was lost in the shuffle of the meandering, pompous writing.

The idea of a stage triumph reasserted itself when Linda went to New York for a television appearance. She was offered the lead in the Columbia-Pictures-backed play *Harbor Lights* opposite Robert Alda, and she was immediately encouraged that this might make the difference in her career. It was a dramatic love story set on Staten Island, and Linda played a young mother torn between her first love and her second husband. "It adds to my age, but that's all right with me," she said. "I'm fed up with costume characters. The fact is that any actress with serious ambitions must sometime put her abilities to the test, not coast along on face and figure alone. This show offers the range to prove my point." Unfortunately the critics didn't agree, and *Harbor Lights* went dark after four performances.

Linda was determend to have a stage success, though, and turned down a western with Jeff Chandler, *Drango,* to go to Florida for a revival of *Tea and Sympathy.* Her reviews were generally good but not as good as she'd hoped for, and she was greatly disheartened.

Linda's personal life took a happy turn, though, when she met airline pilot Merle "Robby" Robertson. A tall, handsome man with charcoal gray hair, who'd once had a romance with Jayne Mansfield, he had an almost boyish charm that immediately attracted Linda. He courted her with an innocent abandon that she'd never known before and attempted to put her life back on a stable basis. When a movie writer sued her former husband, Liebman, over a screenplay he'd done for Linda to star in for Liebman's proposed movie company, Robertson accompanied her to court for the hearing. Attentive and understanding, he triggered romantic images of a kind she'd never experienced before. Her first marriage had been a runaway elopement with a much older man and her second a secretive, whirlwind mistake. Robertson seemed the embodiment of her romantic ideal, and when they soon decided to marry, she was determined to give life to her long dormant fantasies.

They set the date for March 3, 1957, at the Flyer's Chapel in the Mission Inn at Riverside, California. Linda was in the middle of shooting a *Playhouse 90* television show but found time to plan the kind of old-fashioned wedding she'd obviously wanted for so long. She wore a formal wedding gown and veil even though it was her third trip down the aisle, and her daughter Lola, then nine, was the flower girl. The day after the ceremony Linda went back to work while Robertson moved his things from his Redondo Beach apartment into Linda's Bel-Air house. Despite the formal ceremony, the honeymoon had to wait, as usual.

Linda had once told an interviewer that "I mind my business, especially when I am in public. I never dare to take an extra cocktail and just have some silly fun." All that changed once she and Robertson married. Although her career had slowed down to a walk, her drinking habits hadn't, and during the next five years she appeared in only one minor film, *Zero Hour,* for Paramount, which reunited her with old co-star Dana Andrews, whose career was also on the skids. In 1958 she made a rare television appearance on *Pursuit* but it was obvious that her beauty was being sadly ruined by her now-heavy drinking. The fire and promise she'd shown in films like *Summer Storm* and *A Letter to Three Wives* was tragically banked, the luster gone. At thirty-five she was looking decidedly matronly, her figure overweight, making it all too apparent that her romantic dreams were turning into nightmares of frustration and discontent. Her marriage was already beginning to disintegrate and her career was hanging in the balance.

She began getting a reputation in the business as unpredictable, and to counteract that she decided to take a stage offer in 1959 that took her to Chicago for a play called *Late Love.* As opening night approached she became more and more nervous, complaining of fatigue and difficulty in learning her lines. She put in an SOS to her personal physician in California who flew to Chicago and hypnotized her. It worked, too. Linda said, "I've never felt so secure about playing a role," and the *Chicago Daily News* said, "Miss Darnell was entrancing, rather than in trance. [Her] lines were perfect."

Despite this success, though, there were still no movie offers, so Linda tried a new tack; she'd wow them on the nightclub circuit. Returning home she brushed up on dance lessons that harked back to her childhood, and she hired a singing coach. She planned carefully and decided to open her act in July of 1960 at the Town House in Pittsburgh under a veil of secrecy. Linda was frankly scared to death. Oddly enough, the management of the club consented to let her appear without publicity for a nine-day stint. She didn't want any until she was sure of herself, and specifically she didn't want a *Variety* review. (*Variety* did review her, though, and very well, too.) When she finally did consent to an interview, she told reporters, "My true love is TV. I now have a pilot making the rounds about a lady horse owner."

If that was true why was she trying so desperately for a nightclub career? She admitted she'd been well-advised as to what to expect, but since her TV career was so uncertain, she decided to try the clubs anyway. "Joey Bishop told me how it would be. Everything would have a smell and drunks would always bother me." That was one problem Linda didn't have, though, since the club did disastrous business while she was there. Her "no publicity" edict kept not only the press but the public away as well.

By the time the *Variety* review came out it was too late. The local press would likely have been unfavorable to her in any case, since she'd been quoted as saying she was trying out her act "in the sticks." Unfortunately, it never got beyond that, the big money of New York and Las Vegas eluding her.

The disappointment over her nightclub fiasco did little to help Linda's mental state, and upon her return to Hollywood minor disagreements with Robby started flaring into open hostility. He moved out several times until, finally, the marriage collapsed. Robbed of her public personality, she turned more and more to alcohol for solace but found it an uneasy companion. On February 13, 1962, she sued Robertson for separate maintenance saying the forty-four-year-old man had caused her embarrassment and humiliation by acts of cruelty. Several months later he countersued for divorce, stripping away the last vestiges of glamour that clung to her name. He charged that she was habitually drunk and neglectful of her marital duties. The press had a field day, especially when she countercharged that he had been unfaithful to her with a European actress and allegedly had a child by her. It was a messy and undignified swan song for a marriage that she had begun with such high hopes. To try to settle community property and also help pay legal bills, Linda had to sell her beloved ranch in New Mexico, and when the divorce was granted on November 23, 1963, the former Cinderella Girl of the movies was forty-one and at a crisis point.

Lola was in a private school, but when she could she traveled with her mother on the summer stock circuit, Linda's only means of employment. The only movie offer that came her way was a western at Paramount produced in late 1964 by A. C. Lyles, a man who tried to make up for his tiny budgets by hiring as many former big names as possible for his pictures. During those years he utilized what was left of the talent and marquee lure of people like Howard Keel, Jane Russell, Joan Caulfield, Brian Donlevy, John Agar, George Montgomery, Tab Hunter—and Linda Darnell.

The film was called *Black Spurs,* and Linda was surrounded by Rory Calhoun, Terry Moore, Scott Brady, Lon Chaney, and Bruce Cabot. Corseted to a fare-thee-well, she played a saloon hostess again, in a picture she herself described as "a ten-day quickie no one will go to see."

(She was wrong about that. It was released after her death, the tragedy of which brought out many more people than might normally have gone to see "Amber" for the last time. The Darnell they saw, though, was a tarnished version of the dewy original. Her once-perfect face was bloated by drink, her eyes heavily mascaraed, and the high-piled hair too black to be real. It was a sad

A casual Linda the year before she died (1964). JACK KUSTER.

comedown for the girl who was once called "almost too beautiful." Linda never saw the finished film, and perhaps it's better that she didn't.)

In October, after the picture was finished, she went to Chicago for an appearance in *Love out of Town* at the Pheasant Run Playhouse, and while there she looked up her former secretary and still her friend, Jeanne Curtis. They chatted about the old days and the good times, but the visit was brief because Linda was en route to a tour in *Janus* that would wind up in Atlanta the following March. Stage work had always been difficult for her, and she ended the *Janus* tour with a virus infection and was on medication to counteract it. She called Jeanne and then went back to Chicago, where she moved in with Jeanne and the latter's sixteen-year-old daughter, Patricia. Jeanne's husband was away on a business trip to Los Angeles, so the threesome settled in for a long visit.

Shortly after midnight on the morning of April 9, 1965, Linda's virus seemed to be abating. When she noticed that one of her early movies was scheduled for the "Late Show," she jokingly told Jeanne and Patricia about it, saying "Let's have some laughs. Let's stay up and watch *Star Dust.*" They did, watching Linda's third film, almost the story of her life, until 2:30 A.M. When it was over, Jeanne and Patricia went upstairs to their bedrooms while Linda stretched out on the sofa getting ready for sleep.

Though Mrs. Curtis would later say that Linda had giggled all through the film, one wonders what she really thought, seeing herself as she was in 1939—so young and fresh, so full of promise. Whatever went on in her mind—resignation, defeat, a subconscious wish to end it all—will never be known, for Linda Darnell was never able to tell. She fell asleep holding a lighted cigarette, and as she dozed off it fell from her fingers onto the upholstery. In minutes the fabric was ablaze, the flames quickly making an inferno of the living room, searing Linda with second- and third-degree burns over 80 percent of her upper body.

Mrs. Curtis and her daughter were awakened by the smoke and managed to escape serious injury. Patricia jumped from a second-story window while her mother perched on a ledge outside the bathroom until firemen rescued her. A young neighbor, hearing the screams coming from the living room, tried smashing a window to get to the woman trapped within, but the flames drove him back.

Firemen were eventually able to get inside and found Linda huddled behind the sofa. She was alive but unconscious as they carried her to an ambulance and rushed her through the early morning to Skokie Valley Community Hospital. A team of surgeons worked over her for four hours, but little hope was held out that she could survive the terrible burns and shock. Later that day she was transferred to Cook County Hospital's new burn treatment center "in order to provide her with the most comprehensive and specialized care available." A tracheotomy was performed to aid her breathing.

Sixteen-year-old Lola Marley rushed to her mother's bedside from California, and, although Linda couldn't see her because her eyes had swollen shut, she did rally into consciousness for the half hour they spent together. The pretty brunette teenager was robed and masked during the brief visit to deter any danger of infection to her mother, standard procedure in such cases. At the sound of Lola's muffled voice, Linda came around, recognizing it but barely able to communicate with her. It was a heart-rending scene.

After thirty-three hours of suspense, with Linda regaining consciousness again briefly toward the end, she died at 3:25 P.M. Her body was cremated and its ashes buried in a Chicago cemetery following a memorial service attended by a stunned Lola, Jeanne and Patricia Curtis, and an assortment of mostly middle-aged curiosity seekers.*

The tragic circumstances of her death once again riveted the world's attention to Linda Darnell. Reporters called it "the valiant death of a star" and recalled her childhood fear of fire. The little girl from Dallas was gone, and, after the flurry of headlines, few were left to mourn her passing.

FILMOGRAPHY
Linda Darnell

TITLE	YEAR	DIRECTOR	LEADING PLAYERS
Hotel for Women	1939	Gregory Ratoff	Ann Sothern, James Ellison, Jean Rogers, Lynn Bari, June Gayle, Elsa Maxwell, Mary Healy
Daytime Wife	1939	Gregory Ratoff	Tyrone Power, Warren William, Binnie Barnes, Wendy Barrie, Joan Davis, Leonid Kinskey
Star Dust	1940	Walter Lang	John Payne, Roland Young, William Gargan, Charlotte Greenwood, Mary Beth Hughes, Donald Meek
Brigham Young— Frontiersman	1940	Henry Hathaway	Tyrone Power, Dean Jagger, Brian Donlevy, Mary Astor, Jane Darwell, John Carradine
The Mark of Zorro	1940	Rouben Mamoulian	Tyrone Power, Basil Rathbone, Gale Sondergaard, J. Edward Bromberg, Eugene Pallette, Montagu Love
Chad Hanna	1940	Henry King	Henry Fonda, Dorothy Lamour, Jane Darwell, Guy Kibbee, John Carradine
Blood and Sand	1941	Rouben Mamoulian	Tyrone Power, Rita Hayworth, Nazimova, Laird Cregar, Anthony Quinn, John Carradine, Lynn Bari, J. Carroll Naish
Rise and Shine	1941	Allan Dwan	Jack Oakie, George Murphy, Walter

*In September of 1975, Linda's remains were transferred from Chicago to Union Hill Cemetery at Kennett Square, Pennsylvania, as requested in her will. Arrangements were made by Lola, now Mrs. James L. Adams, of New London, Pennsylvania.

TITLE	YEAR	DIRECTOR	LEADING PLAYERS
			Brennan, Sheldon Leonard, Donald Meek, Ruth Donnelly
Loves of Edgar Allan Poe	1942	Harry Lachtman	John Sheppard, Virginia Gilmore, Jane Darwell, Mary Howard, Frank Conway, Henry Morgan
City Without Men	1943	Sidney Salkow	Edgar Buchanan, Michael Duane, Sara Allgood, Glenda Farrell, Leslie Brooks, Doris Dudley, Margaret Hamilton
The Song of Bernadette	1943	Henry King	Jennifer Jones, Charles Bickford, Vincent Price, Lee J. Cobb, William Eythe, Gladys Cooper, Anne Revere
It Happened Tomorrow	1944	René Clair	Dick Powell, Jack Oakie, Edgar Kennedy, John Philliber, George Cleveland
Buffalo Bill	1944	William A. Wellman	Joel McCrea, Maureen O'Hara, Edgar Buchanan, Thomas Mitchell, Anthony Quinn, Sidney Blackmer
Summer Storm	1944	Douglas Sirk	George Sanders, Anna Lee, Edward Everett Horton, Hugo Haas
Sweet and Low Down	1944	Archie Mayo	Benny Goodman and Orchestra, Lynn Bari, Jack Oakie, James Cardwell, Allyn Joslyn
Hangover Square	1945	John Brahm	Laird Cregar, George Sanders, Glenn Langan, Faye Marlowe
The Great John L.	1945	Frank Tuttle	Greg McClure, Barbara Britton, Lee Sullivan, Otto Kruger
Fallen Angel	1945	Otto Preminger	Dana Andrews, Alice Faye, Anne Revere, Charles Bickford, Bruce Cabot, John Carradine
Centennial Summer	1946	Otto Preminger	Jeanne Crain, Cornel Wilde, William Eythe, Walter Brennan, Constance Bennett, Dorothy Gish
Anna and the King of Siam	1946	John Cromwell	Irene Dunne, Rex Harrison, Lee J. Cobb, Gale Sondergaard
My Darling Clementine	1946	John Ford	Henry Fonda, Victor Mature, Walter Brennan, Tim Holt, Ward Bond, Cathy Downs, Alan Mowbray, Jane Darwell
Forever Amber	1947	Otto Preminger	Cornel Wilde, Richard Greene, George Sanders, Glenn Langan, Richard Haydn, Jessica Tandy, Anne Revere, John Russell, Jane Ball, Robert Coote
The Walls of Jericho	1948	John M. Stahl	Cornel Wilde, Anne Baxter, Kirk Douglas, Ann Dvorak, Marjorie Rambeau, Henry Hull
Unfaithfully Yours	1948	Preston Sturges	Rex Harrison, Barbara Lawrence, Rudy Vallee, Kurt Kreuger, Lionel Stander

TITLE	YEAR	DIRECTOR	LEADING PLAYERS
A Letter to Three Wives	1948	Jos. L. Mankiewicz	Jeanne Crain, Ann Sothern, Kirk Douglas, Barbara Lawrence, Connie Gilchrist, Thelma Ritter, Jeffrey Lynn, Celeste Holm
Slattery's Hurricane	1949	Andre de Toth	Richard Widmark, Veronica Lake, John Russell, Gary Merrill
Everybody Does It	1949	Edmund Goulding	Paul Douglas, Celeste Holm, Charles Coburn, Lucille Watson
No Way Out	1950	Jos. L. Mankiewicz	Richard Widmark, Stephen McNally, Sidney Poitier, Ruby Dee
Two Flags West	1950	Robert Wise	Joseph Cotton, Jeff Chandler, Cornel Wilde, Dale Robertson, Jay C. Flippen, Noah Beery, Jr.
The Thirteenth Letter	1951	Otto Preminger	Charles Boyer, Michael Rennie, Constance Smith, Judith Evelyn
The Guy Who Came Back	1951	Joseph Newman	Paul Douglas, Joan Bennett, Don De Fore, Billy Gray, Zero Mostel
The Lady Pays Off	1951	Douglas Sirk	Stephen McNally, Gigi Perreau, Virginia Field, Ann Codee
Island of Desire	1952	Stuart Heisler	Tab Hunter, Donald Gray, John Lauric, Shicla Chong
Night Without Sleep	1952	Roy Baker	Gary Merrill, Hildegarde Neff, Joyce MacKenzie, June Vincent
Blackbeard the Pirate	1952	Raoul Walsh	Robert Newton, William Bendix, Keith Andes, Torin Thatcher, Irene Ryan, Alan Mowbray, Richard Egan
Donne Proibite (U.S. title *Angels of Darkness*)	1953	Guiseppe Amato	Valentina Cortese, Lea Padovani, Guilietta Masina, Anthony Quinn
Second Chance	1953	Rudolph Mate	Robert Mitchum, Jack Palance, Sandro Giglio
This Is My Love	1954	Stuart Heisler	Rick Jason, Dan Duryea, Faith Domergue, Carl "Alfalfa" Switzer
Gli Ultimi Cinque Minuti (U.S. title *The Last Five Minutes*)	1954	Guisseppe Amato	Vittorio de Sica, Rossano Brazzi, Peppino de Filippo
Dakota Incident	1956	Lewis R. Foster	Dale Robertson, John Lund, Ward Bond, Regis Toomey, Skip Homier
Zero Hour	1957	Hall Bartlett	Dana Andrews, Peggy King, Sterling Hayden, Elroy "Crazylegs" Hirsch
Black Spurs	1965	R. G. Springsteen	Rory Calhoun, Scott Brady, Lon Chaney, Bruce Cabot, Richard Arlen, Terry Moore, Patricia Owens, James Brown

Veronica Lake

When they told me I had to do a drunk scene I thought, "How'll I ever pull it off? I've never been drunk in my life."

Veronica Lake speaking to a friend about her screen test for I Wanted Wings.

To each his own. At least I'm not a mainliner, and it's more fun getting high without a needle. At least you can get over booze.

Veronica Lake, quoted in the New York Times, *March 10, 1971.*

From the moment she sauntered across a barroom floor with William Holden on her mind in *I Wanted Wings,* Veronica Lake became the sensation of 1941. With her long blonde hair cascading over half her face, she projected an allure and sexuality that kept male moviegoers away from the popcorn counters, while their girlfriends stampeded to the powder rooms, hairbrushes in hand, to try to duplicate her langourous look. She was an overnight sensation, and the gimmick of her vagrant hair made her an instant idol, one of the most popular female stars of World War II.

When her home studio, Paramount, coupled her with Alan Ladd in *This Gun for Hire* the following year, they created one of the most combustible screen teams of the period. A tiny woman, Lake was magnified by the screen into epic proportions and was so popular and so imitated that the War Department petitioned Paramount to redo her famous mane. So many women working over machines in defense plants were imitating it that it was becoming a hazard not only to them but to the war effort as well.

Ladd and Lake—the pint-sized siren with the peek-a-boo hairdo and husky voice, and the handsome, steely-jawed tough guy—were potent box office, teaming up a total of four times through the forties with *Gun* followed by *The Glass Key* (1942), Raymond Chandler's gritty *The Blue Dahlia* (1946), and finally 1948's

The Veronica Lake the world fell in love with (circa 1941).   THE DOUG MCCLELLAND COLLECTION.

Saigon. That was almost the last film Veronica made for Paramount, for by then her appeal to the moviegoers had almost petered out, due to a series of mostly awful "B" pictures that her studio insisted on throwing her into. A self-professed rebel, when her stardom ended she didn't have many friends in the industry to fall back on, and in 1952 she virtually disappeared overnight from the town that had made her a household word.

For almost ten years no one heard much about Veronica Lake until she surfaced as a barmaid at the Martha Washington Hotel for Women in New York City. The press ate it up, and for a brief moment she was headline news again. The celluloid sorceress of *I Married a Witch* was barely visible in the bloated, strained-looking woman Veronica Lake had become. Liquor, her solace in Hollywood, had long been her solace away from it, and while she managed to work to survive in various summer stock roles over the years, her reincarnation in a hotel bar didn't result in much of a comeback.

The author met her only once, shortly after that, when she was playing the lead role as a fading film star in off-Broadway's *Best Foot Forward,* and I remember her walking toward me after a performance, famous blonde hair pulled tightly back, a look of resignation on her face—was this a friend or an enemy? She was as nervous as I was. The toll of being a Hollywood Love Goddess, especially one with as flimsy a gimmick as her hair, had been an especially difficult one for Veronica Lake to handle. While others were disappointed in not seeing the movie image they remembered, I was saddened to see so much obvious internal struggle still going on inside the woman herself. She was still trying to understand not only that image but the person behind it as well.

Connie Ockleman was only eighteen when she first saw Hollywood in 1938. The family had decided to relocate in better climate due to her stepfather's ill health. She arrived there, after driving across country with her mother, stepfather, and cousin Helen, on a hot, dusty morning in summer, full of the typically youthful dreams of any teenager. Born in Brooklyn on November 14, 1919, she'd spent her youth in that fabled borough and her growing-up years in Miami and at a convent school in Montreal. A Catholic, Connie was already verging on renouncing that religion because of its strictness. She was a rebel at heart, albeit a shy one, and nobody's fool. While the Canadian Mother Superior had once predicted that little Connie would one day be a nun, Connie knew it would never happen. She had her mind on other things.

The newly arrived family settled into a small West Hollywood apartment, and Connie went about the business of making new friends and exploring her newest hometown. She daydreamed about becoming an actress, but her mother took her daydreams seriously. She was shortly enrolled in the Bliss Hayden School on Wilshire Boulevard, practicing her diction and balancing books on her head for posture improvement. Connie did it mostly to please her demanding mother, and frankly never thought she'd make the grade to stardom. About that time the seeds of antagonism were planted between the two that were to grow over the ensuing years, nurtured mainly by the mother's ambitions for her daughter.

One of her friends at the school asked the tiny (five-foot, two-inch) full-bosomed girl to accompany her out to RKO Studios, where she had hopes of landing a bit part in a picture called *Sorority House.* For the fun of it, Connie said yes, and went along. Until then her only public exposure had been as a child, in the starring role in a school play, *Poor Little Rich Girl,* and two appearances in Florida beauty contests. She had come in third in the Miss Miami sweepstakes and then won the Miss Florida prize, only to lose the title when the judges found out she was underage. There was an adult coolness about her, though, and unsurprisingly she too landed a small part in *Sorority House,* and made her official movie debut in that film under the name Constance Keane, her last name coming to her from her new stepfather. It starred Anne Shirley and was directed by John Farrow, but it was a minor film in which Connie didn't have a chance to stand out in the crowd of young girls cast as sorority members. She learned from it, though, and was soon given other bits in *The Wrong Room,* a short with Leon Errol; *All Women Have Secrets;* and, at mighty MGM, in *Forty Little Mothers* with Eddie Cantor.

It was in *Forty Little Mothers* that she affected what later would be known as the hairdo of the century—as Constance Keane, not yet Veronica Lake. Possessed of superfine, naturally blonde hair, Connie had to struggle constantly to keep it under control, yet in one rambunctious scene of the Busby Berkeley-directed *Mothers,* it fell across her face and Berkeley liked the effect enough to argue with Cantor to let it stay. It did, but nobody noticed.

While on the lot, Connie was approached by a producer to make a screen test. At first she thought it was just a come-on, but after being assured it wasn't she decided to match the producer's faith and make it. She later admitted that this was when she was truly bitten by the movie star bug. She unwittingly conveyed this feeling to her mother, who went into ecstasies over her daughter's potential as a movie star. But, over the years, the closer the daughter got to what the mother wanted, the farther apart they grew—a perverse dream come true for each.

In any case, the test was not a successful one, and while Connie was disappointed she was also more determined to make acting work for her—despite the fact that the only job offered during that depressing period was from a porno producer. She also became cognizant of a growing desire to be independent. She was a rebel who wanted to be her own person, and she soon found a way to gain that.

In March of 1940, flowers began arriving daily at her home, always accompanied by an unsigned card. Her suspicious mother pounced on this, but Connie had no idea whom they were from until several weeks later, when the phone rang.

The caller introduced himself as John Detlie, an art director at MGM, who had seen her on the lot and was attracted to her. He invited Connie and her mother to lunch with him at the Brown Derby and the girl, barely out of her teens, was enchanted by the successful, thirty-three-year-old man. His attentiveness increased over the next few weeks, with her mother's approval, and gradually Connie found herself falling in love with him, forseeing a life of liberation with John, her knight in shining armor. It was, perhaps, an unrealistic dream, but Connie wasn't living in a realistic society. Hollywood, in those halcyon days, was the dream capital of the world, and if hers couldn't come true, whose could?

At the same time that she was romanticizing over her future, producer Arthur Hornblow, Jr., was taking steps in another direction. Connie's agent had forwarded her screen test to Hornblow for consideration for the female lead in his upcoming *I Wanted Wings,* one of the biggest productions of the year. At the insistance of his secretary, Hornblow looked at the unsuccessful test and saw something there that intrigued him. He called Connie in to make another test. The scene picked for it was set in a small nightclub where Connie was tipsy, sitting at a table. During the test her elbow slipped off the slick surface and her hair tumbled halfway across her face, obscuring one eye. Trying to keep cool, she plunged ahead with the dialogue and threw her head back, but the hair cascaded again. At the end of the test she felt terrible, positive that her hair had ruined her chances for the plum role of Sally Vaughn, the nightclub singer and mantrap. She was frustrated and furious about that "goddamn hair" and didn't even go to see the test when it was run.

Surprisingly, she got a call from Hornblow who asked her to come see him. He told her simply that he thought she had the makings of a movie star, that she projected the necessary aura of sex he was looking for, and that he wanted her for *I Wanted Wings.* It seems that he was intrigued not only by her face and figure but by her hair as well, sensing in it the trademark that could launch a new sex symbol. What Connie had always thought her greatest detriment suddenly became her greatest asset. A new name was soon to follow, calculated to conjure up fantasies and solidify her image of cool, aloof sexuality, Veronica Lake.

Shooting on the film started in the summer of 1940, on location in Texas. It was traumatic for Veronica to leave Hollywood since, by then, she and John Detlie were very much involved. Her feelings of love were mixed with the fact that he also represented independence from her mother, a combination of emotions which made him more important to her than he should have been. A youngster still trying to find herself, now having to tackle the female lead in a large-budgeted, big-star film, she was saddened by the separation, but she welcomed the challenge of stacking her sensuality against the likes of Bill Holden, Brian Donlevy, and Ray Milland. Not that it didn't frighten her; it did. Her youth was no insurance against actors' ego problems, and to protect herself from being overwhelmed and emotionally overpowered, Veronica consciously developed a tough, cocky shell, behind which the real Connie Keane watched the brand new Veronica Lake go through her paces in front of the camera. The toughness was not an endearing quality; she knew that. But she also knew that the first rule of moviemaking was survival. One scene set in a nightclub called for her to face a sound stage full of actors she had done extra-work with, all of them waiting, she felt, to see her fall flat. When she mentioned this fear to an assistant director, he unwittingly gave her advice that she would carry with her throughout her career in Hollywood. "Fuck 'em," he said, and with that in mind she carried off the scene beautifully.

Speaking long-distance from Texas to Hollywood, she became engaged to John Detlie, and almost as soon as she got back to California to complete the shooting of *Wings,* they eloped. She didn't tell a soul—including her mother and the studio—thus starting a pattern of secrecy that would last most of her Hollywood years.

As she tells of it in *Veronica* (Citadel Press), "We spent our wedding night in a local hotel [in Santa Ana, California]. It was probably the most beautiful moment I'd ever known. I possessed a childish pride at coming to this man as a virgin. And I think he shared the pride with me, or at least respected the way I felt." The next morning as they lay in each other's arms he said, "You're on your way to becoming a star, aren't you?"

"I guess so, Pops," she replied. "At least that's the way Arthur Hornblow feels. Does it bother you?"

"No, not at all," he said, but deep inside, Veronica—or Ronnie, as John preferred to call her—knew that it did.

Midway through production, Mitchell Leisen took over as director of *Wings* and came down hard on Veronica as a result of the antagonism she'd unwittingly built up between herself and several other cast members, especially the other female star, Constance Moore. After a particularly upsetting set-to, she left town for three days to join Detlie on the New Mexico location of a film he was working on. When the studio finally tracked her down, they were none too pleased with her, but by now too much of the film had been shot to replace her, and the studio flacks were already churning out pre-publicity for the movie, which strongly featured her. The response the publicity department had been getting back was positive proof of Veronica's appeal so the studio made peace and kept her in *I Wanted Wings*. She went back and finished the picture, but she'd alienated the studio bosses by her absence. As she later said, "I'd established myself in the hearts and minds of Paramount as a temperamental little brat with the arrogance of a nobody."

When the film opened it was a huge success, proving to be a paean not only to the honor and bravery of the Air Corps but to the beauty of Veronica Lake as well. Her character was an unabashed, self-destructive mantrap, and she invested it with all the fire she could kindle. That fire burned brightly almost from the first instant, and overnight Connie Keane became forever Veronica Lake, with the languid lock of hair disturbing not only the symmetry of her features but the psyches of an entire generation of males as well. Billed seventh, Veronica emerged as a star and a Love Goddess.

Reading her own reviews, Veronica asked her Paramount bosses for a modest salary hike—from $75 per week to $1,000. They compromised at $300. The Lake Look swept the nation, with beauty parlors from Maine to Malibu advertising the Veronica Lake hairstyle. That head of hair temporarily took the nation's mind off the simmering troubles in Europe and was reported on about as extensively as the National Budget. Such startling statistics as how many hairs she had (150,000) and the length of these (varying from seventeen inches in front to twenty-four inches in back and falling about eight inches below her shoulder) were broadcast far and wide, especially in the popular bible of the times, *Life* magazine. That head of hair was a sensation and the beauty underneath it undeniable, yet the talent was totally ignored. Harvard's *Lampoon* voted Veronica the Worst Actress of 1941, while Paramount's publicity men thought up new nicknames for the hairdo of the day, including the Detour Coiffure and the Peeping Pompadour.

Veronica was overwhelmed by the flood of publicity but was smart enough to realize that it should be backed up by another picture. Her impatience in getting one wasn't appreciated by the studio heads, who tried to placate her by saying they were looking for just the right role. Preston Sturges approached them to ask for her as the girl in *Sullivan's Travels,* but the bosses didn't want to sacrifice her glamour for a decidedly unglamorous part that also called for comedic ability. Sturges campaigned, though, and finally sold them on the idea, and a delighted Veronica started work on one of the few films of her career that was truly worthwhile. Today *Sullivan's Travels* is considered a classic, the story of a Hollywood movie director who went out and tried to find real life and in doing so was reported dead and ended up in a Southern prison camp. Veronica, as a starlet he met before the odyssey who tried to accompany him on his adventure, was costumed mostly in baggy pants and sweatshirts, her famous hair pulled up into a boy's cap. It was a risk on Paramount's part to let her play the role, but she pulled it off to unanimously excellent reviews.

Midway through shooting, her bosses found out that she was pregnant, and for a time she almost lost the part. Sturges was furious when he heard, but, after doctor's assurances that she'd be okay, Veronica finished the film. She gave birth to her daughter, Elaine, on August 21, 1941.

Elaine was a beautiful baby but was, initially, a source of conflict for the Detlies when Veronica's mother accused John of possibly ruining Veronica's career by getting her pregnant so soon. Veronica expected her husband to defend himself against Mrs. Keane's onslaught. He didn't, and the ensuing argument made him loose the respect of his young wife. Veronica was particularly affected because she believed that she herself had been an unwanted child, and she was determined to bring her daughter into the world with no such clouds over her. The conflict marked a disintegration in the relationships between John and Veronica, and Veronica and her mother.

Career-wise, though, Veronica was about to take a historic step when Paramount decided to put her in a thriller called *This Gun for Hire* opposite a new young actor, Alan Ladd. It was the beginning of one of the most popular screen teamings of the forties, and Ladd and Lake made sparks fly. Although they got along well offscreen, they never had the romance that was bandied about at the time. Ladd was married to Sue Carol, a former actress turned agent who spent her time pushing his career, and Veronica remained faithful to her husband. But they were kindred spirits, and once the cameras got rolling and the rushes started coming in, the studio heads became conscious of the sexual tension between them on film. And they knew what that could mean at the box office.

At the time production started, *This Gun for Hire* wasn't considered to be much more than an average thriller, but the reception it got from the public made Ladd, and cemented Lake—even though she herself thought it a bit of a formula comedown after her acting success in *Sullivan's Travels*. Again she was a sexy nightclub singer, blonde hair tumbling over her right eye, only this time she was required to do a magic act along with the warbling. That pivotal scene was shot a total of sixty-four times, and take four was the one ultimately used. It opened in the fall of 1942 to mixed reviews but outstanding public acceptance. Today, like *Sullivan's Travels,* it is regarded as a classic of its kind.

So pleased was Paramount that they immediately came up with another vehicle for their new dynamic duo—Dashiell Hammett's *The Glass Key*. Again it was a sexy Veronica that was called for, and she gave it to them. And again it was a hit.

Professionally Veronica was on the way up, but at home it was a different story. John Detlie had married Connie Keane and was finding it increasingly difficult to accept Veronica Lake as his wife. The classic "Good evening, Miss Lake . . . uh . . . Mr. Lake" began happening, and Detlie didn't like it. After carving out his own successful career, and being considerably older than Veronica, he couldn't accept or verbalize his discontent, and the seeds of discord were sown. Another factor was that Veronica was earning more money than her husband, and she delighted in spending it. Everything happened so quickly for her that she felt compelled to keep proving her success, and money was the most tangible proof of it.

After the sizzling sex appeal of Ladd and Lake, Ronnie wanted a change of pace and, again, campaigned vigorously to get the lead in René Clair's *I Married a Witch*. The Frenchman was leery at first, seeing her only as a sexy blonde, but after the first rushes were in, Clair apologized. That movie was another smash hit, but the filming of it was complicated by Veronica's intense dislike for her leading man, Frederic March. From the first there was an innate antagonism between the pair that only deepened as shooting progressed. Veronica, the Brooklyn-born tyro, gave as good as she got; according to her memoirs, one day she had weights sewn into her dress so that when March had to lift her up for one scene, he could barely budge her. When he commented to her later on how much such a tiny woman weighed, she sighed and said, "Big bones." March eventually heard the truth, and he was furious.

Meantime, without telling his wife, Detlie joined the army and was granted a commission as a major with the Camouflage Department District Engineer's office at Fort Lewis in Seattle. He calmly announced over dinner one night that they would all be moving there shortly. Veronica was hurt and angry over his secrecy but, after calming down, agreed to go with him, and they made the move. They were not the typical army family, though, as Veronica's presence in camp was a sensation, and, while Detlie was determined that they live on his salary, she wasn't. They argued over money constantly. They also argued when Veronica accepted an offer to go on a bond-selling trip to New York. John was angered by her acceptance, but she countered by saying that she had every right to do something for her country, just as he had, and went anyway.

When she was barely back, their relationship suffered another jolt when she told him she was returning to Hollywood to star in *So Proudly We Hail,* along with Claudette Colbert, Paulette Goddard, and Sonny Tufts. In the drama of the valiant nurses who served on Bataan and Corregidor, Ronnie was set to play Olivia D'Arcy, a bigot who went to her death clutching a hand grenade as she walked into a Japanese nest. It was a gripping scene, one of her most remembered, and she was justly proud of it and the film as well.

Weekends she'd commute to Seattle, but by now quarrels were a constant part of the Detlies' lives. Shortly after finishing *So Proudly We Hail* she found out she was pregnant again and, at first, was afraid to tell her husband. When she did, he took the news stonily, but Veronica brightened, thinking that another child might help mend their breaking marriage. Before the baby came she was able to squeeze in the filming of *The Hour Before Dawn,* but on the last day of shooting she tripped over a cable on the set and suffered severe hemorrhaging. Her doctors assured her that it wouldn't hurt the baby, but it did. When he was born in July of 1943 there were complications which quickly developed into uremic poisoning. The baby boy, William Anthony, never had a chance, and when Veronica called her husband and begged him to come to them, he refused, stating that he was too busy to get away. The baby died on July 15, seven days after his birth; for Veronica, her marriage died that day, too. Detlie later told her that he didn't believe the baby was his. He and Veronica were divorced the following December.

Personally Veronica was in a state of turmoil but professionally, at least on the surface, she was riding high. The army had voted her their favorite actress and *Life* named her the top female box-office star. These were only blinds, though, because Paramount would soon start putting her into a series of formula movies that capitalized on the Lake Look, but little else. The long slide down had begun, but luckily, she didn't know it at the time. What she did know was that she was free and a beautiful movie star, and after her divorce she decided to have some fun for a change. Hollywood during the war years was a golden playground, and Veronica decided it was time to try a few of the rides.

She was a friend of Howard Hughes; Errol Flynn made a pass at her at a party; and she dated men like director Jean Negulesco and millionaire Aristotle Onassis. She even began entertaining in her own fashion, hostessing kitchen parties at which the biggest female names in town would don aprons and help serve food and drink to guests. The movie magazines had several layouts of Veronica's parties, the rebel in the kitchen pouring scotch while Paulette Goddard labored over a tray of pastries.

Tommy Manville, the madcap marrying millionaire, telegrammed a proposal that included a $100,000 offer—if Veronica would become his wife for three days. She later said that by then she had been almost tempted to take him up on it if it hadn't been for her daughter, Elaine, since her financial situation, complicated by enormous hospital bills from the preceding year, was precarious. Her studio contract was still paying her only $350 per week, and, oddly, her bosses hadn't been coming up with any scripts despite her popularity. The only film she appeared in that year was *Star Spangled Rhythm,* in a cameo part in which she sang the campy "Sweater, Sarong, and a Peek-a-Boo Bang" in a skit with Dorothy Lamour and Paulette Goddard.

As the months stretched out she was becoming increasingly frightened by her inactivity. Things were so bad at one point that she had to leave her house and move in with Rita Beery, Wallace's ex-wife, in an effort to conserve cash.

When the studio finally did come up with a property, she grabbed it, sensing they wouldn't put up with any displays of temperament. More important, she needed the money. It was a Technicolor musical with Sonny Tufts and Marjorie Reynolds called *Bring On the Girls,* also starring Eddie Bracken, with whom Veronica would co-star again in a series of unsophisticated, unfunny comedies. The studio heads had decided what they thought Veronica could do best—be blonde and sexy. As long as it proved profitable for them, that's what they would give the public.

Ronnie's attention was deflected from her career by a hectic love affair with eccentric Hungarian director Andre DeToth, whom she met when he tried—and failed—to get her for a picture. In *Veronica* she described her feelings for him. "He was a charming guy, not unusual for a Hungarian, but overwhelming to me. I'd never been close to a Hungarian before. Had I, I would have known that along with their charm, they're also very childlike, and, in many cases, sadistic." Andre, called Bandi (pronounced Bundy), and Veronica shortly became a very hot gossip item, and they married as soon as her divorce from John Detlie was finalized in December of 1944. DeToth adopted Elaine and the new family settled on a farm in Chatsworth, California.

After an appearance in *Duffy's Tavern,* another all-star musical, and the lead in the innocuous *Hold That Blonde,* again with Eddie Bracken, Veronica began to see the writing on the wall as far as the flexibility of her career was concerned. And it was a very short sentence. Unfortunately her antagonism toward the studio's handling of her career was affecting her performance. She began walking through her roles with little enthusiasm (almost sleepwalking, said several critics), and her fans began pulling away. A former Paramount mailboy remembers during this period that fans would mail in letters enclosing a quarter for an autographed picture. While Alan Ladd kept several secretaries busy faithfully answering those letters and sending out photos, Veronica would sit in her dressing room calmly ripping the corners off hers, shaking the change into a large purse and then throwing the letters away. These people, who had taken the time to write, were permanently alienated.

On the set she began ruffling feathers with her obvious boredom. During the shooting of *Miss Susie Slagle's* in 1945, she was so tired of it all that she blew her lines, said so, and then added, "Why don't we all break and go to the beach?" in the same monotone, so that the camera kept rolling and no one noticed for almost a full minute. Such behavior was not only unprofessional but costly to the studio as well.

She later said that her personal problems kept her mind off her career, but the damage was being done nonetheless, despite her filming activity. Unlike Detlie, DeToth never simmered inside when he was accidentally called "Mr. Lake." He let his anger out, and usually in his wife's direction. When she soon became pregnant, DeToth was obsessed with having a boy, resenting Elaine's beauty and wanting no comparison with a daughter of his—as if Veronica had any control over the situation! They did have a boy, Andre Anthony Michael DeToth, III, whom Veronica instantly nicknamed Mike.

Inexplicably Veronica and the baby didn't get along well. (In her memoirs, she stated that she never really liked the child.) While he was handsome, she later said, "There was a look in his eyes that was frightening to me at times. . . . It was something at odds with itself, a tension threatening to ulcerate and upset the balance of things."

About this time she began her fifth film of 1945, yet another Eddie Bracken musical, *Out of This World.* Veronica was making more money now than ever. Still living at her Chatsworth farm, surrounded by her children and animals, she tried to mask the growing discontent over her career. DeToth assured her that he was looking for just the right part for her, which partially soothed her.

Mike was four months old when Howard Hughes invited Veronica and Bandi to join him on the inaugural flight of his TWA's coast-to-coast service, along with a raft of other stars including Cary Grant, Paulette Goddard, Walter Pidgeon, the William Powells, and the Tyrone Powers. It was a headlined affair, but Bandi managed to make even more headlines after they'd landed in New York. One night at the Stork Club a young man reached out to touch Veronica's hair and DeToth pounced on him and beat him savagely. Sherman Billingsley, boniface of the famed watering hole, threw him out and told him never to come back. It was a messy scene, duly reported by Walter Winchell, at whose table the couple had been sitting just before the incident occurred.

DeToth was a man who didn't care about bad publicity and who also had a supreme disregard for money. Financial worries started stacking up early in their marriage and were one reason Veronica never openly fought with Paramount for better roles. She didn't dare risk a suspension, and her husband's career was not a major one. His temper intruded itself into his work during the forties, and he lost several films because of it. Even these career problems didn't make him listen to his wife's pleas to curtail his spending, and she, out of a misplaced sense of duty, tried to go along with him, even buying him a private plane in 1947 for Valentine's Day. They both took flying lessons and got pilots' licenses, and Veronica would often try to escape her earthbound troubles by solo flights into the blue.

She had bought the plane with the proceeds from the first film her husband directed her in, *Ramrod*, a western and Veronica's first film as a star away from the Paramount lot. Co-starred were Joel McCrea and Preston Foster, with Veronica—hair tied back—playing ranch owner Charlie Ruggles's fiery daughter embroiled in a range dispute. It was a modest success but hardly giant box office.

During its shooting, her stepfather, Hugh Keane, died, causing Veronica both great sadness and trepidation. During his life Keane had been largely responsible for keeping his wife off his stepdaughter's back. Without his placating presence, Veronica feared her mother might try to intrude in her life again, and she was soon to be proven right.

DeToth's habit of spending money increased, with frequent trips abroad on which he refused to take his wife. It was just as well, too, since Paramount called her back for a screen reunion with Alan Ladd in *The Blue Dahlia*, an excellent murder story that briefly rekindled her career. Back in slinky gowns with that wayward hair, Veronica was quite good as hoodlum Howard DaSylva's wife. The picture did very well. Warners had their Bogart and Bacall, and Paramount had their Ladd and Lake, and immediately they shopped around for another picture in which to pair them. This time, though, the scriptwriters were off-center, and the result was *Saigon*. Said Ladd to Lake across the movie ads—"There's nothing cold about you . . . except the gun in your hand." Her reply: "You're too much a man . . . ever to be trusted." Unfortunately the public's trust was faltering too, and the result was a minor effort. It was the last time Ladd and Lake would light up the credits together until television resurrected them on "The Late Show."

After finishing *The Sainted Sisters* with Joan Caulfield, Ronnie found out she was pregnant again. Bandi was pleased but Veronica sank into a minor depression as she looked at a desk top covered with unpaid bills, a situation hardly amenable to the peace of mind she needed. He shortly left for Europe while Veronica tried to bring some money into the house, managing a celebrity bit in *Variety Girl* and signing for *Isn't It Romantic?* to be made after her baby was born.

Because of the state of her nerves, Veronica was confined to the hospital for the two weeks before the baby was due, but her rest was shortlived when reporters started battering on her door with the incredible news that her mother was suing her "for lack of filial love and responsibility." It seems that back in 1943, when she was still married to Detlie, Veronica had made a verbal agreement with her mother to support her and her stepfather for the rest of their lives to the tune of $200 a week. Veronica stuck to it until May of 1948, when her own financial condition made it impossible. Mrs. Keane stated loud and clear that she had sacrificed much, indeed her life savings, to get Veronica's career launched in the acting school, and asked for $17,416 in back payments as well as upping future payments to $500 a week. Veronica's reaction, according to the *New York Daily News* headlines? FILM STAR IN TEARS AS MOTHER SUES.

And indeed she was hysterical over the resurrection of this old dispute. Mrs. Keane had said she was "destitute, indigent, dependent on the charity of others" while her daughter made $4,500 per week. She also named DeToth for "aiding Miss Lake in evading her responsibility." Bandi countered that in the years he'd been married to Veronica, he'd never even met her mother. When Veronica got her emotions under control she admitted to reporters that she hadn't been living up to the verbal agreement because "I'm only supporting my grandmother, my mother-in-law, two children, a nurse, and the servants. And now another baby's due momentarily. I feel awful that a mother and daughter should have this sort of relationship. But I don't want to live my life under a threat."

Ultimately Veronica was advised to make a settlement on her mother to avoid further nasty publicity, and once she did so the feud between mother and daughter was over. Mrs. Keane had indeed spurred her daughter on to a career, but the career never quite lived up to Veronica's expectations. Unreasonably perhaps, she held her mother to blame.

The DeToths' baby daughter Diana was born four days after the headlines, on October 16th, but the child didn't do much toward salvaging the rapidly failing marriage. In the ensuing months Veronica desperately turned to alcohol in an effort to avoid the family problems piling up. It was Bandi who, surprisingly, found a partial solution at Twentieth Century Fox when he got to direct *Slattery's Hurricane* and took Veronica along to star with Linda Darnell and Richard Widmark. It was the best thing that could have happened just then since Paramount had dropped Veronica after *Isn't It Romantic?* The changing times, the end of the movies' Golden Era, and the studio's poor choice of pictures had all added up to diminishing her stature as a valuable property. *Slattery's Hurricane* was a well-intended tribute to hurricane spotters, but despite on-location shooting in Florida, a rarity in those days, it was only a modest success and only a temporary stopgap to the DeToths' troubles.

As creditors began demanding payment of their bills, Veronica became even more desperate. Bandi ignored the money problems and went off to Europe, leaving a frantic wife behind, ever more reliant on a bottle to give her the strength to fight off bill collectors. "I soon found myself spending half of each day pleading, threatening or combining tactics. It was a degrading experience, especially because it was unnecessary. It lasted two years. I did nothing. I didn't try to do anything. No pushing back. No asking why I was no longer in favor with Hollywood. Just a long spiral down into a bottomless well, the only buoy a bottle—of scotch."

In New York to appear on Sid Caesar's *Show of Shows,* Veronica made several stops, including Cartier's, where she began selling off her jewelry in an attempt to keep the household afloat. DeToth was in Europe when a movie offer did come through to go to Mexico for a "B" grade film called *Stronghold.* She grabbed it— "It was a dog but the pay was decent." An amusing thing happened there during shooting when she attended a bullfight one day and was seated in the president's box. "I was all done up in a beautifully tailored red suit with gold hat and shoes.

136

And the Mexicans started shouting 'Veronica! Veronica!' So, naturally, I got up and took bows. I didn't know that they were shouting for the matador to execute a turn called a Veronica.'' That was about the only funny thing that did happen though, for Bandi soon showed up on the set, and they argued long and loud over her cheapening herself by starring in such a low-budget effort. But the arguments were academic because by then the marriage was in ruins. Once they returned home, early in 1951, they had to declare bankruptcy after the IRS seized their house for back taxes.

That act marked the end of Veronica Lake the Love Goddess. Her career, which had started out so gloriously in *I Wanted Wings,* now ground to a halt, smothered in a mountain of unpaid bills and bad publicity. The DeToths officially separated in June, 1951. After that was made public Veronica claimed that picture offers did come in, albeit minor ones, but by then she was thoroughly disenchanted with the town and the people in it, who had typecast her as a siren and

Veronica at the end of her movie career in Slattery's Hurricane *(1949), directed by her husband, Andre DeToth. With John Russell* (right) *and Richard Widmark.* THE DOUG MC CLELLAND COLLECTION.

then never gave her a chance to prove otherwise. She was, whether willing to admit it or not, an artifact of the war years, and the combination of studio negligence and public disavowal had made her as obsolete as a B–29.

She decided to leave Hollywood once and for all. "As I stood ready to board the plane [I said] 'the Hell with you Hollywood. And fuck you too.' " She returned only twice: once to pick up her final divorce papers the following year, and again in 1968 to publicize her memoirs. The ensuing years were difficult once, and for many of them the public neither knew nor seemed to care what had happened to the Peek-a-Boo Blonde who'd sizzled briefly during the dark days of World War II.

She settled in New York's Greenwich Village with her children and for a time did television work there. But the impact of her name on that medium quickly wore thin and she took to the stage, touring in plays like *The Voice of the Turtle* and *Peter Pan*. The children suffered because of her constant traveling and were shuttled back and forth between their father in California and their mother in New York, something she regretted but couldn't avoid. To make ends meet she had to work constantly in out-of-the-way summer stock theaters up and down the eastern seaboard. It was gruelling and a far cry from her pampered days at Paramount, but she suffered with inexperienced actors and undertrained stagehands in an effort to carve out a new career. For a few years she almost succeeded.

In 1955 she briefly made news when she remarried, this time to songwriter Joe McCarthy, in Traverse City, Michigan, where she was appearing in *Affairs of State*. Theirs was a New York romance, though. That city's energy seemed beneficial to her. They had a brownstone on Ninth Street in Greenwich Village, and shortly after the wedding they were joined by her children. The first months of their marriage were spent pub-crawling around Manhattan, and it wasn't long before they both realized that marriage had been a hasty decision. McCarthy resented having the children underfoot all the time; "the only time there was any peace was when we would make a tour of the joints and drink ourselves into a happy but temporary truce. The alcoholic appeasement was fine until the resulting hangovers made things even worse."

The marriage lingered on until 1959, about three and a half years. The last year and a half were spent apart, with the final separation coming after a knock-down argument during which McCarthy kicked Veronica in the back when she tried to use the telephone, and her son, Mike, intervened with a kitchen knife. They both ran out of the house, the fourteen-year-old chasing his stepfather, while Veronica dragged herself back to the phone and called the police. A judge issued a warrant against McCarthy for assault, an action Veronica dropped a few days later when the court ordered McCarthy to stay away from his wife. They filed for a legal separation and the marriage was over.

However, Michael's antics with his friends, including some free-style wood-carving on the dining room walls, resulted in the family's being evicted from the Ninth Street house shortly after that—on twenty-four hours' notice. The girls were in California at the time so she and her son moved in with a friend. Offered a role in a Chicago stage production, mother and son flew out. But Michael soon got in trouble with the police, and an exasperated Veronica sent him back to Andre— only to have Andre ship him back to New York on the first plane. The youngster crossed the country two and a half times in twenty-four hours and never left an airport other than on a plane.

Veronica tried to put some order into the boy's life by scraping together the money for a private school in Connecticut while she looked for a new apartment in New York. All this was complicated by a badly broken ankle suffered at a boisterous party in Queens, when her dancing partner stumbled and they fell to the floor. This required that she spend the next eight months in various casts. "Days on end crawled by me as I spent them dragging myself from the tiny bedroom to the tiny living room at a snail's pace. I had no way of knowing whether my ankle was healing properly. But my biggest concern was over the financial plight I once again found myself facing. There wasn't a cent, the generosity of a few friends buying the groceries and paying the light bill." The accident halted Veronica's stage work completely, and she suffered from a limp for a while after the casts were removed.

The nadir of her life came in 1961. When she was finally able to look for work, the best she could find was a job in a small South Broadway factory pasting felt flowers on lingerie hangers. "When I wasn't pasting flowers, I was pub-crawling around New York with this friend or that friend."

But Hollywood's one-time Cinderella Girl found the factory job thankless and boring, and soon she moved on. In desperate straits again financially, she moved into the Martha Washington Hotel for Women on East 29th Street and applied for a job as a barmaid to pay her rent. She was hired; soon she found herself enjoying her work. The bartenders and the clients liked her, too. Gradually they found out who she was, and when an old movie, a Ladd and Lake scorcher or *I Married a Witch* lit up the television set behind the bar, you could hear a pin drop as the customers swiveled their gaze between the screen goddess and the tiny woman serving them drinks.

After several months, a *New York Post* reporter heard about her being there and went to see for himself, rushing to the telephone breathless with the news that Veronica Lake had been found. Her discovery brought forth a flood of publicity similar to that which Frances Farmer had been accorded a few years earlier when she'd been found in a San Francisco hotel, and instantly the Peek-a-Boo Blonde was news again, and the sob sisters had a field day. At first Veronica was embarrassed by the publicity and tried to explain away her presence there by saying, "I was just filling in for a friend for a few days." Later, in her memoirs, she frankly admitted that she did it for the money. And, ironically, money was what came pouring in once the story broke—from as far away as Japan, where people remembered the pint-sized siren and took pity on her.

"The notes were so sweet and touching," she told the *New York Morning Telegraph*, "and a great many enclosed money, everything from a dollar to ten pounds. It was so heartwarming to know that anybody cared. Of course I had to return all the money. I still have some pride.'' She later declared that one thing she did leave the bar with was a thorough knowledge of mixing drinks, a talent she confessed to exercising often.

Another thing she left with was a new love, a Wisconsin merchant seaman named Andy Elickson. They met one night when Veronica had been instructed to show a boisterous party the door—which included Andy. He showed up later that night, near closing time, and sheepishly took a table in a far corner. Over six feet tall and about 240 pounds, he had the weathered look of a man who faced the elements as part of his regular routine, and she was immediately attracted to him. No Hollywood pretty boy or egomaniac here, ''but as handsome as men should be.''

Later, over fried clams and coffee at an all-night café, he asked her if she'd always been a waitress. ''Nope,'' she replied. ''I was a movie star.'' Somehow he'd never heard of Veronica Lake, and she liked him all the more for it. Since he was separated from his wife but not divorced, the unlikely twosome never spoke of marriage but grasped the happiness they found in each other and appreciated it all the more.

She left the hotel job in April of 1962 and spent some time with Elickson before he had to put out to sea. That October she was offered the job as hostess on the ''Festival of Stars'' television program in Baltimore, introducing old movies and commenting on the Hollywood she'd known. ''Isn't it wonderful? For years all my friends tried to shut me up, and now somebody is paying me to talk!'' The only Lake film station WJZ-TV owned the rights to was *I Married a Witch,* and the night it was shown Veronica ended the program by naming the entire cast, giving her own name last and then, believing the microphone was off, added, ''Whatever happened to her?'' Many viewers watching the tiny lady with the short reddish hair were quick to let her know. The old image of Veronica Lake was undeniably gone, ''but she has the same charm and the same sexy voice,'' a station spokesman said, ''and it's a very popular show.''

During this time Veronica was approached by a firm called State-Wide Restaurants to lend her name to an investment scheme, as president of the firm, no less, which purported to be buying up the option on a hotel and entering the trading stamp business. She was flattered by the offer and for a brief moment thought the idea might bring her some elusive wealth. She quickly became suspicious of the operation, though, and bowed out—just before New York State Attorney General Louis J. Lefkowitz started an investigation that showed it was a bogus business. He called Veronica a dupe and no charges were filed against her. She never made a dime out of it.

Andy Elickson came back from sea, and they picked up where they'd left off. She wanted to be with him so badly, in fact, that she shipped out with him on a brief trip from Tampa, Florida, to Port Arthur, Texas, stowing away from customs inspectors by hiding under a bed in the sick bay. When she got back home Veronica applied for, took tests, and received a merchant marine Z card, vowing that one day she'd use it to work aboard a ship.

Those plans were curtailed, though, in the summer of 1963 when New York newspapers announced she was taking over the lead in the off-Broadway revival of *Best Foot Forward*—as Gale Joy, aging movie queen trying for a comeback. The part hit close to the bone, but she gladly accepted it—her first appearance ever in New York City—and opened on a hot night in late August. I remember sitting in the audience feeling the sense of trepidation that heightened before her entrance, as if the audience didn't really believe she'd be there and, if she was, be able to pull off the performance. The role required singing, dancing, and being thrown around a lot by the chorus boys—all of which she gamely did quite well. Old stills from the forties decorated the stage set of the high school gym, somewhat unkind reminders that much time and travail had gone by between those carefully lit studio sittings and the harshly lit present. At one point she kidded herself with a mocking look over her shoulder at one particularly sultry photo and then turned a "who's she?" look at the audience. She seemed scared as she made her entrance, but the enthusiasm of the audience and the cast members quickly soothed her into an entertaining performance—although even her most die-hard gay fans, of whom there were many in the audience, could find little to remind them of the screen image she'd left behind in Hollywood twelve years before. The press gave her generally favorable notices, sidestepping her faded looks in favor of the energy she so obviously put into the production.

After a few months in the role, Veronica returned to Baltimore and her television chores, flying out weekends to the various ports where Andy would put in. The romance was the most important thing in her life and she worked primarily to finance her flights back and forth. During one of Andy's trips away, in 1964, Alan Ladd died, and to Veronica "it was like losing a piece of jewelry you never wore but enjoyed every time you opened the jewel case."

Once the TV series was over Veronica dropped out of sight for a few years, resurfacing in some unsavory headlines in April of 1965, having been arrested for drunkenness after pounding on the rectory door of St. Mary's Cathedral in Galveston. She had gone there to be with Andy, and once he had sailed she was overcome with loneliness, drinking alone in a waterfront bar. The combination of drink and emotions triggered a longing for the religion she'd abandoned in her youth, and she ran from the bar yelling into the night. When she found the church it was locked for the night, but she noticed the glimmer of light coming from the rectory next door. In desperate need of consolation, she flailed away at the door with all the strength her 100-pound body could muster. Instead of finding solace, however, she was arrested and spent the night in jail. The next morning she paid the twenty-five-dollar fine and was released, telling reporters, "I was sitting around and got to feeling sorry for myself and so I went to the rectory of Father O'Connell. I just wanted to talk to him."

Andy came and went again but when she saw him in February of 1966 in New York there was a great change in him. He was ill with severe disorders of the liver, spleen, kidneys, and bladder. His legs were beginning to swell from water retention, but he wouldn't be hospitalized and also wouldn't stop the drinking that aggravated his condition. Veronica—or Connie, as Andy called her—realized the seriousness of the situation but couldn't convince him to get hospital attention. Guiltily she would slip into the kitchen for a waterglass of scotch and a handful of Clorets to help her cope, and while she was doing that, he was doing the same in the living room.

He refused the idea of surgery and grew progressively worse until finally his family had to be called. They deeply resented his affair with the former movie star, and even as his condition deteriorated Veronica and family members argued back and forth. Finally he had to be taken to a navy hospital on Staten Island, where Veronica was assured she'd be called if the situation became hopeless. "I kissed Andy on the forehead and squeezed his hand before I left. He looked straight into my eyes and smiled. 'You're a good mate, little girl. Damned good. We'll sail together again.'" Those were his last words to her. He died the following day, and his family had his body shipped back to Wisconsin before Veronica could say a final goodbye. When she called there and was advised when the funeral would be, she sent one white rose asking that it be put in his casket. But the flower arrived too late; "He was buried the day before. He took nothing of mine with him. Nothing."

Andy's death left Veronica totally alone. Estranged from her family (by now she was a grandmother three times over via daughter Elaine), she fell back on the only person she could—herself. She moved to Miami and did some theater there, minor comedies like *Goodbye, Charlie,* and tried to piece together a life for herself that included a large group of homosexuals who more or less adopted her. To them the glamour of Veronica Lake was a very live and vibrant thing, and she responded gratefully to their unalloyed affection. She entertained them in her small apartment and played pool with them in local bars. To them she was a movie queen, and hard times couldn't take away that glamour—every *Late Show* was like watching the Phoenix rise—and they never complained about the ashes.

Drinking a lot, Veronica watched television—"'Bonanza' is great and Marshall Dillon really turns me on"—and when she had the money visited friends in New York or the Bahamas. Her relationship with her son, Mike, remained tenuous at best. They simply didn't understand each other or get along, always uneasy in each other's company. She felt he used his famous parents as a crutch against facing up to life, admitting that "his failings are the result of my failings, his father's failings, our combined failings . . . and as guilty as I may be in his upbringing I do wish he'd throw away the crutch."

In 1966 Veronica was offered the starring role in a Canadian movie called *Footsteps in the Snow* and journeyed there to play in the minor film about ski bums and dope dealers. She was paid $10,000 and left without even seeing the rushes. Today it's virtually a lost film, playing, if at all, during TV's insomniac hours of early dawn.

Her second comeback attempt was drastically worse, a Florida-produced horror film originally called *Time Is Terror* and briefly released as *Flesh Feast*. If ever a movie queen suffered a terminal comedown, this was it. In the movie,

Adolf Hitler, alive and well and desiring to return to Germany, consulted a mysterious lady doctor (Veronica) who had a special technique for altering faces—by letting maggots eat them away. The advertising campaign used adjectives like "revolting," "ghastly," "grisly," and "nauseating"—all of which were deservedly applied to the feature presented in "morbid, vivid color." Whereas aging stars like Bette Davis and Joan Crawford had found new leases on tired careers in horror films, there was none of lower quality than Veronica's try at the genre. Filmed by amateurs, it was released in England sometime in 1970, but to the author's knowledge it has never seen the light of an American screen, on television or elsewhere.

While filming it Veronica worked on her memoirs, with Donald Bain, which were published initially in England and then here. Reviews about the ghostwritten book were kind, *The New York Times* mentioning in particular her flashes of "guttersnipe humor," citing as an example her marriage to Bandi DeToth "after a courtship that included such scenes as his belting me in the mouth and then offering me a carving knife with which to cut out his unworthy heart. I didn't accept the invitation. I made a lot of mistakes in my life."

The book proved a boon for Veronica. It sold well and also brought her back to Hollywood where she was welcomed by Rona Barrett and the rest of the press with considerable, if somewhat detached, warmth. They knew her name, but eighteen years was a long time between pictures.

Early in 1969 she went to England and by mid-July was established there, even hustling up a starring role in a play called *Madame Chairman* shortly after Betty Grable had made a West End stab at success in a musical called *Belle Starr*. One critic huffed about the "invasion of blonde matrons from Hollywood," but that didn't deter Veronica from trying to pull off a hit with the meagerly scripted comedy about a widow who assumed control of her late husband's corporation.

It opened in Brighton and shortly thereafter the theater was bombarded with television news crews from as far away as Sweden, all there to interview the former siren. "How did I get here?" she repeated in reply to journalist Bill Gale's question. "I came to England in January to promote my autobiography, *Veronica*, I appeared on a TV interview show, and somebody saw me and decided I'd be good for the lead in this play—and here I am. That's the way things happen to me. Two years ago I went to Freeport in the Bahamas to visit a friend and ended up living there. Came to England for a couple of weeks and now I'm touring in a play."

Her good humor slackened a bit when the subject of her children was broached. "I seldom see them. Elaine, the eldest, is married to a New York advertising man and has three children and, I suppose, lives the good life. Diane, the baby, works as a secretary for the American Embassy in Rome. She's doing very well. And Mike, the last I heard, was living somewhere in upstate New York."

Veronica knew that her starring vehicle was a creaky one but insisted that she wanted it to come into London "with dignity. . . . I'm rewriting the script every day and paying a stenographer out of my own pocket to type the changes so these kids will have time to learn their new lines. You don't know how many times I've wanted to walk out on this show, but I couldn't jeopardize the jobs of ten other actors." Unfortunately her changes couldn't save the production, and after a limited tour it wheezed its last in the provinces, with London still a long way off.

Veronica liked England and her acceptance there, and she settled into a small flat in Ipswich, an hour and a half outside London. She returned to the stage in a revival of *A Streetcar Named Desire* opposite former American TV star Ty "Bronco Lane" Hardin and won respectable reviews for her portrayal of the tormented Blanche Dubois.

On a brief return to New York to promote her book she expanded on the image that made her famous, referring to one book reviewer's reference to her as a sex zombie rather than symbol. "That really names me properly. I was laughing at everybody in all my portraits. I never took that stuff seriously. I will have one of the cleanest obits of any actress. I never did cheesecake like Ann Sheridan or Betty Grable.* I just used my hair." At fifty-one there was little to remind interviewers of her former beauty, but she laughed that away, too—"I earned this face."

She also mentioned possibly writing a cookbook, but said, "It will not specialize in a thousand chocolate chip recipes or what to do with leftover potato chips. It will be simple and fraught with easy dishes to whip up when you're drunk or hungover or both."

In the spring of 1972, she surprised her Florida friends by showing up with an Englishman, Robert Carlton-Munro, whom she soon married. They returned to England, but it wasn't long before these same friends heard from her that the marriage had been a mistake. Drinking bouts and fights had started almost as soon as the wedding ceremony was over, and Veronica decided that she needed to come back home for a while to think things out.

By now her drinking had taken a drastic toll on her health, and during a visit to friends in Burlington, Vermont, on June 26, 1973, she was hospitalized for acute hepatitis. A longtime friend, Bill Roos, was there and in a matter of days knew that the situation was terribly serious. In fact, Veronica Lake never left the hospital alive. She died there on July 7, at the age of fifty-three. "You know, she never thought she was dying," Roos said later. "In the last days she was in the best mood I've seen her in for years. She was turning her life around."

Tragically for Veronica the turning point came too late. Her past caught up with her in that small-town hospital, and yet out of the tragedy appeared the least likely person to mourn her: Mike.

A construction worker in Hawaii at the time, he heard of his mother's death over the radio. He anxiously contacted his father to borrow money to fly east and claim his mother's body, but DeToth turned him down, according to a story in

---

*The studio heads thought her legs were too skinny for that type of publicity.

Veronica in her peaceful English garden in 1970.   LONDON DAILY EXPRESS.

the *National Enquirer.* "He called me some obscene names for even bothering him. He said he'd never gone to his mother's funeral; why should I go to mine?"

Naturally bitter, the twenty-seven-year-old was able to borrow $500 from the local radio station to fly to Vermont to arrange for the cremation his mother wanted, and then to New York for the funeral. His long hair was pulled back in a ponytail, and he was dressed in the casual pants and striped T-shirt he was wearing when he hastily left Hawaii with his eighteen-year-old wife. He sat through the New York service in an apparent daze. He later told reporters of his bitterness, not only against his father "but at all those so-called Hollywood friends who fluttered around my mother when she was a star. None of them turned up at the funeral. None of them sent any flowers. Her four husbands, her two daughters . . . none of them came. I was full of anger as I sat in that little chapel. It was as though nobody cared. She died a lonely and forgotten woman. When I saw my mother's body at the hospital morgue I was heartbroken. She looked so small and lonely."

It had been a five-year estrangement since he last saw her, and seeing her now was heartbreaking. Only thirty mourners showed up for the funeral at the Universal Chapel on East 52nd Street. Veronica had walked out on Hollywood, and at her death few turned out to bid her goodbye. She was a woman who chose to live her life her own way. Once when she was being questioned about her brief career and subsequent tragedies, she announced that she wouldn't have changed any of it—otherwise, "how would I have learned to be a person?"

Her ashes were taken to the Virgin Islands and scattered over the sea that Andy had taught her to love, a fitting resting place for a free spirit who never felt at home in Hollywood or on her pedestal as a Love Goddess.

FILMOGRAPHY
Veronica Lake

TITLE	YEAR	DIRECTOR	LEADING PLAYERS
		(As Constance Keane)	
All Women Have Secrets	1939	Kurt Newmann	Virginia Dale, Jeanne Cagney
Sorority House	1939	John Farrow	Anne Shirley, James Ellison, Barbara Read
Forty Little Mothers	1940	Busby Berkeley	Eddie Cantor, Judith Anderson, Ralph Morgan, Rita Johnson, Bonita Granville
		(As Veronica Lake)	
I Wanted Wings	1941	Mitchell Leisen	Ray Milland, William Holden, Wayne Morris, Brian Donlevy

TITLE	YEAR	DIRECTOR	LEADING PLAYERS
Sullivan's Travels	1941	Preston Sturges	Joel McCrea, Robert Warwick, Franklin Pangborn, William Demarest
This Gun for Hire	1942	Frank Tuttle	Alan Ladd, Robert Preston, Laird Cregar
The Glass Key	1942	Stuart Heisler	Alan Ladd, Brian Donlevy, William Bendix, Bonita Granville
I Married a Witch	1943	René Clair	Frederic March, Cecil Kellaway, Susan Hayward, Robert Benchley, Elizabeth Patterson
Star Spangled Rhythm	1942	George Marshall	An all-star Paramount musical featuring every star on the lot
So Proudly We Hail	1942	Mark Sandrich	Claudette Colbert, Paulette Goddard, Sonny Tufts, George Reeves, Barbara Britton
The Hour Before the Dawn	1944	Frank Tuttle	Franchot Tone, John Sutton, Binnie Barnes
Bring on the Girls	1945	Sidney Lanfield	Eddie Bracken, Sonny Tufts, Marjorie Reynolds
Out of This World	1945	Hal Walker	Eddie Bracken, Diana Lynn, Cass Daley, Florence Bates
Duffy's Tavern	1945	Hal Walker	Barry Sullivan, Bing Crosby, Marjorie Reynolds, Dorothy Lamour, Alan Ladd, Betty Hutton, Robert Benchley, Paulette Goddard, Brian Donlevy
Hold That Blonde	1945	George Marshall	Eddie Bracken, Albert Dekker, George Zucco
Miss Susie Slagle's	1945	John Berry	Sonny Tufts, Joan Caulfield, Lillian Gish, Ray Collins
The Blue Dahlia	1946	George Marshall	Alan Ladd, William Bendix, Howard da Silva, Hugh Beaumont, Doris Dowling
Ramrod	1947	Andre de Toth	Joel McCrea, Arleen Whelan, Preston Foster, Don DeFore, Donald Crisp
Variety Girl	1947	George Marshall	Mary Hatcher, Olga San Juan, De Forest Kelley, William Demarest. Guest stars included Veronica Lake, Gary Cooper, Bing Crosby, Ray Milland, and Bob Hope
The Sainted Sisters	1948	William Russell	Joan Caulfield, Barry Fitzgerald, William Demarest, George Reeves
Saigon	1948	Leslie Fenton	Alan Ladd, Luther Adler, Douglas Dick, Wally Cassell
Isn't It Romantic?	1948	Norman Z. McLeod	Mary Hatcher, Mona Freeman, Billy DeWolfe, Roland Culver, Pearl Bailey
Slattery's Hurricane	1949	Andre de Toth	Richard Widmark, Linda Darnell, John Russell, Gary Merrill

147

THE DECLINE AND FALL OF THE LOVE GODDESSES

TITLE	YEAR	DIRECTOR	LEADING PLAYERS
Stronghold	1952	Steve Sekeley	Zachery Scott, Arturo de Cordova
Footsteps in the Snow	1966	A Canadian production never released in the United States. No information available.	
Flesh Feast (aka Time Is Terror)	1970	Veronica Lake	Phil Philbin, Heather Hughes, Yanka Mann

Betty Hutton

If I could just get it across to every audience, if I could
explain the thrill I get performing, if I could just look at
them out there and tell them: There's nothing I
wouldn't do for you.

Betty Hutton in a 1940 interview.

Now I have to go see casting directors who don't even
know who I am.

*Betty Hutton to Mike Douglas in
February of 1977.*

THEY called her "Bounding Betty," the
"Huttontot," the girl whose energy, if harnessed, could light up New York City.
For over a decade she lit up Paramount musical comedies, moving so fast that one
critic said he couldn't quite tell if she was any good or not!

She was very good while she lasted, streaking through the forties like an out-
of-control meteor and burning herself and her career out in the fifties, a victim of
her own excesses.

A rare combination of sexiness and true comedic talent, with a ricocheting
voice and seemingly boundless energy, Betty was indeed The Blonde Blitz who
not even a giant like Ethel Merman could smother. Betty bounded to Hollywood
from Broadway after 1940's *Panama Hattie,* one of the few stars to emerge from an
Ethel Merman vehicle.

Movie stardom came quickly but not easily for Betty, who was quickly
accepted by war-weary audiences looking for the kind of brash escapism she
excelled in. Hollywood polished her into a goddess, but they never really subdued
the real Betty June Thornburg from Detroit who turned into one of the GIs'
favorite pinup girls. When she wanted to, Betty could be as sexy as Lana, as noisy
as Judy, and as seductive as that other Betty, Grable.

Perhaps her highwater mark was in the 1945 film *Incendiary Blonde,* in which
she interpreted the life of speakeasy queen Texas Guinan. In it she combined a

Betty Hutton when she was Paramount's top glamour blonde (circa 1943).   CHRISTOPHER YOUNG.

sensitive performance (based surely in part on Betty's own childhood speakeasy singing days) with the trademark come-on, ''Hello Suckers!''

Her most dramatic career moment came when she took over the lead in *Annie Get Your Gun* after Judy Garland became ill in 1950. It was a riproaring success, but also marked the period when Betty began being difficult. After a few more films, she walked out on her contract and also out of Hollywood.

The fifties marked a period of ''retirements'' and ''comebacks,'' with each announcement getting less attention. She became a laughing stock, a Hollywood caricature of her former self that no scriptwriter could have invented.

Actually Betty invented herself, but one day she woke up to realize that there were flaws in the machinery—flaws so potentially destructive that no amount of liquor or pills could right them. And Betty tried them all. After awhile even her overdoses became typical press releases. Like the girl she replaced in *Annie Get Your Gun,* Betty Hutton became a joke, and the public, at last, was laughing at her, not with her. But unlike Judy Garland, Betty Hutton has lived on, making sporadic news as a housekeeper in a Rhode Island rectory, resurfacing in Hollywood for yet another comeback, and, finally, in a desperate attempt to shake her troubles and addictions, checking herself into a Hollywood mental institution.

By her own admission, she managed to squander a fortune of some $9 million during a career that blazed like a shooting star from the slums of Detroit to Hollywood superstardom and, finally, back to oblivion.

T HE studio star system, in full swing when Betty Hutton hit Hollywood in 1940, not only remade small town girls like Scranton's Emma Matzo into glamorous Lizabeth Scott but often retailored an up-and-comer's private life as well. And they never did a more inspired job than with Betty's pre-Hollywood days. Initial press releases commented on her spark and verve, but her childhood was hardly talked about except for vague mention that it had been a hard one. What an understatement that was.

Betty June Thornburg was born in Battle Creek, Michigan, on February 26, 1921. ''I never had a father,'' she told Mike Douglas in a poignant 1977 interview. ''I was known as a bastard child, which was rough.'' Her mother was a bootlegger who became an alcoholic, but Betty loved her deeply. When Betty was two, Mrs. Thornburg moved her and her older (by two years) sister, Marion, to a Detroit slum where Betty remembers singing around the kitchen table, her mother playing a battered guitar.

Mrs. Thornburg could only keep sporadic jobs, while Betty and Marion began mini-careers at twenty-five cents an hour. When she was eleven, Betty decided that since she could sing, she'd try and make it pay. So she began singing on street corners and in speakeasies with sawdust on the floor. With her mother's constant insolvency, Betty's contributions to the family came in mighty handy; a good Saturday night might bring in ten dollars.

That lasted for almost four years until Vincent Lopez and his orchestra came to town. At that point he was looking for a female singer and as a publicity stunt decided to hold a contest for the job. Unfortunately, Lopez overestimated the local talent reservoir. Only hillbillies showed up—not a likely candidate in the bunch. Lopez was furious, but a drama critic for the *Detroit Times* remembered Betty. Said the writer, Charlie Gentry, "I've seen a little girl singing in the honky-tonk. Not too good, but not too bad." So in desperation, Lopez signed up Betty June Thornburg.

Her singing style had developed into a haphazard one at best, and she had trouble with Lopez from the outset. Confused, she tried even harder to please him but rarely succeeded. "One of the boys in the band tipped me off that I was going to get the ax," Betty told *Liberty* magazine in 1944. "That's murder. A failure at fifteen. I was burned. Here I was, all set to get to New York in a hurry, and this was going to ruin everything. When I went out to do my number, I was so mad I couldn't sing."

What she did instead was yell, throwing herself around the stage, vaulting on top of the piano, and, for a crashing finale, colliding with the microphone and sending it skidding over. "I tore up the joint. I was solid."

That night marked the premiere of the gyrating Betty Hutton to come. Lopez presented her with a new contract at $65 per week and a new last name via his numerologist. Said Lopez, prophetically, about the name "Hutton," "It has a solid sound. It will be lucky for you. Maybe not in your private life, but in your career."

Lopez worked to amplify Betty's own sense of performing humor, and, by the end of a year's tour, she was being billed as "America's Number One Jitterbug."

After that year she finally made it to New York, scheduled to open with Lopez at Billy Rose's Casa Manana—as the opening act. "Imagine having to compete with steaks, squabs, and breast of chicken under glass. . . . They're smart, New Yorkers. Maybe they won't like the corny stuff I do!" She was scared stiff, but she covered it with even more gyrations, going into her "whirling dervish" routine. For a finale, she grabbed the stage curtain and swung across the stage, singing as she swung. Result? Seven encores. After the show Billy Rose told her not to change anything in her routine but also cautioned her, "Don't tear down my nice new place."

Betty stayed with Lopez several years, honing her talent and enlivening every engagement the orchestra had. During this time she met Bernard Baruch, who became her mentor and friend. (Betty only reached ninth grade as a child.) She also got to meet Al Jolson who tried to calm her own stage fright by telling her that he threw up before every performance and, "If you're not scared, you won't make it out there."

As for Betty's mother, all Betty's success did was make her switch "from beer to Scotch." The problem didn't dissolve as Betty hoped it would. One day in 1940, while Betty was at her lawyer's office discussing a salary dispute she was having with Lopez, a turn of events took place which can only be described as the classic "right place at the right time." Betty's lawyer got a call from Buddy De Sylva, a Broadway entrepreneur who was trying to locate "the dynamic blonde who used to wow them at the Casa Manana" for a part in Ethel Merman's upcoming *Panama Hattie*. "Ah, me," said the lawyer, Abe Berman. "She's sitting here in my office right now."

Betty got the part, and with it came minor Broadway stardom. She and Merman were friendly, and, in fact, Betty wrote Ethel later to express her gratitude for her encouragement. In recent years, though, Betty has insisted on reversing the situation, stating that Merman waited until opening night to cut Betty's big number. It's a story Hutton tells all the time now, but the fact is that Merman did nothing to undermine the newcomer and later gifted her with a ring which was Betty's first piece of important jewelry. In researching *Merman,* writer George Eells found correspondence that corroborates the fact that Betty, if anything, was grateful to Merman. What has made Betty now think the situation was reversed is inexplicable, but there's no doubt that Betty *does* believe it.

After getting *Panama Hattie* on the boards, De Sylva left New York for Hollywood to assume the position of Executive Vice President in charge of production at Paramount Studios, and he wanted Betty with him, promising her that he'd send for her within the year and put her under contract.

She didn't really believe him, took a part in another Broadway musical, *Two for the Show,* and then De Sylva called her westward.

When she got there, Betty was shattered that Hollywood knew nothing about "America's Number One Jitterbug." She, her mother, and her sister Marion set up an apartment, though, and settled in for a long stay, even though Betty's initial contract was for only six months. De Sylva's interest in her was a topic of speculation, with many feeling there was more to it than just employer-employee.

In any case, he debuted Paramount's new blonde bundle of energy opposite Eddie Bracken in the 1942 film *The Fleet's In,* in which Betty established her unique singing style with the mile-a-minute number, "Arthur Murray Taught Me Dancing in a Hurry."

Nobody had to tell Betty Hutton to become a movie star in a hurry because she started that way, immersing herself in the studio routine, studying the daily rushes, and even complaining that she'd like to retake a scene after the director had okayed it.

Instinctively, the creative people around the studio realized Betty's potential and gave her rare leave to improvise in certain scenes. Naturally she gave them the best of what she had. And she improved on that in her next film, *Happy Go Lucky,* in which she played second fiddle to Mary Martin.

But Betty had an unquenchable thirst for stardom and started badgering her boss early on for better parts. When she heard that he'd bought the rights to the life story of Texas Guinan, she stormed into his office demanding to play the lead. As Hutton pulled her new mink coat around her shoulders (seven payments still due), she pounded on his desk, crying, "I look like her, and I talk like her, and I act like her! I climbed the hard way, same as she did. We both sang in gyp joints. I'm a natural for Texas Guinan."

De Sylva patiently explained that the property needed a name in the main role and that he was considering bringing in Ann Sheridan or Barbara Stanwyck for the job. "You don't quite dig me," said Betty. "I'm going to play Texas Guinan. All right, you want a star. Keep it on ice, boss—I'll be back."

She took a giant step toward stardom when she got the lead in *Star Spangled Rhythm,* a lavish musical production with a thin plot revolving around movie studio switchboard operator Betty and gateman Victor Moore—*and* all the stars on Paramount's lot—pulling out all the stops to convince Moore's sailor-on-leave son (Eddie Bracken) that his dad was the head of the studio. It was a noisy wartime hit, highlighted by the appearance of everyone from Veronica Lake to Susan Hayward.

After Betty finished the film, her studio tried to get her to take a two-week vacation at Arrowhead Springs, but she was back the next day. "That terrible quiet set in. It drove me nuts." Reports also gave an insight into her mental attitude at the time, chalking up to natural energy what in looking back seems a clearcut case of hyperactivity. Betty was strung as tight as a two-dollar watch. She took showers because baths took too long, skipped desserts because she didn't like sitting at a table, and, if she didn't fall asleep instantly at night, knocked herself out with sleeping pills.

Her next costar, Bob Hope, in *Let's Face It,* quipped, "If they would put a propeller on Betty Hutton and send her over Germany, the war would be over in no time." Another member of that cast, Marie Windsor, who was then just starting out in the part of a showgirl, recalls, "She was always very popular on the set. Always terribly full of energy. At the time we all thought it was just natural enthusiasm, but in retrospect I think she was a very tense girl."

Betty's nonstop stardom campaign really paid off when Preston Sturges, fresh from hits like *Sullivan's Travels* ('41) and *The Palm Beach Story* ('42), cast her as a smalltown girl named Trudy Kockenlocker who went out on the town one night with a group of servicemen and woke up hungover and married in *The Miracle of Morgan's Creek.* Unfortunately she also found herself pregnant and couldn't remember her groom's name.

It was a sidesplitting comedy—one of Sturges's best—and a huge box office hit. It also lowered the censorship barriers with its somewhat (for the time) racy theme. Critic James Agee commented after viewing *Miracle,* "The Hays [censorship] Office has either been hypnotized into a liberality for which it should be thanked, or has been raped in its sleep."

Sturges had gambled on Betty and won. He'd never seen her on film, only around the studio lot, but as she explained it, "he was sure I had dramatic ability because I acted so much the opposite." It was a comedy performance laced with an enthusiastic tenderness, and, when De Sylva saw the first rushes, he called Betty to tell her the part of Texas Guinan was hers. He also cautioned her to take off some weight "and brush up on your riding."

Betty did both, but before filming started, she completed two other pictures: *And the Angels Sing*—as Dorothy Lamour's sister, with both girls in hot pursuit of bandleader Fred MacMurray—and the patriotic *Here Come the Waves,* with Bing Crosby, in which she played twins, one grave and subdued, the other strictly hustling Hutton.

To say that Betty was blinded by her career seems an understatement. She played the Hollywood dating game, but at twenty-two knew her priorities. And they all came under the heading of *career.* In the few years she'd been in Hollywood, she'd been engaged four times but never took them seriously. She scrupulously returned every engagement ring because she thought diamonds were unlucky when an engagement was broken. She exhibited a straightforward honesty that was almost disconcerting, saying, "If you could treat men you want like you treat men you don't want, you could have any guy in the world."

Her generosity was becoming legend too. She called herself a sucker for a sob story and finally got a business manager who wouldn't let her sign checks. "I spend like a drunken sailor. I get a kick out of helping people. Sort of satisfying to the ego, I guess." The former kid from the slums was now making some $1,250 a week, a far cry from the nickels and dimes of her street-corner youth, which her depression-scarred mother hid in mattresses.

She was also generous with her time when she wasn't filming and spent most of it working for the war effort, traveling back and forth across the country selling bonds with a host of other stars. Even then, however, the process of establishing Betty Hutton as a star never left her mind. In each town, to the chagrin of her glamorous companions, Betty posed with the local mayor, thus ensuring herself front-page exposure from New York to Newport Beach!

Her mother's drinking had tapered off a little after the Thornburgs had settled in Hollywood, and sister Marion worked occasionally in movies herself, but Betty was still the chief breadwinner for the family.

Betty's fan mail began rivaling that of Alan Ladd, but while his was mainly from women, Betty's came by the bushel from servicemen—some 7,000 letters a week by early 1944. She was a pinup favorite of the boys in the barracks, and at the Hollywood Canteen she was one of the most popular stars to entertain the visiting troops. She sang her song from *Happy Go Lucky,* Frank Loesser's "Murder, He Says," there and at various Army posts "about a million times."

When De Sylva's news hit her about the Guinan role, Betty wondered, "Now that I've got it, wouldn't it be funny if I'm a flop?" She tried to cast aside those self-doubts by remembering the studious care with which she'd been researching Guinan's life. While travelling with the Lopez orchestra she'd met the late singer's brother, Tommy, and kept him up all one night talking about his sister. And her hairdresser at the studio was another source of information as he'd once worked for Guinan and regaled Betty with stories by the hour while she baked under the studio dryer.

Though it wasn't released until 1945, *Incendiary Blonde* went before the cameras in October of 1943, teaming Betty with Paramount's new Latin Lover, Arturo DeCordova. It was directed by veteran George Marshall, and he had his hands full when Betty and Arturo started disagreeing. As usual, Betty was determined to turn out a hit, and her energy contrasted sharply with DeCordova's south-of-the-border languor. Fresh out of Mexico, this was his first big picture but one would never have guessed it. "Listen, dollface," Betty finally told him, her patience wearing thin. "You're strictly *manana*. How do you expect to succeed?" Under her withering attention, DeCordova stepped up his pace.

Costars and directors alike were quick to get Betty's opinion, something that soon earned her a reputation for being tactless, to say the least. She shrugged those charges off saying, "I have no time to be subtle and no patience with phony characters."

Incendiary Blonde turned out to be all that Paramount—and Betty—hoped it would be and introduced two songs that would be closely linked with her over the years, "Ragtime Cowboy Joe" and "It Had To Be You." Its success didn't help De Sylva, though, who'd been having problems with Paramount management. He left the studio, by request, in 1945, and Betty was bitterly disappointed. She'd relied on him so much during her first years there, seeing in him both a father figure and a mentor. Once when he asked her what she wanted for Christmas, Betty requested some good books. He gave her 100 classics. She always had qualms about her meager education and privately did her best to upgrade it.

She was also getting tired of the Blonde Bombshell publicity and hired Maggie Ettinger, a high priced and highpowered press agent, to try to dignify her boisterous image. Maggie took Betty under her wing and began introducing her to the right people, schooling her in how to get along with them.

To the public, though, she was still Bounding Betty, and Paramount gave them the Hutton they wanted, letting her play herself in *Duffy's Tavern,* another all-star musical. They also showcased her as a hatcheck girl in *The Stork Club* who befriends a penniless bum (Barry Fitzgerald) who, naturally, turns out to be a millionaire. Betty got to belt out "Doctor, Lawyer, Indian Chief" in it, but the film was mostly a programmer—an "A" budget formula picture.

The hole in Betty's life left by De Sylva's abrupt departure from the Paramount lot became filled later that year when she met a handsome young camera manufacturer named Ted Briskin in a Chicago café. Betty later said she took one look at him and it was love at first sight. She had to have him and, as with her career, pursued him with unabashed ferocity. Briskin, at twenty-eight, was the scion of a successful and socially prominent family and was intrigued by the attentions that Hollywood's frenetic star began lavishing on him. He made several trips to California to see her, and nobody was surprised when they shortly became engaged. Until then Hollywood thought no man could be as important to Betty as her career, but she'd made it clear that if anyone could, it was Briskin. At first Briskin's family was more than a little stunned at his choice of a fiancée, but Betty visited them and charmed them—especially his father. Betty and Ted were married in Chicago on September 3, 1945, but if people expected marriage to take any of the bounce out of Betty, they were very wrong.

Betty's Chicago idyll ended quickly when Paramount called her back for a tepid comedy called *Cross My Heart* with Sonny Tufts, the studio's resident tepid comic. It was a silly business about a girl who just couldn't tell the truth even to the point of confessing to a murder to help her boyfriend. The plot backfired and so did the film. It was hardly the role Betty expected after her success in *Incendiary Blonde*.

Her career frustration didn't help her new marriage, and, after only six months, the couple separated. Briskin wanted Betty to walk away from Hollywood and settle down in Chicago, but this she could not do. The separation didn't last long and they were soon reconciled. "Ted has been after me to give up my career," she explained after their reconciliation. "I love Ted very dearly, but I have worked all my life to get where I am, and I can't give it up. . . . Ted understands now." He tried to anyway, especially when Betty became pregnant. Their first daughter, Lindsay Diane, was born in 1946, and the following year Ted moved his business base from Chicago to Los Angeles to be near them.

Betty's spirits picked up when she started filming *The Perils of Pauline,* a rousing comedy based on the life of silent serial queen Pearl White. While the biographical part of the picture was mostly fiction, a bombastic Betty brought the whole thing off, especially animated in the movie-within-the-movie scenes of Pearl's cliffhanging career. Though it was not another *Incendiary Blonde,* Paramount was pleased with the film's success and, in a fit of enthusiasm, announced that Betty would eventually star in other biographies—stories of Clara Bow, Theda Bara, and Sophie Tucker.

She never made any of those films, but instead turned in a thoughtful acting job as a female Walter Mitty in the 1948 screen version of Elmer Rice's *Dream Girl.* An underrated film, it gave a rare glimpse of Betty the actress. Offscreen she was still Hollywood's madcap blonde, but onscreen and under the proper direction (in this case Mitchell Leisen) she *could* act when properly handled.

Betty rested briefly after the birth of her second daughter, Candice, that year, but was shortly back on the party circuit. She loved having people around her (to her that was acceptance), and the Briskins had a constant social life. Betty loved being a movie star and everything that went with it, even the nonstop hard work—"I hated to go home at night." They moved from one house to another, each one bigger and more lavish than the last—a total of ten houses in five years. Briskin tried to keep up with her, but the pace was a furious one, and he began rebelling against the pattern of nonstop activity his life was falling into. There was another separation, and then a tear-filled reunion capped by a second honeymoon, but it was just a temporary stopgap against the inevitable. He was still asking her to quit the business and settle down, but Betty was adamant. His talk made her "very nervous," and in it she sensed a threat to her hard-won identity. Ted withdrew more and more from her career, her family—whom she still saw a lot of—and her friends. Briskin might have had a valid point about many of Betty's friends. Her outrageous generosity began attracting the "users" of Hollywood, and she was always a sucker for a sob story, loaning money right and left. But these same people shunned her later on when her career collapsed.

In England she was an enormous hit at the London Palladium and came home for *Red, Hot, and Blue,* a noisy musical about a girl breaking into show business and running afoul of gangsters. An old friend, songwriter Frank Loesser, had a bit in it as one of the hoods, and Victor Mature played her boyfriend in his usual stolid manner. Although she was quite pleased with the picture, she immediately began, as usual, looking for something better. An insight into her determination came when Buddy De Sylva, then just recovering from a long illness, sent her a script he wanted her to do to help him get reestablished in the business. She didn't like it and turned her former boss and discoverer down flat. A disappointed De Sylva stopped speaking to her.

The year 1949 was a pivotal one for Betty Hutton, one in which she won greatly and lost just as much. It started off badly when she heard that MGM had purchased the movie rights to Ethel Merman's stage hit *Annie Get Your Gun* for their faltering musical superstar, Judy Garland. Betty was heartbroken. She had pleaded with her own studio to buy it for her, but they wouldn't consider the kind of money MGM was spending for it—a whopping, and for then almost unheard of, sum of $700,000. The project was launched with a maximum of fanfare, but shortly became a plagued project.

The first delay was in finding a suitable leading man. They finally settled on Howard Keel, a newcomer with a big baritone voice whom they'd just contracted at $850 a week. Shortly thereafter, Keel broke his leg, and star Garland and musical director Busby Berkeley began fighting to such an extent that Berkeley was replaced by George Sidney. By May, Judy had recorded the complete soundtrack, and the film was half finished, with $1 million already spent. Then Garland's mental and emotional problems, her fast-fading marriage to Vincente Minelli, and her nonstop work schedule compounded into a nervous breakdown. When she stormed off the set, an irate MGM took her off the picture and put her into a Boston sanitarium.

Desperate to make the film, the studio's first choice as a replacement was Betty Hutton, and Paramount got the call asking that she be loaned to MGM for the choice part. "At first they weren't going to let me do it. I went in with Johnny Hyde, the agent, and I told them I refused to do another picture if I wasn't allowed to do *Annie.* They must have gotten a mint for loaning me, but I didn't care. I had the part. I got it by a fluke," she said in 1977. "I think that's God power. I didn't wish Judy Garland any harm, but that was my part from the beginning." (Hutton also claims that Judy completed the film, but that it was totally unusable and was "canned." She also admits she never saw any of the Garland footage.)

Betty threw herself into the demanding role with a vengeance, prepared to prove that she'd be not only as good as Judy but better. Her complete dedication to the film proved fatal to her marriage. Briskin moved out, moved back in briefly, and then left again. It was an emotional merry-go-round for her, with no brass ring in sight. None that is except *Annie Get Your Gun.*

Despite her own emotional turmoil, she finished the picture. Advance reports were sensational. It was scheduled for release in the spring of 1950. She made headlines before that, however, when in February she filed for divorce. She was awarded a decree without contest on April 4. She told the court that her husband had constantly disapproved of her career and that "When my business associates came to dinner he wouldn't speak to them, which made it very embarrassing for me. Twice during my last picture I fainted as a result of his behavior."

Betty was awarded the eleven-room Brentwood ranch house, which she had had gaudily decorated by a Paramount set designer, and was allotted fifty dollars a month child support.

Betty and Howard Keel hit pay dirt in Annie Get Your Gun *(1950).*
THE DOUG MCCLELLAND COLLECTION.

Annie opened to gigantic box office returns amidst a flood of publicity that garnered Betty terrific reviews and the cover of *Time* magazine. The movie soundtrack, highlighted by Betty and a now-recovered Keel singing Irving Berlin hits like "Anything You Can Do, I Can Do Better," "Doin' What Comes Naturally," and "You Can't Get a Man With a Gun," became a top seller too—happily so, because Betty still gets small royalties from it.

Betty celebrated her hit with some rather manic behavior. She embarked on a romance with actor Robert Sterling, for weeks showering him with gifts and attentions, not to mention many phone calls to producer friends in behalf of his movie career, only to stop seeing him in mid-April of 1950, "because I'm not in a position to get too serious, and we were seeing each other, ya know, every five minutes."

She bought a complete new wardrobe and flew to San Francisco for two frenzied days, singing impromptu in the various night spots she visited. She did the same thing back home at Hollywood's Mogambo, grabbing the microphone and singing the entire score from *Annie Get Your Gun.* After singing to the startled, but obviously happy, audience, she grabbed several men from the floor for some free-for-all dance routines. Outwardly she was living up to her image and seemed to be having a whale of a time doing it.

In the back of her mind, though, lurked the fear of being alone again. "I could marry someone in the business who was higher up than me, or making more," she told *Time,* thoughtfully. "But when a real man comes up against the situation where he gets second billing, he walks. I don't know how I'm going to be happy." *Time* also pointed out that Betty was determined to give her daughters all the things she herself had never had as a child, including a nurse "to change their beautiful dresses five times a day." She knew she was spoiling them outrageously, but they were the daughters of a movie star—part of her image and also part of herself. They'd have the very best.

She was also considering moving again, this time to the old Robert Montgomery mansion on Sunset Boulevard. The reason? Its furnishings looked "musty, as though ancestors had lived in them." Betty never got over the fact that she had been cheated of at least half of hers, considering she didn't even know who her father was.

MGM was so delighted by the way she'd pulled *Annie*'s fat out of the fire that they tried to buy her contract from Paramount, but that studio, after reading her notices and MGM's grosses, wasn't in a selling mood. Instead, they announced that she'd star in the life story of another silent movie star, Mabel Normand. But, like the others, that property was never made.

Instead, they teamed her with Fred Astaire in *Let's Dance,* in which she played a woman trying to win her child's affection back from some stuffy in-laws. It was an ironic parallel. Unbeknownst to Hollywood, Betty was working on a similar situation in her private life, and even the most jaundiced Hollywood observers were taken aback when she and Ted Briskin reconciled again in July. Their divorce was set aside the following month.

For several months they both tried to make the relationship work, for themselves as well as their daughters, but there were too many obstacles in the way. Her businessman husband expected a changed woman, willing to sacrifice at least a part of her celebrity for a normal homelife, but she was a bigger star than ever before, and her ego had expanded to match the billing. She may have won her husband back, but she couldn't keep him. They separated in early December, with Betty once more trekking to the divorce court. This time she wanted more money for the girls, estimating Briskin's yearly income at $40,000 (her own at the time was more than five times that) and saying the fifty dollars per month child support was "wholly insufficient." This time, when the decree came through, it was for keeps.

Betty was the musical queen of Hollywood, the top star on the Paramount lot. Yet, at twenty-nine, she faced the future with a combination of anxiety and determination. She *believed* she was a star, but she also firmly felt that she had to keep proving herself to herself and the public. Off she went to Korea to entertain troops, to New York to replace an again-ailing Judy Garland at the Palace Theater on New Year's Eve (for $100,000, she says), and then back to Hollywood for the starring role in one of her biggest films, *The Greatest Show on Earth,* to be directed by the man she used to greet with "Hi ya, dollface"—Cecil B. De Mille.

DeMille was seventy years old when he turned his attention to life under the Big Top, and the result was the circus picture of all time. For it he tried to assemble the greatest cast on earth, and when he couldn't coerce his *Samson and Delilah* star, Hedy Lamarr, into taking top billing, he got Betty instead. Actually, one wonders how the languorous Lamarr could have pulled off the role of the trapeze high flyer that Betty portrayed with such vigor. Betty played the part of Holly who was in love with circus bossman Charlton Heston, "a guy with sawdust in his veins," with a reckless, yet for her, underplayed, enthusiasm that turned out to be the best acting she ever did.

Betty was totally believable as the girl who would do anything to get into the center ring: fighting Sebastian's (Cornel Wilde) fire with her own intensity, balancing on chairs on the forty-foot trapeze, and trying to keep her balance later when Sebastian tells her she's like "champagne. You make a man dizzy." (De Mille let the old frenetic Betty surface briefly in a trampoline number with Jimmy Stewart called "Be a Jumping Jack.")

It was spectacular entertainment, replete with every De Mille touch the master could muster, including a love triangle, daring duels between Holly and Sebastian on the high wires, euthanasia, and a rousing climax when the circus train is derailed, leaving Betty/Holly to marshal the troupe into a tattered, but determined, band of players for the Greatest Show on Earth.

Much of *Greatest Show* was shot on location at the Ringling Brothers, Barnum and Bailey winter quarters in Sarasota, Florida. There Betty, her children, and her mother set up housekeeping in a local mansion, complete with servants and nannies. For months she trained on the high wires for her role. During one particularly strenuous workout, she injured an arm and had to take painkillers. It was an injury that would change her life. The pain of the injury recurred over the ensuing years, and the pills were never far away.

After its opening, *GSOE* somersaulted onto the Box Office Champions List (number two for a time, to *Gone with the Wind*) and won the Best Picture Oscar for 1952. While not nominated herself, Betty's contributions to the film placed her at a popular peak in an era when many other forties' stars were either scurrying to Europe for film work, marrying Texas oilmen, or fleeing to television. Betty had survived the transition and seemed poised for even greater achievements.

Remembering her success in previous biographical pictures, Paramount decided to team Betty with fledgling Ralph Meeker in *Somebody Loves Me,* the rocky life story of vaudeville star Blossom Seeley. Betty was making $5,000 a week, *every* week, as the queen of the lot. Unfortunately, the make-believe kingdoms of Hollywood are among the most tenuous principalities that ever existed, and more than one star has been dethroned, just when they began feeling their crowns were unshakable.

While making *Somebody Loves Me,* Betty began getting involved with the film's dance director, Charles O'Curran, the first man she'd made news with since a five-day engagement, complete with thirty-two-diamond ring, to producer Norman Krasna in the fall of 1951, shortly after her divorce from Briskin. (At the time she enthused about the quiet-spoken executive, "Isn't it wonderful that such a brilliant man loves me?" When they separated after one of Hollywood's briefest engagements, neither party would say why.) O'Curran, handsome and moustached, was a cultivated man with an eye toward bettering himself. Once he and Betty got together, it may have occurred to him that she might be able to further his own career.

It hadn't started out that way, though, for Betty told Hollywood's then High Priestess of Gossip, Hedda Hopper, "How I hated that man when I first met him. After knocking myself out rehearsing a number, I turned to him and asked 'Well, how'd it look?' He shook his head and said, 'Pretty bad.' Now, I have no humor where my work is concerned; so I flounced off the set and gave notice that I wouldn't be back until that O'Curran character was removed. That only made him needle me more.

"That guy wouldn't put up with my temperament no matter how much I raved and ranted. You know I always sing with my hands spread out. One day Charlie asked, 'Have you got mittens on?' I replied, 'This is the way I work.' He said, 'Well your hands look like a truck driver's.' That burned me. 'It's the way I work,' I shouted. 'I work strong.' 'Well,' said he, 'you won't work strong in any of my numbers. If you don't obey me, my assistant will take over.' Oh it was a battle all right, but I couldn't keep away from Charlie. So we finished the picture and got married."

Betty must have felt she'd finally met her match in a man and he was interested in her career as well as herself; it was hypnotic. Obviously they hadn't fought *all* the time, since O'Curran later said, "I've known Betty six or seven months, and I've been proposing every five or ten minutes of that time." Finally, on St. Patrick's Day of 1952, he proposed to her again during dinner in a Hollywood restaurant. She dared him to charter a plane to take them to Las Vegas, which he promptly did, and they flew there to elope.

Next day, wearing an ice-blue satin cocktail dress and an orchid in her hair, Betty fed her new husband the traditional piece of wedding cake after a chapel ceremony performed by judge Frank McNamee. Her witnesses were Bud Fraker, head of Paramount's still-photograph department and Bea Allen, a studio dance researcher.

Betty and Charlie came home the following day and held a press conference in Betty's Brentwood home into which O'Curran had promptly moved. The bride was vivacious throughout, clutching Charlie's hand as she breathlessly related the story of the dare, the exciting flight to Vegas, and the ceremony. She also tried to cover these impulsive tracks a bit by adding, "We decided to get married some time ago and were trying to arrange a church wedding. We just got tired of waiting." Unfortunately, the church they wanted was the Catholic one, which looked mightily askance at the request, in light of both their previous marital records (O'Curran had been wed before too).

It's interesting, though, that Betty had at least tried to have a Catholic ceremony. She felt a kinship, a solidity about that religion that dated back to her childhood in Detroit when she escaped from the often brutal circumstances of her homelife to hide behind the skirts of the nuns in a nearby convent. Much later it was the Catholic Church that came to her rescue, even though it proved only a temporary respite.

Another wistful statement to a friend provides insight into her emotional makeup. "I don't enjoy being free. I didn't get divorced (from Briskin) because I wanted to."

After a brief rest, Betty flew to New York to follow Judy Garland into the Palace Theater, but it was, overall, not as successful as her previous stint there. Suffering from bursitis (probably brought on by the circus picture injury), she was in pain much of the time, nervous, and in bad voice. She did her best to "wow 'em," though, and returned home to a waiting O'Curran who hugged her tightly as photographers at the airport caught the moment for history. As she announced honeymoon plans, it became apparent that, as usual, Betty's priorities read career first, everything else, including her new groom, second.

She soon told Hedda Hopper, "Charlie says I have a talent for anticipating trouble that'll never happen. You know I'm either way up or way down in mood. But Charlie snaps me out of it. He's my balance wheel." She soon found that she needed one desperately when she launched a campaign at Paramount to have her husband signed as the director of her new film. O'Curran, while very good on the dance floor, was no movie director, especially of the big-budget vehicles Betty starred in. At first her bosses thought she was kidding, but it quickly became apparent she wasn't. Scripts were sent back, and she flatly refused to start work on a project called *Topsy and Eve* without O'Curran at the helm.

Paramount had extended Betty's contract when she went into *The Greatest Show on Earth,* and it still had a year and a half to run. Betty didn't care, and while publicity releases at the time say that she "persuaded" Paramount to let her go, it was common knowledge that she had in effect walked out on them—an unpardonable sin in the eyes of not only Paramount, but of every other major studio in town. By her actions she'd slit the throat of a movie career that, through her dogged persistence and sacrifice, had flourished for almost twelve years. If ever someone blinded by love needed a seeing eye dog, it was Betty during this period, for she alienated every studio executive in town, and it was widely prophesied that she'd never make another film.

Though she issued statements that she'd be going over to MGM, they didn't sign her. Instead she hit the road in an act produced and directed by O'Curran, taking it to New York's Palace for a wildly successful engagement and then on to London's Palladium where she was equally well received. In March of 1954, she was back at the Palace, with O'Curran, her mother, and her sister Marion around for moral support, and she wowed them again. Returning to Hollywood, she quickly realized that the studios were boycotting her, and she issued a statement to the effect that she and her husband were going into independent production. "Charlie and I have formed two corporations named after my two daughters, Lindsay and Candy. The Lindsay Corp. will handle the pictures and personal appearances. The Candy Corp. is for television. I won't do many pictures, but the first will be based on the life story of my idol, Sophie Tucker."

She also let drop that she and O'Curran were preparing a TV show—that they in fact hoped would be *the* TV show of all time. "We don't yet have a format for our TV show, but it'll be filmed and have some sort of dramatic form. It'll also have a period setting." The O'Currans hoped for the kind of TV success that Lucille Ball and Desi Arnaz were then experiencing, but instead of opting for a series, decided to shoot their wad and prestige on a "spectacular"—the first television show to use that title. Produced by Max Liebman, the show Betty and O'Curran hatched was a lavish western musical à la *Annie Get Your Gun* called "Satins and Spurs." Betty would star and O'Curran would direct both her and the dancing.

Rehearsals began, and the pressure was on. O'Curran felt it as much as Betty did, and he encouraged her to turn in the best performance of her career. If she'd faced perils in Pauline, she faced more now, engendered by not only her oversized and demanding ego, but by his as well. And the ironic part of it all was that O'Curran was doing just what Betty wanted him to do in the first place, direct her. But once he'd gotten what he wanted out of her, the temperaments, the suddenly fulfilled egos of both, created a combustible situation. They separated on April 20. When Betty filed for a California divorce, she said, "He had such a violent temper that there were tremendous scenes in front of anyone who might be present.'' Sister Marion was a witness for her, saying, ''I don't see how anyone could live with him.''

After the announced split, Betty went into hiding and then abruptly reconciled with O'Curran, saying, ''I am going to rearrange my whole life now and try to make a go of my marriage.'' The reconciliation lasted one day.

After the divorce action, Betty went to New York to film the show. (Unfortunately, at this disjointed time, she unwisely turned down a chance to play Ado Annie in the movie version of *Oklahoma;* it was the kind of part that just might have made her movie career viable again.) ''Satins and Spurs'' was a mammoth production for those times. It cost $300,000, with Betty getting $50,000, the highest amount ever paid for a television performance up to then.

The press buildup for it was one of the biggest in TV history, but while the fans were waiting to see Betty again after an absence of almost two years, there were many Hollywood executives who were sitting back and waiting for the rebellious star to fall flat on her face.

She didn't disappoint them.

''Satins and Spurs,'' which aired on NBC on September 12, 1954, engendered such reviews as, ''It was regretful that all the effort and money couldn't have gone into something better than this.'' It was a crushing disappointment for Betty, who'd hoped the show would reinstate her as a major star with the public. But, as was becoming a constant thread through her life, she blamed the failure on others, cryptically saying, ''It could have been much better.'' ''Satins and Spurs'' was the kiss of death for any reconciliation between her and O'Curran, for he was, as she saw it, one of the people who had let her down.

It was a subdued Betty who opened the following month at the Desert Inn in Las Vegas—at $25,000 per week for a four-week engagement. In a statement that didn't sound the least bit like the Bounding Blonde of only a few years before, she told the press she was about to retire. ''I've got to quit or blow my top,'' she said about the career she'd pursued with such determination since her youth. ''I had to do something to get noticed. I stood on my head, turned cartwheels, yelled, and screamed,'' she told reporters. ''I can't take the heartbreak anymore. It's not as glamorous as it seems.'' She said her two daughters, then eight and six, were her main reasons for quitting—''I can't bear to have them say once more, 'Mommy, do you have to go away again?' ''

In a rare moment of insight, she admitted that, ''I'm too strong for any man. I can't take it easy. I want everything to be perfect.'' In that perfection she wished to find love and acceptance, albeit the mass affection of an unidentifiable audience. ''If I can just look at them out there and tell them with all my heart 'There's nothing I wouldn't do for you. . . .' ''

On her opening night, she yelled to the crowd, ''This is my last roundup. I'm going to have a good time tonight.'' At the end of her stint, she declared, ''I'm going home, knit, play bridge, and smoke cigarettes . . . and I'm going to love every minute of it.''

As she made these statements, it was gossiped that there was already a new man in her life, Capitol recording executive Alan Livingston, age thirty-eight. She told Louella Parsons, "Alan is in the midst of arranging a financial settlement with his wife. I obtained a California divorce from Charlie six months ago, so I suppose you might say this is a little premature. But I'm going to marry Alan. I am in love with him, and he with me."

Livingston was then making a salary she thought big enough for both of them, and she reiterated that she wasn't fooling around about leaving—"I'm retiring, and this time I intend to make a go of marriage."

She was determined to substitute a private life for a public one, so much so that she decided not to wait for her California divorce to become final. In late February, she went to Las Vegas for a quicker decree on the grounds of "mental cruelty." Three days later, Livingston's wife agreed to a hefty financial settlement and gave him his freedom. Betty and Alan eloped and on March 8, 1955, they were married by the same Las Vegas judge who had joined her with O'Curran less than three years before.

The couple went back to Hollywood and settled into Jack Webb's old house, where Betty took over mothering not only her two girls but Alan's young son and daughter as well. Overnight all her professed dreams had come true, and it was time to get out those knitting needles, call in the girls for those card games, and smoke those cigarettes. Of the three, Betty mostly smoked cigarettes, as she tried to organize the house and coordinate the assorted children who didn't take to each other very well. Alan's son Peter was a sickly child, which added another burden to Betty's shoulders, and it was only a matter of time before her dreams of domesticity got lost in the shuffle of renewed ambition to perform, to get away from those dreams, which were now all too real. When she and Alan lost their expected baby in July, she became even more determined to get back to work and signed with MCA, the huge talent agency, for club work—"I'm still so keyed up I can't sleep at night." The retirement had lasted five months.

Vegas still wanted her, but Hollywood had a long memory over her treatment of Paramount, and it wasn't until the following year that she got an offer to star for Kirk Douglas's Bryna Productions in a small black and white production called *Spring Reunion.*

During an interview, her daughter, Candy, asked a reporter, "Do you know why mother played in *Spring Reunion*? It was because she wanted to show people that she can do dramatic parts." Betty went on, stretching the point almost to the limit. "In four years I read jillions of scripts without finding anything I wanted to do. Then along came *Spring Reunion,* 'This is it!' I said to myself. I sing only once in the film ("That Old Feeling"). I'm a 35-year-old unmarried girl who is dominated by her father. I meet Dana Andrews, and we fall in love."

During the course of the interview, Betty dropped a large hint that she'd give anything to play Nellie Forbush in *South Pacific,* and then proceeded to offer views on her life. "I've had a strange existence. I began working at thirteen to support my family. I had no girlhood in the normal sense. I never dated, never made school friendships or did all the other things so dear to girls. When I married, I was a performer, not a person. I never particularly liked those broad comedy roles, but they were mighty good to me. I don't have to work now, but I enjoy it, so I'll continue. Do I sound like an old lady? I'm not—I only just started young.''

Betty turned in one of the most sensitive performances of her career in *Reunion,* but it was a low-case release and a financial flop. The millions who'd flocked to see Betty Hutton pictures in the forties just weren't going anymore. Previous plans for her to star in a film with Kirk Douglas were scrapped, and, in a desperate attempt to win back audience approval, Betty tried television again. Producer Jess Oppenheimer sank $40,000 into a TV series pilot called ''That's My Mom.'' It was to star Betty as the widowed mother of four kids. Betty looked at the film, decided her character was ''too confining,'' and walked out. It didn't endear her to anyone in the business, and two years later she had to use her own money to launch another series try.

By now there were lots of rumors around Hollywood that things were far from rosy in the Livingston household, but the couple steadfastly denied them. Betty kept working in clubs and had to spend a lot of time on the road, but, as 1958 dawned, things appeared serene. Alan was appointed Vice President in charge of West Coast programming for NBC, and, while no movies came Betty's way, she constantly got big night dub dates. They were apart more often than they were together, and it was increasingly apparent that no man could, or ever would, be able to replace her need for the love of the crowds. The first show of affection she had ever received had been from nameless audiences, and in stardom she'd never been able to buy, on a personal level, the same depth of affection she got from strangers. Husband after husband tried but her emotional need was a peak no man could ever scale.

As always, she demanded perfection, convinced it was necessary to supplant the feelings of unworthiness ingrained in her during her turbulent childhood. And again she stalled at the gate when the elements didn't come together as she wished.

On February 4, Betty exploded the image of a happy family. While appearing in Florida, she told newsmen that her marriage ''is not working out.'' Livingston read about it in the papers and was shocked. ''If that's the way Betty feels, it looks like the end for us.'' Sounding depressed and tired, he admitted, ''Many things beyond our control have gone askew in our married life. There was the pressure of Betty's nightclub engagements, the illness of my little son, Peter, age eight, who is suffering from hemophilia, and the pressure of Betty's two children. . . . These conflicting elements have made it all but impossible for us to have a normal life.'' Betty said she was ''desperately in love'' with her husband, but the breakup was an ''inner family affair that's hard to explain. We haven't seen each other for five weeks.'' She also said she'd like to stay home, but couldn't afford to.

She filed for a divorce, asking that their community property be split down the middle, said she didn't want alimony, and then scooped up her children and her mother for a vacation in Cuba.

Less than a month later, though, the peripatetic blonde told everyone who'd listen that she and Alan had spent a weekend together ironing out their problems and that there'd been a "complete reconciliation."

When Betty had to give up a man in her life, she invariably did two things: she reconciled with him several times, and she always made the reconciliations as public as possible, almost as if reading about her renewed happiness in newsprint would make it more a reality. The same pattern repeated itself with Livingston. Less than four weeks later, the reconciliation was off, only this time Betty wanted him out of their Beverly Hills home (which she said she paid for) and wanted a reasonable alimony based on Livingston's $75,000 a year income. While appearing in Las Vegas in June, she said she'd file for divorce, and friends said that the couple's most severe problems came from the friction between her children and his.

Five days later they were back together again, but this time Betty had a new solution to their problems. She said their problems stemmed from spiritual differences, that she'd recently converted to the Lutheran faith, and that they'd be married again—in church! Even for Hollywood, this was startling, but it's interesting to note that once again religion had seeped back into Betty's life. Livingston wouldn't himself convert but they were remarried in a church ceremony.

The whole affair—conversion, remarriage, ecstatic smiles for the press—came tumbling down a mere nine months later. On April 3, 1959, Betty reinstated her divorce plea charging "mental cruelty" and asked for $3,300 a month living expenses until the divorce became final and a settlement was worked out. Livingston balked. By this time, he'd had enough of Betty's emotional boomeranging and answered her charge by saying she was in good health, made $150,000 a year, and was not entitled to either support or maintenance. Betty flew to Mexico for a divorce, and then refiled in California.

By then she had something else on her mind: her latest TV venture, a series called "Goldie," in which she played a former-showgirl-turned-manicurist who suddenly found herself executrix of a multi-million-dollar estate and the guardian of three spoiled children.

It started in October of 1959, and Betty told the press that the show was terribly important to her. "You don't know what I've been through the past few weeks. And even if I told you, you couldn't print it. Nobody has been on my side. One day I had to stand with my back to the wall and tell everybody to take their cockamamie ideas and go to hell. I'm not going for the buck with this show. I want to be proud of it. If I'm not proud, then I want to be dead. I don't give a hoot if I don't have a dime at the end of the year."

That turned out to be almost the case. Since Betty had invested heavily in her own show in order to get it going, she was determined to make it a success. But she took an odd path toward that end. Not trusting the talent she was paying, she began directing some scenes herself and rewriting others. She brought her own clothes in for costumes and dressed the sets. Her actions became increasingly self-destructive.

Every day at five she'd yell that shooting was over for the day, and out would come the booze and food. Her manic behavior during these sessions meant getting the kids off the set fast before she started letting loose with foul language and worse jokes.

Occasionally Betty would call in a Hollywood character nicknamed "O.K. Freddie" who, upon that signal, would pull out one of the biggest penises that Hollywood had ever seen. It became very chic for a time for party givers to hire him to suddenly display himself, to the consternation/disbelief/delight of the assembled stars. But when Betty called him on the set of her show, actress Joyce Jameson would gather up Betty's TV children, including Gigi Perreau and her little brother, and shepherd them off the set. Another habit Betty quickly formed concerned co-star Tom Conway, George Sanders's brother. Conway, a reformed alcoholic, would have difficulty remembering his lines—that is, until Betty would take him into her dressing room from which he'd soon emerge lighthearted and ready to work.

Another quirk of Betty's was to keep the set very cold. It shortly became known as the coldest set in town because Betty's personal temperature required that it be that way. While others froze, she ran from camera to wardrobe and back again, frantically trying to get *her* show together and thus become the public's darling again. Between takes it was also common practice on the set for any good-looking member of the stage crew to stay as far away from Betty as possible—unless, that is, he wanted to be invited into her dressing room for a "conference."

Somehow, some thirty-seven episodes of the comedy were filmed. By the time the series was wrapped up, Betty was down to ninety pounds. The show was a flop with the public, and Betty was distraught. Her agents hadn't wanted her to do it in the first place, but she'd insisted. "I thought I could pull it off." She says, she lost some $600,000 on the show which she'd hoped "would be an insurance policy for me and my children." Eventually the shows were sold to Desilu, but they've never been rerun.

By January of 1960, she was in the hospital for exhaustion, but she didn't stay there. The shadow of the shattered series hung over her, and she couldn't shake it. Unwisely she accepted a Las Vegas offer and went there tired and in poor voice. She hadn't been able to rehearse, and it was her first major flop there. She later told Mike Douglas, "That was my first big mistake."

Very quickly she became embroiled in an intense affair with jazz trumpeter Pete Candoli, and the ink was barely dry on the Livingston divorce papers when she announced she would marry him. She did, in her favorite wedding town, Las Vegas, on Christmas eve of 1960, in front of a Lutheran minister.

Betty promptly put Pete in her act, and they kicked off their marriage with a hectic tour of England the following month. At the time, Candoli had a cult reputation as a musician's musician and didn't like having to take second place to his more famous wife. That caused bitterness between them from the start, and, after a couple of weeks, arguments about billing and money became commonplace.

In the middle of April, they reached London's Pigalle nightclub. By then the arguments were nonstop and growing in intensity. Betty would compromise a lot, but not her star position. On April 15, she suddenly announced she was flying back to California for an annulment, but it was Candoli who walked out on her and their contract instead. It was a typical can't-live-with-him, can't-live-without-him confrontation for Betty, and the night he left she broke down and wept on the club's stage as she sang "Your Man Is Gone and You've Got the Blues."

They reconciled when she finally returned, but the gossip columns were littered with items about the shakiness of their marriage.

Then, on New Year's Day, 1962, Betty had one of the most traumatic shocks of her life when her mother died in a fire started by a cigarette smoldering in a chair in her Hollywood apartment. Sister Marion was called to the scene, but the news was withheld from Betty because she was pregnant at the time. When she finally was told, Candoli said, "She took it very hard." Over the years, the two women had built up a durable affection (Betty would later say, "I lived for my mother"), and Betty was always trying to overcompensate for the circumstances of her own childhood—those tortured years when mama's kitchen was crowded with strange men drinking bootleg booze while the little blonde girl danced and yelled across the kitchen table. Throughout Betty's years of top stardom and turbulent marriages, she'd fixed on her mother like a storm-tossed ship on a lighthouse beacon, but now the light was out, and there was only Betty herself to find her way through the rocks and shoals of her emotional problems. For years Betty's mother had been a costume-catcher, grabbing her daughter's wardrobe as she made quick changes between numbers. There was no one to catch it anymore.

In June of that year, Betty gave birth to her last daughter, Carolyn, and, for a time, it looked as though the Candolis could make an honest go of their marriage. Betty didn't work as much, content to follow Pete to Vegas for various gigs and occasionally sit in the audience of the "Merv Griffin Show" when he was part of the show's orchestra. She suffered a severe shock, though, when her daughter was in an auto crash while riding with her nurse. Ten month-old Carolyn was severely injured but recovered after extensive surgery.

At the time, Betty was rehearsing for a revival of *Annie Get Your Gun,* opposite Harve Presnell, which opened on the Fourth of July, 1963, at Anaheim, California's, Melodyland Theater. The press was kind about her performance, but it was obvious that much of Betty's old bounce was gone.

The following year she got a comeback break that could have made the difference for her career. She was called to Broadway to replace Carol Burnett for the last week of July in Carol's hit *Fade Out, Fade In,* a spoof of the movie industry.

By then Betty's mental and performing condition was in question. But *Fade Out, Fade In* answered it. Writer Doug McClelland recalls sitting behind David Merrick and an assistant at one performance Merrick attended in order to scout out Betty as successor to Carol Channing in *Hello Dolly.* It was a particularly difficult evening, and Betty dropped lines and song cues all over the place, starting several numbers, only to call a halt, step to the orchestra pit, and say, "Okay, boys, let's try to hit it right this time." Midway through the performance, Merrick looked at his assistant and shook his head, thus planting the kiss of death

170

on Betty Hutton's career. The show's receipts fell drastically during her one week in the role, and what could have been a glorious return to Broadway turned into one of the most publicized fiascos of the year.

Afterwards Betty went back to California, lived in a rented Laguna Beach house with Candoli and Carolyn, and hardly left it for the next two years. (Her other two daughters had gone to live with their father.) The only news she made was when she and her husband were sued by Joe Glazer's Associated Booking Corporation for $6,507 due on a $10,000 promissory note.

In May of 1966, Betty got another chance, albeit a minor one. She was asked to return to her old lot to star in a ten-day quickie western, produced by A. C. Lyles. The salvager of many former big names, Lyles had lined up none other than Howard Keel, her old *Annie* co-star, to play opposite her in a cast which included Broderick Crawford, Scott Brady, Wendell Corey, Tom Drake, and Don "Red" Barry. The film was called *Red Tomahawk,* and was to be her first movie in nine years. When she came back on the Paramount lot for the first time since she'd exited so abruptly in 1952, it was an emotional experience. She took one look at the place filled with memories of her Technicolored triumphs and retreated in tears to her old dressing room. "It's so thrilling, and I'm so scared. It was not a good leavetaking. I had two years to go on my contract and was turning down scripts right and left. I felt that was wrong, so I asked out. I thought I could return to the screen anytime I wanted. I was wrong." Recalling her childhood, Betty told a reporter, "We were finally run out of Lansing. We returned years later for the premiere of *Let's Dance,* the picture I made with Fred Astaire. They had a parade, the mayor came out—the works. Mother said 'At least this time the police are in front of us.'"

The humor lasted about as long as the interview because, when it came time to get down to work, Betty balked. In her mind she was still the star of twenty-years before, and she couldn't, *wouldn't* adjust to the comedown of playing a small role as a saloon hostess named Dakota Lil. She walked off the picture, and another former Paramount Golden Girl, Joan Caulfield, was called in to replace her. It was the last chance Hollywood would ever give Betty.

Her marriage was crumbling around her, and her nerves, even buttressed by pills and alcohol, could no longer be quieted down into a steady work routine. She made a flurry of pathetic newslines—the headline days were over—upon her departure, and Hollywood turned its back on her for good.

Three months later Candoli walked out on her, tired of battling a Betty on the bottle, and the following month it was a thoroughly frightened and disillusioned woman who boarded a plane for Juarez, Mexico, for a quickie divorce. Many were surprised the marriage had lasted as long as it had—six years—but Candoli's devotion to his four-year-old daughter had given him impetus to keep the marriage afloat.

Betty stayed on alone in Laguna with the child, walking on the beach, taking pills to try to stem the recurring pain from her old injury suffered on *The Greatest Show on Earth,* and washing the pills down with liquor. Life was bleak, perhaps the worst it had ever been. Before Betty had always had her career to turn to, but, to all intents and purposes, that was now gone.

Whatever her mental condition, Betty really loved Candoli, only this time there would be no reconciliations such as the ones that dotted her earlier marriages. Candoli came back, but only to see Carolyn, and it was during one of these visits, after an obviously blistering argument, that Betty called the police saying he'd threatened her life. Deputies returned later that evening after getting a call from a "Robert Preston" who "expressed alarm she might take her life." The police had a doctor with them who examined her for barbiturate poisoning, but he said she was under normal sedation and in no danger. When a reporter called the next morning, Betty said, "It's not worth talking about."

A few months later, the owners of the Laguna house paid Betty a visit. After the visit, they sued Betty, accusing her of misrepresenting herself as a person of good repute. They said in their suit that she was "addicted to alcohol and barbiturates" and that the house was a shambles. They asked for $19,400 in damages: $10,000 for false representation, $8,000 for damages to the furnishings, and $1,400 in back rent!

The suit forced Betty to take a long look at her financial situation, and she realized she was in trouble. She decided to get a California divorce from Candoli, which would enable her to ask for "reasonable support for herself and their daughter." She charged him with cruelty which resulted in mental and physical suffering that made it impossible for her to continue the marriage. She was broke, desperate, and bitter, later admitting that during this time she did try to kill herself.

Meanwhile, she countersued the owners of the beach house, slapping them with a libel suit to the tune of $350,000. Eventually the parties settled their dispute, but Betty didn't come out ahead. In fact, she was flat broke and filed for bankruptcy on June 9, 1967. "It's the only way out for Betty," said her lawyer. "She is listing debts of about $150,000 and practically no assets." Her attorney also said she was on the eve of another comeback try and "doesn't want creditors sitting around the table when she takes her next job."

It was a busy month for Betty. On the seventh she got her California divorce and was awarded $700 a month in child support, but only $1.00 a month token alimony. She testified that Candoli was "cold, indifferent, and aloof" and that he was jealous of her as an entertainer. The following morning she slapped him with a personal suit for $34,000, which she claimed they jointly owed creditors, including $25,000 in back taxes, a $1,000 oil bill, and a phone tab of $775 which she needed immediately in order to keep the company from shutting off her service.

She was shattered by it all, and her comeback plans dissolved in a downpour of drug-induced self-pity. She even told friends she was going back home to Michigan—until she realized there was no home to go back to.

In desperation she gave Carolyn over to Candoli, another pride-shattering move, but she had no choice. Alone, she was fast becoming a caricature of her former self, only now the disappointments and the drugs had chipped away at her voice and talent to such a degree that she couldn't get work. She appeared on a local Los Angeles talk show with Maria Cole, the widow of Nat "King" Cole, and poured out her troubles on the air. At the end of the broadcast, she got a call from a producer who offered her $1,000 to be ringmistress at his circus!

Over the next few years there were a few rumors of a comeback or a new act, but they all fizzled out. Betty lived in small apartments or stayed with friends, trading on what luster still clung to her faded name.

In 1972 there was a talk of another film, something called *Poems and Shades of Jersey,* about a retired movie star who murdered her tormenting husband, but it was never made. A San Diego summer stock producer took a chance on her in early 1973 in a play called *Here Today,* but Betty was gone before it opened, canceling out due to a recurrence of her shoulder injury and the medication needed to control it. By now Betty was on pills constantly, taking mood elevators and painkillers and knocking herself out at night with sleeping pills.

In April of 1974, Betty left Hollywood for Massachusetts. She had finally gotten another chance—to star in a small revival of *Annie Get Your Gun* at Boston's Chateau deVille. It was to be her first stage appearance in seven years, and she was terrified, torn by a desperate desire to be good, to be Betty Hutton again, and yet knowing deep inside that that woman no longer existed. She rehearsed for weeks and on opening night pleaded with the producer to keep the reviewers away. She opened the show, but it was a disaster. Shortly afterwards she canceled out of the production and, through AA, checked herself into a Boston hospital—"I didn't want to live." It was in that hospital that she met a Catholic priest named Father Peter Maguire who took pity on the shattered woman and offered her a job as housekeeper in his Portsmouth, Rhode Island, rectory.

She had been there four months when the weekly diocese newspaper, *The Visitor,* ran a story on her which included a poignant interview. "I was broken down and out, without a dime to my name," she told them. "I left Hollywood and landed in New England where I accidentally met Father Maguire. . . . I've had the money, I've had the fame, but I was miserable. Up until ten years ago I was making as much as $150,000 a week, raking in dough hand over fist. Money was no problem. But love was a problem. My marriages have not been happy, my children did not bring me happiness, nothing has brought me true happiness until I discovered Catholicism." Betty had converted to the religion, seeing in it a lifeline to some sort of ordered life. She embraced it fervidly. "Nobody loved me unless I bought them, and so I bought everybody. It wasn't until I came here and experienced the concern of the priests and the simplicity and devotion of the parishioners that I discovered true love really does exist."

It wasn't long before the news got out that the former Blonde Bombshell was scrubbing skillets, and, once it did, reporters descended on the staid rectory, photographing Betty busy at the sink and pouring coffee for the priests. She continuously issued statements that she had, at last, found happiness through Jesus. The publicity brought her 35,000 fan letters which she tried to answer.

The publicity aroused the attention and sympathy of some old show business pals, and, under the leadership of comedian Joey Adams and restaurateur Arthur Roback, a "Betty Hutton Love-In" was planned for the night of June 24 at New York's Riverboat restaurant.

Betty was both elated and scared to death of facing her old friends again, and the evening of the affair, in her room at the Americana, she was so nervous she threatened to throw herself out of the window. Her wig was wrong; her shoes didn't fit; she was frantic. Her friends, the priests, finally got her to the restaurant looking sadly patched together in a feather-trimmed white gown a Portsmouth woman had made for her, and she was in tears throughout the dinner.

Some teenagers greeted her arrival at the restaurant singing her *Annie* hit, "There's No Business Like Show Business," and Betty broke down.

Emcee Adams began the festivities, which included tributes by Cyril Ritchard, Arlene Dahl, Kay Medford, Henny Youngman, and George Jessel, and throughout it all Betty sat at a front table, unable to control her emotions. Long-ago

Betty, converted to Catholicism, working as a cook/housekeeper at a Portsmouth, R.I., rectory (1974).
UNITED PRESS INTERNATIONAL PHOTO.

co-star Eddie Bracken called her long distance, and everyone there tried to buoy up the wavering spirits of the fifty-three-year-old woman whose blonde wig was slightly askew.

When it finally came her turn to take the mike, she said, "I want to thank you for all the love you gave me tonight because I sure need it." The affair raised some $10,000 which was put in the name of St. Anthony's due to Betty's tax problems, and she stated emphatically that, even though "I've been offered open-end contracts and everything," she wasn't planning on trying a comeback. All she wanted to do, she said, was to get back to the rectory, the only haven she'd known in years. "I'll never leave that place."

Unwittingly, however, Betty's well intentioned friends had rekindled her hopes of stardom, and she began dreaming dreams of those $100,000-a-night shows and the glory she'd tasted twenty-five years before. Upon her return to the rectory, the priests noticed a change in her. Soon her desire for the warmth of the spotlight became an obsession, but there were no offers. In the meantime, she was depending more and more on pills to control the excruciating pain in her shoulder, even though she'd already undergone surgery to try to correct it.

In late 1974, she entered Butler Hospital, a Rhode Island psychiatric center, after having a complete nervous breakdown. Father Maguire said she had gotten out of control at the rectory and that she wouldn't be returning there. "The routine here can get rather confining," he said, adding ruefully, "she was a fantastic cook, when she got to it."

After three weeks in the hospital, Betty checked out on New Year's Day of 1975 and disappeared. Benay Venuta, a friend of Betty's from both her Broadway and Hollywood days, had visited her in the hospital and told reporters, "I told her she should get into the Motion Picture Home in California . . . after all, she paid for it. They took it out of her paycheck, and she was making $3,000 a week. I can't get hold of her. I shudder to think what's happening to her, alone and with no money. I keep hoping she'll call. I sit here waiting for her to call."

Betty finally did call someone, but it wasn't Benay. Instead she called columnist Earl Wilson from a motel room in Rhode Island where she was holed up with just a television set for company. All she had in the way of assets was an MGM record royalty check for $540.10. She asked Wilson, "They (the priests) can't absolutely abandon me, can they? I don't have a dime. I became a problem to them. I was put in a psychiatric hospital where my calls were listened in on. Now everything is going to be my fault because I took the pills. The pain was so violent, I had to relieve it." And the $10,000 raised for the rectory by the Love-In? "When it was given to the rectory, I thought it was expressly understood that I was going to stay on there forever. I guess they wanted to back off from me."

Shortly after that phone call, Betty showed up in Hollywood, again intent on making that perfect comeback. Driven by a compulsion to succeed, she moved in with friends and tried to pry open the doors she'd so solidly slammed in the past. But Hollywood had a long memory, and Betty's previous antics had cost her most of her old-time friends. She did land a part on Robert Blake's *Baretta*, but she

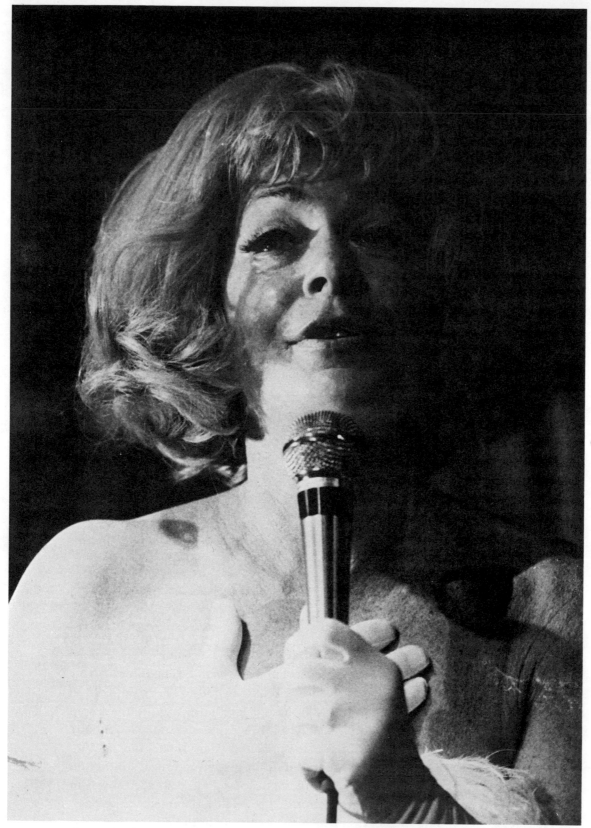

An emotional Betty at her 1974 "Love-In."   UNITED PRESS INTERNATIONAL PHOTO.

caused problems there, and her scenes were cut to one, which lasted only eleven seconds. Another old-timer, Joan Caulfield, was on the same show and got not only a bigger role but bigger billing as well. The only firm offers were for two questionable movies which she turned down, sighing, "I can't take the morality of Hollywood. I've been offered parts, but I just can't do them."

Mike Douglas interviewed her for almost an entire show which aired in February of 1977. It was a meandering, pathetic Betty Hutton the viewers saw. She said that when she'd originally gone to Rhode Island she had wanted to become a nun, "But I just wasn't good enough. It was just too tough a role for me to handle." She declared, "I love my church," and said that the past decade had been a lonely one "because I didn't have the performing thing going. But I found God." She alluded to the fact that she'd been religious as a child, but that "When I got to Hollywood, the religion slowly drained away, and I got in trouble."

Of her four shattered marriages she said, "None of my husbands ever loved me, and they all told me that. When Pete left me, it was such a shock I tried to kill myself with pills." She admitted the only true love she'd previously known had come from audiences, but added, "The tension of performing is so terrific and the fright is so terrific you never really get to know people."

"I wasn't good marriage material—I'd never seen a happy one. I was married to my career. It was my fault. Even my kids suffered terribly because I became so famous. When they became thirteen and fourteen, they knew they were different. Every movie star woman has a rough time with her kids. *They* have a rough time; the mothers die inside. I was a good mother until the girls became seventeen, but when I lost my money they went to live with their father who's now a multimillionaire. You know, the kind of money you can't run out of. One daughter lives in Brentwood, one in Fresno. I have four grandchildren whom I've not seen. I should never have married."

Mike asked Betty to sing, and she did, putting as much energy into her voice as she could muster. She sang "It Had To Be You" from *Incendiary Blonde.* Although she looked surprisingly good, the voice was a mere whisper of its former quality.

She tried to summon up a semblance of good humor, saying "I just got my feet wet in a 'Baretta,'" adding "I'm happy to be back in the business," She seem bemused over the changes that had taken place in the industry, many members of which had forgotten all about Betty Hutton. "Now it's hurry-up time . . . get it done. Now I have to go to see casting directors who don't even know who I am. I have to literally audition for a part, and it's kind of embarrassing."

She announced that she was working on her memoirs to be called *Backstage You Can Have*—"I remember the opening night of *DuBarry Was a Lady* and the empty theater with the janitors sweeping up the dreams."

A few old friends did try to aid Betty. One helped her work on a new act for Los Angeles' *Studio One* nightclub, but it never came off. Bob Hope stepped forward with some money, and in April of 1977, General Studios president Glen Speidel paid her SAG dues for the coming year, and the Actor's Union's "leniency committee" voted to waive the collection of her back dues. Another friend, Don "Red" Barry, got her an actor's pension she didn't even know she was entitled to.

Her appearance on the "Mike Douglas Show" received enormously favorable reaction, according to him, but it didn't lead to any offers. The fans might have remembered the former bombshell, but Hollywood casting directors didn't. She soon returned to Rhode Island and her job at the rectory.

Betty was angry at herself and the rest of the world, and her mood swings were becoming so erratic that she created havoc at the church, totally disrupting the routine.

The priests were rescued when Don Barry, who had taken over as her manager, called with a firm offer from independent producer Clifford Read to star in a San Francisco production of Noel Coward's *Fallen Angel* opposite Hermione Baddeley. She was elated, but along with the elation came a resurfacing of her destructive ego, and, by the time she got off the plane in San Francisco, she was convinced she was a star again. Immediately the temperament spewed forth—the star demands, the star tantrums, were all so out of hand that she lost the part, and the production was scrapped. Again she'd proven to be her own worst enemy.

She called Father Maguire for refuge, but this time his answer was no. Her drug habits and temperament were just too much for him to handle anymore. Furious at this rejection, Betty scribbled off a rambling letter calling him "Jesus Christ Superstar" and renouncing the religion she'd so recently espoused, saying, "I'm now through with the Catholic Church. Don't remember me in your prayers. They mean nothing."

Alone and in despair, she was befriended by Richard J. Moore, vice president of the National Film Society of San Francisco, who, in an attempt to help her, took her in—to his quick dismay. "She's like a railway locomotive charging down the track without an engineer," he told the *National Enquirer*. "She takes pills all the time, pills that would make you think she's drunk, and in quantities that you'd think would kill her. . . . She demands constant attention. She complains and screams that no one understands her. I had to wait on her hand and foot. She can drive a person crazy.

"She kept threatening suicide when she was in her down moods, and once she was going to jump out a window. I stopped her. Then she would sit for days hunched over her blonde wigs, combing them. They seemed to be a symbol of her past life. She'd become a pathetic shadow of the former superstar—only she doesn't know it."

After only nine days, Moore flew with her to Los Angeles where Barry was waiting and, on October 21, 1977, she admitted herself to the psychiatric ward of UCLA Hospital, sadly telling the doctor how desperately she wanted to get off pills and stay off. "I'm out to destroy my life, I know that . . . and I want to live. I want whatever's left of my life to be as good as possible."

She was in the hospital for a while, was quietly released, and dropped out of sight. It wasn't until June of 1978 that she was heard of again when she popped up in Newport, Rhode Island, with a job. The newsflash was partially hopeful—at least she was working again—but almost tragic in its implied desperation. Her job was as a hostess in a jai alai parlor where she greeted guests by singing new lyrics to one of her greatest movie hits. "There's No Business Like Show Business" became "There's No Business Like the Jai Alai Business." The woman who no man or career success could ever make truly happy, who had estranged her children and squandered some $9 million over the years was a star of sorts again, once more.

FILMOGRAPHY

TITLE	YEAR	DIRECTOR	LEADING PLAYERS
The Fleet's In	1942	Victor Schertzinger	Dorothy Lamour, William Holden, Eddie Bracken, Rod Cameron, Leif Erickson
Star Spangled Rhythm	1942	George Marshall	Bing Crosby, Ray Milland, Veronica Lake, Bob Hope, Dorothy Lamour, Susan Hayward, Dick Powell, Alan Ladd, Paulette Goddard, Cecil B. DeMille, Arthur Treacher
Happy Go Lucky	1943	Curtis Bernhardt	Mary Martin, Dick Powell, Eddie Bracken, Rudy Vallee, Mabel Paige
Let's Face It	1943	Sidney Lanfield	Bob Hope, Zasu Pitts, Phyllis Povah, Eve Arden
The Miracle of Morgan's Creek	1944	Preston Sturges	Eddie Bracken, Diana Lynn, Brian Donlevy, William Demarest
And the Angels Sing	1944	George Marshall	Dorothy Lamour, Fred MacMurray, Diana Lynn, Raymond Walburn, Eddie Foy, Jr.
Here Come the Waves	1944	Mark Sandrich	Bing Crosby, Sonny Tufts, Ann Doran
Incendiary Blonde	1945	George Marshall	Arturo de Cordova, Charlie Ruggles, Albert Dekker, Barry Fitzgerald, Mary Phillips
Duffy's Tavern	1945	Hal Walker	Barry Sullivan, Marjorie Reynolds, Bing Crosby, Dorothy Lamour, Alan Ladd, Eddie Bracken, Veronica Lake, Robert Benchley, Paulette Goddard, Brian Donlevy
The Stork Club	1945	Hal Walker	Barry Fitzgerald, Don DeFore, Andy Russell, Iris Adrian, Robert Benchley
Cross My Heart	1946	John Barry	Sonny Tufts, Rhys Williams, Ruth Donnelly, Allan Bridge, Iris Adrian

TITLE	YEAR	DIRECTOR	LEADING PLAYERS
The Perils of Pauline	1947	George Marshall	John Lund, Constance Collier, William Demarest, Billy DeWolfe
Dream Girl	1948	Mitchell Leisen	Macdonald Carey, Virginia Field, Patric Knowles, Walter Abel, Peggy Wood
Red, Hot and Blue	1949	John Farrow	Victor Mature, William Demarest, June Havoc, Frank Loesser, Raymond Walburn
Annie Get Your Gun	1950	George Sidney	Howard Keel, Louis Calhern, Edward Arnold, Keenan Wynn
Let's Dance	1950	Norman Z. McLeod	Fred Astaire, Roland Young, Ruth Warrick, Shepperd Strudwick
Sailor Beware	1951*	Hal Walker	Dean Martin and Jerry Lewis, Corinne Calvet, Marian Marshall, Robert Strauss
Somebody Loves Me	1952	Irving S. Breacher	Ralph Meeker, Adele Jergens, Robert Keith
The Greatest Show on Earth	1952	Cecil B. DeMille	Charlton Heston, Gloria Grahame, Dorothy Lamour, James Stewart, Cornel Wilde, Henry Wilcoxon, Lyle Bettger, Lawrence Tierney
Spring Reunion	1957	Robert Pirosh	Dana Andrews, Jean Hagan, James Gleason, Laura LaPlante

*unbilled guest appearance

Susan Hayward

I realized right away that Hollywood was going to be a tough nut to crack but as soon as I cashed in my return ticket I knew I'd give it my best shot.

Susan Hayward talking about her early Hollywood days after losing the role of Scarlett in Gone with the Wind.

I never thought of myself as an "artiste." I'm a working actress, and, I think, a good one; but what I'm really interested in is the chance to get out there and make believe. Actors are like children, you know; we still like to dress up and play house.

Susan Hayward quoted in the Los Angeles Herald-Examiner *in 1972.*

Susan Hayward was born in Brooklyn and brought from that borough a stubborn sexuality that made her, of all the women labeled Love Goddess, the most pugnaciously earthy. She was able to jump off her pedestal at the drop of a good punch line or the prospect of a challenge. Her insinuating, self-centered beauty, highlighted by a thatch of flaming red hair, made her one of the most distinctive personalities ever to storm across a movie screen. There's scarcely a picture she made, stinkers included, that an audience could walk away from feeling cheated.

Determined to be a star from the first day she set foot in Hollywood to be screen-tested for Scarlett in *Gone with the Wind,* she was one of the most distinctive beauties the town had ever seen, and, while she missed out as the mistress of Tara, she stuck around to carve out one of the most successful careers in movie history, hanging in there past contract days and salad days, always punching, always fighting to make a script or a costume work to her best advantage. In fact, it took the Bible itself to make her hedge her bets. When asked what she thought of doing *David and Bathsheba* in 1951 with Gregory Peck, she quickly replied, "I'd like it a helluva lot better if it was called *Bathsheba and David!*"

Susan Hayward—the sultry starlet (circa 1943).   THE DOUG MCCLELLAND COLLECTION.

That was later in her career, though; at the beginning she took what she could get (like the pallid beauty in the 1939 movie *Beau Geste*), yet underneath those seemingly vapid roles, she kept chiseling away toward a reputation that eventually led to some of the finest characterizations any actress could ask for. She even got a chance to sink her teeth into a Scarlett-type character in 1948, in *Tap Roots*.

Over the years Susan played women on the way up in *Canyon Passage* (1946), and *Tulsa* (1949) and on the way down—literally, in DeMille's *Reap the Wild Wind* (1942), and figuratively, in *Smashup—The Story of a Woman* (1947). In the classic comedy, *I Married a Witch* (1942), she exposed and exploited a gift of sexuality and a talent for bitchiness, qualities she expanded on as she transcended the forties to become one of the biggest box-office stars of the fifties. It was a long and hard climb that took its toll on both her and her family, yet she never complained.

A five-time Best Actress nominee, she finally won her Oscar in 1958 for the brutally frank *I Want To Live*. But with rare exception the rest of her career conformed to dialogue spoken by her in 1954 as Messalina in *Demetrius and the Gladiators*. Looking at Victor Mature over a heavy goblet of wine, she toasted, ''The first glass for thirst, the second for joy, the third, delight, and the fourth, folly.'' Her post-Oscar pictures were mostly follies (although highly profitable ones), with the notable exception of her last, a made-for-television film called *Say Goodbye, Maggie Cole*. In it she had two hours to say goodbye to her fictional late husband, and the world had two hours of prime time to say goodbye to Susan.

Movie fans saw her one last time at the 1974 Academy Awards during the height of her battle against brain cancer. Bolstered by painkillers, she strode onto the stage with Charlton Heston to an outburst of applause that would have been an ovation had she wanted to stand still for it. Instead she did her job with the quick precision of the professional she always was, staying briefly but long remembered.

Susan Hayward never asked for anything in her movie career. She fought for it, and the enviable reward she ultimately reaped was by dint of sheer hard work. She came by that tenacity honestly, for her life was never an easy one from the day she was born Edythe Marrener in a Brooklyn tenement on June 30, 1918. The youngest of three children, her mother favored her older sister, Florence, leaving Edythe pretty much to fend for herself. Her father held various jobs, such as a barker at Coney Island and a subway guard, but was primarily a weak-willed alcoholic who spent a great deal of time doing nothing.

The family was so poor that when Susan/Edythe was struck by a car on her way to grammar school, fracturing both legs and dislocating a hip, the Marreners couldn't afford proper care and took her to a free clinic. For months her mother pulled her to school in a wagon. The bones never knit perfectly, but, like so many other tragedies to come, she turned it into an advantage, developing the hip-rolling walk that later became so much a part of her screen presence. Even though he wasn't strong himself, her father taught her early on that life would be one long fight and that she'd need the resilience of a rubber ball to keep on handling it. The harder life hit her, the higher she'd have to bounce. That advice was his most potent legacy, one she never forgot.

At twelve she became the first female to have a paper route for the *Brooklyn Eagle,* and she persevered at it even though she was constantly heckled by her male competition, who tied tin cans to her borrowed bicycle. They didn't stop her, though, and whatever money she made was squirreled away for the rare treat of going downtown to one of the great movie palaces like Fabian's Fox Theater. These growing-up years gave Susan a lifelong fear of poverty, and much later in her life she'd keep huge amounts of cash in safe deposit boxes scattered around Los Angeles so that she could visit them and play with her money, seeing it as tangible proof against a return to the days when her clothes were patched hand-me-downs. "If my shoes were worn out, I had to stuff cardboard in them."

She later recalled a few happy memories of her Brooklyn childhood, but she admitted that, while it was great being born there, it was better getting out. By the time she graduated from high school, Susan had been dubbed the class actress and had already determined to try to make acting a career. Enrolling in a drama school, paid for by various secretarial jobs and showroom modeling, she was single-minded in her determination to succeed, and neither family nor friends were important enough to distract her. She was a loner, but she chose to be.

Commercial artist Jon Whitcomb used her extensively as a model, and she was said to be the inspiration for his classic "Whitcomb Girls" advertisements. By eighteen, Susan's beauty was blossoming into a spectacular sight with her upturned nose, determined chin, and fiery eyes, not to mention the equally fiery hair that framed it all.

When the search for Scarlett O'Hara was announced by David O. Selznick in 1937, it started a veritable avalanche of beauties, each heading west to capture the prize role of the century. Among the tidal wave of would-be belles was Susan, accompanied by her older sister, Florence. Susan was able to wangle a test, directed by George Cukor, but her extreme youth and lack of acting experience were woefully obvious, especially when stacked against seasoned talents like Paulette Goddard and Margaret Sullivan. She sensed it, too, doubling over into a fit of laughter after completing the confrontation scene with Ashley Wilkes in Twelve Oaks' library, the standard screen test for the role.

Selznick himself told her to forget it and go home, but Susan was undaunted. "I like oranges," she told him, "I think I'll stay." Cashing in her return ticket, she and Florence moved into a small apartment only to be evicted a few months later for lack of rent money. In the meantime her father died of a heart condition and Susan was joined by her mother and older brother Wally. Susan borrowed some money for them to live on from an aunt, and after months of scrounging around Hollywood looking for work, she was given a six-month contract at Warner Brothers.

Her first break came in Busby Berkeley's *Hollywood Hotel* in 1937, with Dick Powell and the then all-powerful gossip columnist Louella Parsons. Parsons was impressed with the brash Brooklyn beauty and incorporated her into her traveling show, "Louella Parsons and her Flying Stars," others of which included Jane Wyman and Ronald Reagan. Susan always made her entrance shouting out, "Anyone here from Brooklyn?"—a line that invariably brought forth a loud audience reaction. It was a fertile training ground for the fledging performer, and she worked hard, keeping to herself offstage, remote from her fellow players. She knew she had a lot to learn and was solely intent on learning it. Socializing could be left until later. She and Parsons built up a strong friendship, though, and the columnist would remain solidly in her corner throughout her career.

Back at Warners Susan Hayward went the starlet route, appearing briefly in several pictures including *The Amazing Dr. Clitterhouse*, *The Sisters* (with Errol Flynn and Bette Davis), and *Girls on Probation,* after which one executive conceded, according to Doug McClelland's excellent *The Complete Life Story of Susan Hayward* (Pinnacle Books), "She had a wonderful mind, but no heart. It took a long time to teach her to cry." At the end of six months they let her go.

That contractual end was a crisis point for Susan, but she scrimped and saved for rent money and got free acting lessons from a believer in her talent. That belief paid off, confirmed by the talent head of Paramount, when she signed for a $200-per-week contract at that studio in 1939. The "neglected Scarlett girl" became one of Paramount's golden circle of promising young players. She debuted for Paramount in *Beau Geste,* beguiling to the tragic brothers (Gary Cooper, Robert Preston, and Ray Milland) at the onset of their foreign legion adventure, and equally beguiling at the finale when Milland alone returned to her. She later described this part by saying, "I waved goodbye to the boys at the beginning and hello to them at the end."

After a few other small parts she won the female lead in *Among the Living* in 1941, a top-notch though low-budget thriller that also starred Albert Dekker and Frances Farmer. As a mercenary flirt, she garnered good reviews—so good, in fact, that the current queens of the Paramount lot were scared to death of her, declaring to the front office that "she's not going to steal *my* picture!"

To calm their leading ladies, Paramount loaned Susan out to Republic for a Judy Canova comedy and, fortuitously, to Columbia for an impressive third-billed part in the Ingrid Bergman movie, *Adam Had Four Sons.* She and Bergman admired each other's talent and independence and got along well—so well that Bergman didn't mind that Susan walked off with the picture as Hester Stoddard, a part that gave her her first of many drunk scenes. Her wicked Hester deserved but didn't get a Best Supporting Actress nomination due primarily to Susan's rebelliousness—"I got the reputation of being, to put it politely, a wave-maker." In fact, she was intensely disliked by directors and most of her co-stars during this period because of her refusal to take guidance and her general aloofness. Though the studio forced her into the cheesecake mill, they couldn't submerge her volatile personality. As an actress and potential box-office property she was valuable, but she chose to find her way to stardom alone. She never forgot Brooklyn and the hand-me-down clothes, and, according to one actor who worked with her at the time, she could "portray a lonely, frustrated, desperate woman because she's experienced those emotions. If you look closely, you'll see they've left scars on her heart." Her innate shyness was a large part of the problem, and "the only way I knew to protect myself was to try and scare people before they scared me."

Susan chafed at the bonds of the star system, the careful grooming of a player from bits to co-star roles to stardom, hopefully, and she fought the front office for more and better parts. She was in a hurry and with her family nagging at her heels, felt compelled to rebel. She was used as a publicity tool for other stars' pictures, often sent her on tour to draw attention to a film she wasn't even in. On these she usually took sister Florence as a companion, but that ended during one tour in the early forties when Susan returned to her New York hotel suite to find it filled with Flo's Flatbush friends. Susan screamed, "How can you do this to me? . . . This is a business trip." When Susan left New York, Florence stayed behind. It was the beginning of a long-standing enmity between the sisters.

After her success in *Adam Had Four Sons,* Susan began being noticed by film exhibitors obviously reacting to the impression she'd made on audiences. At a Paramount sales convention, several exhibitors asked why she wasn't being seen in more studio products. Pouncing on the opportunity, Susan dropped her hostessy opening remarks and instead spoke directly to studio chief Y. Frank Freeman. "Several of you have asked me why I am not in more Paramount pictures and I have never been asked a more interesting question. Why *haven't* I been in more of the studio's pictures? Well, Mr. Freeman, do I get a break or don't I?" The exhibitors cheered, and Freeman took the hint.

Susan's outspokenness seemed to have paid off when she was brought to the attention of Paramount's most important director, Cecil B. DeMille, who cast her as the sweet ingenue in his sweeping saga of Florida shipwreckers, *Reap the Wild Wind.* Filmed in Technicolor, it was one of the biggest moneymakers of 1942, ironically giving the would-be "Scarlett-girl" a chance to use a southern drawl. (Susan wasn't the only one, either; the female lead was played by Paulette Goddard, who, at one point, had the part of Scarlett but lost it when she and Charlie Chaplin refused to clarify their marital situation.) Along with John Wayne, Ray Milland, Goddard, and Robert Preston as her lover, Susan shared in the exuberant reviews that greeted the latest "DeMillestone," winning especially sympathetic ones for her famous death scene, in which she drowned as a stowaway aboard a ship that was wrecked by evil Raymond Massey. It was one of the most effective death scenes ever filmed and one of Hayward's most remembered screen moments. She photographed brilliantly in Technicolor, and, after a rocky start, got on well with the dictatorial DeMille.

Recognizing what they had in Susan, Paramount soon teamed her with Goddard again in *The Forest Rangers,* with Fred MacMurray as the object of both ladies' affections. It was her first major starring role, and she made the most of it as Tana Mason, a wisecracking girl of the woods who wasn't about to let a little thing like his marriage (to Goddard) keep the man she loved away from her. She ultimately lost (but not for lack of trying), giving city girl Goddard a crash course in woodsmanship that she thought would "drive that society 'debit number one' right back to the nightclub circuit." The main thing wrong with the film was how MacMurray could have ignored her in the first place, with her verve and competence dominating every scene she was in except for the pallid fadeout in which Goddard rescued her from a forest fire.

Her next big part was opposite Frederic March and another Brooklyn girl, Veronica Lake, in *I Married a Witch*, a marvelously inventive comedy in which Hayward's natural bitchiness was given full room to flower by French director René Clair. As March's fiancée her part was secondary to Veronica's, but she played it with unrelieved gusto. In the film, Veronica first saw her at the party for her engagement to March, whose ancestors had had her (Lake) burned at the stake. In retaliation, Lake cursed the family by saying that all its men would marry the wrong women. As Veronica peered through a country club window and saw Susan charging around, she gloated, "The curse is working. She has the look of a shrew." Lake eventually met and fell in love with March, breaking the curse and leaving Susan out in the cold—but not before Hayward had a chance to grit her teeth and champ at the bit to a fare-thee-well. The witch won the man but the bitch won every scene she was in.

Susan did the required star-bit in *Star Spangled Rhythm* late in 1942 and then began work on *Hit Parade of 1943* at Republic opposite the virile John Carroll. She and Carroll struck sparks in each other, off the set as well as on, and were soon an item in the gossip columns as steady dates. It was virtually the first time in her Hollywood years that Susan became romantically involved, and speculation mounted as to whether the romance would lead to the altar or not. After the picture was completed, Carroll left for a stint in the service and, the story goes, wrote Hayward to have an engagement ring made. She did, and the ring was so expensive that it ended up busting not only Carroll's bank account but the engagement as well. Susan ended up paying for it herself and wore it for years as a good luck charm, although at first it brought her anything but that. The picture they made together was a mild success, but the romance ended up a flop.

Recovering quickly, Susan made more pictures like *Young and Willing* and the stodgy biography *Jack London,* but in late 1943 she began spending lots of evenings, as almost every other star and starlet was doing, entertaining GIs at the Hollywood Canteen. It was there that she met Jess Barker, a handsome fledgling actor who thus far had broken no records for instant success. A former Broadway actor, (*Magic,* and *You Can't Take It with You*), he was new in Hollywood and looking for a way to get ahead. Until then his main claim to fame was as a gossip-column date of female stars, since most of Hollywood's male contingent was away at the war and escorts were in short supply. Barker was 4-F because of a heart condition. He acted as emcee at the canteen shows. After watching Susan there night after night reprising her "Anybody here from Brooklyn?" yell to an inevitably roaring response, he asked her out, but she refused. Susan read the gossip columns, too. Jess persisted, though, and she eventually gave in to his requests for a date, although it was rumored that the first time he tried to kiss her, the Brooklyn Bombshell socked him squarely in the jaw.

To Susan, Barker must have represented the ultimate gentleman, far removed from her father and the male figures that dominated her childhood in Brooklyn. A Southerner, born in Greenville, South Carolina, in 1914, he had an Ashley Wilkes type of gentility that appealed to her. In short order she personally began playing Scarlett to his Ashley for real, by actively pursing him, just as in *Gone with the Wind.* Susan's mother didn't approve of Barker, though, and for a time Barker himself wasn't sure about the romance either, thinking it might alienate the bobby-sox fans he was gradually attracting with his roles in *Cover Girl* and MGM's *Keep Your Powder Dry.*

Susan wanted him, though, and they eventually announced they'd be married, but before the wedding (at Momma Marrener's insistence, Susan later said) an agreement was drawn up which specified that Susan's earnings would be forever separated from that of her spouse. Barker signed, and the pair were married on July 23, 1944. It was to be one of Hollywood's stormiest marriages. In this instance opposites attracted, but it was an attraction marred by Susan's successful career and Jess's trouble in getting his own off the ground. Coming in at the beginning of an era launching macho types like Kirk Douglas and Burt Lancaster, his Leslie Howard-ish talent never had a chance to be much utilized, let alone developed in stardom. Susan would soon be shooting towards super-stardom in *Canyon Passage* and *Tulsa,* while Jess would be trying to hold his own in Abbott and Costello's *The Time of Their Lives.*

The union was turbulent right from the start, and Susan and Barker actually split up in September after a row on board Steve Cochran's boat. But by then she was pregnant, and they reconciled after two weeks. Susan's pregnancy raised the eyebrows of some Hollywood cynics when she gave birth to twin sons, prematurely, on February 19, 1945—seven months after the wedding. To keep studio publicists and month-counting fans happy, the Barkers' marriage date was "officially" amended to April 23, 1944. The boys were named Gregory and Timothy.

Susan earned the title of Miss Pinup of 1944 but lost in her campaign to grab the part of the adulterous wife in *Double Indemnity* that eventually brought much acclaim—and an Oscar nomination—to Barbara Stanwick. Instead, Paramount threw her into a weepie, *And Now Tomorrow,* opposite Loretta Young and Alan Ladd, who was just back from the war. It was a well-received film, with Hayward getting another crack at the type of man-eating part she'd later corner the market on, as the globe-trotting sister returning home just in time to steal Loretta's fiancé—just moments after Loretta contracted meningitis and went stone deaf! As a doctor, Ladd saved her hearing, but nothing could really save the picture, although Susan got the best reviews of the lot. The film marked the end of her Paramount contract, a period she walked away from with mostly gratifying memories.

She later said that she thought it was her determination to succeed that had helped her to score there, plus the fact that "I was totally reliable and when I was told to be on a set at 9 P.M., I'd be there. . . . I played Loretta Young's sister, Paulette Goddard's cousin, and I lost the boy to Veronica Lake. It was all good training." But she decided she'd had enough of Paramount when Buddy DeSylva, then studio head, refused to loan her out for *Dark Waters,* saying, "You've been rude, snippy and uncooperative with stars and directors. Maybe this will teach you." It taught her it was time to leave, and while they wanted to renew her contract at more money she "told them in no uncertain terms what they could do with their contract."

RKO nabbed her for a murky Manhattan melodrama, *Deadline at Dawn,* put together by former Group Theater members Clifford Odets and Harold Clurman (two men once important in the life of Frances Farmer, who was now incarcerated in a Washington state mental hospital). As a dance hall girl in a Broadway "bunion palace" called The Jungle, Susan exuded an acrid sexuality that would shortly become her trademark. The film got good reviews, and Hayward took another step up the ladder.

Then into her life came the man who would make the difference—producer Walter Wanger. He'd been watching Susan's progress and in 1946 signed her to a personal contract. The two of them developed an intensely ambitious plan to find just the right scripts to showcase her in. (Susan took it seriously, too. Wanger later remarked, "I'd have optioned more books than the New York Public Library if I took everything she wanted.") At last she'd found a producer who listened. She remained forever grateful. The girl who never had anyone to talk to had finally found a listener. (She did take another look at David O. Selznick, who was also interested in her, but when he kept her waiting two hours, she flounced out and over to Wanger.)

Wanger showcased her talent and undeniably ripening beauty in a lusty Technicolor western at Universal, *Canyon Passage.* It was a vigorous story, well told. *The New York Times* called it "a whopping show." It was also a whopping success.

But that was only the beginning. Hayward and Wanger planned to create some of the most potent female movie performances in history, and they started that happy and constructive meeting of the minds with *Smashup—The Story of a Woman.* In the era of female stars such as Bette Davis, Hedy Lamarr, Rita Hayworth, and Olivia DeHavilland, all of whom reigned during the forties, Susan made a large leap toward the front of these comely ranks with *Smashup.* Passed over for *Forever Amber* at Twentieth in favor of that studio's contract beauty, Linda Darnell, she grabbed the script of *Smashup* and ran with it all the way to a Best Actress Academy Award nomination.

As singer "Angie Evans," Susan deteriorated—onscreen—from stardom to alcoholism in a searing performance which many believe to be her best. (Ironically, it's seldom seen on television.) According to biographer McClelland, "Her insight into the drunk's psyche and manner was astonishing, causing many to wonder just how thorough had been her research."

She was bitterly disappointed at losing the Oscar to Loretta Young (for *The Farmer's Daughter*) but vowed she'd be in the running again—and soon.

Not only was *Smashup* the turning point in Susan's career; it was also the first time that she began to feel like an accepted member of the movie community. She'd served a long apprenticeship, and it took her a while to realize that she was finally making the grade. Another first for Hayward was that *Smashup* was the first time she thoroughly enjoyed *making* a movie, getting along with the cast and the crew, and though she worked on the film every day from May 27 until the end of August of 1946, she was never tired or unhappy. Having complete trust in director Stuart Heisler, she instinctively knew that they were turning out something sensational. She said as much in *Photoplay:* "I'm the girl who made all the mistakes in the book but if I hadn't, I never would have fully appreciated that great cooperation from the entire company. I've never been as contented in my life, but it took me seven unfortunate years to learn my lessons and profit by them. I guess no one can really tell another person how to change. You just have to learn for yourself, go through it yourself."

Meanwhile husband Jess's career was limping along with things like *The Daltons Ride Again* and *Scarlet Street,* and there was much talk that all was far from serene in the Barker household. In fact, film roles were so scarce for Jess that Susan bore the brunt of supporting him and their twin sons (and most of her Brooklyn family), and she didn't like it. She had enough fighting on the set and wanted a homelife away from that, with a husband who could support her. Susan had married out of love, but that love was being strongly tested by Barker's inability to find work. There were reports that Susan was drinking heavily, but she never got out of control in public because she and Barker seldom went out. She preferred staying at home, reading countless books in search of a possible script rather than socializing with her new-found peers. Also there was the realization that as long as she was married to Barker, it would be her career that kept the family together, and she concentrated on it even more after the success of *Smashup.* While other stars from her old Paramount fold—like Lake, Goddard, and Lamour—were finding their careers starting to wind down, Susan stood poised at the top.

As part of her plan to be taken seriously from now on, Susan announced, after completing her next film (a melodrama with Robert Young called *They Won't Believe Me*), that she was no longer available for cheesecake layouts. The starlet phase was definitely behind her, and they did believe her when she said it.

Susan's next production with Wanger was *The Lost Moment,* an underrated drama that had her the mistress of a crumbling Venetian palazzo that held the answer to the mysterious death of a poet from long ago. She was lush and believable as she played a split personality—the severe, almost shrewish niece of Agnes Moorehead, and the young vivacious woman Moorehead once was as the dead poet's mistress, coming to life by night to play the piano and read his musty love letters.

Director Martin Gabel warned the crew not to talk to Susan during production, saying that since she was playing a schizophrenic she had to maintain an isolated mood. When Hayward heard this she erupted in a typically effective Flatbush manner and hit him over the head with a lamp—"and to this day I've never felt sorry." She herself disliked the film and upon seeing it redubbed it *The Lost Hour and a Half. Moment* was Gabel's only try at screen directing—no small wonder, after tangling with Susan.

Wanger then gave her her chance at the Scarlett-like role of Morna Dabney in the Technicolored *Tap Roots* in 1948. She gave her character a fire and insight that made many wonder what she could have done as Scarlett if she had been just a few years older and more experienced when she'd stood before George Cukor's cameras for her first screen test.

After her next film, *The Saxon Charm,* an average account of the life of an unscrupulous Broadway producer (played by Robert Montgomery), Susan had it written into her future contracts that her hair could not be cut unless she agreed. *Charm* was the first picture in which the public got to see a short-haired Hayward —the film's only redeeming quality.

She desperately wanted the lead in *The Snake Pit,* and mentor Wanger met with Fox chief Darryl F. Zanuck in an attempt to get it for her. He didn't succeed, but when Zanuck saw her latest film, *Tulsa,* in which she played a fiesty oil queen, he decided he wanted her and offered Wanger $200,000 for her contract, guaranteeing Susan a similar sum yearly. Between them Wanger and Susan decided it was a good step for her to take, and she took it. They were to remain fast friends, however, and Susan never did forget that he was the man who listened.

In the late forties the specter of television was stalking the mansions of Beverly Hills, and a star under contract—especially a contract as good as Susan's —was a better bet than a freelance actress to snare one of the decreasing number of good available parts. She moved onto the Fox lot determined to be one of the survivors, in fact, the greatest of them all.

Zanuck knew what he had in Susan, too, and gave her a meaty debut in *House of Strangers,* directed by Joseph L. Mankiewicz. As a fast-running society playgirl, Susan quickly cut to a walk after meeting Richard Conte, the one good son (of four) of Italian banker Edward G. Robinson. When the bad sons ganged up to dethrone Robinson from his bank presidency, Conte tried to save him by bribing a juror and got tossed into prison after being betrayed by his brothers. In a rare display of screen patience, Susan waited for Conte for seven years, until his release. In this rich and robust story, the sexual attraction between the pair was so instantly and persistently strong that perhaps it wasn't such a surprise that she waited after all.

At this point in her career Susan was approaching a security she'd never known before. Although her family life was constricted by her husband's lack of income and the growing burden that put on their relationship, the public Susan Hayward never looked better. Over at Sam Goldwyn's studio she made one of the films for which she's most fondly remembered, the tear-jerking *My Foolish Heart.* Based on J. D. Salinger's famous short story "Uncle Wiggily in Connecticut," it gave her the opportunity to combine all the pieces of her screen persona into one soaring, if at times sudsy, whole. Susan liked the script so much she okayed taking second billing to Dana Andrews, who played the college lover who swept her off her feet, got her pregnant and then promptly got himself killed in an air-field explosion. Susan then tricked another beau into marrying her, but the union went sour fast because she was never able to get over her first love, an affair highlighted—constantly—by the throbbing strains of the title song. As the college girl she was fresh and innocent and, later, as the unhappy wife, she ran the gamut from melancholia to dipsomania in a bravura display of emotional fireworks bright enough to garner her a Best Actress Oscar nomination for 1949.

She lost the award but returned to Fox as its number-one star. Betty Grable's appeal was beginning to fade, and newcomer Marilyn Monroe was still several years away from stardom, but at that moment and for several years to come it was Hayward who topped the studio's box-office list. Competition for top roles was cutthroat, and Susan barely relaxed during this period. As if to compensate for a less-than-happy homelife, she continued throwing herself into her career and, although she had a top business manager and agent, she made all the final decisions herself. She reportedly told a friend then, "My life is fair game for anybody. I spent an unhappy, penniless childhood in Brooklyn. I had to slug my way up in a place called Hollywood where people love to trample you to death. I don't relax because I don't know how. Life is too short to relax."

She launched a powerhouse decade of movie hits with *I'd Climb the Highest Mountain,* the story of a backwoods preacher and his wife set in the wilds of Georgia circa 1900. William Lundigan, an otherwise middling actor, had one of the best roles of his career as the circuit preacher, his soft-spoken charm and good looks just the right complement for her often forthright city-bred behavior, as when she speedily dispatches wealthy widow Lynn Bari, who took to calling her husband over for what Susan thought was one too many spiritual conferences. Filmed on location in Georgia, Susan was charmed by both the state and its people, a fact that would greatly affect her later life.

It was a good, perhaps excellent, movie but not one of Susan's favorites. When a reporter told her in 1972 that it was one of his favorite Hayward portrayals, she scoffed, "You gotta be kidding. I never saw myself as much of a preacher's wife. I didn't like wearing all those pretty dresses or having to be so genteel."

Soon after, she got a chance at the kind of woman she enjoyed playing. *Rawhide,* a terse and tense Western, teamed her with Tyrone Power, just back from several years of making films abroad. She was Vinnie Holt, a riverboat entertainer heading east with her young niece to start a new life, only to get sidetracked at an 1880s relay station where Power worked. When a gang of outlaws took over the premises, they assumed that Power, Susan, and little Judy Ann Dunn were a family and held them captive. The plot concerned their escaping the villains, with Susan neatly accomplishing that when she shot Jack Elam as he was about to finish off Power. Ty's part was one of the first western anti-heroes, a man out to save his own skin, and a great departure from his usually heroic screen image.

As in television today, success breeds endless imitations. When Cecil B. DeMille made *Samson and Delilah* with Victor Mature and Hedy Lamarr in 1949, its enormous box-office success sent Hollywood executives scrambling through the pages of the good book looking for suitable male-female combinations to be fleshed out for the Technicolor screen. As Fox's first lady it was inevitable that Susan would eventually don the robes of one of the Bible's slightly tarnished females, Bathsheba in *David and Bathsheba.*

In this plodding movie—almost nonspectacle—it took a lot of patience for Susan to sit back smiling and simpering gratefully while an uninspired Gregory Peck, as David, seduced her, sent her husband off to be killed, and then claimed her for his own. Naturally this behavior set off a wide-screen drought and famine that soon had the high priests (led by Raymond Massey—who else?) demanding her death, by stoning no less, as an adulteress. Peck then stormed the Holy of Holies and gained forgiveness, and as the rains poured down he and Susan were reunited for a soggy finale (in more ways than one). Though it was one of the top grossers of the year, it proved that when it came to the scriptures, De Mille was still tops in the distillation of sex and salvation.

Susan thanked God (and her own determination) when she got the lead role in the excellently done exposé of New York's garment industry, *I Can Get It for You Wholesale.* In her fourth picture of 1951, she was the woman on the make in the garment jungle and gave a performance of "blistering intensity" as Harriet Boyd, a top model who decided to open her own dress company. Stepping over family, boyfriend (Dan Dailey), and former pals in the process, she almost brought them all to ruin with her ambition before a turnabout into Dailey's arms at the fadeout. The production was filmed largely on location in her hometown of New York, and the place seemed to trigger emotions in Susan that helped greatly in her portrayal of Harriet, the hard-hitting, success-ridden businesswoman. There's no record that Susan visited her old neighborhood in Brooklyn. That was one place where she had no desire to return. If her old friends wanted to see Susan Hayward they could go to the Brooklyn Paramount—and pay for it.

Susan was a girl whose emotions were always bubbling just beneath the surface of her Irish skin, and when she felt it expedient, they exploded in whatever direction she thought necessary. Her constant work schedule was a marvel to many in Hollywood, almost as if she were happier on a sound stage than in her own house. Her initial shyness had contributed a lot to her general attitude of aloofness, not to mention the fact that she wore glasses off-camera because she was nearsighted, another contributing factor to her growing reputation as a loner. There was still more than a spark of rebelliousness in her and it's said that, when she reached the superstar stage, whenever she was approached by studio executives she'd say, "Whatever it is, the answer is no!" She liked working, though— loved it, in fact—so much so that she told a reporter she was jealous of actors who worked every day. "I don't like a picture on which I work a couple of days and then am off for a couple. . . . Some day I'll do a picture in which I play all the roles."

Despite her newly won superstar label, Hayward never tried to further her husband's career. It was as if she believed in "every man for himself." She'd use her influence to fight for better scripts, better production values, and better co-stars, but her husband was never one of the latter. While she made four pictures in one year, he hadn't worked since 1950 in a minor movie called *The Milkman*. The rumors were growing that the Barker household in Sherman Oaks was getting shakier and shakier. There had been several break-ups already, one in 1947 that almost reached the divorce stage, but Susan kept hoping that the man she married would turn out to be just that—a man in every sense of the word, including supporting his family.

Susan capped off 1951 by putting her handprints in the forecourt of Grauman's Chinese Theater, an event suitably publicized. No doubt the thought crossed her mind as she posed happily for photographers that the closest her husband would likely get to the forecourt would be as a tourist.

As befitted the queen of the lot, Susan's next film was a skillfully tailored, three-hankie biography of singer Jane Froman, who had been tragically injured in a 1943 plane accident that almost severed her right leg and resulted in many operations (which engendered an overflow of public concern and interest that made her newsworthy long after the accident).

Once Susan safely got the part away from Jeanne Crain, who'd begged Fox-head Zanuck for it, she prepared with the discipline of a boxer going for the heavyweight crown, taking vocal lessons with Elsie Janis, playing Froman records constantly at home, and rehearsing eight hours a day at the studio. Froman was delighted that Susan would be playing her but was slightly spooked when she found her huddled in a corner of the recording studio watching her intently as Froman sang the twenty-six song soundtrack. "It was uncanny!" she later said. "When I saw the rushes I was astounded by her pantomime." So right did Susan want her performance to be that she cut her luxuriant hair shorter to Froman's length.

Her portrayal was so dynamic in *With a Song in My Heart* that it was one of the ten most popular pictures of 1952 and won her third Academy Award nomination as Best Actress. She personally liked it so much that it was the first time she allowed her twin sons to see her onscreen. Thelma Ritter added greatly to the proceedings as Froman's maid, to whom Susan says a classic line— "Clancey, they're gonna yank my leg off." Susan lost the Oscar to Shirley Booth's touching *Come Back, Little Sheba,* but she did earn the distinction of being awarded *Photoplay's* Gold Medal as "the nation's most-enjoyed actress during 1952."

Susan finished the year with two good—and popular—outdoor films, *The Snows of Kilimanjaro* with Gregory Peck and Ava Gardner, and *The Lusty Men* opposite Bob Mitchum as a rodeo rider. The first was middling Hemingway with the juicy female scenes all going to Gardner, but the second, directed by Hollywood maverick Nicolas Ray, has become something of a classic over the years.

But Susan didn't just make movies that year. She finally relented and returned to Brooklyn for a widely publicized visit to her old neighborhood. Clad in a mink coat and dragging on countless cigarettes, she stubbed them out long enough to give an apple to one of her old teachers at Prospect Heights High School. She was accompanied by Barker, who was always referred to in the news stories as simply, "Miss Hayward's husband." What a keen delight she must have felt to float back home as a movie queen—and what a keener delight to leave it all behind, floating away again in her limousine, mink intact and the past buried. Back on the west coast she learned that her *Song* fan mail had outnumbered that of Fox's blonde musical queen, Betty Grable—no mean feat.

Susan also took time out that year to make her views very plain indeed about actors and politics. Stars were coming out right and left for Eisenhower and Stevenson, but she would have none of it. "I think that an entertainer—a person who makes his living by pleasing the most people—has a responsibility to his bosses not to alienate factions of that group that might go and see him in a motion picture." She added that she had an intense interest in her country "and in politics, but I will not put my views on other people. . . . I don't think it's right for me to stand up and make speeches." A far cry from those of Vanessa Redgrave and Jane Fonda two and a half decades later!

Ironically Susan did get her pretty red head into politics of a sort with her next film, *The President's Lady,* the story of Andrew Jackson (Charlton Heston) and his pipe-smoking backwoods wife, Rachel. In the sweeping film, which brought out a spontaneous chemistry between its larger-than-life stars, she gave a touching edge to the portrait of the lady who'd married Jackson before her divorce was final and had suffered social ostracism for the rest of her days.

Fox teamed her again with Mitchum in *White Witch Doctor*—although all Susan got to see of Africa were rear projections of process shots—after which she felt she deserved a vacation. She and Barker left for Europe in May, leaving the twins with her mother. When she got back she did a syndicated piece on her trip and experiences—but never once mentioned her husband. "I bought a Jaguar and motored through France, Italy, and Spain. One incident in Paris I'll always remember. I was strolling on the Champs Elysees when a little girl turned and cried, 'Oh maman, voici Jane Froman!' I was ham enough to get a big kick out of that for both Jane and myself.''

The trip fell on the Barkers' ninth anniversary but if it was an attempt at a second honeymoon to somehow mend the widening rift between them, it didn't work out. Susan's old friend and mentor, Louella Parsons, broke the news on July 24 that Susan was filing for a divorce. Three days before the not unexpected announcement the couple had been to a party together and things seemed relatively placid. But seven days before that all hell had broken loose at the Barkers' Sherman Oaks house, and the lurid recounting of it all at the pre-divorce hearing the following February made headlines for days.

Until the announcement that she wanted out of her marriage, Susan had constantly defended her husband as a great actor who just hadn't gotten the right breaks. Her loyalty, until the end, had remained steadfast, at least in public, but, despite Susan's desire to end it all, Barker did his best to try to keep them together. As they unfolded, the details made him look like a heel while Susan emerged the battle-scarred heroine, albeit as feisty a one as she'd ever played onscreen.

Barker moved out, and within two months Susan was trying to forget the whole mess by going back to work, getting her second chance at biblical posturing as the evil Messalina in the lavishly vulgar but highly entertaining sequel to *The Robe, Demetrius and the Gladiators.*

The strain of the upcoming divorce was already beginning to show, and her co-star, Victor Mature, mentioned that she was so distracted that they were barely on speaking terms—"Susan acts like she's a hundred years old." Hardboiled, lascivious, speculating through sequined veils about the prowess of Mature outside the gladiator's arena, she wa remarkably subdued—whether swaying through a marketplace in a chiffon-draped litter carried by muscular Nubians, swishing through Caligula's court, or ultimately seducing Mature in a seaside villa steaming with hot sex on a summer night. There were scenes—such as one with Jay Robinson, recreating his Caligula role from *The Robe*—where she held her own against the relish with which he played his part, something that might have overwhelmed any less an actress. In all she evidenced an audacious beauty coupled with a wetlipped sensuality, doing with Messalina what Lamarr had done with Delilah and what Turner was about to do in *The Prodigal.*

In her bitterly contested divorce suit, Susan charged 'mental cruelty,'' but Barker hotly denied the charges, saying that he was intensely in love with his wife and wanted a reconciliation.

In November of 1953 they went to court for a compatibility hearing, but after the much-publicized histrionics of a court assistant who didn't get her picture taken with the famous couple (Susan had to calm *her* down), the Barkers left very much unreconciled. When a reporter asked Susan what their chances were of getting back together, she snapped, "It takes two to tango."

Barker's main worry was the marital agreement he'd signed forever separating their incomes. (He later said he was too busy buying the cake to really read it.) The following morning he countersued for a share in the $400,000 worth of community property, saying he felt it was due him since he and his wife had filed joint income tax returns over the years which, with his unstable career and her burgeoning one, had saved her a great deal of money.

Susan hired the best attorneys she could find and then left for Mexico to film *The Garden of Evil* with Gary Cooper. While she was gone Barker tried to pull a fast one and moved back into the Sherman Oaks house, saying that Susan's mother wasn't taking proper care of his sons in their mother's absence, insinuating that Susan herself wasn't a proper mother. He was quickly cited for contempt of court for making that move, but the forthcoming testimony was a welter of accusations that flew fast and furiously over the reputation of a lady who had always tried to keep her private life private.

The pre-divorce hearing was set for February 25, 1954, and Susan approached it with great trepidation. She knew what she'd be called upon to do and say. In all her films she had seldom run across such a seamy plot.

It seems that the final breakdown began on the night of July 16. It had been a pretty normal evening for them with the "usual two drinks" before dinner and more later as they sat around watching television. That's about as much as either party admitted as fact, for after that their stories differed, the end result being news stories with headlines screaming FILM BEAUTY TELLS FLEEING IN THE NUDE.

According to Susan, Barker had gone out for the evening papers and came back about 11 P.M., finding her sitting in the living room in a terrycloth robe "with nothing underneath." "I sleep in the raw," she explained. They began talking about Hollywood families, and the story quickly came around to their own.

She testified: "I said, 'If you don't love me and you don't want to do what I consider proper [go to work], why don't you leave me?'

"Mr. Barker answered, 'You're a good meal ticket!'

"I told him: "I don't understand you. I think you're very queer!'

"Then he walked over to me and slapped me in the face. I tried to cover my face with my arms and he slapped me again. He threw me on the floor, pulled up my terrycloth robe and beat me." (Doctors the following day attested to the fact that she indeed had bruises "mostly on [her] fanny.")

As the judge cautioned her to relax and calm down, Susan—dressed in a beige suit with mink-trimmed sleeves, a cigarette and a kleenex clutched in her black-gloved hands—continued telling how she had started crying that night as the argument deepened, running past midnight and into the early morning hours.

Finally, "I ran out into the back garden. I just wanted to get away. But he caught up with me, forced me into the house again. I struggled to get to the telephone to call the police. As I was reaching for the phone, he said 'I'll cool you off.'

"He grabbed me and took me to the pool. He threw me in and the heavy robe pulled me under." She added that she had worked her way out of the robe, and at this point a sobbing Susan was asked by her lawyer if she had been in fear

197

of her life. "I certainly was!" she cried. Then, calming slightly, she went on with her story. "I realized I wasn't dealing with a normal person. He was enraged. I decided to keep still for fear he would hurt me." When she could break away, she said, she had pulled herself out of the pool and run naked across the garden into the house.

"He followed me. He pushed me into the bedroom and told me to stay there. He left the room and I went to the closet and put on some clothes. I went to the kitchen door—I wanted to go out the driveway and to freedom." At this point she broke down again, apologizing softly, "I'm sorry. I hate to tell these things."

After a five-minute recess during which she regained her composure, Susan went on, saying how Barker had hurled her back across the kitchen "with such force the momentum carried me all the way to the living room." Then she had run out the front door screaming for help, but "the next thing I remember, he was beating me, and picked me up and threw me over a hedge." A neighbor had heard the by-now 3 A.M. commotion and called the police, who arrived as Susan and Barker were struggling for the phone. An awakened houseguest, actress Martha Little, looked on in horror, pleading with Jess to stop.

She had refused to sign a complaint and had merely asked the officers to summon a taxi to take her to her mother's home for the night. X-rays taken the following day showed no broken bones, but the black eye he gave her lasted for two weeks. Barker had left the house the following day and had never lived there again.

Barker's version was that Susan, after more than just a few drinks, had made slurs about his manhood that summer night, recalling an undetailed childhood incident that goaded him into slapping her. She bit him on the arm and ran for it. He admitted he had chased her outside but only to bring her back and put her to bed, "but she got up again and ran out nude. It was then that he had said he would "cool her off," and tossed her into the pool. He also said he had tried to help her out of it instead of trying to drown her. Barker's lawyers tried hard to make Susan the heavy, saying that she consistently drank too much and had goaded him on other occasions as well.

For example, the lawyer said, when Barker showed up the following Labor Day to talk to her about a reconciliation, she was lying by the pool with guests after consuming a pitcher of scotch. Susan's version of that day was that Jess had shown up and had indeed talked about a reconciliation, but she had said it was impossible and asked him to leave. He said he wouldn't until he "was good and ready. He was standing near me. I had a cigarette in my hand, and I have a temper. I said: 'I'd like to push this cigarette in your face!' He replied: 'You haven't the guts.' Whereupon I pushed the cigarette in his face. He struck me. I grabbed a scotch and water and threw it in his face. It was wrong and I know it, but I was mad and I was provoked."

Another enigmatic figure to surface in all of this—as he had in the lives of almost every other Love Goddess—was Howard Hughes. Hughes testified that he had wanted Susan for the lead in his $6 million, super-production of *The Conquerer* and that he'd been at the house in Barker's absence.

Barker's lawyer questioned the husband on the stand about Hughes, starting by asking if his sons' attitudes toward him had changed any since the break-up. "They've been quite silent toward me. They did tell me that a man who had called at the house to see their mother had been introduced to them as 'Mr. Magic.' They told me that he had a long black chin. And when I asked who this man might be, they said 'His name is Howard Hughes, and he said he was going to take us for an airplane ride, but mother said we shouldn't tell you his name.' "

Called back to the stand, Susan admitted that Hughes had been at her home —"He flew in to discuss some script changes." She also admitted she'd introduced Greg and Tim to him as "Mr. Howard and his name is magic, that is what I told the boys. And I told them he does many things, flies planes and the like." She also firmly denied having told the boys to keep the meeting a secret from their father.

The judge granted custody of the children to Susan, but Barker still tried to throw up as many legal roadblocks as possible. In March he tried but failed to stop her from taking them on location with her to Utah, where she was filming Hughes's epic.

The formal divorce trial in June rehashed all the lurid details of that last evening of the Barker marriage. It went on for four days, and Susan was obliged to go through the whole testimony again. She appeared in court alone, clad in black, and when reporters asked her to take off her dark glasses she sighed and said, "Not today." They shot her picture anyway, as she walked stiffly away from an arms-crossed, intently staring Barker, who told them he was still hoping for a reconciliation.

She'd flown in from the rigorous location in Utah for the trial, and she was obviously tired. She broke down and almost fainted at one point, the humiliation of her private life being replayed across TV screens and newspapers obviously too much for her. Her fierce Irish pride was taking a severe beating, and the delayed reaction from it all was yet to surface.

Another thing she feared was seeing half of her hard-earned money flow away to Barker, who said that one of the main problems in their marriage was a role reversal because of her success. "She was more fortunate than I in the business— she became a star." Susan contended that he slept late, bought cheap groceries, and refused to look for work.

Barker's lawyer did his best at the end of the four-day trial, mixing his metaphors a bit as he pleaded with the judge to "Melt the ice in the heart of that woman with a legal whip. . . . A river of gold has blinded that woman to her responsibilities to her children and to her husband." Susan missed his eloquence, though, for she'd skipped the last day of court to return to work on *The Conqueror*.

Barker was offered an out-of-court settlement of $100,000 in cash, but he refused it, gambling on winning half of everything Susan had. He lost, and when the divorce decree was handed down, he walked away from the marriage with nothing more than the family station wagon. (Ironically, the notoriety of the divorce did get him some minor movie offers. Barker finally went to work—he had to!)

Also, he was instructed to stay away from Susan's house except for the days he was allowed to visit his sons. Susan was ordered to pay his legal fees, however, but that $3,500 bill was little enough to ensure her freedom and her fortune.

By the end of August she was hard at work again on another major spectacular, *Untamed*, playing Katie O'Neill, an Irish lass who found herself battling Zulus in South Africa while gradually working her way into the elusive affections of Tyrone Power. It was a gigantic production set in the days of the settling of the Dutch on the dark continent, and stars like Jane Wyman, Joan Crawford, and Lana Turner (especially) had wanted to play in it. It was a natural for Hayward, though, and she got the plum, although it was a physically difficult role.

Hard work never hindered her enthusiasm though, and on the set she was a changed person, warm and outgoing, the demons exorcised with the divorce behind her. She even joked, "Forever is usually the theme song of marriage, but to me it's the theme song of divorce."

She even talked about a renewed private life to columnist Dorothy Manners, but she was her usual pragmatic self about what that would entail. "I pity the poor devil who takes me out in public the first time. We'll both be so miserable. I haven't had a 'date' in so long I hardly know how to talk to a man except career-wise. And I'm sure he will be uncomfortable with all the romance rumors the most casual dinner engagements will bring forth." Despite the unhappy memories of the Sherman Oaks house, Susan said she had no plans to move because she didn't want to uproot her sons. As to the future, "I'll take it as it comes along. . . . I'm grateful for the good which falls my way and pray for strength to handle the bad things."

She soon needed a bit of that strength when she tried to take the twins with her on location to Hong Kong for *Soldier of Fortune* with Clark Gable. Barker intervened and this time won, so Susan turned down the film. Barker's action created a new animosity between them, but the studio wanted her for the picture and let her shoot all her scenes in the action adventure on Fox's backlot Hong Kong.

Grace Kelly had originally been set for the part, but she had already retired and left for Monaco. The resultant combination of Gable and Hayward should have sparked a bigger fire than it did in this picture, but it was interesting to observe, at long last, the would-be Scarlett with the original Rhett. She even got herself carried up a flight of stairs by Gable, in this instance the entrance to a Hong Kong restaurant called the Peacock where he took her to talk over her search for husband Gene Barry who was missing in China. While Gable was, by then, well past his Rhett Butler peak, she was every inch the fiery adversary who, had time not intervened, could have been his Scarlett. Anna Sten, a one-time

Goldwyn discovery, appeared briefly as a tired and hungry whore, willing to hand out information for a meal. The elements were there but the script really wasn't. Even today, though, it's worth watching.

Barker still couldn't believe that Susan had divorced him, and, since it required a year for the interlocutory decree to become final under California law, he petitioned for a reversal, lost, and then petitioned that Susan pay for his petition. He lost that round, too, but it was all increasingly nerve-wracking for Susan, who was about to start one of the most demanding roles of her career, that of Lillian Roth in *I'll Cry Tomorrow.*

Susan's nonstop work schedule, the strain of the divorce, and the added wrangling over the twins soon worked together to bring her to a point of despair. She was finishing *Soldier of Fortune* at Fox while she was starting *I'll Cry Tomorrow* at MGM, and her new part added another tension, for she was an actress who often adapted to the character she was playing, delving deeply into the tragedies as well as the triumphs. In this case they were those of a famous singer whose career had skidded into a bottle, and who was never really able to reclaim it.

She threw herself into the part with an energy that surpassed even that of *With a Song in My Heart.* She had campaigned for the role by telling then-Metro-chief Dore Schary that it was made for her, that it combined the best elements of two of her Oscar nominated films—and two of her favorites—*Smashup* and *With a Song in My Heart.* Her vigorous arguments quickly put little June Allyson and big Jane Russell, Schary's considerations, right out of the ball game.

As had happened earlier with Jane Froman, one of Susan's biggest allies was Lillian Roth, who, also like Froman, marveled at the way Susan was able to crawl under her skin to better get to know the woman inside. Susan met Lillian in Las Vegas. "She visited me again at the Beverly Hills Hotel in Hollywood. It was in the early afternoon and she arrived in her black Chinese pajamas with a coat thrown over them," Roth wrote in her sequel, *Beyond My Worth.* "We talked for several hours. By the time she left, I didn't know whether she was imitating me or I was emulating her. We were both so emotional about things that when we faced each other it was almost like looking in a mirror."

Unlike *With a Song in My Heart,* though, Susan did her own vocalizing in *I'll Cry Tomorrow,* an added strain that necessitated long hours of extra work but was a challenge she wanted. Always trying to improve, to expand, she was unwittingly overburdening herself in the process.

And then back into her life came Barker, flush from finishing a minor western, *Kentucky Rifle.* Again he wanted to talk reconciliation, and Susan agreed to meet with him, with her lawyer present, in a bungalow at the Ambassador Hotel. It was a secret meeting that quickly turned into a free-for-all shouting match. Susan was still greatly upset over the Hong Kong incident, taking it as a slur on her abilities as a competent mother, while Barker harped increasingly on the twins being used in a tug of war between them.

After the meeting he took off for New Orleans to promote his new picture, but not before telling reporters, "Susan will never talk to me unless she wants something. She won't speak to me when I come out to pick up the boys. She won't even let the servants speak to me. The children see this and other things, and it has to be bad for them. I admit I blew up at the finish of the meeting. We had gotten absolutely nowhere. I said some unpleasant things but they had been on my chest for two years."

Susan stated: "I have my reasons for not seeing Jess alone. We are two diametrically opposed people. In the past, when we have been alone, violence has resulted. . . . As for the children, I think I am a good mother. I believe the boys are in better shape than they have ever been before."

Thirty-six hours later Susan was greatly despondent over the whole mess. She put her sons to bed, in good spirits according to later reports, and curled up with the shooting script of *I'll Cry Tomorrow*. A note on the kitchen table read, "Please awaken me at 11:30 A.M. Miss H."

As the April night wore on, the tensions grew, mounting steadily. Susan recounted the confusions of her life, especially with Barker. What did it all mean? She took some sleeping pills but still found herself slipping into uncontrollable emotion. She took some more pills. At around three in the morning she phoned her mother, hysterical, her voice slurred by drugs. She said only, "Mother, you'll be well taken care of." Unable to get any more out of her than that, Mrs. Marrener hung up and called the police saying, "My daughter is Susan Hayward. I'm afraid she's going to commit suicide."

Two Van Nuys detectives rushed to the house on Longridge Avenue. After they rang the doorbell they heard someone mumble, "Yeah, yeah," and then silence. Going around to the patio they kicked in a French door and found Susan, clad in filmy blue pajamas and a white housecoat, slumped unconscious on the living room floor. Near her prostrate body were two empty pill bottles.

Susan was breathing so hard, almost gasping, that the detectives decided they couldn't wait for an ambulance and rushed her in their car, siren screaming, to a nearby hospital where a doctor pumped her stomach and administered oxygen. "It was a close one," a doctor said the next day as front-page pictures showed her being carried into the hospital.

Mrs. Marrener laid the blame for her daughter's attempted suicide squarely on Barker's shoulders, telling Louella Parsons, "He just won't let her alone." Susan's brother, Walter, told newsmen, "I don't know why she did it. You can assume anything. She seemed happy when I saw her about a week ago. She was always close-mouthed about her troubles with Barker, even with relatives."

Susan's personal physician had her transferred to Cedars of Lebanon Hospital when she came out of a three-hour coma and was out of danger. She rested there several days. Surprisingly she opened her hospital room to reporters and posed, smiling sexily, in a negligee.

When Barker heard the news he broke down, crying, "I love her, I love her." He flew back from New Orleans immediately, but Susan's doctors wouldn't let him see her, saying his presence would only upset her more.

Susan said it was an accident, but it would seem that, for a few minutes at least, the tough lady of the movies had come face-to-face with herself and wanted out. She was an extremely private person, and few knew how upsetting the events of the past two days had been until it was almost too late—until Susan made that call for help, even though she disguised it as a call of farewell.

Susan went back to work almost immediately upon her discharge from the hospital, channeling all her energy into what many believe is her most potent screen performance (*I Want To Live,* notwithstanding). *I'll Cry Tomorrow* was the high water mark in her career of "women in trouble," and with the life of Lillian Roth there was trouble aplenty, starting with that first drink and going on to a series of husbands ranging from bland to sadistic. Along the way Susan sang, with unrelieved gusto, such songs as "Happiness Is Just a Thing Called Joe," "Sing You Sinners," and "Red Red Robin." Metro was so impressed that they released a single of "Just One of Those Things" with the flip side the original "I'll Cry Tomorrow," as well as a full soundtrack album, both of which did remarkably well.

Her performance as the alcoholic singer brought in rave reviews and yet another Academy Award nomination, and this time Susan thought she'd get it at last. She was heartsick when she lost to Anna Magnani but, as she told *After Dark* magazine, "I managed not to shed any tears until everything was over and my company had gone home. Then I sat down and had a good cry."

During the shooting and afterwards Susan was seeing a lot of Don "Red" Barry, a former "B" western star of the forties and a bit player in *Tomorrow.* He and Hayward were soon coupled in headlines when she was surprised at his house over breakfast one morning by the arrival of another friend of his, starlet Jil Jarmyn. Jarmyn later stated—with the same attorney who'd represented Barker in his divorce suit—that she'd stopped by "for coffee" but her appearance obviously riled pajama-clad Susan to such an extent that Jarmyn filed an assault and battery charge against her. Susan later told reporters that she too had just stopped by for coffee, which caused much tongue-wagging, the most loquacious of which belonged to Marlene Dietrich, who remarked, "Dat Bawwy must serve good coffee!" After a burst of publicity that did nothing for her career, Jarmyn dropped the suit.

For a fleeting moment Susan almost continued her movie career as a singing star by letting it be known that she'd love playing Nellie Forbush in *South Pacific.* A lot of stars from Betty Hutton on up wanted it, but Susan ran into the picture's director, Joshua Logan, at a party and said she'd do anything for the part. Said Josh, "Anything?" Said Susan, "Anything." Said Josh, "Will you test for it?" Said Susan, "Absolutely not." That ended that, and eventually Mitzi Gaynor got the coveted role.

Fox had put Susan on suspension in 1956 for turning down *Hilda Crane,* (a wise move on Susan's part) but inexplicably she also turned down a role— perhaps roles is a better word—that could have won her an Oscar sooner—in *The Three Faces of Eve.*

Perhaps it was because Susan had fallen in love with a man who, for once, made her think of him ahead of her career. She once said her ideal man needed "reliability, tenderness, strength, and an equal income." She found all of these qualities in a Georgia businessman named Floyd Eaton Chalkley. She met him at a Christmas party in 1956 and married him less than three months later. They were introduced by another Georgian, "Uncle" Harvey Hester whom Susan "adopted" after he played a small part in *I'd Climb the Highest Mountain* some years before and they'd become fast friends.

When Susan saw something she wanted, she went after it, only Chalkley didn't need all that much persuasion. The tall, handsome former FBI agent turned millionaire attorney and gentlemen farmer fell hard and fast for the redhead from Brooklyn. He was ten years her senior. They eloped like youngsters to Phoenix on the spur of the moment on February 9, 1957. It was the beginning of what she'd later call "the happiest period I've ever known."

After the phenomenal success of *I'll Cry Tomorrow,* Susan didn't film again for some time, but she wasn't off the screen, thanks to Howard Hughes. After almost two years of work he finally let the public see *The Conqueror,* his mighty tale of Mongol king Genghis Khan, played by America's mightiest hero, John Wayne. In the film, directed by former movie hoofer Dick Powell, the public was asked to swallow Susan as Bortai, a Tartar princess captured by Khan en route to her wedding—and almost two hours later finally winning her for himself.

If Hughes was out to dethrone Cecil B. DeMille, he failed. Susan's sword dance, which took her six weeks to learn, was climaxed by one of the weapons quivering in a post just inches from Wayne's heavily moustached face. Clad in standard captured-princess garb, she performed the dance with unabashed sensuality.

Hughes later bought back the negative when he sold RKO Pictures, and the film is very seldom seen today, which is too bad, for it contains some quite dazzling nonsense.

Her new marriage changed Susan deeply. She was embarking on a new period of her life with "Eaton," as she called Chalkley, and the vistas were limitless. He built her a lavish new house on 450 acres of his Georgia land in Carrollton and introduced her to deep sea fishing in Florida. Every year they went to the Irish Hunt (shades of her old *Untamed*), and he formed a corporation with Susan as president to develop movie properties, motels, and restaurants. Susan loved the simple Georgia life, and the natives liked her, too, because she was just like any of them, down-to-earth, interested, and, as she told her maid, who paraphrased her, Georgia people "was more sincere and whatever they say they be really meaning." The twins went to school there and Susan reflected, "Women are soft. They're only hard until they meet the right man and fall in love. Then it all changes. Any woman would put true love before a career."

For a time it looked almost as though Susan would. She was choosey after *I'll Cry Tomorrow,* but in 1957 she finally decided on a new project, a comedy with rock-jawed Kirk Douglas called *Top Secret Affair.* She was the best thing in it,

The night of her life—Susan with her Oscar for I Want To Live *(1959).*
THE DOUG MCCLELLAND COLLECTION.

playing Dottie Peale, head honcho of a magazine empire who set out to find the real story about spotless soldier Melville Goodwin (Douglas). Susan looked rather bloated after two years of inactivity, and the film was hardly the success everyone had hoped for. She herself later called it "a bomb."

After a few months back on the farm, Susan found a story she knew could be the mother load—*I Want To Live,* the tale of Barbara Graham, a convicted murderess who'd been executed in the California gas chamber for robbing and killing an elderly housewife. It was brought to her attention by her former mentor Walter Wanger, then coming off several flop pictures, but, thanks to Susan's promptly agreeing to star in it, he was able to raise financing for the film, which was based mainly on the executed B-girl's letters and the extensive newspaper stories about her.

Wanger had served time in jail in the early fifties for shooting wife Joan Bennett's agent, Jennings Lang, in the groin. Ever since his incarceration Wanger had been convinced that the penal system was the nation's number one disgrace. In *I Want To Live* he planned on exposing it, and the sad story of Miss Graham proved the perfect opportunity.

Susan wanted it from the start. "I read the outline and was fascinated by the contradictory traits of personality in the strangely controversial woman who had an extraordinary effect on everyone she met. She was first a juvenile, then an adult delinquent, arrested on bad check charges, perjury, soliciting, and a flood of misdemeanors. But somewhere along the line she was a good wife and mother. I read her letters, often literate, sometimes profound. She loved poetry and music, both jazz and classical. None of this seemed to square with the picture drawn of her at the time of the trial. I studied the trial transcript. I began to wonder myself whether she was really guilty or innocent. I became so fascinated by the woman that I simply had to play her."

And play her she did with all the pathos, weakness, and strength combined in a heart-wrenching performance that literally makes one's nerves tingle—especially at the end, as Graham waits out her own death watch. Susan finally won her Oscar for it, over such heavyweight performers as Elizabeth Taylor for *Cat on a Hot Tin Roof* and Rosalind Russell for the classic *Auntie Mame.* Many fans will never forget that long run she took to the stage to collect her golden statue which, she said, "I won for my three men," meaning Eaton and her sons, to whom she was now closer than ever before. Although Susan had won several major awards, including the New York Film Critics and the Golden Globe, she later told her husband that after twenty-eight years of hard work, she'd finally "climbed on top of that dungheap" that part of her felt Hollywood was—and always had been.

A few years later someone asked Susan her personal views of capital punishment, to which she replied, "My own feelings . . . are simply that if somebody murdered the man I loved and didn't get the death penalty, I'd murder him or her myself!"

I Want To Live was not the start of a roll of hits for her, for her next two,

Woman Obsessed and *Thunder in the Sun,* were terrible flops that not even her Oscar-winning prestige could salvage. Thinking a comedy might be the ticket, she starred with James Mason in the not-very-funny film *The Marriage-Go-Round.* Based on a racy Broadway play about a professor who was picked by a nubile student (Julie Newmar) to father his child while his wife tried to adjust to it all, the original play, which starred Charles Boyer and Claudette Colbert, was considerably censored for its transition to the Technicolor screen. Newmar played her stage role again, and Susan looked a trifle mature as her opposition. At best the fun was flabby.

But movies were now only an occasional job and no longer an obsession. In 1959 she told an interviewer, "I don't miss Hollywood at all, not even my psychiatrist. The career doesn't interest me very much, and more and more I ask why I make any pictures at all."

Hayward fans were delighted that she did though, for her next one was a return to the type of woman she'd long personified on the screen. As Ada Dallas, "a sharecropper's kid off the Delta Road," she told off a bunch of snooty women after she had worked her way up from a southern whorehouse to the governor's mansion on the arm of Dean Martin. In *Ada,* Martin managed a believable performance as the guitar-strumming, easy-going "good old boy" who was maneuvered into the state capitol by the machinations of wily Wilfred Hyde-White. When he was injured in an explosion, Susan stepped into his office and proceeded to let everyone in sight know just who was boss. One reviewer called her a "redheaded switchblade" in the part, and, while it wasn't going to win her any awards, it was a big money-maker and proved that domestic tranquillity hadn't banked the Hayward fire for keeps.

Ross Hunter, the savior of many a languishing career in the fifties (Lana Turner, Jane Wyman, Virginia Grey, et al), signed her for a glossy remake of that time-honored weeper *Back Street* in 1961. In this case the career in question was far from languishing, but she greatly benefited by Hunter's lavish touch, playing a fashion designer who, in her youth, fell in love with soldier John Gavin only to lose him to the war and find him again, much later on a crowded Manhattan street, very much married to an alcoholic socialite played by Vera Miles. Thus began their back street affair—only, with the Hunter touch, it was carried on everyplace else but there, including Susan's very own French chateau. Susan looked magnificent in an Academy nominated wardrobe by Jean Louis, of Rita Hayworth's *Put the Blame on Mame* fame. The film turned into one of the year's least critically liked but most publicly popular films.

Hunter had to talk her into doing *Back Street.* She had always preferred parts where she had to struggle, but she fiercely defended it after it was completed, saying, "These days, unless you have incest and a couple of rapings, the critics are not impressed. . . . *Back Street* is a love story. It's simple old-fashioned love. And I think audiences have liked it. You don't feel dirty when you come out of the theater."

The Chalkleys liked to travel, which seems the only reason she would have made her next picture, a murder/melodrama of the tiredest sort, with the improbable title *I Thank a Fool*. Produced in England and Ireland in 1962, it paired her with Peter Finch in a mixed-up tale of maybe-it-was-murder, maybe-it-wasn't. After seeing it twice, this viewer still can't figure it out. Perhaps part of the blame can be laid to the fact that throughout the picture she and director Robert Stevens didn't get along at all. In a later interview she referred to him simply as "that man." Fortunately, few have ever seen the film.

Ironically Susan's next part was one that would ultimately prove tragically prophetic—that of an heiress dying of brain cancer in the 1963 glossy remake of *Dark Victory*. Reviewers called it a real tear-jerker, but there was a warmth and fire, a mature glamour about Susan's personality that shone through. A gigantic hit for Bette Davis in 1939, the plot was suitably adopted to the sixties in this made-in-Britain production. Originally called *Summer Flight*, but released as *Stolen Hours*, it's a difficult movie to watch now in light of the tragedy that befell Hayward, but it's lushly made and lovingly photographed, and when Susan (the society playgirl) found out about her condition, she projected just the right shade of go-to-hell spirit. As in the original she fell in love with the doctor who diagnosed her condition, and they settled into idyllic happiness on the Cornish coast for the last few months of her life.

There were no displays of temperament on the Shepperton Studio set, and while not working Susan spent quiet hours in her dressing room knitting Eaton a sweater. As with every picture she had made since she married him, Eaton sent her yellow roses every day.

Every actress does trash if the price is right. This is just what Susan did the following year, in 1964, when she took the starring role in *Where Love Has Gone*, based on the Harold Robbins novel that he, in turn, had based on the inflammatory Lana Turner-Cheryl Crane sex-murder scandal of 1958. Susan had long admired Bette Davis and finally would get a chance to lock horns onscreen with the formidable actress, a lady who has always kept her opinions as public as possible. When this author asked her what she thought of Susan's remake of Davis's favorite film, *Dark Victory*, there was a long, smoke-filled pause, after which Bette said crisply, "There are some pictures that should *never* be remade!" Because of this and other things—Susan was often called a "young Bette Davis" —fireworks were expected. Luckily the script called for the ladies, playing mother and daughter, to hate each other anyway, so whatever happened off-camera could only be transmuted to heady emotion on.

Although the story line was a rip-off of the Turner affair, here the lady in question was a famous scupltress instead of a movie queen. Lana herself made no public comment on either the book or the movie, retiring in her later years to a position of silence. "Why fight it and thereby publicize it" became Lana's motto.

When Doug McClelland did his biography of Hayward, he asked Davis pointblank what had happened between them. Davis said, "It is with sadness I tell you Miss Hayward was utterly unkind to me on *Where Love Has Gone.* The title was prophetic. There was no one whose performances I admired more *up* to working with Miss Hayward, and if I said otherwise, when Miss Hayward reads your book she would know I was dishonest.''

Hayward countered that Davis had demanded the last few pages—including the pivotal death scene—be rewritten because she (Davis) felt she couldn't commit suicide with less than two pages of dialogue. ''So we flipped a coin—I lost, and won the death scene,'' which had her race into her sculpting studio and stab herself with an artist's scalpel.

The script was awful to begin with and, as the film's director later admitted, the stars were jealous of each other. ''Susan was frightened of Bette who can come on very very strong if she likes. And, much as I like her, Bette didn't help any.'' Davis's star-mania was still in full flag in the early sixties, which had seen her re-emerge in hits like *Whatever Happened to Baby Jane?* and *Dead Ringer,* and Susan was afraid she'd walk away with the picture. The old fighting spirit had returned to Hayward, and eventually, after numerous demands by Davis for script changes, Susan simply stormed the front offices and said, in effect, 'I shoot the script I signed for or I don't shoot at all.' Susan won, but the film, glossy and star-filled as it was, turned into a compromise that didn't set any records at the box-office. Both stars walked away with their fat salary checks as quickly as possible. Both considered the film low-points of their careers.

For the next two years Susan reveled in her homelife. She apparently felt she had proven just about everything she'd set out to prove and she seemed content being a blue-jeaned, bandanaed housewife to Eaton. He taught her how to ride horseback, and to sail and fish from their place in Fort Lauderdale, relaxing in the mutual enjoyment of mature love for each other.

Susan was still leery of strangers, though, as a representative of a Fort Lauderdale civic association quickly found out when she visited the star and got sidetracked into discussing Susan's furniture rather than her business.

''What did you want to see me about?'' Susan finally growled, a cigarette dangling from her mouth.

''Joining the association.''

''What's it cost?''

When told, Susan said, ''I'll join. Send me a bill and can the chitchat; it bores me.''

She felt that people were more interested in the movie star than in the person underneath. It's ''either the name or the money. That's what they want. Or they want me to be a monkey on a goddam stick and I'm tired of that.''

When Joseph L. Mankiewicz, her old friend from *House of Strangers,* asked her to take a lead role in his new comedy, to be filmed in Venice, Italy, she readily agreed. Called *The Honey Pot,* it was an updated version of *Volpone* and cast her with Rex Harrison as the presumed-to-be-dying millionaire, Cliff Robertson as his Mosca and Edie Adams and the langorous Capucine as two women in his life, summoned along with Susan to say goodbye. As Lone Star Sheridan, Hayward had the juiciest role of the lot (which also included Maggie Smith as her nurse, a specialist in complaining women.)

Shooting was interrupted in late 1965 when Susan got the news that her husband was in a Florida hospital with hepatitis. It was the most severe shock she'd had since the death of her mother in 1958, and she flew home immediately to be with him.

When Susan got to Fort Lauderdale, she found him in Holy Cross Hospital in low spirits. After two weeks he felt he was dying and wanted to go home to Georgia. Susan refused to believe this but decided to humor him anyway. She took him home.

Chalkley, a devout Catholic, burned with a stubborn concern about what would happen to her if he should die since she refused to have anything to do with religion. They had been married in an Episcopalian ceremony (Chalkley was divorced), and on his deathbed he must have realized his spiritual situation. In the eyes of the church whose mass he attended almost every day, he wasn't really married to Susan at all. Though he cleared his conscience of this at his deathbed confession, he worried about Susan's spiritual future, telling her about the Catholic religion and its view of the afterlife. Susan was talking to him when he died.

According to Ron Nelson, her closest friend in later years, when she realized he was dead ''she locked herself in the bathroom and yelled her lungs out. After about ten minutes, she opened the door and came out composed. She turned to Dr. Leonard Erdman, who'd attended Eaton, and said, 'Okay doc, what do I do next?'''

She buried him in a small Georgia cemetery on the grounds of a Catholic church they'd endowed. Then she went back to Italy to finish her film, which had been shot around her, because ''my husband wouldn't have been very proud of me if I hadn't finished what I'd already started.'' For the first time since she'd met Eaton ten years before, there was no bouquet of yellow roses to greet her in the morning.

Five months later she traveled alone and incognito to East Liberty, Pennsylvania, to a Catholic priest who had been a friend of her husband. With his help she converted to Catholicism and later told her friend Nelson, ''I hope to Christ there is something to reincarnation because I want to see Eaton again.''

Returning to Georgia, she found the memories there too fierce, too compelling to live with, so she sold their two vast spreads and moved permanently to Fort Lauderdale, venturing from there the following year to replace Judy Garland in *The Valley of the Dolls*.

During those private months she'd rarely left the house, grieving like an eighteenth-century widow, said one friend, and drinking heavily—saying she needed Beefeater martinis served in brandy snifters the size of goldfish bowls ''to get blown away.''

When Garland couldn't go on, an SOS brought Hayward back to Hollywood for one of the most vulgar movies ever made about the movies. Based on Jacqueline Susann's torrid novel, the only really good thing about it was Susan. In a paucity of scenes (four) she nonetheless succeeded in establishing a character that had many similarities to her own. Purported to be an Ethel Merman-type Broadway star, "a barracuda," she conveyed very much a Susan Hayward-type movie star, still in there pitching, determined to earn applause, yet at the end wondering, "What the hell happened?"

Bette Davis and Jane Wyman had both wanted the part, but it was Hayward's all the way. She brought a hard-shelled earnestness to it that Garland could never have done. And for a mere two weeks' work, the $50,000 she was paid made it palatable for her to sit still at a kickoff press conference and listen to starlet Barbara Parkins introduce her as "one of my co-stars." Susan took the money, along with most of the reviews, and ran back to Florida.

She stayed there, too, living in a ninth-floor luxury apartment surrounded by artifacts of her life. One huge closet was filled with costumes from her various movie roles—the oil-covered dress from *Tulsa,* and a Lillian Roth cocktail dress, among others. And the brandy snifter was always full.

In 1968 producer Marty Rackin called her to kid her about hanging out in Sun City and offered her the lead in a Las Vegas version of the Broadway musical *Mame.* She took him up on it and worked incredibly hard to get herself in shape for the demanding role. Choreographer Oona White worked tirelessly with her to get her into condition, and while Susan worried about her dancing, she didn't initially worry about her voice. She should have, though, for that was what ultimately tripped her up. She wanted the movie role badly and felt that if she could pull off the Vegas version she'd have a good shot at it. But after ninety-six performances—two a night—her voice failed her, and her doctors advised her to get out. (The author has a prized possession—an invitation to a run-through of the show at New York's Winter Garden Theater on Sunday, December 15, 1968. The performance never came off. Susan canceled at the last minute because of a cold, which, according to Doug McClelland, had perhaps settled in her feet.)

Susan cried at a press conference, saying that she'd "never copped out on a job in my life" and got a standing ovation from the cast and crew who had worked with her, and felt for her. She threw them a name-brand liquor party, saying, "I want to go out in style and say thank-you in style." At fifty, the still-striking redhead did just that.

When replacement Celeste Holm came in to take over the part, the feisty beauty told the newcomer that she'd be working with some great people. Ms. Holm agreed offhandedly, according to writer Frank Greve, to which La Hayward replied, "I don't think you heard me right. They're great people, and if I ever hear of your abusing them, so help me, I'll come here and kick your ass back to Toledo, Ohio." After writing "Celeste Who?" on her dressing-room mirror in grease pencil, Susan, still seething, exited from her stage career for a return to Fort Lauderdale and seclusion.

She turned down the Mrs. Robinson role in *The Graduate* as being "unsuit-able" and for a few years little was seen of her. During that time, Susan sat back and read *The Wall Street Journal* (she'd sold off her husband's holdings for millions) and *Photoplay,* and every once in a while she would make a trip to the Southeast Everglades Bank to fondle the approximately $400,000 in cash she kept there. She told her friend Nelson, "I just like to touch it. . . . I like to count it." She liked the Florida life—"I can get to things I never had enough time for before, like music and reading. I keep busy. People from all over the world come and visit me. And I never want to be too far away from my fishing."

Her twin sons had graduated from Georgia Military Academy and had gone on to college, Greg to be a veterinarian and Tim a Hollywood publicist. (Many years later, when she may have suspected she was dying, she played a trick on them. Cutting up newspapers to the size of dollar bills, she put a few real bills on top and left this note in a paper bag in her safe deposit box: "Where did all the dough go? I spent it, what the hell did you think?")

After Eaton's death she was closer to her sons than ever, but as had always been her way, she didn't spoil them. Both boys had to help pay for their educations themselves. Susan had never gotten a free ride, and she felt it was good that her boys learn to fend for themselves early on.

In 1971 a fire started by a lighted cigarette roared through her apartment while she slept. She was quick-witted enough to make her way to the balcony and was tying blankets there for a lifeline when firemen rescued her. The experience shook Susan out of herself, and she decided that perhaps it was time to restart her stalled life. Her old friend Marty Rackin offered her a part in a western called *The Revengers* and she took it. She wanted to pay him back at least partially for dropping out of *Mame* several years before, and she took the Screen-Actors-Guild minimum—$487—which helped get the picture made. It wasn't much of a return for her though, despite a cast that included Bill Holden and Ernest Borgnine.

After finishing *The Revengers* she got the lead in a television movie called *Heat of Anger* when Barbara Stanwyck had to drop out due to illness. It was a projected pilot for a series about a lady lawyer and her eager-beaver young assistant, played by James Stacey, and it gave Susan a crash course in television. She told *TV Guide,* "I was frenzied when I had to learn ten pages of dialogue every day, instead of the three pages we used to do in films, but I soon found out I was able to handle it. Fortunately, my brain is in good shape."

Tragically, it wasn't. In 1972 Susan began to experience piercing headaches. She attributed them to too much drinking and shrugged them off. She did another television movie, an excellent drama about a lady doctor trying to come to grips with her sudden widowhood by taking a job in a Chicago slum. It was a part worthy of her, and she played it with enormous gusto. It felt good to be working again, and even the hectic pace of television didn't slow her down, nor did the headaches. The end result was a poignant, Emmy-worthy performance, but Susan didn't even get a nomination. Nobody knew at the time that it would be the last movie she'd make. Called *Say Goodbye, Maggie Cole,* it turned out to be the world's chance to say goodbye to Susan as one of the most captivating actresses of all time.

Audiences got one last glimpse of the complete woman that spring when, ironically, she and George Peppard presented the Emmy Awards for Best Actor and Actress in a Single Performance. As she began reciting the nominees' names, their photographs flashed onscreen—just a bit behind tempo. Flashed Susan, "I'm waiting."

In December of 1972 she checked into Georgetown University Hospital in Washington, D.C., because of her increasing headaches. The doctors there told her the horrifying news that they'd found some twenty lesions in her brain. She told them they were crazy.

The following April, back in Beverly Hills, she collapsed while attending a party. She was taken to Century City Hospital under the name of Margaret Redding, but friends were told she was in Cedars of Lebanon. Her need for privacy was enormous as she came face to face with the inescapable fact that she was deathly ill. Like so many other times in her life, Susan fought back with all the strength she could muster. When she was released in May, the five-foot, one-inch star weighed only eighty-five pounds. Chemotherapy had robbed her of her beautiful hair and she wore a red wig to conceal its loss.

Rumors about the seriousness of her illness swamped the town, but no one got confirmation from Susan. Though confined to a wheelchair most of the time, smoking one Newport after another, she decided that she'd survive, even as Nelson was told by her doctor, "It could be a week, it could be a month, but she's going to die." He predicted the fourth of July, which turned out to be a terrible weekend. This author remembers it well, for over that holiday weekend in 1973, death claimed Betty Grable and Veronica Lake. Susan was rumored to be the third in one of Hollywood's oldest superstitions: death by threes.

After some weeks Susan left the hospital for home. "Fantastic accuracy" in radiation had halted the spread of the brain tumors, and she was in remission. She knew all along she'd be okay. It was a bunch of baloney, and in October she reported for tests at Massachusetts General Hospital, sure that the results would be positive. They weren't. Her friend Nelson met her when she came back to Fort Lauderdale for three weeks before returning to Hollywood. "I met the plane and thought she'd missed it. All the passengers had gotten off and no Susan. The passage was empty, and then she came. A nurse was holding her. She wore a sable coat and dark glasses. She was dragging her right foot."

They went to his house and Susan signaled for a drink, a request to which her nurse furiously shook her head "No." "Who the hell says I can't drink?" Susan snapped. "I can do anything I please." After three hefty shots of Chivas Regal, she collapsed. Nelson said later that then he let himself cry.

By the end of the year Susan was really dragging her leg. Except for her arm, she was paralyzed on her right side. There was a large tumor growing on the left side of her brain, according to her doctors, and there was no doubt that it would travel across to the right side and paraylze her totally. But within months, despite her resistance to further chemotherapy, she was in remission again. In fact, she was feeling so chipper that she happily accepted an invitation to be an Oscar presenter at the upcoming ceremonies.

Dress designer Nolan Miller concocted a high-necked, black-sequined gown with long lace sleeves, which effectively covered her now-paralyzed right hand. She came on with Charlton Heston, and it was one of the most emotion-filled moments in Oscar's history. Had she allowed it, the applause that greeted her would have grown into a standing ovation, but Susan wouldn't let it. She immediately launched into listing the nominees, thereby quelling the audience. She didn't want Hollywood to have that long a look at her, to pity her.

Buttressed by a massive dose of Dilantin to ward off possible seizure, she said her piece and, in effect, said goodbye, just as Helen Lawson said in *Valley of the Dolls*—"I'll go out the way I came in." Coming offstage she murmured, "Well, that's the last time I pull that off."

By July her brain seizures had become longer and more frequent. She went into Emory University Hospital in Atlanta for exploratory surgery. She issued no public statements but told Nelson, "It's just that I've got rocks in my head and doctors have a machine that detects them. I've known I had rocks in my head for a long time."

At first her therapy was so good that the doctors thought the tumors were benign, but when they came in with the bad news from pathology she told Nelson, "If he's gonna tell me what I think he's gonna tell me, I think you'd better leave." He heard her screams of disbelief and then went in to comfort her, asking if she'd like to talk. "Nothing to talk about, is there?" she asked, announcing, "I'm going home to Fort Lauderdale and I'm going to act as though it never happened."

By summer of 1974 Susan was confined to a wheelchair, her legs in braces to keep the brittle bones from breaking. Her hands were shaking too badly for her to hold a cigarette, but she burned up several carpets trying. At night she and Nelson watched television until the early hours, and once she said, "The night *has* a thousand eyes, doesn't it?"

"Are you afraid?" he asked.

"Let's put it this way—I feel more comfortable sleeping in the daytime."

In September she was back in Emory, where a brain scan showed rapid tumor growth. Doctors concluded that she would soon lose her speech and her memory, and because she explicitly forbade "intravenous or any other lifesaving crap," she'd die once she could no longer swallow. She was in the hospital for weeks and went into a coma, but rallied after four days. Susan was putting up the fight of her life. She had no illusions this time, though, and realized that the end was coming soon. She told Nelson, "I don't want anybody to push me over the brink, and I don't want anybody to hold me back."

Since Eaton had died in Florida, Susan didn't want to go back there. She had Nelson charter a private plane in Atlanta to take her to Hollywood and her mansion high over Culver City. Before they boarded the plane they made a

Susan in one of her last public appearances (1974).   EMILY BARNEY.

"survival pact." He had a serious heart condition, and she told him, "Look, they *think* I've got cancer. We *know* you've had a heart attack. Make a deal? We won't talk about that crap anymore, but let's keep this special thing we've got till one of us kicks the bucket. If it's you, I'll try to be there. If it's me, you goddam better well be or I'll haunt you."

She allowed none of her old friends to see her with the exception of Barbara Stanwyck and Katharine Hepburn. The rest she turned away as the days slipped by and her condition deteriorated.

Finally she called her son Greg in Florida and told him, "You know, I'm dying." It was the first time she'd admitted it to him. He asked what he could do. "Oh, you're a veterinarian, and I thought you might be able to fix up this old horse." After some small talk she said, "This is my nickel so I'm signing off now. I really want you to remember something, though. Remember that I love you."

Her other son, Tim, came over, and they quietly arranged that he take over her extensive financial affairs. "It's the right thing," she whispered. "You're my son." Then, he recalls, "She said she loved me, and whimpered and collapsed."

As predicted, Susan could no longer swallow food, and the last ten days of her life passed without her eating. Three days after she had talked to her sons, the end finally came, Susan's paralyzed hand desperately wrapped around a large onyx crucifix given her by Pope John XXIII. It was two o'clock on the afternoon of March 14, 1975.

Her physician, Dr. Siegel, said of her will to live, "There was no other case like it, nothing in the medical literature. It was amazing to live that long with this type of lesion. She was one of the great fighters. I've never seen anything like it." But then, what else could anyone expect of Susan Hayward?

Tim followed her instructions and had her quietly buried beside Eaton in Carrollton, Georgia. The local people who'd loved her lined the roads respectfully as the hearse pulled into the small churchyard and Susan was laid next to the man she'd loved so desperately. She'd come home to her adopted countryside to stay.

FILMOGRAPHY

Susan Hayward

TITLE	YEAR	DIRECTOR	LEADING PLAYERS
Hollywood Hotel	1937	Busby Berkeley	Dick Powell, Rosemary Lane, Lola Lane, Louella Parsons, Glenda Farrell
The Amazing Dr. Clitterhouse	1938	Anatole Litvak	Edward G. Robinson, Claire Trevor, Humphrey Bogart, Gale Page
The Sisters	1938	Anatole Litvak	Bette Davis, Errol Flynn, Anita Louise, Ian Hunter

TITLE	YEAR	DIRECTOR	LEADING PLAYERS
Comet over Broadway	1938	Busby Berkeley	Kay Francis, Ian Hunter, John Litel
Campus Cinderella	1938	Noel Smith	Johnnie Davis, Penny Singleton
Girls on Probation	1938	William McGann	Jane Bryan, Ronald Reagan
Beau Geste	1939	William A. Wellman	Gary Cooper, Ray Milland, Robert Preston, Brian Donlevy, Broderick Crawford
Our Leading Citizen	1939	Alfred Santell	Bob Burns
$1,000 a Touchdown	1939	James Hogan	Martha Raye, Joe E. Brown, Eric Blore
Among the Living	1941	Stuart Heisler	Albert Dekker, Harry Carey, Frances Farmer, Maude Eburne
Sis Hopkins	1941	Joseph Santley	Judy Canova, Charles Butterworth, Bob Crosby and Orchestra with the Bobcats
Adam Had Four Sons	1941	Gregory Ratoff	Ingrid Bergman, Warner Baxter, Richard Denning, Fay Wray, Johnny Downs
Reap the Wild Wind	1942	Cecil B. DeMille	Paulette Goddard, Ray Milland, John Wayne, Robert Preston, Raymond Massey, Hedda Hopper
The Forest Rangers	1942	George Marshall	Fred MacMurray, Paulette Goddard, Albert Dekker, Lynne Overman, Eugene Pallette
I Married a Witch	1942	René Clair	Frederic March, Veronica Lake, Robert Benchley, Cecil Kellaway, Elizabeth Patterson
A Letter from Bataan	1942	William H. Pine	Richard Arlen, Janet Beecher, Jimmy Lydon
Star Spangled Rhythm	1942	George Marshall	An all-star Paramount musical featuring every star on the lot
Hit Parade of 1943	1943	Albert S. Rogell	John Carroll, Eve Arden, Gail Patrick, Walter Catlett
Young and Willing	1943	Edward H. Griffith	William Holden, Eddie Bracken, Barbara Britton, Robert Benchley
Jack London	1943	Alfred Santell	Michael O'Shea, Osa Massen, Virginia Mayo
Skirmish on the Home Front	1944	For U.S. Government Office of War Information	Alan Ladd, Betty Hutton, William Bendix
And Now Tomorrow	1944	Irving Pichel	Alan Ladd, Loretta Young, Barry Sullivan, Beulah Bondi, Cecil Kellaway
The Fighting Seabees	1944	Edward Ludwig	John Wayne, Dennis O'Keefe, William Frawley
The Hairy Ape	1944	Alfred Santell	William Bendix, John Loder, Dorothy Comingore
Deadline at Dawn	1946	Harold Clurman	Bill Williams, Paul Lukas, Joseph Calleia, Osa Massen, Lola Lane

TITLE	YEAR	DIRECTOR	LEADING PLAYERS
Canyon Passage	1946	Jacques Tourneur	Dana Andrews, Brain Donlevy, Hoagy Carmichael
Smashup, The Story of a Woman	1947	Stuart Heisler	Lee Bowman, Eddie Albert, Marsha Hunt, Carl Esmond
They Won't Believe Me	1947	Irving Pichel	Robert Young, Jane Greer, Rita Johnson, Tom Powers
The Lost Moment	1947	Martin Gabel	Robert Cummings, Agnes Moorehead, Joan Lorring
Tap Roots	1948	George Marshall	Van Heflin, Ward Bond, Boris Karloff, Julie London
The Saxon Charm	1948	Claude Binyon	Robert Montgomery, John Payne, Audrey Totter, Harry Morgan, Harry Von Zell
Tulsa	1949	Stuart Heisler	Robert Preston, Pedro Armendariz, Chill Wills
House of Strangers	1949	Joseph L. Mankiewicz	Edward G. Robinson, Richard Conte, Luther Adler, Efrem Zimbalist, Jr.
My Foolish Heart	1949	Mark Robson	Dana Andrews, Kent Smith, Robert Keith, Jessie Royce Landis, Lois Wheeler
I'd Climb the Highest Mountain	1951	Henry King	William Lundigan, Lynn Bari, Rory Calhoun, Alexander Knox, Gene Lockhart
Rawhide	1951	Henry Hathaway	Tyrone Power, Hugh Marlowe, Dean Jagger, Jack Elam
David and Bathsheba	1951	Henry King	Gregory Peck, Raymond Massey, Jayne Meadows, Kieron Moore
I Can Get It for You Wholesale	1951	Michael Gordon	Dan Dailey, George Sanders, Sam Jaffe
With a Song in My Heart	1952	Walter Lang	David Wayne, Rory Calhoun, Thelma Ritter, Robert Wagner, Una Merkel
The Snows of Kilimanjaro	1952	Henry King	Gregory Peck, Ava Gardner, Hildegarde Neff, Leo G. Carroll
The Lusty Men	1952	Nicholas Ray	Robert Mitchum, Arthur Kennedy, Arthur Hunnicutt
The President's Lady	1953	Henry Levin	Charlton Heston, Fay Bainter, John McIntire
White Witch Doctor	1953	Henry Hathaway	Robert Mitchum, Walter Slezak, Michael Ansara
Demetrius and the Gladiators	1954	Delmer Davies	Victor Mature, Michael Rennie, Debra Paget, Ann Bancroft, Jay Robinson, Richard Egan
Garden of Evil	1954	Henry Hathaway	Gary Cooper, Richard Widmark, Hugh Marlowe, Cameron Mitchell, Rita Moreno

TITLE	YEAR	DIRECTOR	LEADING PLAYERS
Untamed	1955	Henry King	Tyrone Power, Richard Egan, Agnes Moorehead, Rita Moreno, John Justin
Soldier of Fortune	1955	Edward Dmytryk	Clark Gable, Gene Barry, Michael Rennie, Anna Sten
I'll Cry Tomorrow	1955	Daniel Mann	Jo Van Fleet, Richard Conte, Eddie Albert, Don Taylor, Margo, Virginia Gregg
The Conqueror	1956	Dick Powell	John Wayne, Agnes Moorehead, Pedro Armendariz, Thomas Gomez, Ted DeCorsia
Top Secret Affair	1957	H. C. Potter	Kirk Douglas, Paul Stewart, Jim Backus, Roland Winters, Charles Lane
I Want To Live!	1958	Robert Wise	Simon Oakland, Virginia Vincent, Theodore Bikel, Alice Backes
Woman Obsessed	1959	Henry Hathaway	Stephen Boyd, Theodore Bikel, Dennis Holmes, Barbara Nichols
Thunder in the Sun	1959	Russell Rouse	Jeff Chandler, Jacques Bergerac, Blanche Yurka, Carl Esmond
The Marriage-Go-Round	1960	Walter Lang	James Mason, Julie Newmar, Robert Paige
Ada	1961	Daniel Mann	Dean Martin, Wilfred Hyde-White, Ralph Meeker, Martin Balsam
Back Street	1961	David Miller	John Gavin, Vera Miles, Virginia Grey, Reginald Gardiner, Natalie Schafer, Charles Drake
I Thank a Fool	1962	Robert Stevens	Peter Finch, Diane Cilento, Cyril Cusack, Kieron Moore
Stolen Hours	1963	Daniel Petrie	Michael Craig, Edward Judd, Diane Baker
Where Love Has Gone	1964	Edward Dmytryk	Bette Davis, Michael Conners, Joey Heatherton, Jane Greer, Anne Seymour
The Honey Pot	1967	Joseph L. Mankiewicz	Rex Harrison, Maggie Smith, Capucine, Cliff Robertson, Edie Adams
Valley of the Dolls	1967	Mark Robson	Barbara Parkins, Patty Duke, Sharon Tate, Paul Burke, Tony Scotti, Lee Grant, Martin Milner
Heat of Anger Movie for Television	1972	Don Taylor	James Stacey, Lee J. Cobb, Fritz Weaver
The Revengers	1972	Daniel Mann	William Holden, Ernest Borgnine, Woody Strode, Arthur Hunnicutt
Say Goodbye, Maggie Cole Movie for Television	1972	Jud Taylor	Darren McGavin, Beverly Garland, Dane Clark, Michael Constantine, Jeanette Nolan

219

Dorothy Dandridge

I'll get that part if it's the last thing I do.

*Dorothy Dandridge, upon hearing
that the role of Carmen Jones was
up for grabs.*

In case of my death—to whomever discovers it—don't
remove anything I have on—scarf, gown, or underwear.
Cremate me right away. If I have anything, money,
furniture, give it to my mother Ruby Dandridge. She
will know what to do.

*Written by Dorothy Dandridge and
given to her business manager, Earl
Mills, on May 21, 1965, shortly
before her death.*

IF any decade was able to produce and
then attempt to handle a black sex symbol, it was the 1950s. It was a time of racial
movement when millions of white Americans looked across their backyards and
saw blacks moving in next door. It was a time when both races would begin to
accept a black movie goddess on the movie screen. The actress who made the
breakthrough was a classically beautiful, lightskinned, singer-turned-dancer
named Dorothy Dandridge.

After some half-dozen movie roles in the late forties and early fifties, Dorothy
blazed across the screen as Otto Preminger's *Carmen Jones* in 1954, lighting a fire
of sexuality that made her an international star and the first black woman to be
nominated for a Best Actress Oscar. At a time when it was no longer believable
for a Jeanne Crain to play a black (as she did in 1949 in *Pinky*), Dorothy filtered
through the layers of color as surely as a dollop of cream in a glass of chocolate
milk. And as she shortly found out, it wasn't easy.

Lena Horne learned that lesson a decade earlier in several MGM musicals,
most of which found her clinging to a pillar in self-contained numbers easily
excised for Southern audiences not yet ready for an overt black sex symbol. She
was more elegantly beautiful than Dandridge, but for the times her eroticism was

Dorothy Dandridge and Harry Belafonte in Carmen Jones *(1954).*
THE DOUG MCCLELLAND COLLECTION

more threatening than appealing. As late as 1951, Lena was denied the chance to play the doomed mulatto, Julie, in *Show Boat,* but when Dorothy burst upon the scene as a full-fledged sex object a few years later, there was scarcely a way to avoid her being just that.

Ironically, though, just when she attained the impossible dream of being the first black leading lady, Dorothy found it equally impossible to continue, for what roles could she play? Typecast as a turbulent lady of loose morals because of *Carmen Jones* and *Porgy and Bess,* she was a victim of her own fame as much as its celebrant. Her film career ended at the end of the fifties because, in the violent sixties to follow, there was no place for the tragic mulatto image to survive, let alone flourish. All that remained for Dorothy Dandridge were five years of increasing disappointment, rejection and tragedy.

Later, actresses like Cicely Tyson could play dramatic heroines, as in *Sounder* and *The Autobiography of Miss Jane Pittman,* but Dorothy was trapped in the mold of sexuality, an object of fantasy to blacks and whites alike. It was a fantasy which turned into a reality she soon found too unrewarding to continue.

UNHAPPINESS marked Dorothy Dandridge even before her birth in Cleveland, Ohio, on November 11, 1922. Her father had disappeared, leaving her mother, Ruby, to raise Dorothy and her older sister Vivian. Her father's disappearance led to rumors later in her life that he had been a white man. That would explain her undeniably mulatto complexion which would prove a benefit career-wise, but ultimately a great personal problem.

A hardworking woman, Ruby tried to make up for the absence of a husband by involving herself deeply in church activities. One night she was to deliver a sermon at church, but fell ill and prodded tiny Dorothy to do it in her stead. The three year old did it so successfully that other churches heard about the child preacher. Ruby teamed her up with Vivian, and they became The Wonder Kids. While Ruby worked hard as a restaurant cook, her daughters entertained church-goers all over Cleveland.

When they were invited to appear at a Baptist conference in the South, Mrs. Dandridge gave her permission, providing their expenses were paid. That appearance created an even bigger demand for the children's services—so big in fact that Ruby quit her job, hired a piano player, and started out on a tour of southern churches that would last five years.

In 1930, caught in the grip of the Depression like millions of others, Ruby made the decision to move her family to California, where they settled in a forty-dollar-a-month apartment in the Watts section of Los Angeles. The next few years, the ones children usually spend playing and going to school, were primarily work years for Ruby's girls, with Dorothy gradually getting small parts in various films. Pretty, bright, and anxious to please with her outgoing personality, Dorothy started attracting attention at a young age. Although all she saw of the white world was movie backlots and sound stages, her developing sexuality was at odds with the prevailing attitude towards blacks. While Dorothy appreciated—and understood—the fact that she would some day be a beauty, that fact also made her realize she'd be a more prominent target for the lust, insecurities, and subsequent angers of then and future employers. Without a father, she also knew that she'd have to defend herself all by herself.

Though she sometimes pretended that her father was a very important man back East, she never told the story well enough to be believed. In Watts there were already too many stories floating around in vain attempts at welding together disappointments and shattered dreams into some kind of palatable reality.

The squalor of the ghetto and the rampant alcoholism and attendant weakening of family fiber made Dorothy a total nondrinker in her youth, so repugnant to her were its effects on her neighbors. Later in life she never drank in public, and, while she subsequently developed a serious alcohol problem bred by her own frustrations and broken dreams, she drank in private. From her teenage years and even before, Dorothy carried herself like a lady at all times—and people gradually accepted her as one.

Throughout these formative years, Dorothy and her sister had a formidable ally in their mother. Ruby Dandridge was determined that her children would escape the ghetto life, and, with her own career just beginning in the movies—as the second favorite maid after Hattie McDaniel—she decided that the world of entertainment would be the quickest way out.

After enrolling the girls in dancing school as a career back-up, Ruby scouted out a third talented youngster, Etta Jones, and formed a group called The Dandridge Sisters. She entered them in a Los Angeles radio station contest which they won by doing an imitation of the Andrew Sisters. Dorothy had already played bit parts in several pictures, including *A Day at the Races* with the Marx Brothers in 1937, and the following year the Sisters landed a spot in Dick Powell's *Going Places*—a prophetic title for Dorothy in particular.

By this time, Ruby Dandridge was beginning to get steady work in radio and as a movie extra. Her work kept her too busy to take care of her daughters and Etta during their singing tours, so she hired a woman to chaperone them. A martinet whom the girls were instructed to call "aunt," the woman governed the girls' lives strictly—Dorothy's in particular—especially stressing the fact that Dorothy's burgeoning sexuality was something to be held in check at all times.

One night when Dorothy returned home from a date later than she'd been told to, the woman verbally assaulted her, calling her names and accusing her of having had sex with her friend. To find out, the woman ripped off a horrified Dorothy's dress and forcibly probed inside her to find out whether or not her virginity was still intact. It was a harrowing experience for the young girl, and it reinforced her own feelings of self-recrimination and remorse. What had she done wrong? She felt as guilty as if she had had sex, and it became an episode that would haunt her later on. As Dorothy told Earl Mills, later her manager and lover and the author of *Dorothy Dandridge—A Portrait in Black* (Holloway House, 1970), "She was often brutal and always threatening . . . she wanted to take credit for making me successful, but on the other hand she hated to see me succeed. I was always a target for her. She did everything she could to destroy me. It made it harder for me to cope with society later on."

After finishing *Going Places,* the Dandridge Sisters were booked into Harlem's famous Cotton Club, where Dorothy met a handsome young black tap dancer, Harold Nicholas, one-half of the Nicholas Brothers. He was impressed by the unspoiled freshness of the beautiful girl and began courting her in earnest after they both returned to Hollywood, where they appeared together in the "Chattanooga Choo Choo" number in *Sun Valley Serenade.* The film was one of the bigger hits of 1941, in which Glenn Miller debuted the song which would be his first million selling record.

Nicholas had a reputation around the Hollywood black community as a ladies' man, but Dorothy didn't listen to the rumors of his constant romantic adventures. She'd met him at a crucial point in her life—after *Sun Valley Serenade* the Sisters had joined the Jimmy Lunceford band, and shortly thereafter Etta announced she was leaving the group to be married. This triggered romantic thoughts in Dorothy's brain, and she innocently fell in love with Harold before they'd even exchanged their first kiss.

With an MGM contract for the Nicholas Brothers act in his hip pocket, Harold Nicholas felt financially secure. They were married on November 2, 1942 —seven days short of her twentieth birthday. Unfortunately, while he envisioned the glamour of Hollywood nights, his wife envisioned quiet nights in Hollywood, making a home for them both while he danced in Metro musicals and she worked part time in pictures like *Bahama Passage, Lady from Louisiana,* and *The Drums of the Congo.* That same year she joined Duke Ellington's musical show, *Jump for Joy,* and prophetically sang "I Got It Bad and That Ain't Good." Mama Ruby was busy making *Cabin in the Sky* for MGM with Mantan Moreland, Ethel Waters, Rex Ingram, and the gorgeous Lena Horne, leaving Dorothy with no one to turn to at one of the most troubled times of her life.

Marriage and happiness. It all seemed so simple; to Dorothy, the first led to the second. But it wasn't so simple after all. Their wedding night was one of pain and frustration for Dorothy. She loved Harold but was sexually frigid, and the union was a rocky one from the moment she took off her wedding dress.

They soon reached a compromise. Dorothy took care of the house, which she loved doing, while Harold started seeing some of his old girlfriends. Despite her outward serenity, sex was a difficult thing for Dorothy, due largely to the fear of it engendered by her earlier experience with her chaperone. And while Harold was far from happy with the situation, he nonetheless felt it balanced out by his growing status in the black community due mainly to his beautiful wife. The chasm between the two widened when Dorothy became pregnant, and used her pregnancy as an excuse to avoid sleeping with her husband at all.

What was left of her dreams of a simple life of home and hearth were completely shattered when, after the birth of her daughter, Harolyn, it was discovered the child was brain-damaged. Dorothy had to face that awful realization alone, as Harold was touring Europe. It was a brutal time for her emotionally. In a desperate effort to reverse the truth, she took the child from doctor to doctor, hoping for another verdict, but it was always the same—mental retardation.

This tragedy, which should have brought the couple together, actually drove the couple apart. Dorothy blamed herself, Harold, even God, and, as the child grew, she carried a snapshot of Harolyn as she had looked as a one year old: wide-eyed and seemingly perfect.

Harold wrote to her saying that he liked Paris so much that he was staying there and that she should expect no more money from him. A realist, he knew that a future with Dorothy and a mentally crippled child was simply not for him. Meanwhile, Dorothy was finding it impossible to accept the reality of her child's disability and her own disintegrated marriage. She constantly asked herself, "Why? Why? Why?" She couldn't concentrate on getting her own career back together, and, as her money ran out, she skirted dangerously near a nervous breakdown. By 1947 she was clearly at a crisis point. But there was no one there to listen or help, even on that dark day when doctors told her, finally, that her child would always have the mentality of a four year old.

Ironically, at this point Dorothy's childhood nemesis—her "aunt"—showed up and suggested that the child be institutionalized, a thought that horrified Dorothy. In a desperate bid for time and hoping it would change the inevitable, Dorothy gave Harolyn over to the woman to take care of while she tried to pull her life together. She knew no miracle would happen and that the child would eventually have to be sent away, as she ultimately was.

With responsibility of Harolyn at least temporarily off her shoulders, although it would never leave her mind, Dorothy was able to take stock of herself and try to come to a decision about what her next step should be. Her faith in herself and her singing talent were both extremely shaky, but, happily, there was someone about to step into her life who would reawaken her self-confidence and her career—musician Phil Moore, a composer and arranger who had once worked with the Dandridge Sisters in New York.

He encouraged and helped her put together a new singing act, and, as they worked closely together on it, their interests gradually changed from purely professional to romantic as well. He was able to give her the enthusiasm, confidence, and affection of which she was in such short supply, and managed to find her a spot with the Desi Arnaz band, then playing at the Mogambo, when Desi's regular vocalist became ill. It was too soon, though. Dorothy's voice wasn't ready yet. Desi's own singer took back her job as soon as she recovered.

Depressed, Dorothy felt that she'd let down not only herself and Phil, but the black community—whose respect she would always court but be only sporadically sure of.

A friend of Phil's, producer Sol Lesser, was putting together *Tarzan's Peril* with Lex Barker, and there was a role as a jungle princess in it that was perfect for Dorothy. She tested and got the part, and, when it was released in 1951, she caused a minor furor. At one point, she was tied spread-eagle on the ground, writhing in supposed agony, but projecting a blatant sexuality that piqued not only Tarzan's interest, but that of everyone else as well.

At Columbia she played an athlete's wife in *The Harlem Globetrotters*. With her voice by now honed to a new sultry sharpness by a series of dates at small L.A. clubs, she accepted a booking at London's Café de Paris, along with her old friend Phil Moore. Her impact was spectacular enough to result in her long hoped for personal success. Unfortunately, the audience wanted more of Dorothy than of Moore, and as he gradually withdrew into the background of the act, their personal relationship began disintegrating. A respected musician who had worked for years with Lena Horne, his ego was wounded, and the silences between them became increasingly longer. When Dorothy returned home, she was distraught over the breakup. Grateful to Moore for what he'd done for her professionally, she wanted to remain his friend, although by now she had finally reached the point where she felt she could step out on a stage alone and take control. Moore did stay on as Dorothy's musical arranger, and she signed with a personal manager. Together they set their sights on the hottest spot in Hollywood—the Mogambo.

The Mogambo management, after signing her for a two-week stay, capitalized on her beauty and her London success by sending out elaborate brochures, complete with sultry pictures, which stated that Dorothy Dandridge was like a living Kinsey Report! *Life* magazine covered the opening and called her the most beautiful singer since Lena Horne, a comparison that made Dorothy swell with pride. More important, though, was the approval she got from *Ebony*, the leading black magazine, which not only raved about her beauty and talent, but also called her a credit to her race, thus quelling the fears that had built up when she'd heard rumors that many blacks thought her a snob and accused her of going "over to the white side." Unfortunately, Dorothy was so sensitive to *anything* said about her that she was constantly worrying and tried to keep everyone happy, an almost hopeless task.

Shortly thereafter, she set a record when she became the first black entertainer to open at New York's Waldorf-Astoria Hotel. Once again the reviews were glowing.

Back home, her manager got a call from MGM's Dore Schary who had seen Dorothy onscreen and onstage and wanted to talk about her playing the lead in a small-budgeted, but prestigious, film he was planning called *Bright Road*. The film would focus on the problems of blacks and have a primarily Negro cast to be headed up, hopefully, by Dorothy. She would play the part of a schoolteacher, and, while it was not a glamorous role, she grabbed it and projected an elegant simplicity in her attempts to reach out and help a wayward student. Harry Belafonte was also in the cast, and the news of the picture caused widespread excitement and speculation in the black community. As always, Dorothy worried about whether or not she could succeed and worked hard on the role, turning herself into the character with an artistry that quickly convinced Schary he hadn't been wrong in his choice of the virtually untried actress. The tragedy of her own daughter added yet another dimension to her performance, a personal touch that only she could interpret.

Another and, as it turned out, easier confrontation came during a singing engagement in Cleveland, her hometown, when she was approached by a handsome, distinguished-looking black man who introduced himself as Cyril Dandridge, her father. The residue of resentment that had built up over the years of her fatherless childhood was swept away as they talked, warily at first, and then more confidently as they got to know one another. He wanted nothing from her other than for her to know how proud he was of her growing success. Remarried, he'd built a new life for himself and wished Dorothy the same kind of contentment he'd found. Although it was a happy reunion, they were never to meet or talk again after this short interlude. But it marked the solution of one of Dorothy's personal mysteries. She found out from this meeting that she was one-quarter white.

The critical success of *Bright Road* restored a great deal of Dorothy's self-confidence, so badly shaken by her tragic marriage. MGM was so pleased with her picture work that Louis B. Mayer personally guaranteed her stardom. Unfortunately, Mayer's days as studio chief were running out, and he wasn't able to live up to his promise. She appeared in a small part in *Remains To Be Seen* in 1953, but the star buildup he'd promised never materialized.

After a wildly successful return engagement at the Mogambo, Dorothy thought the time was ripe to get back into movies. Her determination was fired when she heard of a project between Twentieth Century Fox's Darryl F. Zanuck and independent producer Otto Preminger—a black movie musical called *Carmen Jones*.

An innovative project to say the least, it would obviously be a major groundbreaking film, as well as a star-making vehicle for the title player. First cast was Pearl Bailey as Carmen's girlfriend, Frankie, and then Harry Belafonte was signed to play the tragic G.I., Joe, the soldier who falls for the black temptress and finally strangles her in a jealous rage when she leaves him for a prize fighter. The big question mark was who would play the lead, and Dorothy decided that it would be she—no matter what.

Her manager approached Preminger who was very lukewarm. Dorothy was furious when she heard that and reacted with a vengeance when Preminger suggested she test instead for the part of Joe's sweet girlfriend Cindy Lou. At the time a singer named Joyce Bryant was considered the top candidate for Carmen, but Preminger hadn't reckoned with a determined Dorothy.

Preminger came to see her perform at New York's La Vie En Rose, but her classy delivery convinced him even more that "I can't see her in a parachute factory or a sleazy Chicago hotel room with an A.W.O.L. soldier." Then he tested Lena Horne for the part, something Dorothy could almost live with considering the respect she had for the singer. But secretly she began to devise a strategy. Through Ingo Preminger, Otto's agent brother, Dorothy got a face-to-face interview with Otto. He still thought she was more Cindy Lou than Carmen, saying she was "too much like Loretta Young," despite her protestations that "I can play a whore. I'm an actress. I can play a whore as well as a nun. . . . I'm not a Cindy. You don't know what I've gone through."

From his office she went to the Max Factor studio and borrowed a whorish, messy black wig. From there she went home, took off her brassiere, and put on an off-the-shoulder blouse, a black satin skirt slit up the thigh, and high-heeled pumps. She looked at herself in the mirror and knew for sure that whether she got Carmen or not, she'd never get Cindy Lou.

Preminger was speechless when she swaggered sexily into his office, put one high-heeled foot up on the edge of a chair and stared him down. So flabbergasted was he that he consented to let her test for the title role. She tested the famous scene in the Chicago hotel where a humbled Joe is reduced to painting Carmen's toenails before she goes out with another man; it cinched the deal. "It is remarkable," Preminger muttered over and over during the test as he witnessed the transformation Dorothy had pulled off. He was so taken by her that before long they were embarked on an affair, an on-again, off-again thing which would last several years.

Before production began, however, Dorothy had to fly to Rio de Janeiro to fulfill a singing engagement there, and she fell hopelessly in love with a Brazilian millionaire. Feeling more comfortable there, she mixed easily with the upper class society types who picked up on the rising star. Romantic that she was, she believed her new admirer's protestations of love and returned them wholeheartedly, writing home to friends that she felt as if she'd fallen into a make-believe fantasy that she prayed would never end. Unfortunately, it proved to be just that when she learned that he was a married man who wanted her as his mistress, not his wife. She never saw him again after he made that proposition, and she was so badly shaken by it that she went to a local doctor who prescribed sedatives which she began downing at an alarming rate. When she'd finished her singing stint and returned home, she was emotionally depleted and distraught and soon started psychotherapy to try to regain her equilibrium. She had been willing to give up her career for him, but only as his wife. Now she turned back onto the path of ambition so boldly laid out by Otto Preminger. If she couldn't have a happy home and a husband, then by God she would have international stardom.

Carmen Jones was fashioned by Preminger to be a drama with music rather than a straight-out musical. In making it he cut out much of what had been onstage in the Oscar Hammerstein-scripted Broadway revue, going back to the original story of *Carmen* by Prosper Merimee and updating it to World War II. Initially he had a hard time getting the picture off the ground, until Zanuck came to his rescue. Other producers had shied away, citing the box office flops of previous black films such as *Cabin in the Sky* and *Green Pastures*. Zanuck had been impressed with Otto's having pulled off the controversial *The Moon Is Blue*—a censorship landmark for its time containing such heretofore unheard (onscreen at least) words as "virgin" and "pregnant." He was immediately enthusiastic about this new venture, even though his board of directors at Twentieth advised against it. The most he could get them to part with for a budget was a paltry $750,000, which meant that the entire film would have to be wrapped up in a mere four weeks.

Once she'd landed the role, Dorothy began suffering grave doubts as to whether she could pull it off. These intensified to such a degree that the day before shooting was to start, she called her manager and informed him, quietly, that she wasn't going to do the film after all. Getting the part, she told him, proved that she was capable of it, so why take on the burden of carrying an entire production on her shoulders? Naturally he was frantic at this inexplicable change of heart and, with her psychiatrist in tow, spent the whole day trying to convince her that she could do it, citing the fact that it would give her a chance to finally prove herself as an actress, as well as give her the reputation she'd long stated she wanted so badly. But like a self-destructive child, she stubbornly insisted that she'd proven herself already. They talked until 3 A.M., but she remained adamant, and, when her manager drove over at 5:30 to take her to the studio, he still wasn't sure if she'd be willing to go ahead or not.

She was, and she laughed off the whole escapade by saying she was just nervous and, "You know how I am." The self-destructive child had been put to rest, at least for the time being.

Dorothy was disappointed when Preminger informed her that her voice, while undeniably good, wasn't up to the operatic standards of the Bizet score and that she was to be dubbed in the finished product by a young opera student named Marilyn Horne. If Dorothy had had weeks to rehearse, she could have done it herself, but there just wasn't that kind of time, and, as it was, the dubbing required long hours of practice with a teacher so that she looked onscreen as if she were indeed singing the turbulent melodies.

The pace set by Preminger was a furious one, and Dorothy, sensing his total dedication to the film and her performance in it, worked long hours trying to please him. Every morning they'd view the rushes of the preceding day, and he'd caution her about this or that. Since it was being shot in Cinemascope, every gesture was magnified, and he was always telling her to go more slowly, to take more time, that Carmen would never rush. Under his tutelage, her characterization as the vain and tormented beauty grew steadily, combining an elemental sexuality with a calculating confidence and an unmistakable vulnerability. A man who inspired fear in the hearts of even the most seasoned actors, Preminger realized that that was not the way to handle his newest star. He was, instead, overly patient with her, happily working on scenes with her long after the other cast members had gone home, or willing to talk them over at a quiet dinner.

In him Dorothy saw a strong, positive, and important man, and she bent her will accordingly, letting him take full control and also letting him solve her problems. He dug her out of herself, and, as the weeks wore on, their attachment grew to be more than just that of director-star. Preminger never became involved with his leading ladies while a film was in production, but when the shooting was finished, he and Dorothy began dating, albeit quietly. In the early fifties it was still shocking for a white man to be seen openly with a Negro woman, no matter how beautiful or famous she was. Also, Otto's estranged wife had been making the Hollywood rounds with Michael Rennie, a man Dorothy had dated once or twice (as she had Peter Lawford, who eventually became a close friend), so instead of chancing the crossing of paths, Otto opted for quiet dinners, teaching Dorothy the elements of gourmet cooking along the way. He also bought her clothes and fine art, and helped her select a mansion suitable for a star when the time came—and it was coming fast.

On the set she remained aloof from everyone. The only friend Dorothy made was Pearl Bailey, preferring to stay locked up in her dressing room when not needed on the set. The dedication of Dorothy and the single-mindedness of her director paid off when *Carmen Jones* opened at New York's Rivoli Theater on October 28, 1954. Dorothy had already seen the film at a sneak preview in California and was racked with doubts over her performance, telling Preminger of the dozens of places where she thought she could have done better. With an uncharacteristic kindness, he tried to calm her fears. As the trade reviews came in, she was gradually convinced that she'd done more than a good job. As Carmen she shouted, clawed, and fought her way into movie history.

The night of the premiere Dorothy arrived at the theater alone. She had just done a television show and was scheduled to go on the "Steve Allen Show" afterwards. Ruby, her mother, was busy in Hollywood, but sister Vivian was there. When Dorothy alighted from her limousine, the curious crowd let out a resounding roar which Dorothy acknowledged with a curious, detached radiance, almost as if what happened next was beyond her control and all she could do was continue hoping the results would be worthwhile. They were, as the New York newspapers glowingly responded to the film and the dynamically beautiful lady in the title role, an appropriate climax to the standing ovation she'd received at the premiere's end. *Time* and *Newsweek* both heralded the film, and *Life* magazine put Dorothy on its cover, the first time a black woman had been given that honor. In doing that they said, "Of all the divas of grand opera—from Emma Calvé of the 90s to Rise Stevens—who have decorated the title role of Carmen and have in turn been made famous by it, none was ever so decorative or will reach nation-wide fame so quickly as the sultry young lady on *Life*'s cover this week."

Preminger stood by with "I told you sos," and Dorothy basked in the greatest wave of approval she'd ever had. For a flashing moment, all the frustrations and torments were bathed away by the soothing waters of acceptance and, finally, stardom.

She willingly went on the road to attend other major city premieres, and Fox, sensing they had a new star on their hands, especially after she was nominated for an Academy Award as Best Actress of 1954, signed her to a three-year contract in March of 1955, guaranteeing her a picture a year, with a salary escalating from $75,000 to $125,000 per picture. It was a nonexclusive contract that would allow her to take outside work as well, as Fox already sensed that it might be difficult to find enough good parts for a black Love Goddess.

Dorothy was the first black actress ever to be nominated for the Best Actress Award, and her competition was formidable: Judy Garland for *A Star Is Born,* Grace Kelly for *The Country Girl,* Audrey Hepburn for *Sabrina,* and Jane Wyman for *Magnificent Obsession.* Clad in a white-yellow satin gown, she stood nervously backstage at New York's Century Theater (the televised award show was split between Los Angeles and New York that year) waiting to present the Best Editing Award. She wanted to win desperately and was riding yet another crest of fame. She was in New York because she was headlining at the Waldorf-Astoria, another black first, and had recently been named one of the five most beautiful women in the world by an association of Hollywood photographers. She'd memorized a simple speech just in case she won, and, if she couldn't win, she honestly hoped that her friend Judy Garland would. Sister Vivian was there with her and before the ceremonies Dorothy had mentioned how far they'd come from the Wonder Children. After presenting her award (won by Gene Milford for *On The Water-front*), she hovered nervously backstage watching while Marlon Brando won Best Actor for the same picture, as did Elia Kazan as Best Director. The crucial moment was suddenly on top of her as she saw William Holden walk on camera with that magic envelope in his hand. Without preamble he opened it and announced, ''Grace Kelly for *The Country Girl.*''

Later that night in her Waldorf Towers suite, over a dinner of chittlins sent in from her favorite Harlem restaurant, she told friends that while she'd lost that night, someday she'd walk off with the gold statue in her hands. At the time her optimism seemed both reasonable and possible.

By then her affair with Preminger was amounting to something of a standoff, since she was so busy touring and performing. At the start she'd been lighthearted about it all, casual almost, but now she was beginning to miss a love relationship. She had worked so hard to get up there, and there was no one to share her success with her. An exhaustive schedule found her either working, rehearsing, or sleeping.

After conquering New York, Dorothy was booked into the Riviera Hotel in Las Vegas at $20,000 a week and soon thereafter began getting lots of attention from the maître d' of the main room. He was a handsome, greying white man named Jack Dennison. At night, after she'd finished her show, he would send up elaborate dinners for her served by several waiters. He also made sure that fresh flowers were always in her dressing room. She relished the attention, especially since her relationship with Preminger seemed to be approaching a dead end, and her longtime friendship with Peter Lawford was already dead. She was vulnerable to the suave attentions of a man like Dennison, and, before she finished her engagement, they had become emotionally involved. To Dennison, Dorothy was not only a star, but a desirable woman who crossed both black and white worlds. To blacks, she was the epitome of *their* sexuality, and to whites she represented the ultimate, forbidden fantasy.

And Dorothy knew that too. When *Confidential* magazine published a shocking story which claimed that she had willingly let herself be seduced by a white musician in the woods behind a Nevada resort, she became the first major star to fight back against the slander rag. Seeing the story as an affront to not only her reputation but to that of black women everywhere, she hit the publishers with a whopping $2 million lawsuit. After a long drawn out case which included a court appearance in August of 1957, she eventually won a settlement of $10,000. It took enormous courage to fight the monthly scandal sheet, then at its peak as a ripper-apart of Hollywood reputations from Clark Gable's to Ava Gardner's. The victory was one of the few she would taste. Even though she'd been advised that the story was "good publicity," she was determined to dispell the idea that she was an "easy lay." Her friendships with Preminger, Lawford, and currently Dennison didn't help her cause, but she couldn't be dissuaded, and came out of it vindicated, complete with a printed retraction and apology.

She was triumphant in newsprint, but not on the screen, as Fox had indeed been having a hard time finding a script for her, and two years had gone by since *Carmen Jones.*

Later in 1957 there was great excitement when producer Lester Cowan announced that Dorothy would star in the film version of William Dufty's bestseller, *Lady Sings the Blues,* the story of the tragic Billie Holliday. As Dufty, now married to Gloria Swanson, recalls, "She was obviously our first choice to play Billie, even though I didn't think she had enough of Billie's soul, her special, raunchy blackness. But Lester Cowan wanted her, and Walter Reade, the man who was putting up the money, also wanted her, very badly. Dandridge had never seen Holliday perform. There was never any question but that Billie would do the soundtrack for the film, and we even for a time considered Ava Gardner for the part. (Author's note: obviously because Miss Gardner had played the mulatto Julie in *Showboat* six years before.) And Lana Turner, since I always felt color blind about the part in that respect. Dorothy was definitely the number one choice of the producers, but the project collapsed. There was general unhappiness about it. A recording strike was going on, and Billie would have had to record in Mexico or Europe." There were, in fact, all sorts of problems.

Considering the version that surfaced in the early seventies starring Diana Ross, it remains a shame that Dorothy Dandridge didn't get a chance to play the role, since she'd have likely taken the part and run with it to the Academy Award that was her dream.

Studio heads searched desperately for roles to showcase their new star, and she was indeed announced for several other interesting projects. When they were setting up the lavish *The King and I* in 1955, Dorothy was announced to play the part of the concubine Tuptim, and there was also mention of a musical remake of the old Claudette Colbert picture *Under Two Flags*. Rita Moreno got the part in the first, and the second picture was never made.

Most intriguing, though, was the studio announcement that Dorothy would star as Lola Cola in their planned remake of Marlene Dietrich's *The Blue Angel*. It would have been a daring step to translate the femme fatale from German blonde to American black, but they ultimately opted instead to market a "new Dietrich," Mai Britt, in a less-than-successful 1959 production.

Fox finally found the right property for her—the controversial *Island in the Sun* —which required that she fly to Jamaica for location filming. Also starring would be James Mason, Joan Fontaine, Harry Belafonte (Dorothy's *Carmen Jones* co-star), and Joan Collins, but Dorothy received the lion's share of publicity because her role was the most talked about. She was set to play opposite British actor John Justin in the first interracial romance ever to be filmed by a major producer. Zanuck himself was masterminding the production, hoping to find in it the same kind of critical approval, box office success, and sympathetic understanding of *Gentlemen's Agreement,* the 1947 film that had so candidly explored anti-Semitism.

Before Dorothy left, Dennison flew into Los Angeles to spend his days off with her in her Hollywood Hills mansion off Sunset Boulevard, and, as their affair intensified, he began using the one word that she most wanted to hear—marriage. He had regaled her with a story of how his only other real love had been a Negro girl who died, and this made him more attractive to Dorothy. When it came time for her to leave, she was in love with him, and it was ironic that the part she would be playing onscreen should so closely parallel her personal life.

While she was in Jamaica, Dorothy and Dennison kept in daily touch via long distance calls which often left her sad because of the misunderstandings they would have over the cables. She was having her problems on the film, too, as the black/white romance was a very touchy subject and no one knew how to handle it. Compromises in dialogue came constantly, the most ludicrous being when Dorothy's "I love you" to Justin was transmuted into "You know how I feel." There were also personal complications with Harry Belafonte who, according to Dorothy's manager, made it clear early on that he'd like to intensify their offcamera relationship. While it's a usual, almost casual, thing for stars to pair off, especially on remote locations, Dorothy would have none of it. She loved Jack and prided herself on being a one-man woman. Belafonte solved the problem by sending for his white girlfriend, a former Katherine Dunham dancer, whom he ultimately married.

The high point of the film comes when sophisticated Margot (Dorothy) sheds her couturier clothes to take part in a native Limbo contest, an event that Dorothy threw herself into with the abandon of the jungle princess she'd played earlier in *Tarzan's Peril.* It was, in essence, the sexual high-water mark of *Island in the Sun,* with Dorothy writhing under the ever-lowering bar with the agility of a black Terpsichore, much to the delight of locals hired as extras for the scene. She

Dorothy as the tragic Margot in Island in the Sun *(1957).*   AUTHOR'S COLLECTION.

obviously thrived in that particular spotlight: the epitome of sex in a society that, for once, truly appreciated her.

Offcamera, as was her pattern, she kept mostly to herself except for her friendship with James Mason, who gave her acting lessons which she would later utilize in another film they made together. By now she was so emotionally involved with Dennison that it had escalated to a point where she asked to be let off the production for a couple of weeks so she could see him and straighten things out. Because of weather problems, the filming of *Island* was to be completed in London, so Zanuck gave her permission to take some time off. She flew to New York where Jack met her.

When she arrived, she was upset both personally and professionally. She wasn't happy with the way her movie character, Margot Seaton, was emerging in the daily rushes, declaring that it seemed impossible for studio executives to think of an island girl as anything but a stockings-rolled-halfway-down prostitute. That worried her enormously and didn't add any serenity to the reunion, since the spectre of public acceptance was still foremost in her priorities. Dennison soon returned to Hollywood, while Dorothy went off to England to finish filming *Island in the Sun*. From there she made a radiant appearance at the Cannes Film Festival in May, 1957, on the arm of German actor Curt Jurgens.

In Europe she felt a different kind of acceptance than she did in her own country. She was treated like a star and like a lady—and no one looked askance at her choice of male partners. *Island* premiered in June of 1957 and was a giant box office hit, despite its many compromises. Yet in spite of the film's success, Fox still didn't know what to do with her, so Dorothy stayed on in Europe, signing with MGM in November to star with James Mason in *The Decks Ran Red*. A muddled sea adventure of mutiny and intrigue, the film offered Dorothy a thankless role as Mahia, wife of the ship's black cook and the only woman on board. It gave her many windswept closeups, but little chance to act. As usual, there was a near-rape scene involving Dorothy and mutineer Stuart Whitman, but there was little contact made. Though paid $75,000 for doing it, Dorothy walked through the role with a mostly perplexed look on her face.

She got another offer (at even more money—$125,000) to play the part of an exotic half-caste in *Tamango* opposite Curt Jurgens. She took the part, wanting to work and liking the possibilities of the role which had her on board a slave ship and lusted after by its white captain, Jurgens. This time there was no opposition to love scenes between the stars—but only for the European market. Two versions of the intimate scenes were shot, the tamer ones used in the American release. Even with this precaution, though, the French producers couldn't find a major American company to distribute the film, and, while it did well in Europe, it was hardly seen stateside. This intolerance saddened Dorothy, but she was gradually becoming resigned to it. She worked hard on the film, learning French phonetically for the European release print. "I didn't speak the language, but I was determined to do my best. It was the most difficult job I ever did."

Happily, Hollywood beckoned her home at this point for Sam Goldwyn's $6,000,000 production of the classic *Porgy and Bess,* to be directed by Otto Preminger. She was delighted by the prospect of starring in the hugely budgeted musical and also to be working with Preminger again. While their affair had run its course, they were still good friends, and she looked forward to being a part of his life, at least professionally, again. Sidney Poitier was cast as Porgy, and her good friend Pearl Bailey was signed for Maria, while Sammy Davis Jr. nabbed the snappy Sportin' Life part.

It took a completed script to get all these stars to sign for the film, for when it was first announced, there were loud outcries from the Negro community. They felt that *Porgy and Bess* could do nothing but solidify the already prevalent Negro stereotypes; images they thought should be forgotten rather than spread across the wide screen. Preminger and screenplay writer N. Richard Nash, however, delivered a finished project that satisfied the stars. As Catfish Row's torrid Bess, Dorothy would again play the good girl who strays, the tragic beauty, and she prepared for it with an awesome intensity, determined to make it an even bigger success than *Carmen Jones.* The film was not without its enemies, though, and just before shooting was to start, a mysterious fire destroyed most of the sets on the Goldwyn lot, causing an eight-week delay. As Dorothy later said, she ''felt like a race horse ready at the starting post, and suddenly told to go back to the stable and eat some oats. I had been preparing for the picture, and I was all ready emotionally. Where will I put all this energy? I feel artistically stymied.''

Dennison by now had eschewed Las Vegas for Hollywood and had opened a restaurant on Sunset Strip in partnership with Sammy Davis Jr. He and Dorothy had resumed their romance, but the strain of the picture's delay took its toll on their personal life. While she had not publicly announced she was serious about him, she pointedly told Sheilah Graham that there was a man in the picture but that the relationship was not without its problems, a major one being the haunting memory of her first marital disaster. ''I must say there is a particular admirer, but I was very disappointed the first time. I'm not sure that career women can be happily married. We expect too much. One thing is very important to me. It is not necessary to be agreed with, just understood. And where this particular man in my life is concerned, it is very important that he understands me and the life I lead. It's all very fine to be admired and for your husband to be proud of you on screen, but he has to realize that when you are concentrating on a role you are not always in a mood to talk or to go places or even be very polite. And right now my work comes first, and the man I marry would have to know this. With my friends I can pick up and leave any time I want to. I couldn't do this with a husband. And that is why I am taking my time about marrying again.''

The production of *Porgy and Bess* was a lengthy one, and, again, she willingly surrendered herself to the advice and direction of Preminger, repeating the trust she'd placed in him during *Carmen Jones.* She desperately wanted the movie to be a success—remember her vow to get an Academy Award?—and worked tirelessly on it. One problem that gives a piercing insight into Dorothy's mental outlook at the time became immediately apparent during rehearsals. As Otto Preminger tells it in his memoirs (*Preminger—An Autobiography,* Doubleday), she came to him distraught after a day spent rehearsing the scene in which Bess is raped by Crown, played by Brock Peters. " 'Otto,' she said, sounding very upset, 'you must recast him. I can't stand that man.' "

"Dorothy, are you out of your mind? You're not casting the film, I am. I think Brock Peters will be very good in the part. I know he's not ready yet, but you're not perfect in everything you're doing.' She got more upset. She kept saying she couldn't work with him. 'When he puts his hands on me I can't bear it,' she cried hysterically. It went on for about fifteen minutes, at the end of which she exclaimed, 'And—and—and he's so black!'

"I calmed her down, and Peters continued in the part, but her tortured 'he's so black' revealed to me the tragedy of Dorothy Dandridge. She was divorced from a black man who had fathered her retarded child. From then on, she avoided black men. For her love affairs, she always chose white men."

Despite this personal problem, Dorothy was a stunning Bess, sweeping gorgeously across the screen in costumes by Irene Sharaff and walking off with the picture in the process. Sinuous, sexy, with the cast of quiet despair to her beautiful face, she dominated the screen, dwarfing all her co-stars, including Poitier, and also walked off with a Golden Globe Award as Best Actress in a Musical given by the Hollywood Foreign Press Association. But that was yet to come.

After wrapping *Porgy and Bess,* Dorothy flew to Spain to star with Trevor Howard in *Malaga,* also known as *Moment of Danger,* pursued almost instantly by Dennison who now had marriage very much on his mind. He must have appeared stronger to her now, hemmed in as she shortly was in the thankless movie role of Gianna, a woman of questionable ancestry, abandoned by Edmund Purdom and rescued by Howard. There were no love scenes between Dorothy and Howard, although the need of them was obvious from the storyline. It was a frustrating acting experience for her, and she walked through it looking dejected. Dennison was there for support, though, and he used his position well, promising that if she married him he'd make sure these kinds of roles would stop and that he would bring fresh promise to her career. And she believed him.

By the time they returned home, Dorothy went public and announced that she and Jack Dennison were to wed. The silver-haired restaurateur and a smiling Dorothy posed happily for photographers at the Los Angeles City Hall when they applied for a marriage license on June 21, 1959. They were married on the following day at the Greek Orthodox Cathedral of St. Sophia in Hollywood. They honeymooned in New York, where Dorothy was set to appear at the premiere of *Porgy and Bess.*

One of the first thigns Dennison did was take over her career, curtly firing her long-time mentor, Earl Mills, the man who'd maneuvered her to stardom. Like many another star, Dorothy wanted to totally depend on her husband, both emotionally and financially, and willingly agreed to let him handle her affairs. It was a terrible mistake. He may have promised that she'd never have to take compromising roles such as in *Malaga* and *Tamango* again, but what she didn't know at the time was that she'd never complete another movie at all, compromising or not.

At first things went smoothly. She was ecstatic at the success of *Porgy and Bess* and with her Golden Globe Best Actress Award, and for a few months she was convinced that she'd be deluged with picture offers. None came, however, although there was brief talk at Fox of starring her in their mammoth remake of *Cleopatra*. By now, though, Dorothy knew that, historically true or not, that coveted part would go to a white woman, not to her. She told that to Rouben Mamoulian, the film's initial director: "They'd never let you get away with it. They'll talk you out of it. It would take too much guts to use a Negro in the part."

During her successful years, Dorothy, with a childhood fear of poverty, had saved a great deal of money which she needed not only to keep her daughter in a private mental hospital, but also to insure her own future. Once married to Dennison, that changed. When he took over her career, he took over her finances as well. She stated, "Ours is not a young love. We have a wonderful understanding," and trusted him with her money which he promptly began investing in a variety of enterprises, none very successful.

Dorothy's career was stalled, and she began drinking. She couldn't figure out why she wasn't getting at least singing work since "I have a nice voice and it's pleasant. It's got a lot of soul in it. Besides, people seem to like to look at me." Gradually, though, she realized that her marriage to a white man was causing her to be boycotted in the business. While others, like Lena Horne and Pearl Bailey, could pull off a black/white marriage, Dorothy's tempestuous screen reputation as everybody's good time girl worked against her. The bitterness and the drinking increased. She was making most of the financial contributions to the marriage, and that cut further into their relationship. More went out in expenses and speculations than was coming in. Dennison's nightclub was no great success, but that didn't stop him from living like a movie star's husband—in her house.

Things deteriorated badly over the next two years, but there seemed one bright spot late in 1961 when she was offered a starring part opposite French idol Alain Delon in a European picture about the life of Marco Polo. A still exists of her in oriental costume on the set of this movie in Belgrade, Yugoslavia, laughing with Delon. Unfortunately, the film was scrapped midway through production, and she came home in a deep depression.

Almost immediately she filed for a divorce from Dennison, realizing that things were getting no better between them. She charged him with having a volatile temper and said that she had not worked during their three-year marriage "because of this hassle." She added sadly, "Everything changed the day we were married." The divorce proceedings were traumatic to her, and all she wanted was her freedom. She asked no alimony.

Unfortunately the end of that traumatic three years brought only more despair. The very day of her divorce there was a knock on her door, and her daughter, Harolyn, was unceremoniously dumped on her doorstep by the private hospital in which Dorothy could no longer afford to keep her. In time the girl became violent, and Dorothy had no choice but to have her committed to the Camarillo State Hospital. It broke her heart to do it, but there was just no other way. Harolyn was still there upon her mother's death.

Desperate, Dorothy got in touch with Earl Mills who agreed to try to revive her career, but by this time she was in poor health physically and emotionally, as well as financially. He was distressed to see her looking ill and relying on liquor and pills to get her through this terrible period. He stuck with her, though, and was a friend when she needed one. "I was shocked to learn of her very poor health and that her new doctor gave her pills for everything—energy pills, relaxants, sleeping pills. . . . She was constantly at the doctor's, but she didn't quit."

On April 26, 1963, there was no other choice for Dorothy but to declare bankruptcy. On that day she appeared in court, but she was not the Dorothy Dandridge the public remembered. With her hair pulled back, wearing a high-necked dress and sunglasses to cover a black eye she said she'd gotten in a fall, she was haggard and woebegone, a million light years away from the fiery Carmen of a scant nine years before. She claimed that bad investments, primarily an oil deal in which she'd lost $150,000, had forced her to take this humiliating step, and she listed debts totalling $127,994 to some seventy-seven creditors from hotels to laundries to supermarkets. Her assets, she said, were $5,000. She also stated that many of her debts were mutually accrued with her ex-husband and asked that Dennison be required to pay some $14,600.

Mills's first job was to get Dorothy healthy again, and, at a Mexican ranch, he helped wean her away from the medications and alcohol and work on her nightclub act, going over the songs that had made her famous, like "What Is This Thing Called Love" and "Blow Out the Candle." She was anxious to make a comeback, feeling that she'd disappointed her people by her disastrous second marriage and subsequent bankruptcy. But she was also depressed about the possibility of pulling it off. Mills tried to soothe her as she started the slow climb back, highlighted by an impressive appearance as the tragic mulatto Julie in a summer stock production of *Showboat,* starring Kathryn Grayson. A few international singing engagements in Japan and South America followed, and, by the beginning of 1965, things were looking better than they had in some time.

In the middle of that year she was booked to open at New York's Basin Street East on September 10, followed by an appearance on the "Ed Sullivan Show." What made that news even more meaningful to her was that Basin Street East was formerly La Vie En Rose, the club from which she'd first conquered New York in 1952. She vowed to do it again, saying "I'm going to set New York on their ears." It was the chance she was waiting for, but deep inside were troublesome depressions and a lack of self-confidence. After all, she was forty-two. Could she, she thought, revive the sexiness and talent that had been the cornerstone of her earlier career? It haunted her despite her outward optimism.

A Mexican film producer contacted Mills rearegarding two films for a total salary of $100,000, and an exhilarated Dorothy prepared to fly to Oaxaca, Mexico, to talk about an appearance on Mexican television. However, the day before departure she turned her ankle going down a flight of steps in a gym, and all during the trip she complained of how it hurt her. When she and Mills returned to Los Angeles, they saw a doctor on September 7. He confirmed that she'd suffered a tiny fracture and recommended she come back the next day to have it set and a cast put on. She was very upset by this but calmed down when he said she'd only be in the cast a short time and that it wouldn't stall her New York opening.

Mills took her home to her small West Hollywood apartment (her Beverly Hills mansion had been swept away in the bankruptcy) on Fountain Avenue and arranged to pick her up early the following morning to take her to the hospital. She spent the evening talking with a friend and chatting a long time over the phone with her mother Ruby. She then arranged her clothes and stayed up late packing. At 7:15 the following morning she called Mills and asked him to set back the appointment so she could sleep a little longer. He rearranged it and called her back. "You know how I am about these things," she said, "I'll sleep for a while and I'll be fine." Those were her last words, as far as anyone knows.

When Mills tried to reach her by phone later that morning, there was no answer. Around mid-day he drove over to her apartment. There was no answer at the door either. Thinking she'd decided to cancel her appointment and sleep longer, he left. He came back again at 2 P.M. Still no answer. With a premonition that something was wrong, he tried his key to the apartment. It was locked from inside by a chain. He tried to push it open, but finally had to get a tire iron from his car to break it free.

Dorothy was lying on the bathroom floor, nude except for a blue scarf wrapped about her head. Cuddled with her face resting on her hands, she looked like she was sleeping. Mills felt her hand, and she was cold. He called her doctor and an ambulance, but the medical team only punctuated the dreadful realization he was feeling. Dorothy was dead. The ambulance driver called the county sheriff. "Sheriff," he said, "we've got a cold one. Her name is Dorothy Dandridge. She's that colored singer, isn't she?"

During this emotion-charged scene, shortly heightened by the appearance of a desperate Ruby, Mills remembered the note she had given him in May of that year which stated, "In case of my death—to whomever discovers it—don't remove anything I have on—scarf, gown, or underwear. Cremate me right away. If I have anything, money, furniture, give it to my mother Ruby Dandridge. She will know what to do. Dorothy Dandridge." She'd given it to him saying, "You keep it, Earl, because I know you will be the one who discovers me." It was eventually filed as her last will and testament.

It was determined that she had been dead about two hours when Mills found her. She had bathed, powdered, and applied deodorant before dying. The burning question, especially in light of the scrawled note which was immediately made

Dorothy as a dope-addicted singer in a TV drama shortly before her death (1962).
AUTHOR'S COLLECTION.

public, was *how* did she die; did she commit suicide? Those rumors swept Hollywood, but were shortly squelched when the Los Angeles County Coroner's Office opined that she had died of a rare embolism, that locked off the blood passages at the lungs and brain with tiny pieces of fat that had flaked off the bone marrow in her fractured right foot.

Her funeral, at the Little Church of the Flowers at Forest Lawn, was followed by cremation. Peter Lawford was the most prominent star in attendance. A tragedy, everyone agreed, especially coming so fast on the heels of the good news about the upsurge of her career—which had also included an offer for her autobiography with an advance of $10,000. In death, Hollywood rhapsodized about the talent and the promise they had so sadly and tragically neglected.

However, not many weeks went by before Dorothy made headlines again, when, as a result of extensive toxicological analysis by the Armed Forces Institute of Pathology working with samples from the autopsy, a startling discovery was made. Dorothy had not died of an embolism, but rather from a drug overdose of an anti-depressant called Tofranil. Suddenly the question of suicide again reared its head, since the overuse of an anti-depressant seemed an unlikely cause of accidental death. A psychological autopsy was then done by a team of psychiatrists, but they couldn't arrive at a sufficient motive in light of her recent career promise. The question remains unanswered to this day, and the only person who could answer it is dead.

Caught by a sex image in the fifties and imprisoned by the same image in the sixties, an era that seemingly didn't want it any longer, Dorothy Dandridge died just two months short of her forty-third birthday, not cognizant of what she'd done for the image, and for the emergence, of the black woman onscreen. The uncertainty of her acceptance by her own people had been a constant nagging weight. Coupled with personal guilt over her private life, it's possible, in the end, she felt she couldn't really gain their approval or further her career. Until the day she died, her comeback had been primarily on paper. Within hours of her death she was to have opened in New York. She would have had to start proving herself all over again; the talking was finished. One wonders what her final thoughts were; were they of the tragedies or the possibilities? Only one thing is certain. She died too soon.

Dorothy never won her Oscar, but she did indeed carve out a special niche for herself in the pantheon of gods and goddesses of Hollywood. More important, in death she won the acceptance she had craved so hard in life.

On February 20, 1977, she was posthumously inducted into the Black Filmmakers Hall of Fame at the annual Oscar Micheaux Awards presentation in Oakland, California, by former co-worker and old friend Joel Fluellen. "It's an intense pleasure for me," he said, "to be able to share with you some of my memories of the next entry. She was Margot in *Island in the Sun;* she was Bess in *Porgy and Bess;* she *was,*" he paused emotionally, "Carmen." A huge screen behind him suddenly lit up with Dorothy perched anxiously in a jeep with Harry

Belafonte, who was getting ready to cart her off after a riot at the parachute factory. ''You mean you really gonna take me to jail?'' she asks.

''You won't be in for long,'' he replies.

''A minute's too long for me!'' she retorts, eyes flashing on the Cinemascope screen. ''I can't stand bein' cooped up.''

Fluellen continued after the clip faded out and the applause died down, ''She had so much to give, and she gave so much. Dorothy Dandridge gave to every Civil Rights cause. She gave graciously, bountifully, happily. Dorothy fought for integrated parts in the motion picture industry on every level and for all minorities, and especially for black women. She was my friend and I know this. We who knew Dorothy Dandridge loved her.''

The award was accepted by Vivian Dandridge, one half of The Wonder Kids of so long ago. ''I regret that my sister isn't alive to be here and participate in this wonderful, wonderful affair. I want to thank the black filmmakers for her. She would have enjoyed this night so much.

''I loved my sister very deeply. She was a dedicated actress and helped open doors for young actors, and I hope that contribution at least will be remembered.'' As if in answer, the orchestra struck up ''Again,'' the love theme from *Island in the Sun,* the last lines of which go, ''Again, this couldn't happen again. This happens once in a lifetime, but never, never again.'' Holding back her tears, Vivian walked off the stage.

FILMOGRAPHY
Dorothy Dandridge

TITLE	YEAR	DIRECTOR	LEADING PLAYERS
A Day at the Races	1937	Sam Wood	Groucho, Harpo and Chico Marx, Allan Jones, Maureen O'Sullivan, Margaret Dumont
Going Places	1939	Ray Enright	Dick Powell, Anita Louise, Allen Jenkins, Ronald Reagan
Lady from Louisiana	1941	Bernard Vorhaus	John Wayne, Osa Massen, Ray Middleton
Sun Valley Serenade	1941	H. Bruce Humberstone	Sonja Henie, John Payne, Glenn Miller and orchestra, Milton Berle
Bahama Passage	1941	Edward Griffith	Madeleine Carroll, Sterling Hayden, Flora Robsen, Leo G. Carroll
Sundown	1941	Henry Hathaway	Gene Tierney, Bruce Cabot, George Sanders, Harry Carey
Drums of the Congo	1941	Christy Cabanne	Ona Munson, Don Terry, Stuart Erwin

TITLE	YEAR	DIRECTOR	LEADING PLAYERS
The Hit Parade of 1943	1943	Albert S. Rogell	Susan Hayward, John Carroll, Eve Arden, Gail Patrick, Walter Catlett
Ebony Parade	1947	George Spelvin	Count Basie and orchestra, Cab Calloway, June Richmond, the Mills Brothers
Tarzan's Peril	1951	Byron Haskin	Les Barker, Virginia Huston
The Harlem Globetrotters	1951	Phil Brown	Thomas Gomez, Bill Walker, Angela Clarke, the Harlem Globetrotters
Bright Road	1953	Gerald Mayer	Harry Belafonte, Robert Horton, Philip Hepburn
Remains To Be Seen	1953	Don Weis	June Allyson, Angela Lansbury, Van Johnson, Louis Calhern
Carmen Jones	1954	Otto Preminger	Harry Belafonte, Pearl Bailey, Diahann Carroll, Olga James, Brock Peters
Island in the Sun	1957	Robert Rossen	James Mason, Joan Collins, Stephen Boyd, Joan Fontaine, Harry Belafonte, John Justin
The Decks Ran Red (aka *Infamy at Sea*)	1957	Andrew L. Stone	James Mason, Broderick Crawford, Stuart Whitman
Tamango	1957	John Barry	Curt Jurgens, Jean Servais, Roger Hanin
Porgy and Bess	1959	Otto Preminger	Sidney Poitier, Pearl Bailey, Sammy Davis, Jr., Brock Peters, Diahann Carroll
Malaga (aka *Moment of Danger*)	1961	Laslo Benedek	Trevor Howard, Edmund Purdom, Michael Hordern

Jayne Mansfield

This girl I play has the most fabulous body in the world, but she's unaware of her sex appeal. All she wants to be is a wife and mother, but sex keeps getting in the way. She's like me, you might say. . . . It's a perfect part for me because I understand the girl so well. She's like me, you know, the personality of a June Allyson with a fabulous figure.

Jayne Mansfield explaining her character in her debut movie, The Girl Can't Help It.

I dream of the day when I can stay home and have a little time like other people to do things I like to do. I want to be just a woman, not a breadwinner, but I have to keep working so the money will come in to support my children.

Jayne Mansfield talking to a friend the week before her death in July 1967.

For a girl from the unlikely hometown of Bryn Mawr, Pennsylvania, Jayne Mansfield parleyed a photogenic face and an incredibly well-endowed body into the fulfillment of the fantasy of movie stardom in the richest sense of the term. Her looks, coupled with an uncanny gift for personal publicity—and a certain amount of comedic ability largely overlooked in the few major movies she starred in—made hers one of the most publicized figures of the fifties. In fact, there was scarcely a figure more public! While Marilyn Monroe, the goddess Jayne hoped to unseat at the box office, fretted about becoming an accepted dramatic actress, Jayne plunged, clad and unclad, into the publicity pool reserved for movie blondes, and for a while at least, topped Monroe in the press department, if not in the one labeled talent. When Monroe was busy elsewhere, journalists always knew they had only to telephone Jayne for yet another parade through her Sunset Boulevard pink palace, with muscleman husband Mickey Hargitay on hand to playfully dunk her in his handmade, heart-shaped swimming pool complete with their entwined names mosaicked across its bottom.

A publicity photo of Jayne Mansfield shortly after she arrived in Hollywood (1953).
AUTHOR'S COLLECTION.

Ironically, Jayne conquered something that Monroe was never able to—Broadway—since it was there that she was seen and signed by Twentieth Century Fox (MM's home studio) when executives caught her take-off of Marilyn in *Will Success Spoil Rock Hunter?* (1957). They promptly signed her to the standard seven-year contract and promised the world a new Monroe, but the public was hardly fooled. Jayne Mansfield was soon to find out that stardom was something earned by performance onscreen as well as off.

When she died in a ghastly auto crash in June of 1967, she had become a parody of herself, the leftover sweater queen of the fumbling fifties trying desperately to find a new niche in a new era of openness that had made sweater queens about as popular as Edsels. Her brand of peek-a-boo sex was outdated. Unlike Monroe—mercifully dead by then—she tried to bend herself to the changing times but by the end had buried her career under a bakers' dozen scrapbooks of marriages, divorces, scandals, terrible movies and—always perhaps most important to her—magazine covers from *Confidential* to the *National Enquirer.* Unfortunately those cover blurbs, like her career, were only flash and surface with no substance underneath.

J AYNE's mother was obsessed with having a child, and, after losing her first at birth, a son, she took no chances when she became pregnant again in the middle of 1932. When she was born on April 19, 1933, Vera Jayne Palmer weighed in at nine pounds, ten ounces, and was delivered by Caesarean section. Doctors anticipated that her mother—also named Vera—would take a while to recuperate, but she was up and around in a matter of days, so happy was she at the healthy birth of the only child she'd ever bear.

They moved to Phillipsburg, Pennsylvania, a small town, and Jayne's early childhood was happy, with both parents coddling her as she quickly grew from precious to precocious. Papa Herbert Palmer, an attorney, bought little Vera Jayne a Shirley Temple songbook, and long before she started kindergarten she was well up on the Temple ditties and films. "I always knew I'd be just as big as Shirley Temple," she later said. "She was my ideal. From the moment I saw her movies, I knew I was going to be a big star, too." Egged on by her demonstrative mother, who promised trips to the movies complete with lollipops and ice cream, Jayne drank it all in.

She had inherited her enthusiasm from her father, who declared after an early, promising political venture, "I'm going to be President some day."

Unfortunately, he never got a chance to try. The young lawyer died of a heart attack when Jayne was only three. But from him she interited her determination, once described as being "the strongest career drive of anyone in show business," and from his early death came her never-ending search for male approval. A famous Hollywood lawyer would later say, "She was like Will

Rogers. She never met a man she didn't like.'' So the pattern was set when she was barely old enough to walk—men and fame were to be the constant goals of her life.

Widowed, Vera Palmer quit her job as a teacher and married Harry Peers in St. Louis in 1939, the halfway point between her home in Pennsylvania and his in Dallas. Even today their house is part home and part memorial of their famous daughter, a girl Harry remembers, according to Martha Sexton's excellent *Jayne Mansfield and the American Fifties,* as having the vocabulary of a twelve-year-old by the time she was four. Although she was later to play the ultimate dumb blonde, Jayne was anything but. In school she excelled in foreign languages, especially French and Spanish, but she grew up rather a shy girl in spite of the fact that her looks were sensational from a very early age. She exercised vigorously in school to further develop her figure, sure all the while that every step she took would eventually lead to Hollywood and fame.

From her mother and stepfather she acquired still another quality, shrewdness, and later made full use of it, promoting herself everything from refrigerators to fur coats. Her cautious parents—who a husband of Jayne's later said had kept "the first nickel they ever made"—instilled this shrewdness in her, as potent a legacy as anyone could wish for. In 1945 she showed one of the first of many manifestations of it when she wrote a letter to the Swan Soap Company and told them she was the mother of triplets, Sammy, Pammy, and Jammy, and they replied not only with a congratulatory letter but with a case of the then-rationed commodity.

Another part of Jayne's personality that would never change was that from girlhood on she was absolutely starstruck, and in high school her bedroom walls were papered with pictures from fan magazines. Her favorite star was Johnny Weissmuller, the movies' brawny Tarzan, evidence of her early appreciation of good-looking, muscular men. A good student at Highland Park High, her primary reason for studying hard was to please her mother and thus reap rewards. A good mark might mean a new skirt or a special outing. An open, friendly girl with attractive, brunette hair and flashing teeth, Jayne was never particularly popular in school, never a member of the ruling clique of personality girls, but then with Harry dropping her off in the morning and Vera there to pick her up every afternoon there was hardly time for her to make many friends. Instead, along with the few close girlfriends she did have, she became an incurable romantic, resorting to daydreams instead of the real thing, which was quite all right with her parents.

Unfortunately, and not surprisingly, the tight rein on which young Jayne was held finally snapped back at sixteen, when she met a twenty-year-old college freshman named Paul Mansfield. Tall and good-looking, he was a singer, and he used to spend hours romancing her over the phone by singing the latest hits. One night he brought his whole group over to serenade her, and from then on he was the center of her small universe. He also soon made her pregnant. Vera and Harry were naturally horrified when they heard the news, but in the moral climate of the times, abortion was out of the question. There was nothing they could do but see to it that the couple were secretly married, on May 6, 1950. Jayne graduated from high school the following month, but it wasn't until then that her parents relented and had a small party for the newlyweds.

Jayne stayed home to await the birth of their baby, Jayne Marie, born the following November, and then she and the baby followed Paul to the University of Texas at Austin. She enrolled for three reasons: Paul's being there, her parents' expectations, and the fact that it was a glamorous thing for her to do. In the space of a few short months she'd covered a lot of ground, from unworldly high school girl to wife and mother to married college student.

To her dismay, however, she discovered that her married status cut her off from much of the university's social life. At seventeen she found herself saddled with the enormous responsibility of a husband and baby, and the other students found her hard to accept as just one of the girls. The Mansfields lived in a tiny apartment with only one chair and ate out a lot since Jayne's mother had never shown her the way around a kitchen much beyond teaching her how to make terrific fudge. She enrolled in some drama courses but didn't get a chance to perform, since all the parts went to the seniors. She took it very seriously, nonetheless, and the idea began forming that perhaps she could have a career as an actress. The childhood idea made as much sense now as then; and besides, her natural and increasingly spectacular body was becoming a constant source of attention, so why not capitalize on it? Her forty-one-inch bustline looked even bigger because of her large ribcage, and, since society's standards told her she was extraordinary, she dressed accordingly in tight clothes, which never failed to create a commotion wherever she and Paul went. The sight of her pushing Jayne Marie around the campus in her baby carriage became a familiar spectacle. She and Vera became closer than ever during this period because Jayne was more than willing to let her mother help in raising Jayne Marie. Jayne, at seventeen, had other things on her mind once she'd made up her mind she wanted to be a famous star.

Paul Mansfield was drafted early in 1952, but before he was shipped overseas Jayne extracted his promise that as soon as he returned they would head for California, where she was sure her dream would come true. The more real that dream became, the more unreal was her position as just Mrs. Mansfield. She'd fallen in love with and married an ''older'' man, a singer, a college man. The reality, though, proved hardly as glamorous as she'd naively expected it to be, and the marriage began to strain in both directions. Paul wasn't enthusiastic about either her blossoming exhibitionism or her desire to be an actress, but he did promise to give her a six-month try.

With Paul gone, Jayne moved back to her parents' home to wait it out, but at his insistence she soon moved into her own small apartment near Southern Methodist University, where she took more drama courses. He tried to make her independent of Vera and Harry, but his plan didn't work out too well, for she was a constant visitor to their house, popping in and out at will. She took her courses seriously and her body, as well, and in 1952, after stints as a nude model for the university life-drawing classes and some photographic work, she was named Miss Photoflash, a prophetic title. By the spring of 1954, when Paul returned, Jayne's ambition had only solidified, and before he had his uniform packed away she was reminding him of his promise. Within days they were ready to go to California. Vera packed them a lunch of fried chicken and potato salad, and they were off. Later Jayne breathlessly described the scene when she and Paul crossed the California border, remembering how she had broken into tears, made Paul stop her red Buick, and had gotten out and kissed the ground, whispering, "I am home."

And in a unique way she was, for Hollywood at that time was the only place where a girl with her looks could forge a career like the one she was sure she'd have. In her mind she'd always lived there, only now she could compete in reality for the rewards she knew would come her way. After all, she'd read all the magazines and Sunday supplements, and she believed them. After being such a great consumer of Hollywood hype, she knew she could now be a purveyor of even more.

Her husband, on the other hand, found Hollywood a bewildering place, and finding work there was almost impossible. He wanted to return home after three months, but his wife would have none of it, for by then she was assaulting various film studios in search of a contract. A minor milestone was reached when she got an agent who advised her to dye her dark hair platinum blonde, thus entering her into the burgeoning ranks of flaxen-haired contenders for the throne of Marilyn Monroe.

Jayne didn't waste a minute trying to mold herself in the expected Hollywood image. When she came into $5,000 from a family trust fund, she promptly spent most of it as a down payment on a Beverly Hills house. She soon found herself living there with her child but without her husband, though, when Paul packed up and moved back to Texas. Jayne's six months were up, but she really had never had any intention of going back at all.

Instead she threw herself into the Hollywood whirlwind that was waiting to carry her to notoriety. She met a public relations man who saw in her an opportunity to create his most farout publicity stunts. The first was to dress her in a tight red outfit in which she distributed his Christmas bottles of whiskey among reporters at various L.A. papers. It was a sensational success, and the next day her picture was in the papers, beginning a relationship between Jayne and the press that would last through the thickest years of her stardom and the thinnest years of her decline. Reporters loved her, and even when she became a big star, they could reach her at any time of the day or night for a story. Jayne was sure that the first commandment of stardom was "Be kind to reporters," and she strove to keep it the rest of her life.

She was anxious for fame and followed to the letter every publicity scheme her PR man devised, including one that had her flying to Florida for the premiere of Jane Russell's *Underwater* and making a startling appearance in a bikini at the hotel pool. The top was one of the many self-destructing ones she would always wear over the years to come, and that day it promptly fell off in the pool. Pictures of her wearing it made newspapers all over the country, and shots of her scrambling ing to reclaim it made more than a few private collections. When Russell finally showed up, the photographers were out of film, and Jayne had upped her progress towards sexual recognition another notch.

While she didn't have quite the IQ of 163 that she was forever bandying about, Jayne was no one's fool except perhaps her own. She believed that the basic credo for stardom was to become well-known; such things as acting talent would come naturally. Friendly, easygoing, and punctuating every other line with her gasping squeal, she used her notable sex appeal in any way she thought would help her. In the mid-fifties, peek-a-boo sex was still in style—led, of course, by Marilyn Monroe. In her heart, Jayne felt she had everything Monroe had and then some, and this total self-confidence helped her circumvent the outright silliness of many of her projects, such as her availability to take on every beauty queen title that could be drummed up. And she collected a formidable mantle full of cups and plaques, among them Miss Queen of the Chihuahua Show, Miss Nylon, Miss Texas Tomato, and Miss Electric Switch. She once remarked that the only honor she declined was Miss Roquefort Cheese, because it didn't sound right.

Along with her Beverly Hills address, Jayne made a down payment on a pink Jaguar, the first item of the color she would soon embrace as her personal trademark. She loved the car but also knew that having it was good business and, in fact, never separated her career from her personal life. She lived her career twenty-four hours a day and never let a lover or a husband get in the way. In her mind, her private and public selves were one.

And why shouldn't she think that way, since her publicity seemed to be paying off? She signed with Warner Brothers for $250 per week but got only small parts in three movies, *Pete Kelly's Blues, Illegal,* and *Hell on Frisco Bay.* Offscreen she quickly wore out her welcome at Warners with her over-enthusiasm, prompted by her willingness to act on any and all suggestions, no matter how vulgar or pedestrian, that would get her name and figure in front of the public. She bothered the studio publicity department constantly with suggestions and proposals, many of which she'd carry out even after they'd turn them down, including a life-size inflatable Mansfield swimming pool float. It was all grist for Jayne's publicity mill, but the studio soon decided that she was more of a freak than an actress with star potential. How could they take her seriously when almost every day a newspaper picture would pop out at them with Jayne cutting the ribbon at still another supermarket, bowling alley, or fried chicken franchise?

Jayne's agent at the time, Bill Shiffrin, then came up with a property he thought would make her a star, a play about to be produced on Broadway called *Will Success Spoil Rock Hunter?,* a spoof of the movie industry that required a Marilyn-Monroe-type for a lead role. Jayne's reaction, however, was dismay, because to her, Broadway was a far cry from the movie sound stage where she so desperately wanted to make history. Equally unenthusiastic was the studio, for when Shiffrin suggested to Warners that they lend her out for a movie called *The Burglar,* to be shot in Pennsylvania, then let her go on to do the play and come back an exploitable Broadway success, they chose to drop her option instead. Jayne was heartsick at first and for once listened to some good advice when told never to let anyone ever know she'd been dropped. She always said afterwards that she had left them to go to New York for *Rock Hunter.*

With Jayne Marie in tow, she soon reported for *The Burglar* in Philadelphia, a lukewarm thriller with Dan Duryea, and then set out for New York where the producers of the play were anxiously awaiting her. They'd seen only her photos but had cabled back, "If she can talk, she's got the part."

Jayne did indeed get the part, and the similarity between the character and herself was outstandingly obvious from the first. She was playing a star, and after the reviews were in she was one—and gloried in every minute of it. An ironic moment came on opening night when the producers were told that Marilyn Monroe was planning on coming to see Walter Matthau and Orson Bean, two friends in the cast. Fortunately she was talked out of it, and the focus of attention was Jayne, from the moment the curtain rose on her towel-clad body lying on a massage table until it lowered two hours later. She was the best thing about the comedy, and her every gasp and squeal helped propel it to immediate hit status.

The New York press were as ecstatic over Jayne as the Hollywood contingent had been, and during the year-long run of the play she made the papers constantly. Every night she'd stand at the stage door until every fan had gotten his snapshot and autograph, no matter how cold the weather might be or how early she had to be up the next morning. Backstage, though, was a different story. Her naturally undisciplined manner didn't make for good offstage etiquette, and she'd often show up at the theater just minutes before curtain time. More than once she opened the play nude except for the tiny towel since she hated wearing the body stocking that was her basic costume. Since she always took seriously what was written about her, the stage manager devised a scheme to get her to act more professionally by threatening to tell the press what a shambles she was creating backstage. The result was that Jayne was on time and letter perfect for the next several months.

Meanwhile Jayne reveled in her newly acquired star status and, again, was willing to involve herself in any scheme to keep it alive and well. The columnists loved her, *Life* magazine loved her, and, most important, the fans did, too, calling out to her from trucks and taxicabs whenever she'd take one of her many traffic-stalling walks down Broadway. Her advisers tried to make her steer clear of some of her more outlandish concepts of life and love, feeling that laughter dampens sexual interest and that if she got too funny, she'd stop being sexy. A few gems did slip through, though, such as when she told *Life* how she enjoyed roasting turkeys because "they're so good when they're cooked, you know."

Her native thriftiness asserted itself, too, and during her time in New York she promoted a formidable array of star trappings, from free hairdos to fur coats,

Jayne at the peak of fame, fortune, and stunning physique (circa 1957).
THE DOUG MCCLELLAND COLLECTION.

in particular a full-length mink that she would drag around on even the hottest days. She needed these symbols to prove to herself that she was a successful star, but the more she got, the more she needed in order to bolster her self-confidence. Promoting herself became a full-time offstage job. More grocery stores. More chicken franchises. Anything, in fact, that would get her photographed and proclaimed again as the hottest ticket in town. And since her career did indeed rest on her personality, there was never time enough for her to relax. Jayne Mansfield was performing twenty-four hours a day.

One of the victims was little Jayne Marie, who spent most of that year in her mother's dressing room or playing in the street outside the stage door. They lived in a small apartment on West 55th Street, and Jayne Marie was often looked after by various fans of Jayne's who'd become close to her, the photo and autograph hounds who showed up nightly because they knew they'd always be welcomed into her dressing room. In an ill-advised effort to see more of her daughter, Jayne would often bring her along on dates, parking her in the ladies' rooms of various supper clubs. Jayne Marie relished every dollop of affection she got, though, and never complained; she was terribly proud of her mother. Jayne needed her child's approval as well, interpreting it as the kind of approval she never got from Vera, who had demanded perfection in school, in deportment. Jayne herself only demanded that her daughter love her. In fact, both were happy with their relationship, as unorthodox as it might have been, until Paul Mansfield rocked the boat by starting a suit to get custody of the child, claiming that Jayne was an unfit mother. He based the claim on an almost nude photo of her in a February 1956 *Playboy* article. Jayne was heartsick at the possibility of losing her daughter, and furious at the bad press the affair might engender. She fought back, regaling reporters with details of her life with Jayne Marie and telling how every night before tucking her in she read the child a Bible story. Paul countered that Jayne caused him "pain, anguish, and distress" but he didn't get Jayne Marie. The couple divorced on October 24, 1956.

Before that divorce Jayne had become embroiled in what was to be the longest-lasting affair of her life. It began the previous May when she'd gone with *Rock Hunter* composer Jules Styne to the Latin Quarter to see Mae West's act. At the time Mae's back-up consisted of seven muscle-bound chorus boys, one of whom caught Jayne's eye. He was Mickey Hargitay, a six-foot-two former Mr. Universe. Weighing some 230 outrageously muscled pounds, the curly-haired Hungarian with his fifty-two-inch chest expansion lit a fire in her that was soon to burn into headlines. The first night, between shows, they exchanged telephone numbers, and on their next meeting—themselves. Together they journeyed to Brooklyn the following day where Jayne picked up an honor as Blossom Queen; but the real news was in the photographs of the already amorous couple that covered the front page of the *Daily News* the following morning. They announced they'd fallen in love.

When La West realized the romance was serious, the roof fell in. She threatened to fire Mickey if he didn't leave Jayne at once, angered not only by the press she thought they were getting at her expense but also because she had a thing for Mickey herself. In Washington, later in the tour, West called a press conference at which Mickey was supposed to deny his affection for Jayne and say it was all publicity and all over. Instead he declared his love in even stronger terms, enraging Mae's bodyguard, who then attacked him. In the ensuing uproar, West got pushed to the floor, where she sat declaring, "You can't do this to me. I'm an institution!" But Jayne won the round and the day, in absentia, when she observed to the press that she'd always been brought up to respect her elders. Mae fired Mickey, calling him last year's model in the muscle department, and he flew back to New York and Jayne. As would be the case from now on, it was a much publicized reunion.

They moved in together, and to Mickey it was the fulfillment of every dream a red-blooded boy could have. A one-time adagio dancer, he could hardly believe that Jayne had fallen in love with him. He loved her desperately and was willing to sacrifice his own identity to help substantiate hers. She saw him as a perfect consort and took enormous pride in the physique she felt was her masculine counterpart. She relished the impact they made together in public, and on more than one occasion willingly showed her affection for him by what amounted to heavy-petting at parties—after, of course, he'd lifted her over his head like a much-loved dumbbell. To Jayne he was a magnificent toy, constantly wound up to make her happy, and to Mickey she was the embodiment of female sensuality. It was eventually to be a marriage made, if not made in heaven, certainly in headlines.

They continued making New York newspapers juicier until Hollywood called Jayne back home to star in the movie version of *Rock Hunter,* to be preceded by another comedy, *The Girl Can't Help It.* Against her agent's advice, she signed a contract with Twentieth Century Fox at $1,250 a week, preferrng the stability of a studio to being a freelance actress. Her Warner Brothers episode was forgotten, and her exit from New York was typically Mansfield. She boarded her flight wearing a black scarf wrapped around her blonde head, the darkest sunglasses she could find, and her full-length mink, which she thought was only proper for a budding movie star traveling incognito.

While Mickey went to work building a swimming pool on the Wanda Park Drive property, Jayne starred in her first film, a raffish, vulgar story of a nice simple girl whose gangster boyfriend insisted she have a career in show business. Co-starring Tom Ewell, it had all the subtlety of a steamroller, awash with sight gags such as milk bottles exploding as Jayne walked down the street, or ice cubes melting on sight of her. As a showcase for her body, it was nothing if not right to the point, but as the real debut of the successor (hopefully) to Marilyn Monroe it was tastelessly overblown. From *The Girl Can't Help It* she went directly into a version of John Steinbeck's *The Wayward Bus* and was better playing a more serious role than just a giggly blonde. What could have changed her career was the lead in *Anatomy of a Murder,* the classic Otto Preminger film, but it didn't work out, and Lee Remick got the part instead.

Jayne was delighted with her movie star status, though, and didn't fret over the roles that were offered her. She was determined to keep working, for she felt that was the only way she could keep the Mansfield balloon afloat. One piece of good fortune did come her way in early 1957, though, when she came into an inheritance of over $100,000 from the estate of her grandfather, Elmer Palmer.

Unlike Paul before him, Mickey loved Hollywood, but his prime interest in it remained Jayne and her comforts. He took time off from fixing up her house to play the brawny star of a jungle series in the movie version of *Will Success Spoil Rock Hunter?* that started filming that winter. It had been rewritten to make fun of the television industry rather than the movies, though, and Tony Randall was Jayne's co-star in what remains quite a funny picture. Like most of her other co-stars, he remembers her with great fondness. "She was funny. She wasn't a great actress or anything like that, but she was very amusing. She said funny things all day long. I remember there was a dog on the set and he wasn't behaving well. He wouldn't do anything right. I said, 'They ought to drug that damn dog the way they used to,' and she said, 'Oh, no. They're not allowed to ever since the Pure Food and Dog Act.' She was genuinely funny and much brighter than most people think."

Mixed in with her movie work were the usual number of publicity gimmicks. When a manufacturer tried to market a bust-developing cream called Zoom and used her name in the ads, she immediately sued him, but when Ed Sullivan discovered she'd studied the violin as a child and asked her to play it on her show she promptly agreed and did surprisingly well.

Rock Hunter was another blatant exploitation of Mansfield's physical charms, and she was quite good in it. There was talk around the studio that she might star in *Can-Can,* but Shirley MacLaine got the part. After that Jayne took the leading role opposite one of her all-time favorite stars, Cary Grant, in a tepid comedy called *Kiss Them for Me.* She was strongly advised against doing it, for it was simply another caricature role, only this time the blonde got to carry around a copy of *Fortune* magazine throughout so that people would think she was smart. Not even the magazine, Cary Grant, or the script could help her on the picture, one of the few failures that Grant ever starred in. She was determined to do it, though, and in making it made a serious mistake. As an inducement there had been hints about her playing Jean Harlow, another idol of hers, but, even when she found out that Fox never really intended to make it with her, she still went ahead with *Kiss Them.* To co-star with Cary Grant was worth anything to her, and co-workers recall that she sometimes acted like a tourist on her own set, never totally sure that all this was happening to her. And she kept believing that she needed to work, no matter how ill-suited the property might be.

When Mickey finally finished the pool, Jayne ran an invitation to its christening in a Beverly Hills newspaper, and hundreds of people crammed into her house to see her lolling in the gallons of pink champagne the pool had been filled with and to admire Mickey's handiwork, highlighted by a ceramic rendition of Jayne adorning the bottom.

After she had made four pictures back to back, Fox decided to send Jayne on a European good will tour, which resulted in mob scenes all over the continent. In London she was presented to the queen, appearing in a highnecked, champagne-colored, silk jersey with a slit up the side to make curtseying easier. Said Jayne afterwards, in obvious awe, "Everything about her was so marvelous—from the first moment she came in and the band played 'My Country 'Tis of Thee.'" Suffice it to say that the queen was equally impressed.

In her own mind Jayne had formulated a plan to ensure her future success, winning over the general population segment by segment, but naturally starting with the men. Next came the women, and then, in the tradition of Monroe, she planned on making a stab at the intellectuals. To accomplish the first segment a constant force-feeding of Mansfield cheesecake was put forth, and the more of it the better. She and Mickey, in matching leopard bikinis, worked out a little act called "The Bird," in which Jayne would lie stomach-down on one of his massive palms while he raised her slowly up over his head. That trick created lots of comments, especially when they started doing it in public.

But her most fantastic publicity coup happened the night she upstaged Sophia Loren, then quite new to Hollywood and being introduced to the press. Jayne showed up at the press party in a gown cut down to her nipple line, and before Sophia could say "arrivederci" Jayne had pulled and tugged at the dress so much that one breast popped out as she leaned over to greet the Italian import. Photos of Sophia looking askance at Jayne's bare breast made front pages in newspapers everywhere, and those that didn't print the photo told the tale over and over again. When Loren commented that she would never wear a dress like that, Jayne retorted that maybe she couldn't. Again it was an exercise in Jayne's growing narcissism, a quality she treated as a virtue by taking constant care of herself. She knew what her main assets were and had no intention of depreciating them!

Part of Jayne's popularity, in the studio heads' minds, was because she was still single, but that was a status Jayne herself was not happy with. She wanted to marry Mickey, to be "respectable" again, and she planned the nuptials with all the enthusiasm and bravado of P. T. Barnum preparing a new show. At first she said she wanted a small wedding, but as the time drew near the ceremony expanded in all directions, such as one pronouncement that she'd like to be married at the beach in a white satin bikini. They set the date for January 13, 1958, just after their return from touring the Far East with Bob Hope, and they finally settled on a glass church in Palos Verdes for the ceremony itself. The happy couple sent out pink invitations to their many friends, half of whom were reporters, and Jayne had concocted a pink lace wedding gown skin tight to the knee and then bottomed off by an explosion of flounces. She could barely walk in it, and the sight of her edging her way down aisle drove the five thousand fans outside the glass walls almost berserk. Happily for the badly shaken minister, it was a short ceremony.

After a honeymoon that included a Dallas welcome from a delighted Vera and Harry, Jayne and Mickey journeyed on to Las Vegas for a six-week stand at the Tropicana where she proved in short order that what Mae West needed seven men for, she could accomplish with one. She had designed her own costume of mostly movable sequins that moved in the right or wrong direction at her will, and Mickey had a chance to brush up on his adagio skills, throwing her around the stage in simulated passion to the healthy tune of $20,000 a week. But that was for Jayne: Mickey earned only $5,000 weekly, still a healthy figure for a man who just months before was virtually part of the scenery.

By now, the Fox bosses were at a loss as to what to do with their new glamour girl. Monroe had returned to the fold after her New York "theatah" fling and was back on the lot, so they sent Jayne to Spain to star opposite British actor Kenneth More in *The Sheriff of Fractured Jaw*. At the time it seemed the wisest thing to do since the box-office figures had thus far proved that Jayne was more successful as a tabloid favorite than as a movie star. Jayne saw it as a complete change of pace, issuing statements as to how it would bring out facets of her talent

All of Hollywood and almost all of Jayne show up to greet Sophia Loren (1957). A bemused Clifton Webb looks on. UNITED PRESS INTERNATIONAL PHOTO.

heretofore unseen or unappreciated. Three months pregnant, she was tightly corseted to play a saloon hostess who fell for a meek undercover agent investigating gunrunning to Indians. For the first time in memory, her personal life took precedence over her public life, and she declined cheesecake offers because "I don't think this is the time for it." Unfortunately the end result of the filming was so inauspicious at the box-office that it hardly mattered. She tried to compensate for the public's ambivalence by concentrating on her coming child and her new home, a vintage 1929 Holmby Hills mansion once owned by Rudy Vallee. Three stories of California stucco situated on legendary Sunset Boulevard, it was soon to gain new fame as Jayne's pink palace. She said it was a present from Mickey. In reality it was bought from her grandfather's bequest and the sale of her old house. Yet with J & M entwined on the new grillwork of the entrance gates, it seemed the perfect home for America's most perfect couple; in her mind, at least, that's what they were.

When Mickey's ex-wife, Mary Birge Hargitay, read about all this opulence, she tried to get an increase in the twenty-dollar-a-week child support payments that he'd been paying for their daughter. Since Jayne had consciously worked at inflating Mickey's career and moneymaking potential, she was caught up short and the pair had to retrench publicly, saying that life in the pink palace was hardly royal and that, in fact, they were sleeping on a mattress on the floor because there was no furniture. They also issued a statement that little Jayne Marie cost them only seventy-one dollars a month and that it was supplemented by the most important thing of all a child needs, love. As usual the denouement was in Jayne's favor. While Mickey had to cough up more money per month for his daughter, the publicity started a groundswell of free furniture and appliances, a staggering total of $150,000 in promoted goods in all. Naturally the suppliers received a great deal of publicity for their goods. One item was a $15,000 garbage disposal that Jayne herself drummed up after appearing with its manufacturer on "The Mike Douglas Show." Another time she got a very expensive chair by telling the furniture store owner she'd sit in his window for an afternoon signing autographs.

As for Mickey, he was happiest working on fixing up the palace, redoing bathrooms, laying carpets, installing chandeliers, and working overtime entwining his initial with Jayne's, almost as if he believed that the more often she saw them that way, the more she'd come to believe they could never be separated. The predominant color was pink, of course, with Jayne's other trademark represented by her heart-shaped swimming pool. A greater joy to her came on December 21, 1958, when her son, Miklos, was born a week late, weighing in at a very healthy 9 pounds, 9½ ounces. Ecstatic, she bought Mickey a bracelet engraved, "Chained to you forever."

Jayne Mansfield never did anything in half measures, and the fall she suffered from public favor was equally massive. By 1959 she had become a joke. Sexy still, in a Daisy Mae way, but to be taken seriously? Not at all.

From the United States she journeyed south to a Brazilian film festival and excited both fans and headlines there, getting her clothes torn off while stalwart Mickey stood within an arm's length ready to whisk her away to a hotel room. Her reputation had preceded her, but she didn't know that advance promotion was all that was keeping her going, keeping her hot. She tried her best to live up to the fantasies expected of her, and the excitement her appearances engendered obviously thrilled her. But she didn't know that it was spurious attention. Jayne was fast becoming everybody's cheap thrill.

As that happened, criticism of her became more and more overt. Increasingly censured for doing what she'd always wanted to do and what she expected that people wanted her to do, she became a squealing paradox who had reached the point of believing the publicity she'd worked so many hours to engender. As long as it was in print, it was okay with Jayne. In 1959 she fired the men who had helped mold her into a commodity, mistakenly sure that she could now carry the ball of her notoriety and dribble it into her home court. Unlike her blonde contemporaries, Marilyn Monroe and Kim Novak, Jayne never tried to act, never held out for a part that would or could test her other than obvious talents. Without strong advisers, she relied more and more on Mickey, although she never really gave him a chance to carry out his decisions. He tried, but she only listened when she wanted to.

Her career was sinking fast, and she journeyed to England for a couple of independent quickies when Fox dropped her option. In both of them, *The Challenge* with Anthony Quayle and *Too Hot To Handle* with Leo Genn, her acting was deemed "tepid and at times ludicrous" by *Variety*. They were rarely seen in the United States. Mickey still had plans for a joint career with Jayne, and later that year they went to Italy to star together in a "hysterical" drama called *The Loves of Hercules*. Jayne was pregnant again at this point but that didn't deter her from accepting the offer of the film. Packing up her children and her chihuahuas, the Hargitays were off to Rome. Mickey was Hercules and Jayne played two parts, one as a tribal queen in a black wig, and the other as an Amazon queen in a red wig, alternating from submissive love object, black-haired, to domineering seductress, in red hair.

Back home she hit the public-appearance trail again while awaiting the birth of her third child, racking up a good deal of money traveling from telethon to shopping center. Zoltan Hargitay was born on August 1, 1960, but by that time the Hargitay marriage had begun its long slide downward. Jayne began drinking too much and seeing other men after the euphoric effects of having baby Zoltan had worn off. Mickey tried to help her, but she wasn't having any, and, in fact, was drinking primarily to put a little excitement back in her life. Mickey loved her, but he wasn't the most stimulating of men even at the best of times, and his stolid devotion had begun to bore Jayne. She also drank because the truth about her career problems was finally beginning to penetrate the thick shell of self-delusion she'd been developing for the past five years. For about five minutes she considered eschewing further cheesecake and publicity stunts and going back to classes at the Actor's Studio, but she was afraid that her desire to be taken seriously would threaten the image that she did have, however ludicrous it was becoming. She finally decided it would be better to stick with what she had rather than take a chance on something new.

Mickey started a barbell business but left it to join her in Rome for a silly comedy called *It Happened in Athens*. They returned to find themselves being audited by the IRS, who had caught on to the fact that Jayne was notoriously late in declaring many of those fees for supermarket and bowling alley openings, which she always insisted on taking in cash. It was the beginning of a running battle between the blonde and the tax men that would flare up from then on until her death.

At twenty-eight, she was already beginning to hedge about her age, and she dressed up her budding daughter to look about eight years old instead of her real eleven. She even joked to the child that "one day you're going to have to start being my sister." That was a mistake, because later, when Jayne Marie did indeed act that way, Jayne found it even harder to accept. When Jayne Marie reached puberty she was competition instead of sister or daughter.

After finishing her role in *The George Raft Story,* Jayne and Mickey left in February of 1962 for a vacation in Nassau, which shortly produced more sensational headlines when, after an afternoon of waterskiing, they never showed up for a scheduled press conference. After a nightlong search, their overturned boat was found the following morning, and for a few breathless moments it appeared that Jayne Mansfield had been lost for good. But later that day she, Mickey, and their hotel's publicity man were found on a rocky atoll. The consensus of opinion was that Jayne and the PR man had concocted the scheme, planning on being found before sundown, in time to meet the press. But the scheme backfired. She was hospitalized briefly for an assortment of shipwreck injuries, including exposure and mosquito bites.

No sooner had those half-hearted newsflashes died down than Jayne stirred up a few others by suddenly announcing that she and Mickey were divorcing. In her typical method of breaking news, Jayne informed the press before she told Mickey, who found it out when newsmen accosted him outside the pink palace, where he was busy trimming hedges. It all blew over in eighteen hours with a reunion by the heartshaped pool, with Jayne telling reporters that they had quarreled about taking the children to Rome, where she was to make *Panic Button* with Maurice Chevalier. It seems that Mickey had wanted her all to himself for once, but she wouldn't hear of it; thus, the breakup. As usual Mickey ended up losing the battle, and in early May the entire family was off to Italy.

Despite the presence of Chevalier and Eleanor Parker, *Panic Button* was another minor picture. But Jayne couldn't have cared less about its quality as she threw herself into the decadent atmosphere of Rome and the arms of the picture's producer, Enrico Bomba, in that order. The twist was the dance of the hour in the early sixties, and Jayne mastered it quickly on the nightclub floors with Bomba— often, incredibly, chaperoned by Mickey, who'd sit glowering in the corner while his wife swung herself out of several dress tops with her latest lover. Naturally the *papparazzi* were having a field day snapping the fallout, and reporters were kept busy when she started making unveiled hints that perhaps Bomba could do for her what Carlo Ponti had done for Sophia Loren. There were fights with Mickey and more headlines, and finally they were home where Jayne again announced she'd divorce Mickey. Despite the fact that Bomba was already married with two children, Jayne told the press that he'd proposed to her and that, in preparation for the wedding, she was studying Catholicism, an announcement that caused more than one lump to appear in clerics' throats.

This time, it appeared that Jayne meant what she said and she and Mickey soon signed separation papers and agreed to a Mexican divorce. He still desperately loved her but felt he couldn't stand in the way of her latest fantasy, her need for a strong man to guide and resuscitate her sagging career, something that was becoming more and more of a concern to her. Unlike other actresses such as Kim Novak, who opted for a quiet semi-retirement when her heyday was over, Jayne's career was all she had. The public and the private selves were totally one, and without a constant drama going on in her personal life she didn't have a grasp on reality in either self. The affair with Bomba eventually grounded out in New York, and she rushed back to Mickey and the thirty-five newsmen who accompanied him to meet her at the Los Angeles airport.

The reunion didn't last long, but for a short while it assuaged her contorted ego. To cement their reconciliation, they signed to co-star again in *Promises, Promises,* an independent quickie produced by comedian Tommy Noonan, which would pit Jayne's charms against those of another notorious blonde, Marie "The Body" MacDonald. Marie never had much of a career onscreen either, but her offscreen antics, such as her highly publicized kidnapping in 1957, had made her name recognizable. Jayne soon grabbed the lion's share of publicity, though, by posing nude for *Playboy* in what were billed as scenes from the upcoming picture, purportedly the first time a major name had posed unclothed *after* hitting stardom. The picture was a dismal failure even with her exposed charms, and all she really got from it was some gossip about an affair with Noonan (which purportedly lasted four weeks), and a handslap from Hedda Hopper for the nudity.

Now Jayne was in a quandary about what to do next, either professionally or personally. The movie magazine covers she'd so carefully stacked up over the years were collapsing around her like a house of glossy cards. The reconciliation with Mickey wasn't working, and she'd spent many evenings hanging out in a Sunset Strip bar, asking the piano player over and over to play her favorite song, *Fly Me to the Moon.*

Jayne had flown to the moon and played among the stars of her favorite heaven, Hollywood, but the trip back was destined to be a miserably unhappy one. Bolstered by champagne, she'd appear in a nightclub only to be followed to the club by Mickey, which invariably ended in a fight. It soon became a predictably self-destructive game, played almost nightly and highlighted by a desperate narcissism and need for attention on Jayne's part that was tame in comparison to the naive determination that had started her on her career.

By February of 1963, she was again telling newsmen her marriage was over and, as usual, Mickey was taken by surprise. Jayne began an affair with singer Nelson Sardelli, whom she'd met while performing in a second-rate nightclub in Biloxi, Mississippi. With him in tow she flew that June to Juarez, Mexico, to pick up her divorce from Mickey. This time it was Sardelli who started making marriage noises, even though he was already very much married at the time. Unfortunately he took his affair with Jayne too seriously, and after a fistfight with her male secretary (while Jayne was out opening yet another supermarket) the affair fell rapidly to pieces.

By now Jayne was grabbing at straws, one of which was a German film called, incredibly, *Homesick for St. Paul,* and she flew there to make it. Confused and totally unsure of herself at this point, there was only one thing she could count on—the imminent birth of another child. Needing a strong shoulder, she called Mickey, who quickly joined her in Europe with the children. Then they traveled en masse to Budapest, where they picked up Mickey's mother and brought her home with them. Trying to sort out her personal mess, Jayne announced her pregnancy upon her return, saying, somewhat lamely, that she and Mickey were still legally married in California and that they'd planned the baby all the time. Knowing of her closeness with Sardelli, there were many doubters, but it's a credit to Jayne's still-potent appeal to reporters that the story was at least circulated, thus assuaging her guilt and saving her reputation from an out-and-out mauling at the hands of her critics. Mickey and Jayne revived their nightclub act, adding a striptease for Jayne, and played the Dunes in Las Vegas. Appearing in public was, as usual, proof to Jayne that they had indeed reunited.

Mickey Hargitay might be emerging in these pages as a musclebound simpleton, but the basic unvarnished truth was that he was totally in love with his wife and would continue to play the suffering fool to her golden goddess anytime she wished him to. Raised as a Catholic, it was undeniably difficult for him to overlook her indiscretions, but he chose to do so, always hoping, always waiting for the time Jayne would need him again, as he was sure she would. In late January of 1964, Jayne gave birth to a daughter in Hollywood and named her Mariska Magdolna, after Mickey's mother.

The euphoria that always accompanied the birth of a child for Jayne was shorter-lived this time, and before long they were hitting the nightspots again. One quote of Mickey's deserves repeating regarding these sojourns: "She is deeply religious in many ways but is one of the best twisters in the country. She does not consider it undignified or forbidden." Again Mickey's faith in Jayne as both a goddess and a down-to-earth woman asserted itself in her defense.

Their quarreling erupted again, and it was an uneasy crew who motored east that May to Yonkers, where the couple were set to star in a production of *Bus Stop,* ironically Marilyn Monroe's most personally successful screen performance. To Jayne and Mickey, though, by this time it must have seemed like just another slightly run down, rip-off engagement. But it proved to be much more than that once Jayne met the show's director, Matt Cimber. Jayne was impressed with his

Italian good looks, his physique, his talent as a director and the fact that he claimed an IQ of 165—two points higher than the one she'd been flaunting for so long. All these attributes combined made her think that, finally, she had found a man who could make positive sense of Jayne Mansfield.

It didn't take Cimber long to size her up, both her weaknesses and her potential, and he decided that the time was ripe for plucking her once and for all away from Mickey. He appreciated her name value and later admitted, "It wasn't a great romance, but we made each other laugh." For Jayne, at the time, that must have seemed enough, for she quickly fell under his verbose spell.

Born in Brooklyn as Thomas Vitale Ottaviano, Cimber had changed his name after attending Syracuse University. He was twenty-eight when he met Jayne. Soon he was taking over not only her career but her life as well. Jayne hardly struggled, and she was soon waving around that "he'll do for me what Ponti did for Loren" banner that she'd previously used on Enrico Bomba.

When Jayne told Mickey that she wanted out again from their marriage—by now totally unrewarding and stifling to them both—he willingly agreed. Over the years, however, he had picked up some of the Mansfield shrewdnes, and he was concerned about the validity not only of their Mexican divorce but of subsequent business deals he had made as well. Cimber and Jayne eventually had to make a healthy settlement on him, which included money and property. As her manager/husband, he had sacrificed whatever acting career he might have hoped for and felt that he was due a portion of the money they'd jointly earned. Ironically, once he divorced Jayne he did get offers to appear in European movies, usually the preserve and often the graveyard of former American movie names. In August Jayne filed suit to have the Mexican divorce formally recognized by California courts, and she also sought custody of Miklos, Zoltan, and Mariska.

For a moment Mickey considered a custody battle, but instead he decided not to fight the woman he loved. As before, if what she thought she wanted was what she really wanted, he would go along with it, as much as it hurt.

Once Cimber was sure that the Mexican divorce would hold up against legal scrutiny, he and Jayne flew to Baja California where they were married on September 24. It was a ceremony in great contrast to the circus that had surrounded her marriage to Mickey. This time instead of clawing crowds outside of a glass church, there was only one witness, Matt's lawyer.

Vera and Harry Peers thought that Cimber was an opportunist, and while their affection for Mickey was on the wane, they felt that Matt would take their daughter away from them, and, to an extent, he did just that. After Jayne had tearfully cleared out her belongings from the pink palace, occasionally highlighted by emotional intrusions by Mickey, the newlyweds finally got away from California and set up housekeeping in an east side New York townhouse. Outwardly at least, Jayne seemed determined that this marriage would mark a new beginning for her in every respect. When newsmen asked about the new house she told them definitely that it wouldn't have anything either pink or heartshaped in it, "except me.'' She still owned the pink palace, though, and they eventually moved back there.

The marriage of Matt and Mansfield was a stormy one thanks in large part to Mickey. Jayne changed Mariska's name to Maria, in light of Matt's Italian background, which only added fuel to an already smoldering fire. New York reporters were treated to yet another field day when the husband and the ex-husband met on East 72nd Street during a visit between Mickey and his children. By now Mickey had learned, among other lessons, that publicity was a key factor in one-upmanship, so he showed up for the reunion with a group of photographers. One word led to another, a punch was thrown, and mini-skirted Jayne ended up refereeing a fight between husbands number two and number three in the middle of the thoroughfare, a fact that must have tickled a small portion of her headline-hungry heart. The ensuing stories, though, were ridiculous for all concerned. Jayne contended that Mickey had been bombarding her with love

Affectionate newlyweds greet the press when Jayne introduces new husband, Matt Cimber, after divorce from Mickey Hargitay (1964). UNITED PRESS INTERNATIONAL PHOTO.

letters while he was in Europe making a film capitalizing on his muscles and his fame as the ex-Mr. Mansfield. She clubbed him below the belt with statements such as, "I've never been happier. I always dreamed about falling in love. I didn't think it existed, but I was wrong. I never knew it was possible to be so happy." She attempted to cement that news by announcing another pregnancy in January of 1965, with Cimber punctuating her statement by adding, "Everything good is happening to us."

Unfortunately for Jayne, the changes in the sexual climate of the sixties, as compared to the decade before, when she started, were stacking up against her. Everything good *wasn't* happening to her. Her leering, giggly brand of sensuality was fast becoming passé in the freewheeling era about to start. The sexual revolution was imminent, and she was to be a victim of it although she did put up a fight. One kiss of death came when Beatle Paul McCartney referred to the thirty-two-year-old actress as "an old bag" in a 1965 *Playboy* interview. For years that magazine had made the most of Mansfield cheesecake, but when people heard this spokesman of the new age, they listened.

It also soon became all too obvious that Cimber would be no Ponti to her Sophia Loren. True, he did maneuver an Italian film for her but it was a quickie called *Primitive Love*. Television wanted her for the movie-star role in the incubating *Gilligan's Island* series, which might have given her career a new lease, but Cimber thought the pay was too low and refused. She remained a popular talk show guest, although it was increasingly apparent that she wasn't being taken for anything but a reliably wacky character. One memorable night on the *Tonight Show* she was pitted against Zsa Zsa Gabor. Jayne was still playing the let's-be-naughty sex kitten in white go-go boots and micro-miniskirt, while Gabor proffered her usually savvy, begowned sex appeal. Jayne came out of the encounter a sorry second, constantly outwitted and outflanked by the seasoned purveyor of mature sex. It was an interesting confrontation in that both ladies had started their careers outrageously, but Gabor had been canny enough to change with the times and allow her image to mature, while Jayne simply stuck with her original one. The bubbles of the sex kitten were becoming distinctly flat.

Jayne and Matt's son, Anthony Richard Cimber, was born in October of 1965, in L.A.'s Cedars of Lebanon Hospital. Instead of producing normal motherly feelings, however, this child brought forth a sense of overprotective fear in Jayne, and the marriage began to suffer from it immediately. She became increasingly possessive of Matt, whose irritation proliferated when he took stock of her other children's upbringing and education. Jayne Marie, for example, had much more experience painting her mother's fingernails than studying her homework, which had been fine with Jayne, who still valued her daughter's simple approval. The two were on a first-name basis, and Jayne Marie didn't seem to mind the childish costumes in which her mother continued to deck her out. She thought they were best friends.

Another sad development after Anthony's birth was Jayne's return to the bottle; Matt later stated that she'd gone on a diet consisting of one cup of beef bouillion, one bottle of bourbon, and one bottle of champagne a day. He was a teetotaler himself, too smart to get caught up in the unrewarding side effects of liquor, so it was Jayne Marie who did the bartending. Matt was terribly unhappy with this entire situation, but Jayne's will won out. After all, she was paying the bills. Alcohol helped reinforce her notions and fantasies about herself—that she was still the young and sensational movie star, the successor to Marilyn Monroe. In her mind, she'd manufactured herself to be a goddess, and she relied more and more on liquor to keep her on her own pedestal. It helped obscure the facts and pump up the dreams of drama and glamour, which she needed more at that time than she seemed to need food.

Matt tried to interest the important movie moguls in her again, but Jayne's reputation was too far gone by then, and only quickie producers would sign her. For them she made *The Fat Spy* in Florida, with Phyllis Diller and the late Jack E. Leonard, and *The Las Vegas Hillbillies,* produced by Matt himself. Early in 1966, she played New York's famed Latin Quarter for $11,000 a week and did good business sitting on the credit-card customers' laps and cooing her songs.

Offstage, though, the drinking was getting heavier, taking an inexorable toll on her marriage. Matt continued to disapprove of the way she treated Jayne Marie, whom she often woke up in the middle of the night to tend bar, and whom she generally expected to wait on her hand and foot doing manicures and pedicures. Their domestic situation reached a boiling point later that year, and Jayne moved out of the townhouse and into a hotel, where she was soon joined by Mickey Hargitay, who'd flown to her side as soon as the news of her split had reached him in Rome. As usual, his first consideration was her welfare, and, according to Cimber, he moved into the hotel with her accompanied by a male friend from Italy. Mickey told reporters that he was there to protect Jayne from Matt, that he never had felt he wasn't married to her, and that he'd "never been out of love with her."

Jayne formally separated from Matt in July, and, although she said they would continue on a star-manager basis, she almost immediately filed for a divorce, charging "extreme cruelty and grievous mental suffering." An associate of his accompanied her to Colombia for the opening there of *The Fat Spy* and later testified in a suit Matt instigated to get custody of his son that she had had a very wild time of it there, as evidenced by the souvenir she brought back with her, a twenty-year-old named Douglas Olivares. When Matt got wind of this return, he grabbed his son out of the pink palace and whisked him off to his grandmother's house.

When he showed up at the palace to discuss the situation with Jayne, Matt found her surrounded by more than a dozen drinking partners, with the children serving the drinks. Matt said she couldn't have the baby back, but shortly thereafter he lent her $50,000 to bail her out with the IRS. In September she opened at a downtown Las Vegas hotel, a far cry from the top places that she and Mickey had played, taking Olivares along with her as her recording secretary. It was quite a feat, considering that the young man couldn't speak, let alone write, English.

During the custody fight with Matt, Jayne engaged the services of a dynamic lawyer named Sam Brody, who had once worked for Melvin Belli and had helped in the defense of Jack Ruby. Married and the father of two children himself, the younger of whom was three, Brody was considered by his peers to be a tough, top-notch attorney. Yet when he met Jayne, he quickly became putty in her hands. Her habits, her dogs—the chihuahuas she had always doted on and always kept with her—her children, and her glamour all combined to blind him to virtually everything including his own growing career. Almost overnight he eschewed the rest of it for Jayne and was soon following her around, stuffed animals in hand, to look after her. Assuming an almost dictatorial interest in her affairs, he personally pitted himself against Matt in the custody battle for little Anthony and, as before, Mickey got lost in the shuffle of Jayne's priorities.

She sensed early on that Brody would be her champion in helping uphold (to herself, at least) her reputation as a good and worthwhile mother, and she used her sexuality to keep him close. Together they attended the San Francisco Film Festival, uninvited, where Jayne showed up in a breakaway dress and found herself turned away by the festival's director, who said, "Madame, I don't know how much a pound you are charging, but whatever it is I will pay it if you will leave." The days when Jayne could overtake and overwhelm a premiere, as she'd done years before with Jane Russell's *Underwater*—in which she didn't even appear —were plainly long gone.

From San Francisco Jayne and Brody went to Canada, and during that time an all too obviously physical relationship asserted itself, and Jayne had the black and blue marks to prove it. In place of love, her escalated need for attention made her all too willing to accept brutality as a sign of attention. And Brody was there to provide it.

In November, Jayne made her next-to-last sympathetic headlines when her six-year-old son, Zoltan, was grabbed and mauled by a presumably tame lion during a personal appearance at Jungleland, a zoo in the San Fernando Valley. It was an appalling accident that resulted in severe facial and head injuries to the child, who had been posing with Jayne and Miklos. Doctors worked for hours to repair the child's face and relieve pressure on the brain, while his mother wailed outside the operating room with Brody on hand to try to calm her hysteria. By then Mickey Hargitay had given up the fight and was back in Rome, but Brody was there to see her through the crisis. Jayne phoned Mickey to report the accident, with her next coin going to call her publicity man who, on her instructions, started releasing daily reports on Zoltan's recovery. As before, Jayne couldn't separate reality from the printed page, but she had also reached a point where she was showing up at the hospital so drunk that she was eventually barred from returning. Also, she and Brody had reportedly upset the entire place with their now common battles. Her absence at the hospital was explained to the press as an attack of viral pneumonia.

Mickey returned from Rome, Zoltan rallied, and Jayne called a press conference at the pink palace on Christmas morning, the day of the child's release from the hospital. As an attestation to her friendship with the press, over thirty-five reporters showed up and took countless pictures of the injured child, his mother, his father, and Sam Brody. Only when Jayne saw the stories in black and white on the front pages did Zoltan's recovery become truly believable to her.

As 1967 began, Jayne was more intense about the future than ever before. Her life was by now a maze of legal battles, custody suits, movie litigation over broken contracts, and Sam Brody, the man she hoped would lead her out of this wilderness and back to the childhood dream of movie-stardom that she always, and only, wanted. Part of her obviously knew that this dream was unlikely to come true, as her drinking increased along with her exhibitionism. Sam Brody's wife sued him for divorce and child support while he and Jayne toured Europe, loving, fighting, and making up from Stockholm to London—where Jayne startled Parliament by showing up in an outrageous mini-skirt and teased hair. Both their divorces were to be finalized that July, and they announced their plans to wed as soon as the legalities were settled, this despite the fact that while in London it was rumored that she had a brief fling with singer Englebert Humperdinck, who would later buy her pink palace. Like others, though, that romance was only a ploy to keep Sam totally devoted to her, a fact he declared with every bruise and every kiss. One nightclub engagement in England had to be canceled because her legs were too bruised for her to appear in the brief costume the customers expected her to wear.

When Jayne and Brody got back home to Hollywood it was to an even more unsavory pile of press clippings after Jayne Marie showed up at the West Los Angeles police station one night covered with welts and bruises that she blamed on Brody. She said that he'd beaten her, and she wanted sanctuary. When questioned, Jayne said that her daughter had been chastized because they had found a naked boy in the girl's closet. Jayne Marie said that the boy was there because she thought her mother might be interested in him, but Jayne didn't buy that story and apparently had lashed out against her daughter, urging Brody to use a leather belt on her. Jayne had thought of herself as her daughter's friend and equal, but, when confronted by the youngster's unabashed sexuality, she couldn't take it. She couldn't believe that her sixteen-year-old daughter was—or could be—interested in sex. It made Jayne seem older, too old to be the goddess she still was in her own mind. As a result, she sent Jayne Marie to live with relatives.

Trying to pick up her career, Jayne packed up bags, baggage, dogs, Sam, and her three youngest children for a return engagement at Gus Stevens's night-club in Biloxi. It was a successful opening considering the slightly seedy surroundings. On the night of June 28, 1967, finishing early, Jayne packed them all plus a driver into a 1966 Buick and headed for New Orleans, where she had a television interview set for early the next morning.

It was a long drive, and after a while Jayne put the children to sleep on the back seat while she, the driver and Brody sat up front. Ahead of them, a mosquito-spraying machine was moving slowly down the highway, spreading a dense fog behind it. Jayne's driver, a nineteen-year-old named Ronald Harrison, drove into the mist too fast to see the trailer truck in front of him in time. The vehicles collided, the truck slicing off the top of the Buick as neatly as a machete against a jungle palm. Harrison and Sam were killed when their bodies were flung to the highway. Jayne was decapitated before her body hit the asphalt, landing some feet away. The children miraculously survived, however, and were found whimpering in the wreckage under a pile of luggage that had been thrown forward from the trunk.

One of the dogs was also killed. A gruesome photograph of its bloody body lying conspicuously next to a broken Scotch bottle appears in Kenneth Anger's *Hollywood Babylon* (Straight Arrow Books).

It was a horrifying end for Jayne Mansfield, yet it was also, in a bizarre way, an appropriate one, for it gained her a last set of sympathetic headlines. From coast to coast, her widely smiling face, circa 1956, greeted the country's readers the next morning beneath the grisly news story. For an instant she was remembered as the girl who was to have been the new Marilyn Monroe, and also for an instant the past was revived in its simplicity. She was the good girl once again, who'd worked hard to make her dreams come true—who had, in fact, sacrificed everything to make the dreams a reality.

In death she had the same enemies and the same friends as in life. Mae West later told a writer that "she was full of evil. She was so full of evil that one day she exploded and her head went one way and her body went another." But her friends were there, too, a grief-stricken Mickey in particular. Mickey and the Peerses joined forces against Matt Cimber in a fight over her body and where it would be buried. Cimber said Hollywood; the family and Mickey said she'd always wanted to be buried in her hometown. That's where Mickey finally took her, back to Pennsylvania to the Fairview Cemetery in Pen Argyl.

The coffin was covered with a blanket of roses with a large heart in the middle. Mickey threw himself on the coffin, weeping, and kissed it. After he'd been pulled away, it was slowly lowered into the ground taking with it a lady whose only real problem was that she had set out to make news but in the long run couldn't differentiate between the press release and the truth.

Today a huge, heart-shaped headstone marks the place where Jayne rests. Her children, sent off to their respective fathers at the time of her death, are all grown now. In 1976 Jayne Marie attempted to duplicate her mother's image by posing for *Playboy,* but it was obvious that the quality of sexual ingenuousness her mother had once had was missing. For all her shortcomings and incessant narcissism, Jayne Mansfield was and remains an American original.

FILMOGRAPHY
Jayne Mansfield

TITLE	YEAR	DIRECTOR	LEADING PLAYERS
The Female Jungle (aka *Hangover*)	1954	Bruno De Sota	Lawrence Tierney, John Carradine
Pete Kelly's Blues	1955	Jack Webb	Jack Webb, Janet Leigh, Edmond O'Brien, Peggy Lee, Andy Devine, Lee Marvin
Illegal	1955	Lewis Allen	Edward G. Robinson, Nina Foch, Hugh Marlowe, Albert Dekker
Hell on Frisco Bay	1955	Frank Tuttle	Alan Ladd, Edward G. Robinson, Joanne Dru, William Demarest, Fay Wray
The Burglar	1956	Paul Wendkos	Dan Duryea, Martha Vickers, Mickey Shaughnessy
The Girl Can't Help It	1957	Frank Tashlin	Tom Ewell, Edmond O'Brien, Julie London
The Wayward Bus	1957	Victor Vicas	Joan Collins, Dan Dailey, Rick Jason
Will Success Spoil Rock Hunter?	1957	Frank Tashlin	Tony Randall, Joan Blondell, Betsy Drake, John Williams
Kiss Them for Me	1957	Stanley Donen	Cary Grant, Suzy Parker, Larry Blyden, Ray Walston
The Sheriff of Fractured Jaw	1958	Raoul Walsh	Kenneth More, Henry Hull, William Campbell, Robert Morley
Too Hot To Handle	1960	Terence Young	Leo Genn, Carl Boehm
The Challenge	1960	John Gilling	Anthony Quayle, Carl Mohner, Edward Judd
The Loves of Hercules	1960		Co-starred Mickey Hargitay. Never theatrically released in the U.S. No details
It Happened in Athens	1960	Andrew Marton	Trax Colton, Bob Mathias
The George Raft Story	1961	Joseph M. Newman	Ray Danton, Barbara Nichols, Julie London, Neville Brand
Panic Button	1962	George Sherman	Maurice Chevalier, Eleanor Parker, Michael Conners, Akim Tamiroff
Promises, Promises!	1963	Tommy Noonan	Tommy Noonan, Marie MacDonald, Mickey Hargitay.
Homesick for St. Paul (*Heimweh nach St Pauli*)	1963		Co-starred with German singer Freddy Quinn. Never released in the U.S. No details
Spree (aka *Here's Las Vegas*)	1964	Mitchell Leisen	Vic Damone, Juliet Prowse
Primitive Love (*L'Amore Primitivo*)	1964		Not released in the U.S. No details

TITLE	YEAR	DIRECTOR	LEADING PLAYERS
Single Room Furnished	1965	Matt Cimber	Fabian Dean, Dorothy Keller Released in 1967
Las Vegas Hillbillys	1966	Arthur C. Pierce	Ferlin Husky, Mamie Van Doren
The Fat Spy	1966	Joseph Cates	Jack E. Leonard, Jordan Christopher, Phyllis Diller
A Guide for the Married Man	1967	Gene Kelly	Walter Matthau, Robert Morse, Inger Stevens, Louis Nye

The Last Goddess --
Marilyn Monroe

I'm not going back into that fucking film until [Billy] Wilder reshoots my opening. When Marilyn Monroe comes into a room, nobody's going to be looking at Tony Curtis playing Joan Crawford. They're going to be looking at Marilyn Monroe.

Marilyn Monroe in 1959, after walking off the set of Some Like It Hot.

MARILYN Monroe has become a legend for many reasons. She was the last of Hollywood's Golden Goddesses and rightly so as the industry could hardly bear another one as spoiled and selfish, as self-destructive, and as surprisingly vulnerable as she was. From the moment her famous calendar picture exploded upon the public scene, Marilyn Monroe was *the* sex symbol of the fifties. Her initials—MM—became as famous as FDR's or JFK's.

At first her studio bosses thought that the picture would ruin her newly blossoming career, but the effect was just the opposite, especially when a contrite Marilyn explained she'd posed in the nude to pay the rent. A former factory-worker-turned-model with one husband, James Dougherty, already behind her, Marilyn circumvented her haphazard past and steadily rose higher in the Hollywood sky.

After her mother's nervous breakdown and subsequent hospitalizations, Marilyn (born Norma Jean Baker in 1926) suffered an anguished childhood filled with foster homes and temporary parents. That childhood would leave emotional scars that lasted her lifetime.

When she was discovered working in a defense plant and subsequently show-cased in a variety of ''men's'' magazines, she'd already married the older

Marilyn: the apogee of the Love Goddess (1954).　THE DOUG MCCLELLAND COLLECTION.

Dougherty who was serving in World War II. By the time he returned, though, it was to a new Norma Jean, a girl now hopelessly bitten by the movie star bug. Her new ambitions caused the marriage to collapse, but they were viable and potent enough to land her a $125-a-week starlet's contract at Fox late in 1946.

At first she was just one of many optimistic blondes, and success was far from instantaneous. Fox dropped her after one small role in the 1947 film *Dangerous Years,* but she was able to land small parts at other studios such as Columbia, where she decorated a "B" musical, *Ladies of the Chorus,* in 1948.

It took two more years of struggling through small parts before she got two showcase roles: as Louis Calhern's mistress in *The Asphalt Jungle* and as Miss Caswell in *All About Eve,* the trenchant classic about backstage theater life. As "a graduate of the Copacabana School of Dramatic Art," she held her own against the formidable Bette Davis, Anne Baxter, and the urbane George Sanders. Those two films marked her as a Golden Girl on the go, and it wasn't long before Fox resigned her and began showcasing her in their films.

When they were convinced that the famed calendar incident wasn't going to hurt her burgeoning appeal, Fox starred her as a psychotic babysitter opposite Richard Widmark in *Don't Bother To Knock.* That was in 1952, the same year she appeared in *We're Not Married, O'Henry's Full House,* and *Monkey Business* with Cary Grant.

Marilyn achieved stardom relatively late, at twenty-four, and resented the climb that others had seemingly made faster and easier. The struggle to climb the slippery slope to a real movie career began taking its toll almost from the beginning, expressing itself in dependence on others, particularly her drama coach, Natasha Lytess, tardiness, temperament, and rampant narcissism.

This narcissism surfaced in her first major film role, the starring part in 1953's *Niagara.* There was one scene in a motel room where she got up out of bed and went to the bathroom for a shower. Marilyn insisted on playing the scene in the nude, even though her body was fully reflected in the glass door each time she approached it. The director finally gave in and let her do it that way, and then had to have extra work done on darkening the film to get it past the censors.

Actor Max Showalter worked on that picture with her—as did her then acting coach Natasha Lytess. Max recalls that even then her narcissism was bouyant. From his adjoining room in the Niagara Falls Hotel, he would see her standing naked in front of her window, while crowds of men collected in the street below, gaping upwards. Then she'd run into Showalter's room complaining that people wouldn't leave her alone and that she was astounded by it. Said Max: "Well, for God's sake, Marilyn, put some clothes on." It was obvious, though, that she relished the attention, though late at night she'd rush into Showalter's room and jump in bed with him, pleading, "Don't do anything but just hold me."

Lytess was her mentor, and Marilyn never delivered a line directly to another actor, but always to Lytess's shadow standing near the cameras. Marilyn always waited for the nod of Lytess's head "yes" or "no," depending on the older woman's reaction. That decided whether there'd be a retake or not.

The results were both confusing and electric, for at the initial showing of *Niagara,* in the scene where Marilyn unveiled her famous walk in that tight red dress, audiences laughed because it was so totally unexpected and new to them.

It didn't stay that way long, though, and they soon came to love it, as she came to expand on it in pictures like *Gentlemen Prefer Blondes,* 1953; *How To Marry a Millionaire,* also that year; *River of No Return,* 1954; and that same year, *There's No Business Like Show Business.*

1954 also saw Marilyn enter into a shortlived and headline-making marriage to "Joltin' Joe" DiMaggio. An old-fashioned man, Joe wanted Marilyn to give up her newly carved stardom, and, from the first, the famous pair argued about it. Marilyn had worked too hard and too long to give it up, and chauvinistic Joe gradually realized he was fighting a tougher battle than he'd ever fought in Yankee Stadium. One of their final arguments occurred during the New York location filming of *The Seven Year Itch,* when Joe objected to his wife's legs being

A nubile Marilyn with Bette Davis and George Sanders in the classic All About Eve *(1950).*
THE DOUG McCLELLAND COLLECTION.

276

exposed (shocking in those days) by a wind machine. The film was one of her most popular, but by the time of its release, the marriage was dead. DiMaggio never stopped loving her, though, nor did she ever really forget him, despite the twists and turns she encountered in her life, a life filled with obstacles, many of which Marilyn herself constructed.

Being a movie star wasn't enough for Marilyn. She wanted to be accepted as an actress too. In 1953, she'd pointedly told newsmen that while Jane Russell might be making much more money for their film together, "The title is *Gentlemen Prefer Blondes,* after all, and I'm the blonde!"

She chucked all that, though, and walked away from Fox for New York and a straightbacked chair in the over-publicized and over-vaunted Actor's Studio. There the golden creampuff of the movies tried to transform herself, via classes, into a tree, a fog, or an anxious lady waiting for an elevator.

When the ire of Fox stockholders and the reality of her own precarious financial position became apparent, Marilyn relented and returned to Hollywood, buttressed by a new cast of supporting characters, including photographer Milton Greene and Lee and Paula Strasberg, the founders of the Actor's Studio. Paula became her new mentor, choreographing Marilyn's private life, as well as exerting a powerful influence on her career. Paula would stand next to the camera, signaling and offering suggestions to Josh Logan, the director of Marilyn's new movie, the very satisfying *Bus Stop.*

Marilyn's acting was undeniably better, but the toll it was taking on the studio's nerves made them wonder if it was worth while. Max Showalter worked on *Bus Stop,* too, and recalls how she one day pulled him aside and told him, almost fearfully, "How I wish we could just run away and talk about *Niagara* and the good times we had, but I can't. I can't talk to any of my old friends anymore."

She continued battling the studio, the Goddess against Goliath, over the parts she'd play and thus played few. She was off the screen for two years before going to England amidst wild fanfare to make *The Prince and the Showgirl* opposite Laurence Olivier. Their acting styles didn't match at all, and the resultant film wasn't the success it should have been.

By then she was married to Arthur Miller, the prestigious playwright, a classic example of opposites attracting—for a while. At first Marilyn thought she'd found a man who wasn't just interested in her sexual image, for in truth that image was a lie. Marilyn never liked the sex act all that much—it hurt. Ironic that the symbol of ultimate bedability should in private steer so clear of the bed. Miller was going to be her intellectual Svengali, filling his Trilby's educational gaps with his own erudition. He ended up as the keeper of her sleeping pills—but that came later.

Before that came director Billy Wilder, a Teutonic master of stinging comedy, who signed Marilyn to star in his 1959 comedy, *Some Like It Hot.* A perfectionist, he expected total professionalism from Marilyn (why he thought he'd get it where others hadn't remains to be seen) and hated her when she didn't, or couldn't, deliver it. The film, with an overweight and constantly overwrought star, took months to film.

Playing Sugar Kane, Marilyn got to project a robust sexuality and was genuinely funny in the part, but the delays she caused endeared her to no one—especially co-star Tony Curtis. For one take, she required forty-two tries, during each one of which Curtis had to munch on a fresh chicken leg. It was a very long time before he could look at another chicken leg. In addition, Curtis, a seasoned *movie* actor and a product of the Universal Pictures assembly line of the early 1950s, had been trained to get it right the first time out. As the takes accumulated, he lost spontaneity, while Marilyn gained it, almost feeding off his energy. Naturally, Wilder went with her good takes rather than his. Even so, Curtis managed a very good performance in what's now considered a classic comedy. Marilyn was extraordinarily good, but by then her personal publicity was turning sour. Her bad habits were becoming not just Hollywood legend, but public truth, as each argument, each minor breakdown, was chronicled and commented on in the press. The film was a hit, but her next one—*Let's Make Love* with Yves Montand—almost polished off her career in one fell swoop.

By the time they started filming, Miller was doling out the sleeping pills, and Marilyn's once fabulous figure was distorted by overweight, while her eyes were distorted by the drugs. With the gradual breakdown of the studio system, these habits became known to the public, whereas in the past, a Love Goddess could do almost anything, and the studio—protective father/investor—would cover it up. Tony Randall, a co-star of *Let's Make Love,* recalled to this author what it was like to work with her during this period. "She was so nervous before each shot that her body would be covered with Kleenex to keep her dry. Then, just as the director called for a shot, she'd shake them off like a wet puppy dog and rush onto the set."

Directed with the no-longer-light touch of George Cukor, the film's main claim to notoriety was the affair between Marilyn and Montand. The studio even publicized this—an unheard of thing in the forties—because they knew the film was a dog and thought the publicity could only help at the box office.

The highly publicized affair didn't help the movie after all, and *Let's Make Love* was a virtually uncontested flop. Marilyn was reaching the point, like Rita Hayworth and Lana Turner before her, and Elizabeth Taylor yet to come, where people were still highly interested in reading about her, but were no longer very anxious to pay money to see her. The decline was in full swing.

Ironically, Marilyn was symbolically on screen in Billy Wilder's *The Apartment* later that year. He frankly detested her after working with her and had a running gag in *The Apartment* about a girl who "looked just like Marilyn Monroe." He cast Joyce Jameson as "the girl," outfitted her in one of Monroe's costumes from *Some Like It Hot,* and let her loose, to coo throughout the picture in an uncanny Monroe takeoff. As far as Wilder was concerned, the score was settled.

Marilyn and Miller were committed to making *The Misfits* which he'd been working on for several years as a vehicle especially for her. The film was directed by John Huston and Marilyn teamed with her childhood idol, Clark Gable, along with Actor's Studio graduate Eli Wallach, stalwart Thelma Ritter, and Montgomery Clift, whose career had been very hit and miss for the past few years.

Marilyn and Monty were kindred spirits, two wounded birds helping each other toward nest and safety. Before *The Misfits* they had almost worked together in *Bus Stop,* but at that time Monty thought she was just another sexpot and turned the chance down. It would have been a magnificent teaming, both of them at the top of their beauty and powers. When they finally did come together five years later, the fire in both had been severely beaten down by the emotional storms that had raged around them. Like Marilyn, Monty was totally dependent on drugs and alcohol to survive, and, also like Marilyn, he thought his part in *The*

A wistful Marilyn looks out at the world (1955).   THE DOUG MCCLELLAND COLLECTION.

Misfits would bring him back to stability and stardom, both of which had eluded him for several years.

By then, Marilyn's lateness was fact instead of rumor, and shooting days slipped by on the hot Nevada location while she tried to pull herself out of pill-induced comas. Miller had been tailor-making the part of Roslyn, the fragile divorcée, for three years, but he was by now at the end of his marital rope, and everybody soon knew it. The union between the Love Goddess and the Intellectual was almost dead. *The Misfits*—an apt title if ever there was one—was the relationship's final punctuation mark.

The parallels between Marilyn and Monty were strong and obvious. Monty was forever grappling with personal demons while Marilyn fought the violent insecurity and self-doubts which, by this point, had virtually destroyed her career, not to mention her life.

Miller noticed the similarities between them immediately and in Robert LaGuardia's *Monty* (Arbor House) said: "Neither one knew when and how to make the compromises that had to be made in the movies they appeared in. So they would make drastic compromises at the wrong time and refuse to make the ones that would have been helpful at the right time. But Monty was less paranoid than Marilyn. He was a little better capable of running his life and could continue to work, no matter what the conditions. He was far more advanced as a technician and could be more objective about his performance because of his theater background.

"Marilyn had never been onstage, had never learned the discipline he learned. She was a native talent who was trying to find some way of rationalizing it and controlling it. . . . The Actor's Studio disfigured a lot of her working career. It didn't support her. It didn't make her feel secure with her talents. It always left her with a feeling that she wished someone was there to tell her what to do. . . . After all, before the Studio she was a very good comedienne. In *The Misfits*, her performance as a dramatic actress was extraordinary, but I'm not sure if all that torture was worth the result—all that agony. It's not worth anything."

Marilyn's performance as the disillusioned Roslyn was indeed incandescent. She carved a carefully etched portrait of an unhappy woman, in Reno for a divorce, who got picked up by a group of mustangers headed by Gable. They in turn picked up a broken-down rodeo rider played by Clift. Marilyn's and Monty's big scene together was a five-minute take during which Monty's Perce woozily told her how he had lost his family ranch and turned to bronc-riding for a livelihood. It was to be the longest single scene in the film, and all concerned expected it to take days to shoot with those two unpredictable personalities. It didn't.

They did it in one day. Marilyn cradled Monty's battered head in her lap as he poured out his tale. She demanded that the set be cleared of everyone but the absolutely necessary technicians, even banning the still photographer so the clicking of his camera wouldn't distract them.

Both stars approached the scene with trepidation, yet, in a rare moment of self-confidence—wasn't Monty an as big, if not bigger, victim of the movie industry than she?—it was Marilyn who pulled the lengthy scene off, helping Monty through it. It took three tries to get the first take, since both actors had lengthy speeches requiring absolute synchronization. Marilyn told Monty how good he was. Monty listened, savoring the praise like a parched leaf savors a rainshower. Marilyn blew the next take, and Monty the one after that, and they collapsed against each other, laughing, and relieving the tensions inside. The sixth take was letter perfect, and Huston had his scene, one of the picture's most intimate, and, in retrospect, one of the most endearing of both their careers.

When *The Misfits* finally wrapped, Marilyn and Miller made public their plans to divorce. Soon she was alone again, drifting back to Hollywood where she began the downdraft of her life.

Makeup man George Masters knew her during this period. In fact, he concocted that last white-blonde look the public remembers of her at the end of her life. When this author interviewed Masters for *Celebrity* magazine, he gave an insight into her state of mind by relating the story of a flight they took together. During the flight, a stewardess asked the handsome blond if he was Marilyn's brother. Marilyn couldn't stand the idea of anyone looking like her, and from then on she kept nagging him to dye his hair black. George refused. Marilyn wouldn't budge, and it was the end of their relationship.

There was then a stint in the Payne Whitney mental clinic in New York from which she emerged ghostly and withdrawn. *The Misfits* opened to generally disappointing reviews, and, back at Fox, they decided to star her in a tired remake of a thirties comedy now to be called *Something's Got To Give*. (Jean Arthur had originally starred in it as *Too Many Husbands*. Later, after Marilyn's death, it was reshaped into a Doris Day vehicle.)

Marilyn's personal life after her divorce from Miller had been a point of constant controversy, but one thing is certain, she was in no condition to make a film. Heavily into pills washed down with Dom Perignon, she moved into a ranch-style house on Fifth Helena Drive in Brentwood. She lived there alone, except for her housekeeper, Mrs. Eunice Murray.

The film was trouble laden from the first day of production—which Marilyn missed, by the way—and got worse as the weeks went by. She started it with a low-grade fever, and, in three weeks, appeared on the set only six days, and then not on time. Though doctors assured Fox she was honestly ill, that excuse went out the window when she flew to New York City in the middle of May 1962 to sing the sultriest "Happy Birthday" of all time to President John F. Kennedy in front of 20,000 guests at Madison Square Garden.

The studio was furious and was on the verge of firing her when she unexpectedly showed up and went to work with a minor vengeance, stripping off her flesh-colored swimsuit to swim for hours in the studio pool for a pivotal scene. On Friday, June 1, she had a birthday party on the set, and she appeared happy, for a change, as she exulted over the sparkler-studded cake. On Monday and Tuesday she didn't show up for work, though, and Fox suspended the movie. On Thursday she was fired from the film for "willful violation of contract," and shortly after that co-star Dean Martin walked off when they tried to substitute Lee Remick. He wanted Marilyn or nobody.

After a brief visit to New York City, Marilyn holed up in her uncompleted house, surrounded by boxes and cartons containing the detritus of a disordered life. Finally it was agreed that she'd return to work in September when Martin had finished some nightclub work, to complete *Something's Got To Give*. But that September was a long way off.

Faithful Joe DiMaggio reentered her life. He had never really left it, always maintaining some sort of contact via friends like Frank Sinatra. But it was only a sporadic relationship. Joe had passed through the fire of being "Mr. Monroe" once and wasn't about to do it again. Most of her nights were spent alone. Through the friendship of Peter Lawford, she'd met the Kennedys, John and Robert, and, according to some reports, had had an affair with Bobby. Other people say it was the President himself she was really interested in, and, shortly before her death, she told her old friend Bob Slatzer, author of *The Life and Curious Death of Marilyn Monroe* (Pinnacle Books) that she just might call a news conference and name some names. Slatzer cautioned her against threatening Bobby Kennedy, but she just laughed. This was her last conversation with Slatzer, two days before she died.

The night of Marilyn Monroe's death contains some of the most outrageous elements that any screenwriter could have devised: mystery, suspense, self-defeat, suicide, and suspected murder. It's as if another script were being acted out, some cheap overdone melodrama full of banal facts and fantasies.

Marilyn was always a romantic. Who's to say that she wasn't, that hot summer night, entertaining the wildest of delusions to calm her restlessness—like becoming the First Lady of the country? Marilyn had, in effect, blown *Something's Got To Give* by going to New York to sing for Kennedy's birthday party. She followed "Happy Birthday" with a special rendition of "Thanks for the Memories"—"and all the things you've done." As Norman Mailer says in his *Marilyn* (Grosset and Dunlap), "She sounds like she knows him awful well!"

Perhaps she couldn't sleep that last night. She seldom could without massive doses of Nembutal, the drug her physician had switched her back on to the preceding day.

The night wore on as the stack of Frank Sinatra records played on the stereo in her bedroom. She was lonely, and she reached for the telephone, her constant lifeline during empty tortured nights.

Marilyn made many calls that dark night, but obviously couldn't get through to the person she wanted. Was it JFK? No one knows because the following morning, while Marilyn lay dead on a cold mortuary slab, the notations of her phone calls were carefully snipped from the telephone company records. Ironically, the phone company later submitted a bill to her estate for $209.00 worth of toll calls—but no one knows to whom they were made.

The Golden Idol at whose altar millions of men had worshipped died naked and alone on August 6, 1962, the telephone still in her hand.

The coroner's verdict, however disputed, was barbiturate overdose. DiMaggio stepped in to handle the funeral arrangements, but there were no Kennedys or Lawfords or Sinatras invited. To this day, a single red rose is delivered daily and placed in a vase attached to the small crypt where she lies in Westwood Village Mortuary in Los Angeles. DiMaggio has set up a trust fund to make sure that when he himself is no longer here, the red rose will be.

Others have been interested in the crypt and the plots near it. In 1977, a report came out that one crypt, just to the side of Marilyn, was up for sale by a private owner for $25,000. What morbid sexual fantasy could be conjured up by such a purchase? Even in death, Marilyn proved a valuable commodity.

And what if she had lived, this ultimate symbol of a dead decade? What would she be doing now? Would she have gone to Europe and starred for Bergman in some black and white study of middle-aged moral chaos?

Would she, like Ava Gardner, have compromised any serious acting hopes by taking small flashy roles for huge sums of money that would allow her to hole up in a London townhouse, no longer worrying, or caring, who had top billing?

Would she, like Gene Tierney, be married to a millionaire and live in a gaudy Texas suburb in a mansion built by her husband's other famous wife, Hedy Lamarr?

Would she be like Hedy herself, alone after six headlined marriages, living in a small New York apartment surrounded by eight-by-ten glossies of the glory days?

Would she have been like the other fifties Golden Girl, Kim Novak, who, safely and happily married and lived in relative seclusion, ventures forth from the rocky expanses of Big Sur every year or so for a TV movie role, for which she gets top billing, even though her beauty is now disguised by overweight?

Would she be living alone in a small Hollywood apartment scrambling for small parts in television shows and ''B'' movies, the luster permanently extinguished, the dream tarnishing by the day?

Or would she have followed the path of insanity that threaded through her family like a vagrant tapeworm, eating from within?

Unfortunately, we'll never know, for the exquisite flame that was Marilyn was snuffed out too soon, either by her own hand of by that of another.

Marilyn's life and loves have been dissected, scrutinized, biographied, and examined in such minute detail that there seems no stone left unturned. But there will be, and speculation upon how her life ended, whether by accident or secret government plot, will never truly end until, perhaps, enough of the people involved have died and the final truth emerges.

Meanwhile, what has been left behind is an image captured and held in dozens of film cans, an image that can be resurrected continually, and that continues to delight and surprise us, whether it masquerades under the name of Lorelei Lee of *Gentlemen Prefer Blondes* or as *Bus Stop's* Cherie.

The image captured in these silver receptacles is perhaps the real Marilyn Monroe, for, as she often said, the camera was her only true lover. She made love

Marilyn walks away from the set of Something's Got To Give *into the twilight of history (1962)*.
THE DOUG MCCLELLAND COLLECTION.

to it, fought with it, often ignored it, and ultimately, gave in to its embrace. Those moments of mutual surrender are perhaps the only true legacy of a Love Goddess. The snippets that remain of *Something's Got To Give* offer what may have been a new Monroe, her white-blonde beauty slightly distracted as she wandered through an opulent set in a tight print dress for a costume test. She pauses, looks up at the camera, laughs, walks, and turns around, smiling over her shoulder. Thin and langourous in those brief scenes, she seems to promise so much. She'd come a long way from being the golddigging "Little Girl From Little Rock" in *Gentlemen Prefer Blondes*, but we'll never know how much further she could have gone.

FILMOGRAPHY
Marilyn Monroe

TITLE	YEAR	DIRECTOR	LEADING PLAYERS
Dangerous Years	1947	Arthur Pierson	Billy Halop, Ann E. Todd, Jerome Cowan
Ladies of the Chorus	1948	Phil Karlson	Adele Jergens, Rand Brooks, Nana Bryant
Love Happy	1949	David Miller	Harpo, Chico and Groucho Marx, Ilone Massey, Vera-Ellen
A Ticket to Tomahawk	1950	Richard Sale	Dan Dailey, Anne Baxter, Rory Calhoun, Walter Brennan
The Asphalt Jungle	1950	John Huston	Sterling Hayden, Louis Calhern, Jean Hagen, Sam Jaffe
All About Eve	1950	Joseph L. Mankiewicz	Bette Davis, Gary Merrill, Anne Baxter, Thelma Ritter, George Sanders
Right Cross	1950	John Sturges	June Allyson, Dick Powell, Lionel Barrymore, Ricardo Montalban
The Fireball	1950	Tay Garnett	Mickey Rooney, Pat O'Brien, Beverly Tyler
Hometown Story	1951	Arthur Pierson	Jeffrey Lynn, Marjorie Reynolds, Donald Crisp, Alan Hale, Jr.
As Young As You Feel	1951	Harmon Jones	Monty Wooley, Thelma Ritter, David Wayne, Jean Peters, Constance Bennett
Love Nest	1951	Joseph M. Newman	June Haver, William Lundigan, Frank Fay, Jack Paar
Let's Make It Legal	1951	Richard Sale	Claudette Colbert, Macdonald Carey, Zachary Scott, Robert Wagner
Clash By Night	1952	Fritz Lang	Barbara Stanwyck, Paul Douglas, Robert Ryan, Keith Andes
We're Not Married	1952	Edmund Goulding	Ginger Rogers, Fred Allen, Victor Moore, Paul Douglas, David Wayne
Dont Bother To Knock	1952	Robert Baker	Richard Widmark, Anne Bancroft

TITLE	YEAR	DIRECTOR	LEADING PLAYERS
Monkey Business	1952	Howard Hawks	Cary Grant, Ginger Rogers, Charles Coburn, Hugh Marlowe
O'Henry's Full House	1952	Henry Hathaway, Howard Hawks, Henry King, Henry Koster, Jean Negulesco. Monroe segment directed by Henry Koster.	Fred Allen, Anne Baxter, Charles Laughton, Gregory Ratoff, Jeanne Crain, Jean Peters
Niagara	1953	Henry Hathaway	Joseph Cotten, Jean Peters, Don Wilson, Max Showalter
Gentlemen Prefer Blondes	1953	Howard Hawks	Jane Russell, Tommy Noonan, Charles Coburn, George Winslow, Norma Varden
How To Marry a Millionaire	1953	Jean Negulesco	Betty Grable, Lauren Bacall, William Powell, Rory Calhoun, David Wayne
River of No Return	1954	Otto Preminger	Robert Mitchum, Rory Calhoun, Tommy Rettig
There's No Business Like Show Business	1954	Walter Lang	Dan Dailey, Ethel Merman, Donald O'Conner, Mitzi Gaynor
The Seven-Year Itch	1955	Billy Wilder	Tom Ewell, Evelyn Keyes, Sonny Tufts
Bus Stop	1956	Joshua Logan	Don Murray, Eileen Heckart, Arthur O'Connell, Hope Lange, Betty Field
The Prince and the Show Girl	1957	Laurence Olivier	Laurence Olivier, Sybil Thorndike, Jeremy Spencer
Some Like It Hot	1959	Billy Wilder	Tony Curtis, Jack Lemmon, Joe E. Brown, George Raft, Pat O'Brien, Joan Shawlee
Let's Make Love	1960	George Cukor	Yves Montand, Tony Randall, Frankie Vaughn, David Burns
The Misfits	1961	John Huston	Clarke Gable, Montgomery Clift, Thelma Ritter, Eli Wallach